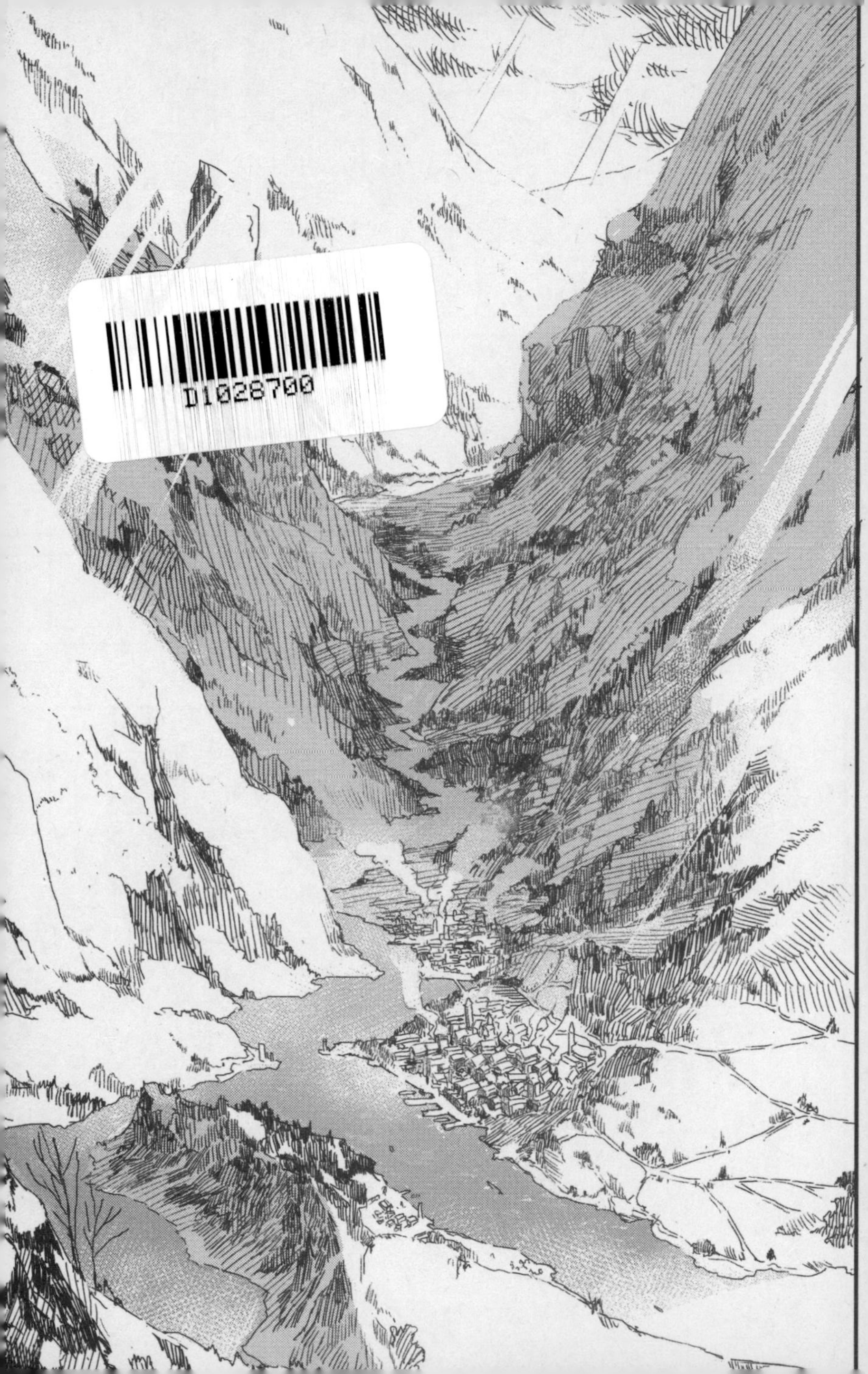

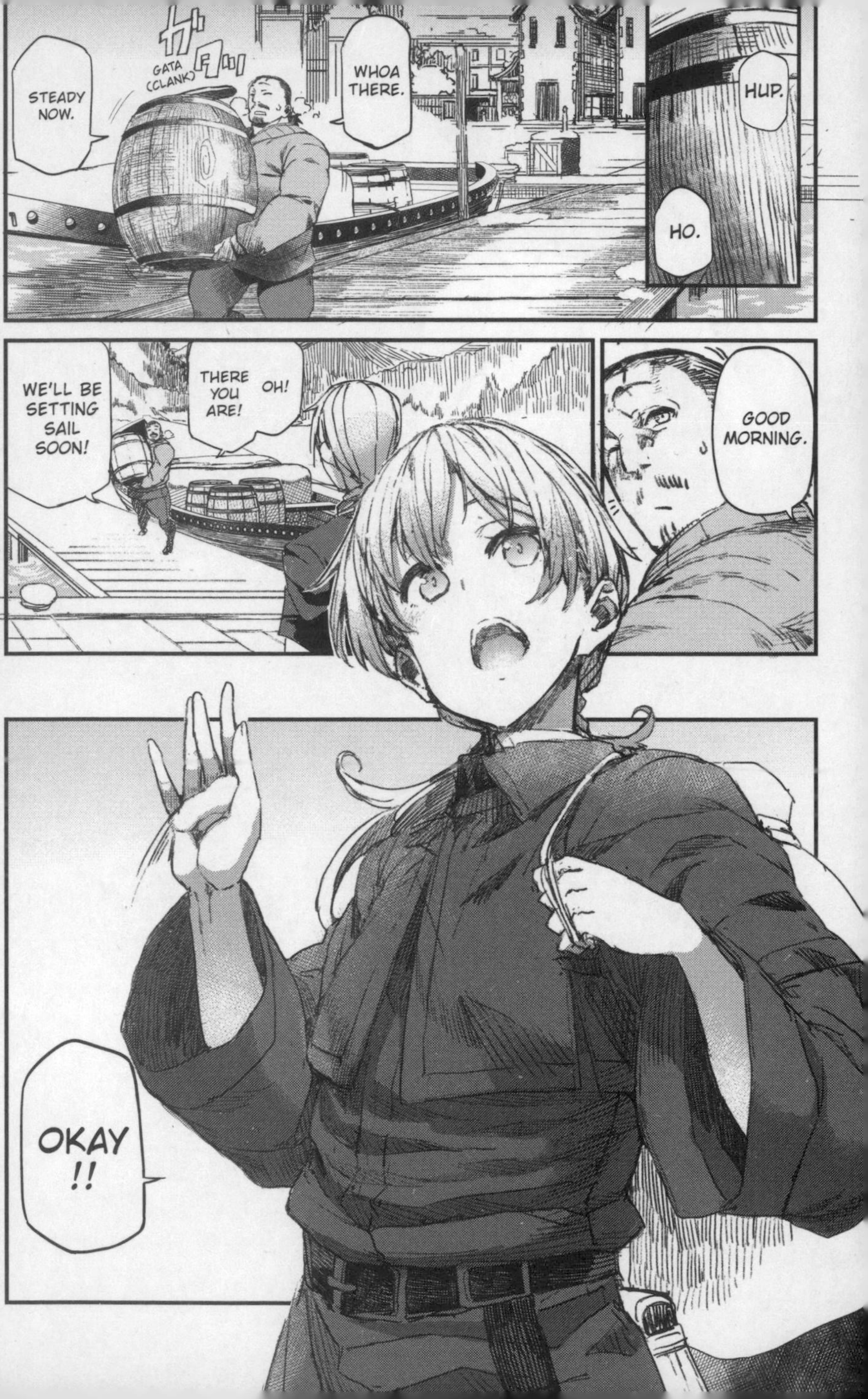
HUP.
HO.
WHOA THERE.
GATA (CLANK)
STEADY NOW.
GOOD MORNING.
OH!
THERE YOU ARE!
WE'LL BE SETTING SAIL SOON!
OKAY !!

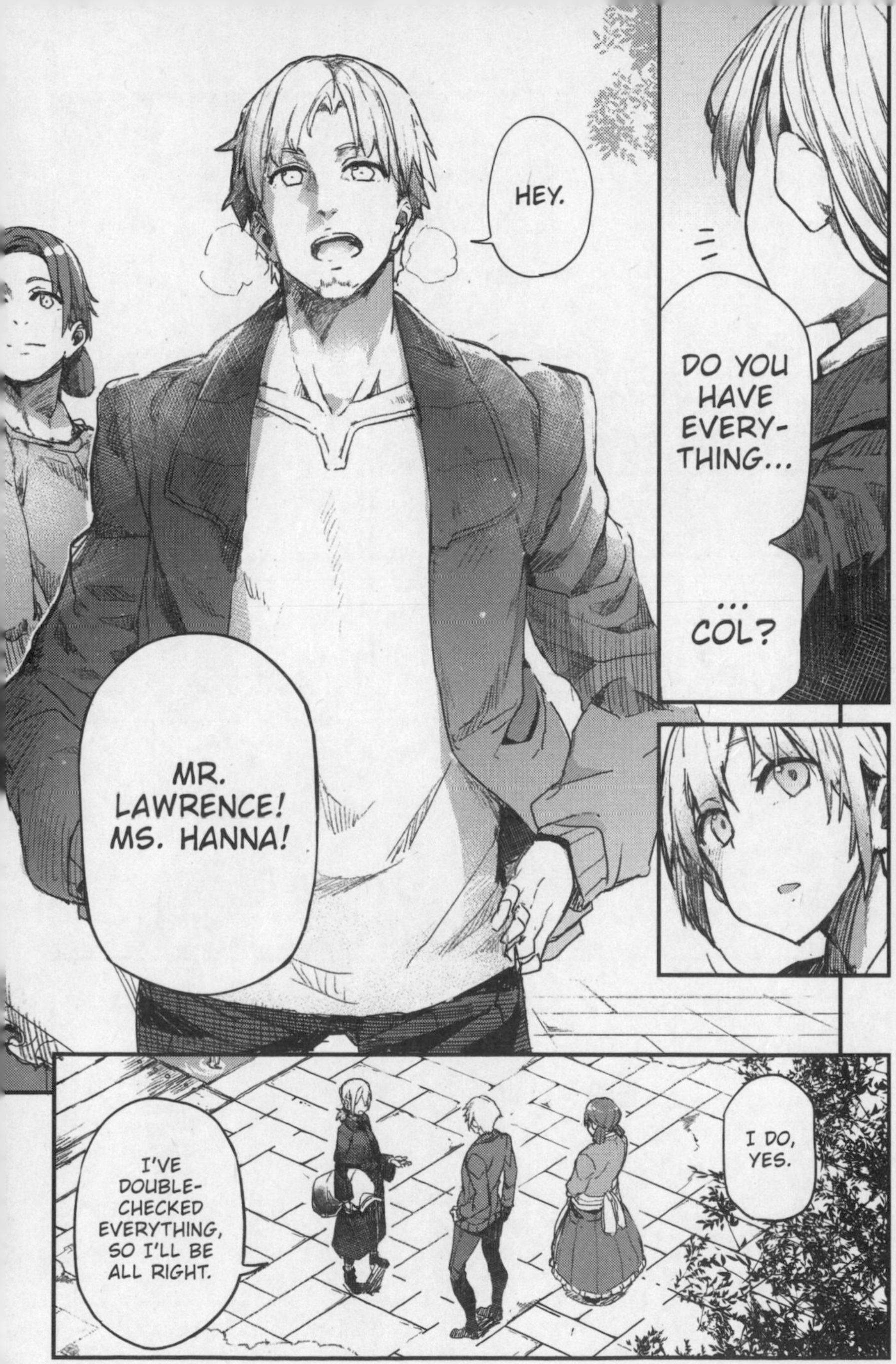
DO YOU HAVE EVERY-THING...
...COL?
HEY.
MR. LAWRENCE! MS. HANNA!
I DO, YES.
I'VE DOUBLE-CHECKED EVERYTHING, SO I'LL BE ALL RIGHT.

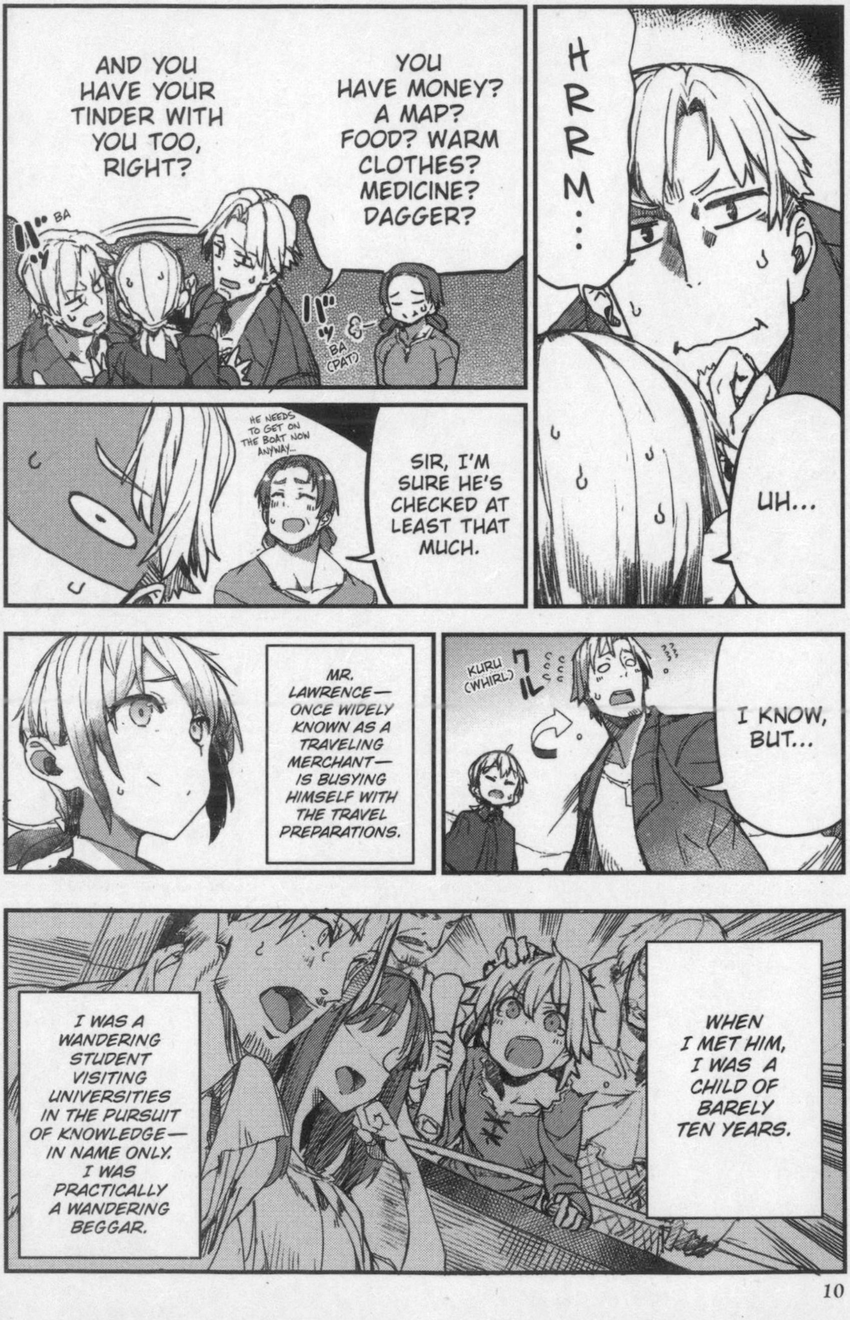
HRRM...
UH...
YOU HAVE MONEY? A MAP? FOOD? WARM CLOTHES? MEDICINE? DAGGER?
AND YOU HAVE YOUR TINDER WITH YOU TOO, RIGHT?
BA
BA (PAT)
SIR, I'M SURE HE'S CHECKED AT LEAST THAT MUCH.
HE NEEDS TO GET ON THE BOAT NOW ANYWAY...
I KNOW, BUT...
KURU (WHIRL)
MR. LAWRENCE—ONCE WIDELY KNOWN AS A TRAVELING MERCHANT—IS BUSYING HIMSELF WITH THE TRAVEL PREPARATIONS.
WHEN I MET HIM, I WAS A CHILD OF BARELY TEN YEARS.
I WAS A WANDERING STUDENT VISITING UNIVERSITIES IN THE PURSUIT OF KNOWLEDGE—IN NAME ONLY. I WAS PRACTICALLY A WANDERING BEGGAR.

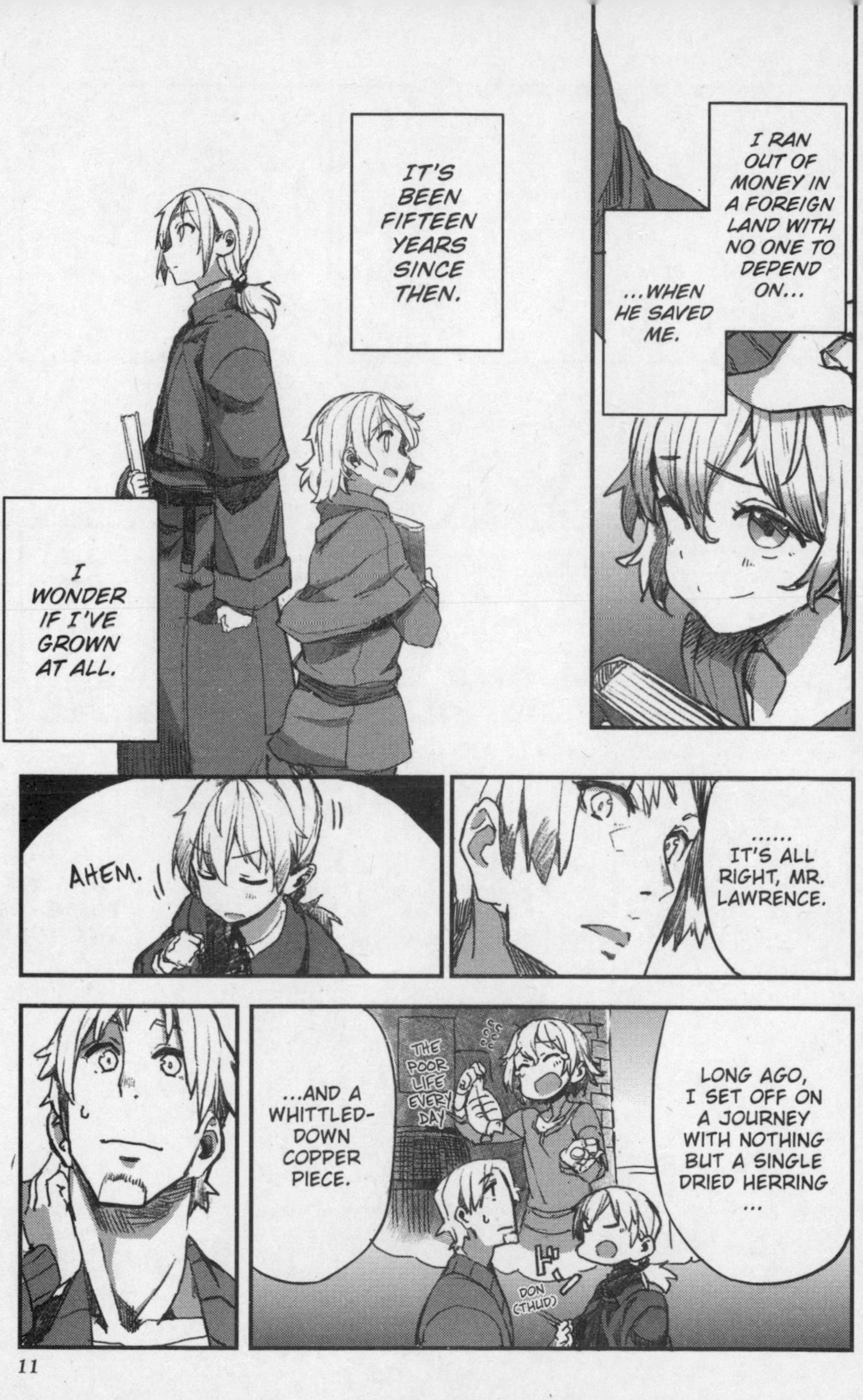
I RAN OUT OF MONEY IN A FOREIGN LAND WITH NO ONE TO DEPEND ON...
...WHEN HE SAVED ME.
IT'S BEEN FIFTEEN YEARS SINCE THEN.
I WONDER IF I'VE GROWN AT ALL.
...... IT'S ALL RIGHT, MR. LAWRENCE.
AHEM.
LONG AGO, I SET OFF ON A JOURNEY WITH NOTHING BUT A SINGLE DRIED HERRING ...
...AND A WHITTLED-DOWN COPPER PIECE.
THE POOR LIFE EVERY DAY
DON (THUD)

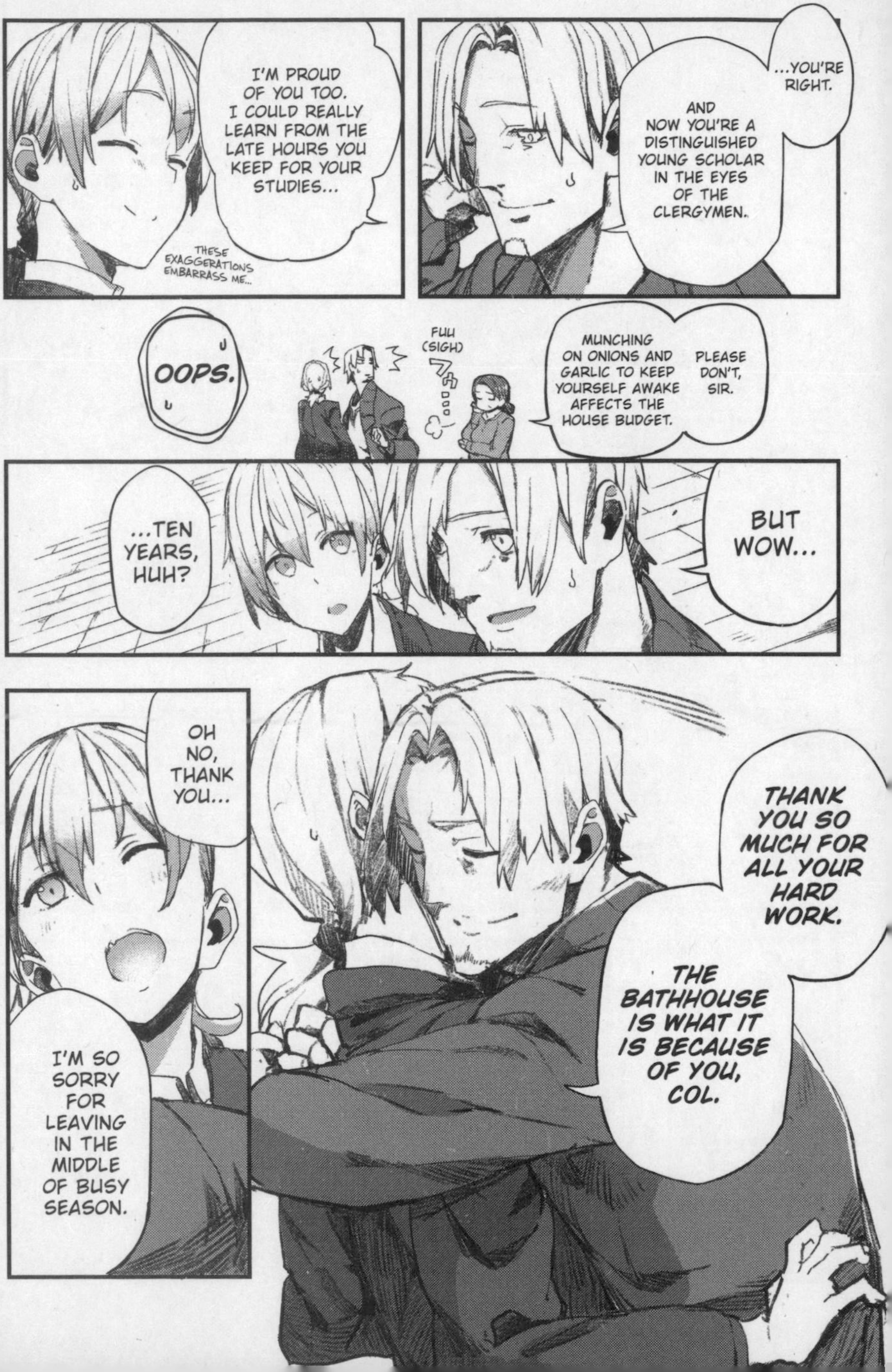
...YOU'RE RIGHT.
AND NOW YOU'RE A DISTINGUISHED YOUNG SCHOLAR IN THE EYES OF THE CLERGYMEN.
I'M PROUD OF YOU TOO. I COULD REALLY LEARN FROM THE LATE HOURS YOU KEEP FOR YOUR STUDIES...
THESE EXAGGERATIONS EMBARRASS ME...
PLEASE DON'T, SIR.
MUNCHING ON ONIONS AND GARLIC TO KEEP YOURSELF AWAKE AFFECTS THE HOUSE BUDGET.
FUU (SIGH)
OOPS.
BUT WOW...
...TEN YEARS, HUH?
THANK YOU SO MUCH FOR ALL YOUR HARD WORK.
THE BATHHOUSE IS WHAT IT IS BECAUSE OF YOU, COL.
OH NO, THANK YOU...
I'M SO SORRY FOR LEAVING IN THE MIDDLE OF BUSY SEASON.

HEY, IF YOU GO SOUTH AND MAKE IT BIG...

...AT LEAST LET US KNOW!

SEE THE MONEY...

AND...

...AREN'T HERE TO SEE YOU OFF.

...I'M SORRY THE GIRLS...

MS. HOLO ALREADY SAID HER GOOD-BYES TO ME A WEEK AGO.

IT'S ALL RIGHT.

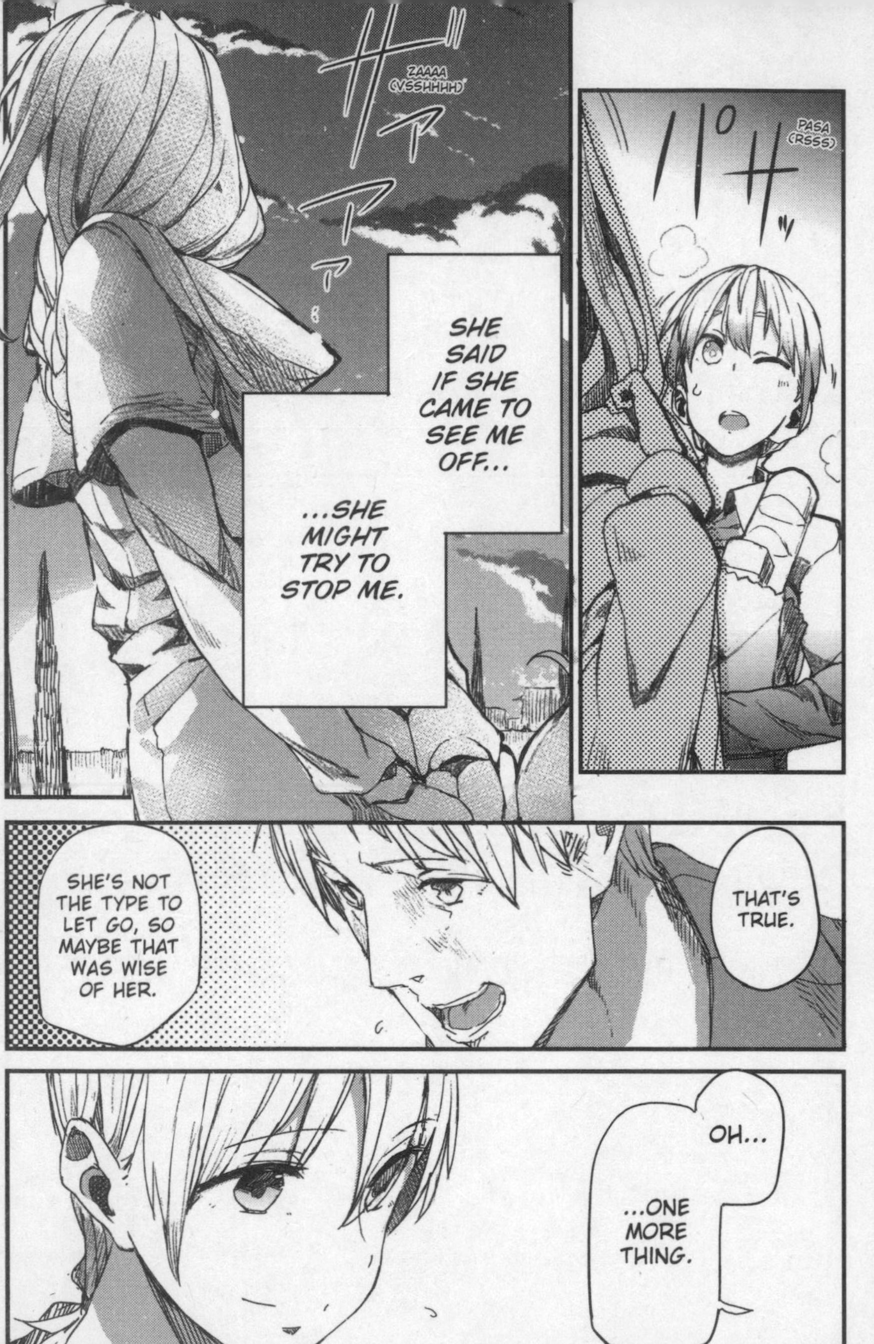
PASA (RSSS)
ZAAAA (VSSHHHH)
SHE SAID IF SHE CAME TO SEE ME OFF...
...SHE MIGHT TRY TO STOP ME.
THAT'S TRUE.
SHE'S NOT THE TYPE TO LET GO, SO MAYBE THAT WAS WISE OF HER.
OH...
...ONE MORE THING.

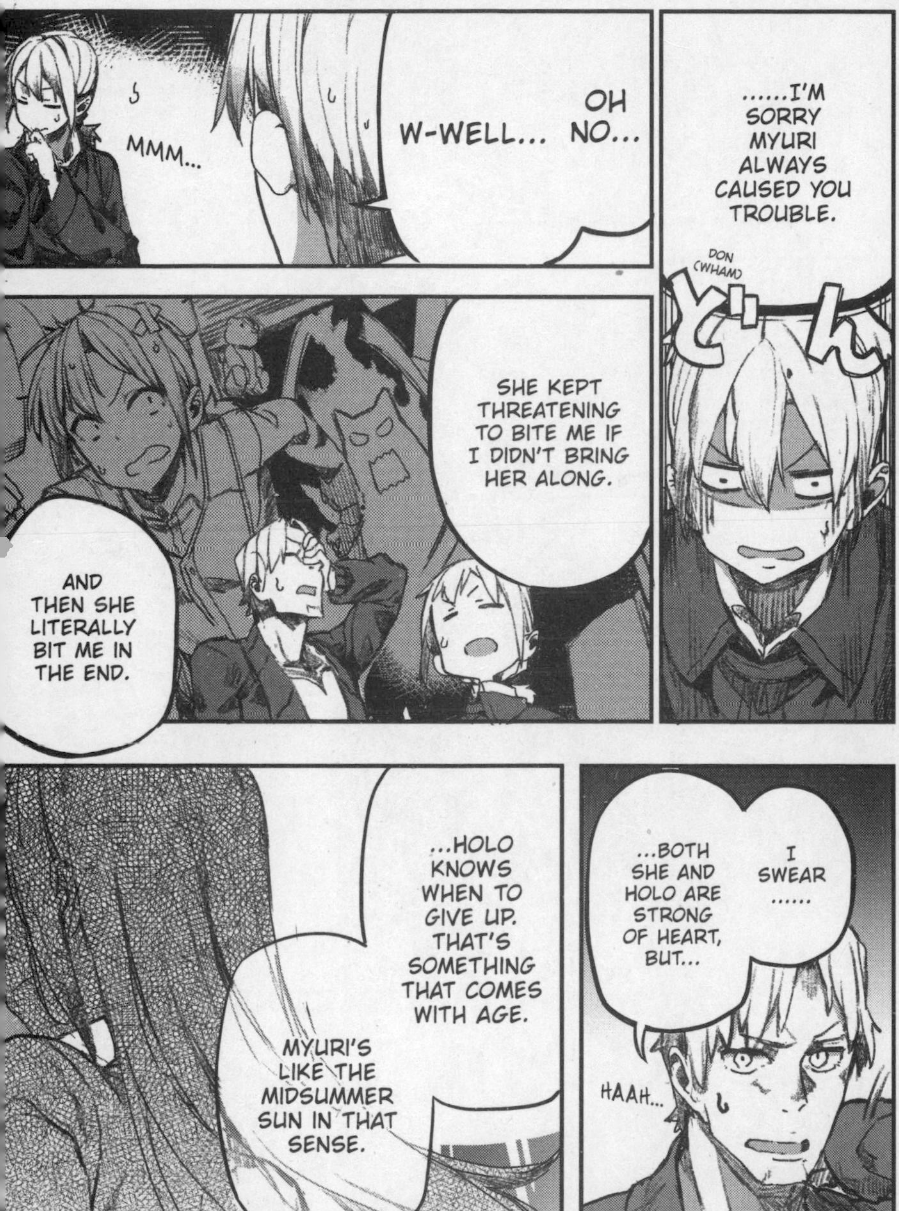
......I'M SORRY MYURI ALWAYS CAUSED YOU TROUBLE.
DON (WHAM)
どん
OH NO...
W-WELL...
MMM...
SHE KEPT THREATENING TO BITE ME IF I DIDN'T BRING HER ALONG.
AND THEN SHE LITERALLY BIT ME IN THE END.
I SWEAR ......
...BOTH SHE AND HOLO ARE STRONG OF HEART, BUT...
HAAH...
...HOLO KNOWS WHEN TO GIVE UP. THAT'S SOMETHING THAT COMES WITH AGE.
MYURI'S LIKE THE MIDSUMMER SUN IN THAT SENSE.

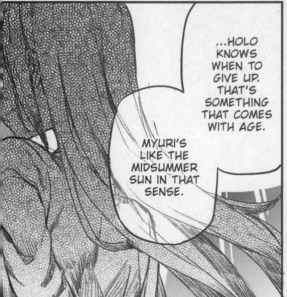

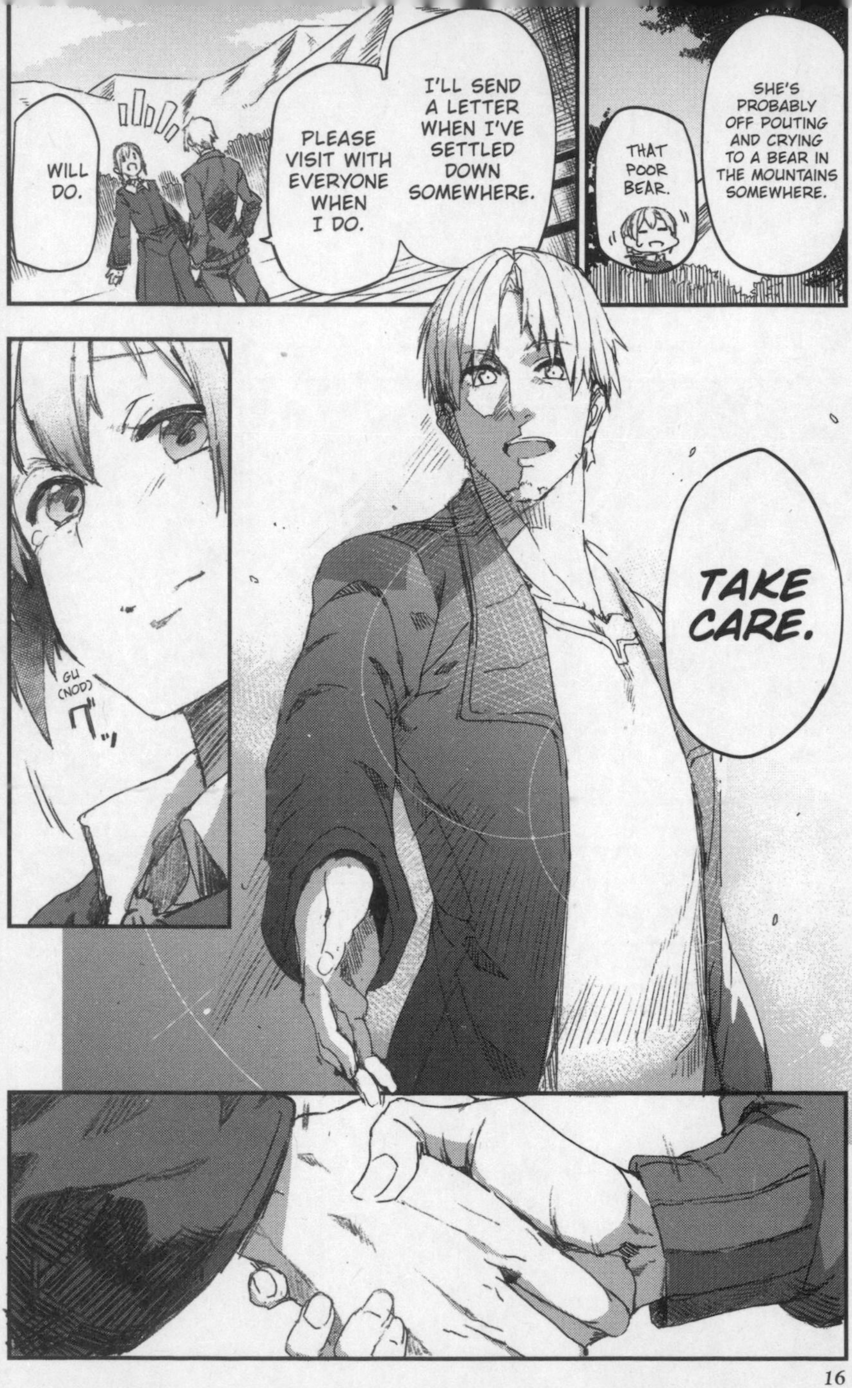

SHE'S PROBABLY OFF POUTING AND CRYING TO A BEAR IN THE MOUNTAINS SOMEWHERE.
THAT POOR BEAR.
I'LL SEND A LETTER WHEN I'VE SETTLED DOWN SOMEWHERE.
PLEASE VISIT WITH EVERYONE WHEN I DO.
WILL DO.
TAKE CARE.
GU (NOD)
グッ

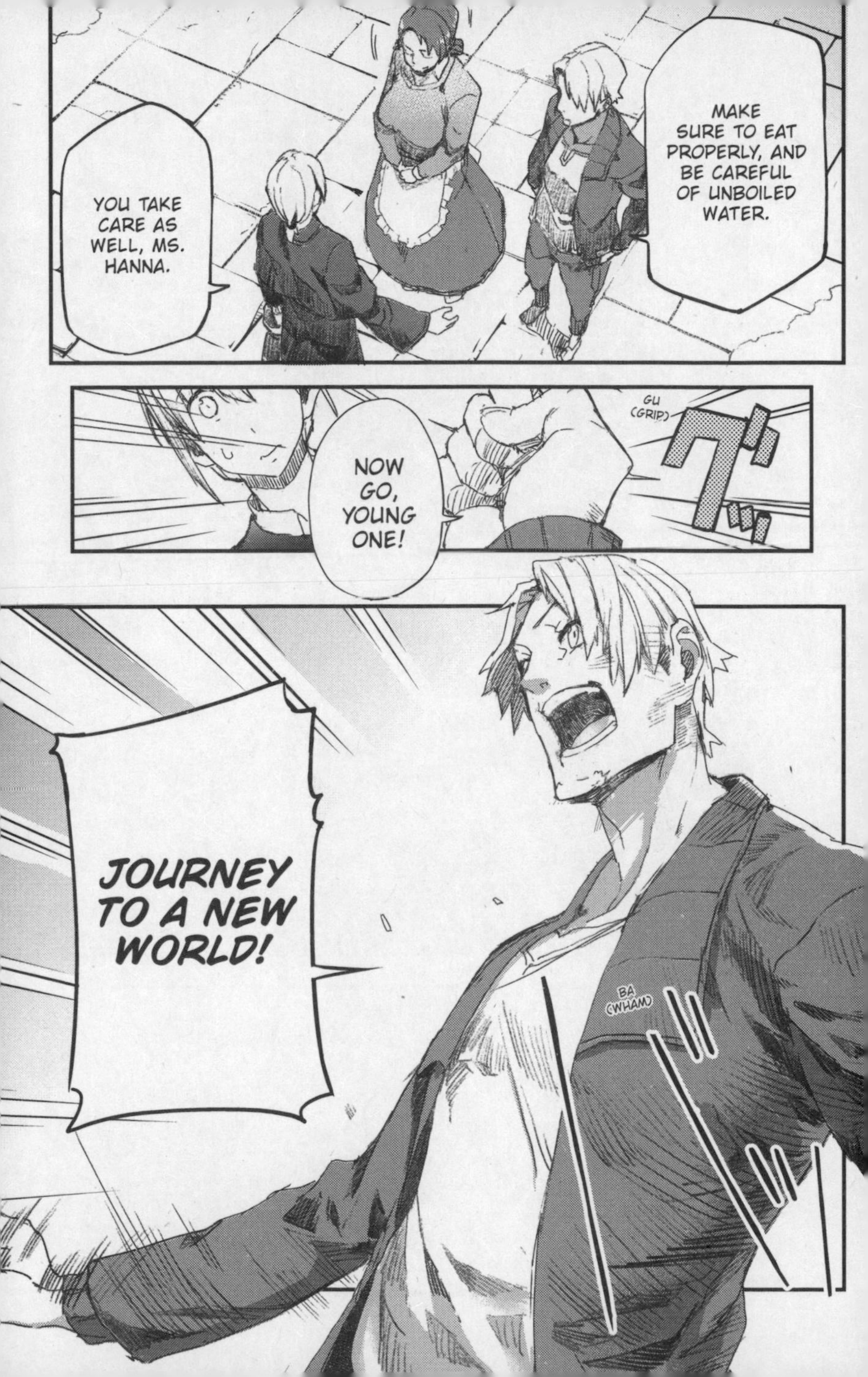
MAKE SURE TO EAT PROPERLY, AND BE CAREFUL OF UNBOILED WATER.
YOU TAKE CARE AS WELL, MS. HANNA.
GU (GRIP)
NOW GO, YOUNG ONE!
BA (WHAM)
JOURNEY TO A NEW WORLD!

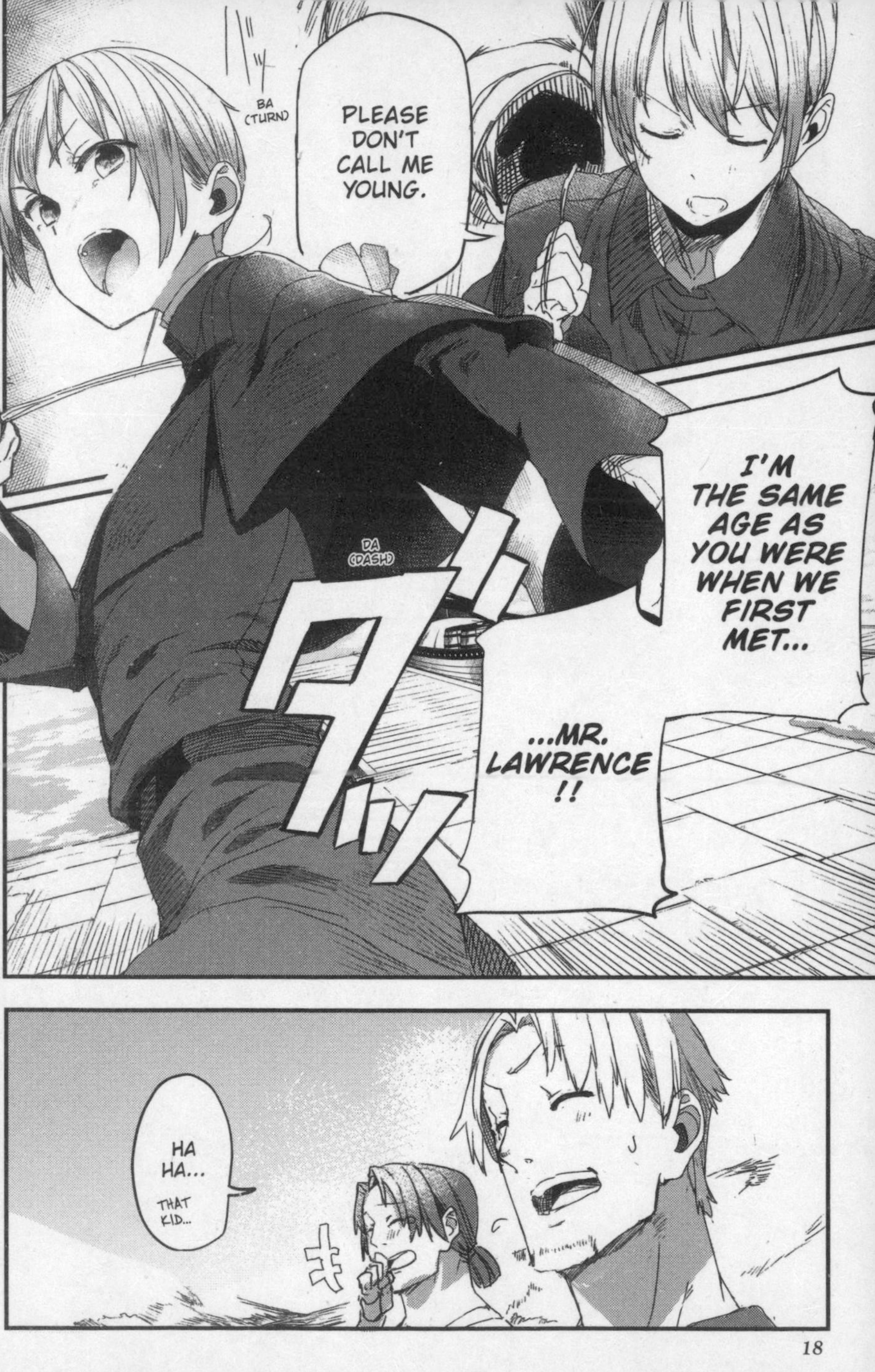
PLEASE DON'T CALL ME YOUNG.
BA (TURN)
I'M THE SAME AGE AS YOU WERE WHEN WE FIRST MET...
DA (DASH)
...MR. LAWRENCE!!
HA HA...
THAT KID...

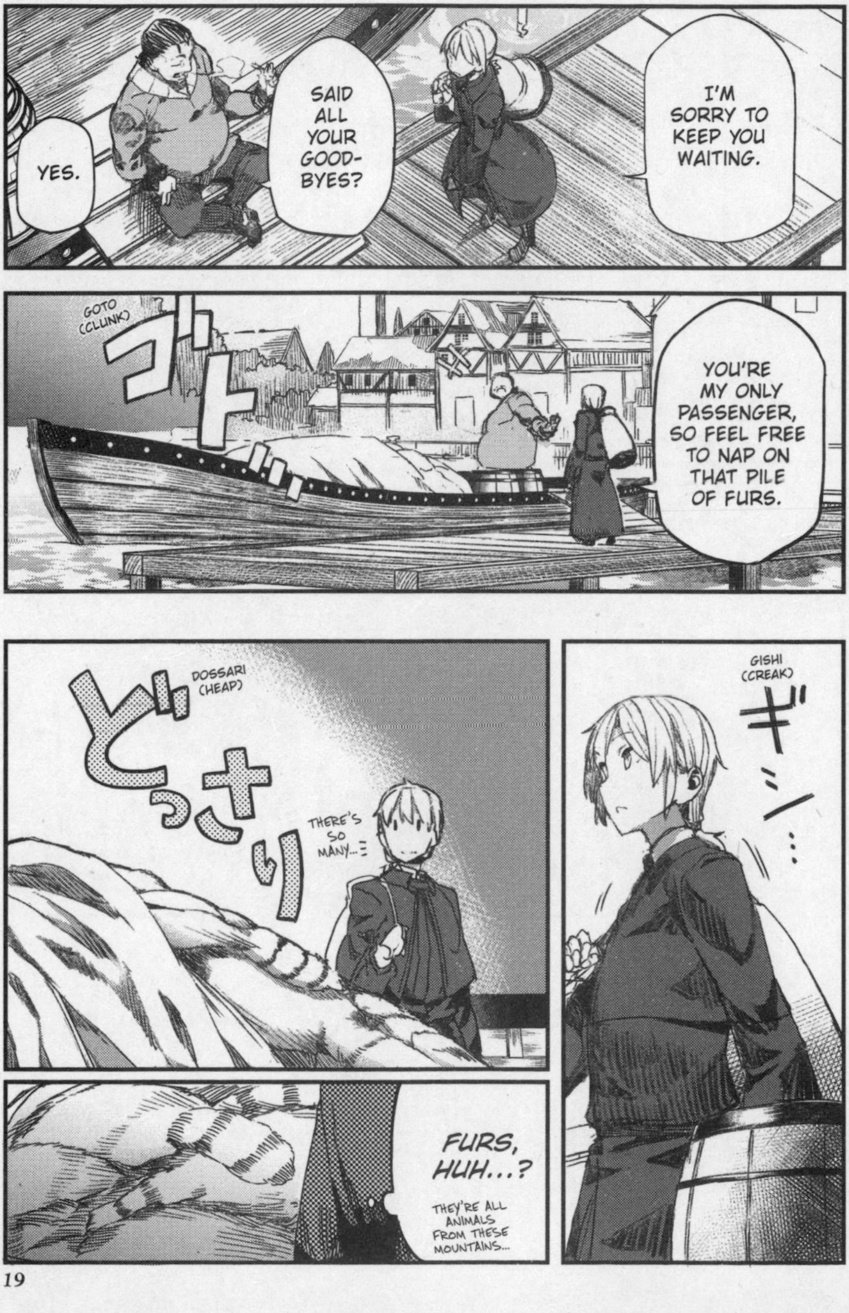

I'M SORRY TO KEEP YOU WAITING.
SAID ALL YOUR GOOD-BYES?
YES.
YOU'RE MY ONLY PASSENGER, SO FEEL FREE TO NAP ON THAT PILE OF FURS.
GOTO (CLUNK)
GISHI (CREAK)
DOSSARI (HEAP)
THERE'S SO MANY...
FURS, HUH...?
THEY'RE ALL ANIMALS FROM THESE MOUNTAINS...

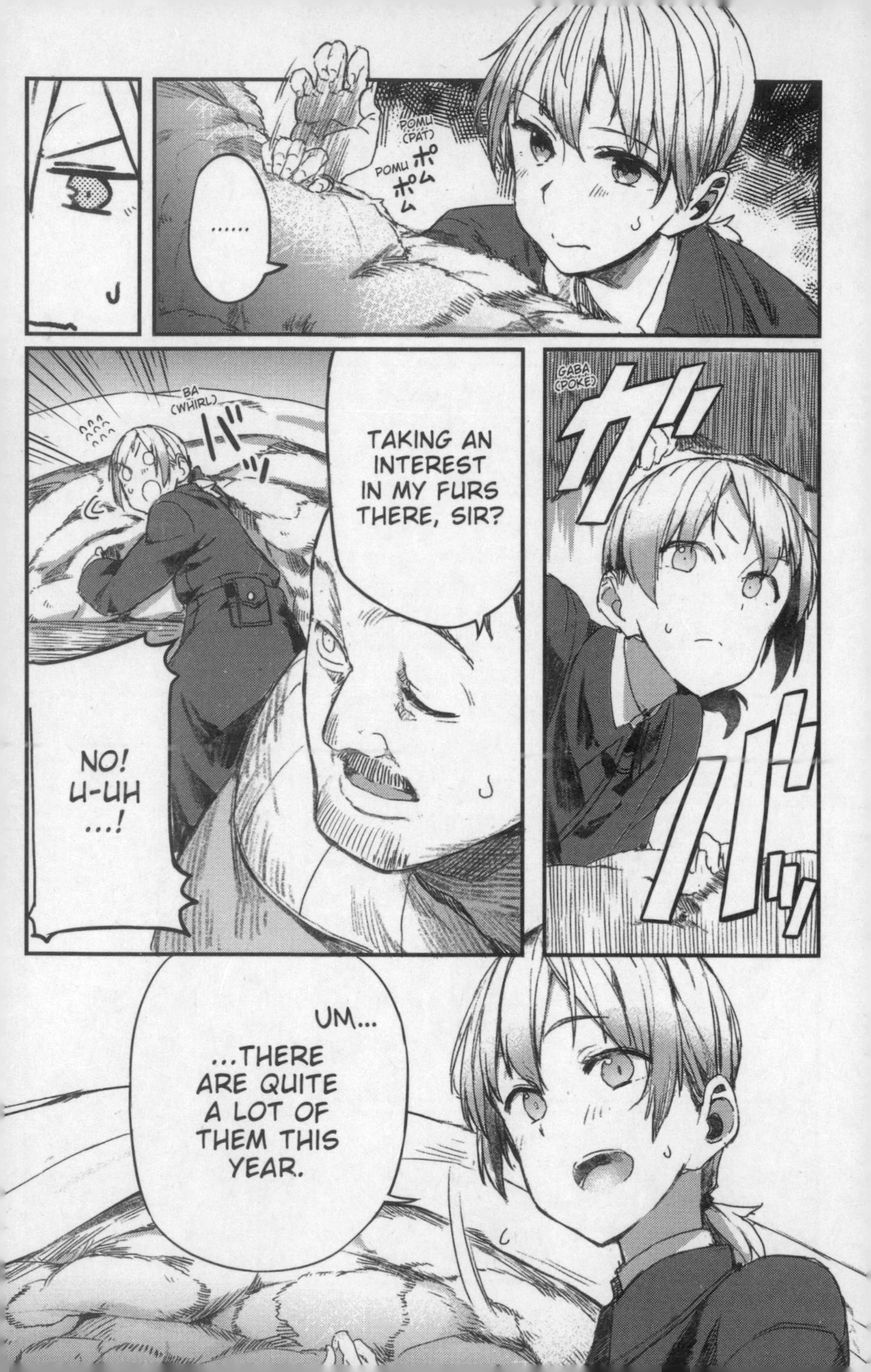

POMU (PAT) ポム
POMU ポム
......
GABA (POKE)
ガバッ
BA (WHIRL) バッ
TAKING AN INTEREST IN MY FURS THERE, SIR?
NO! U-UH ...!
UM...
...THERE ARE QUITE A LOT OF THEM THIS YEAR.

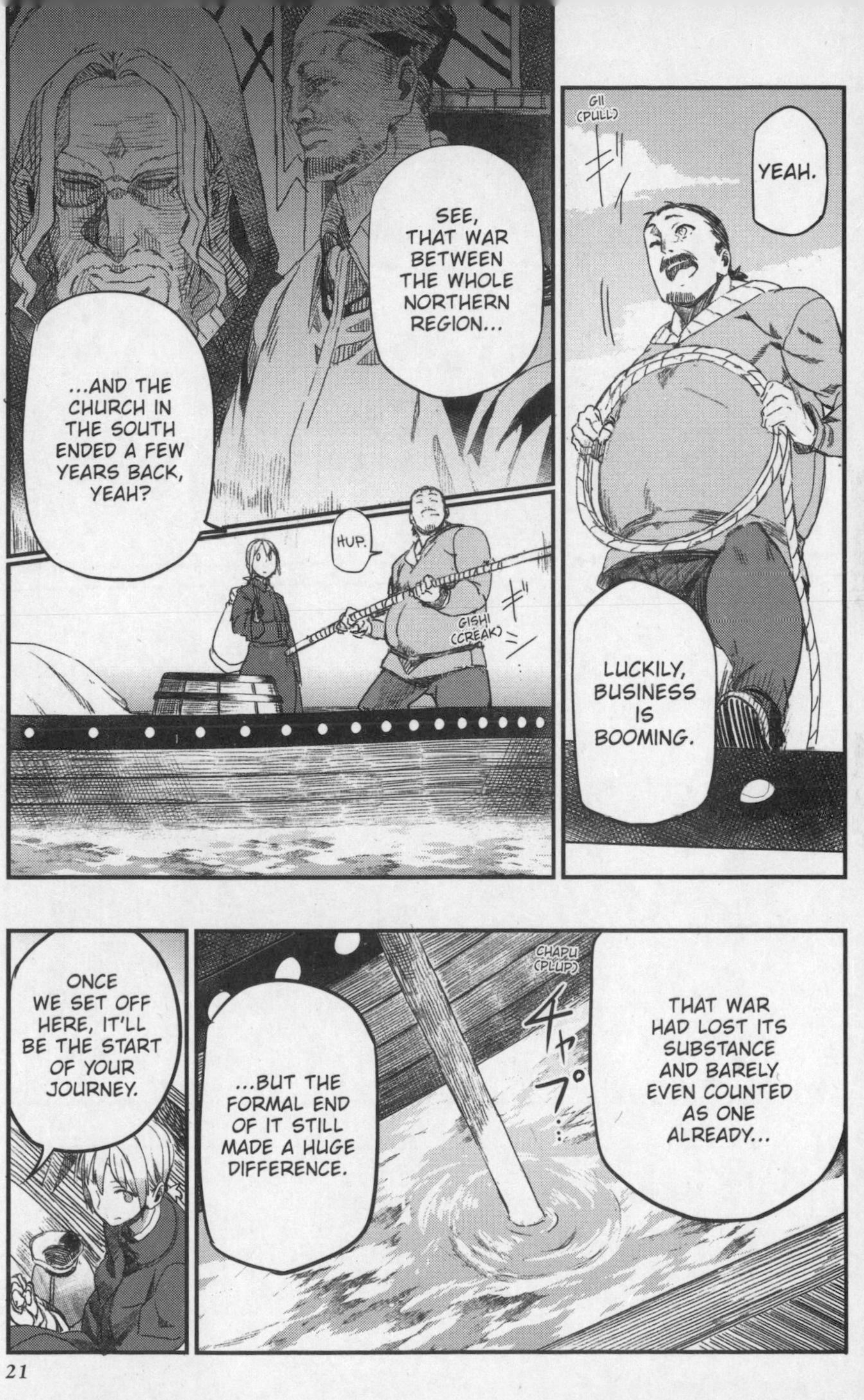
GII (PULL)
YEAH.
LUCKILY, BUSINESS IS BOOMING.
SEE, THAT WAR BETWEEN THE WHOLE NORTHERN REGION...
...AND THE CHURCH IN THE SOUTH ENDED A FEW YEARS BACK, YEAH?
HUP.
GISHI (CREAK)
CHAPU (PLUP)
THAT WAR HAD LOST ITS SUBSTANCE AND BARELY EVEN COUNTED AS ONE ALREADY...
...BUT THE FORMAL END OF IT STILL MADE A HUGE DIFFERENCE.
ONCE WE SET OFF HERE, IT'LL BE THE START OF YOUR JOURNEY.

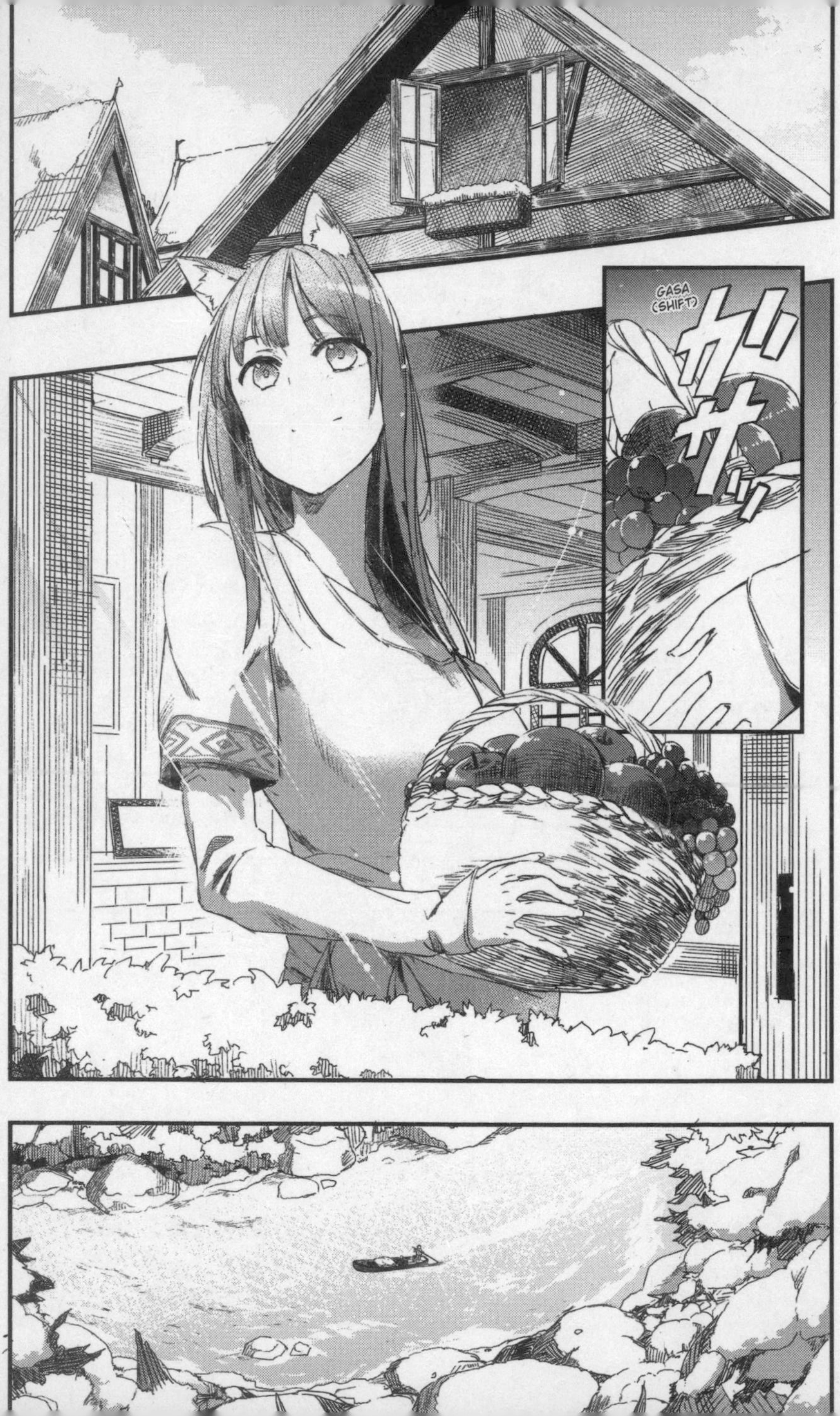
GASA
(SHIFT)
ガサッ

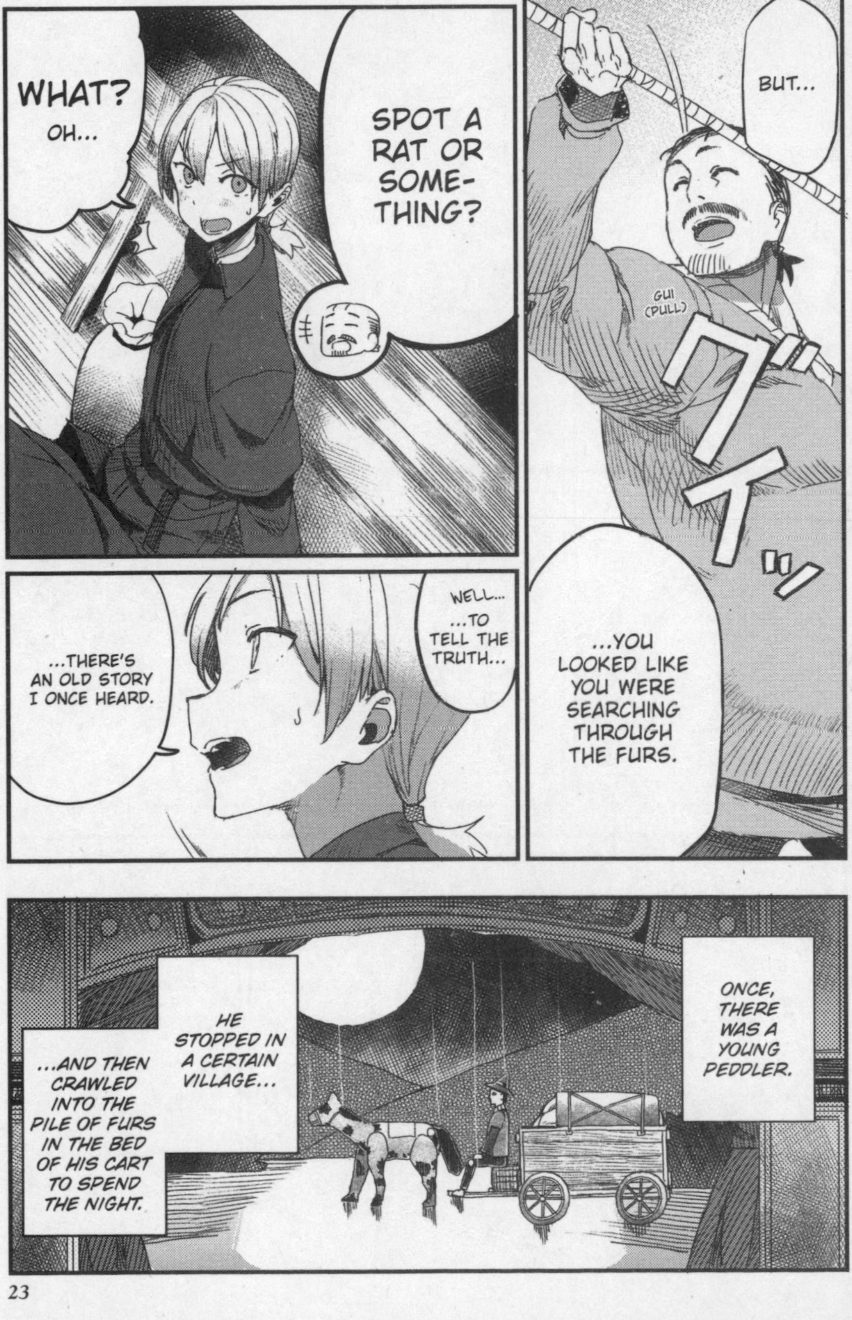
BUT...
GUI (PULL)
...YOU LOOKED LIKE YOU WERE SEARCHING THROUGH THE FURS.
SPOT A RAT OR SOME-THING?
WHAT? OH...
WELL... ...TO TELL THE TRUTH...
...THERE'S AN OLD STORY I ONCE HEARD.
ONCE, THERE WAS A YOUNG PEDDLER.
HE STOPPED IN A CERTAIN VILLAGE...
...AND THEN CRAWLED INTO THE PILE OF FURS IN THE BED OF HIS CART TO SPEND THE NIGHT.

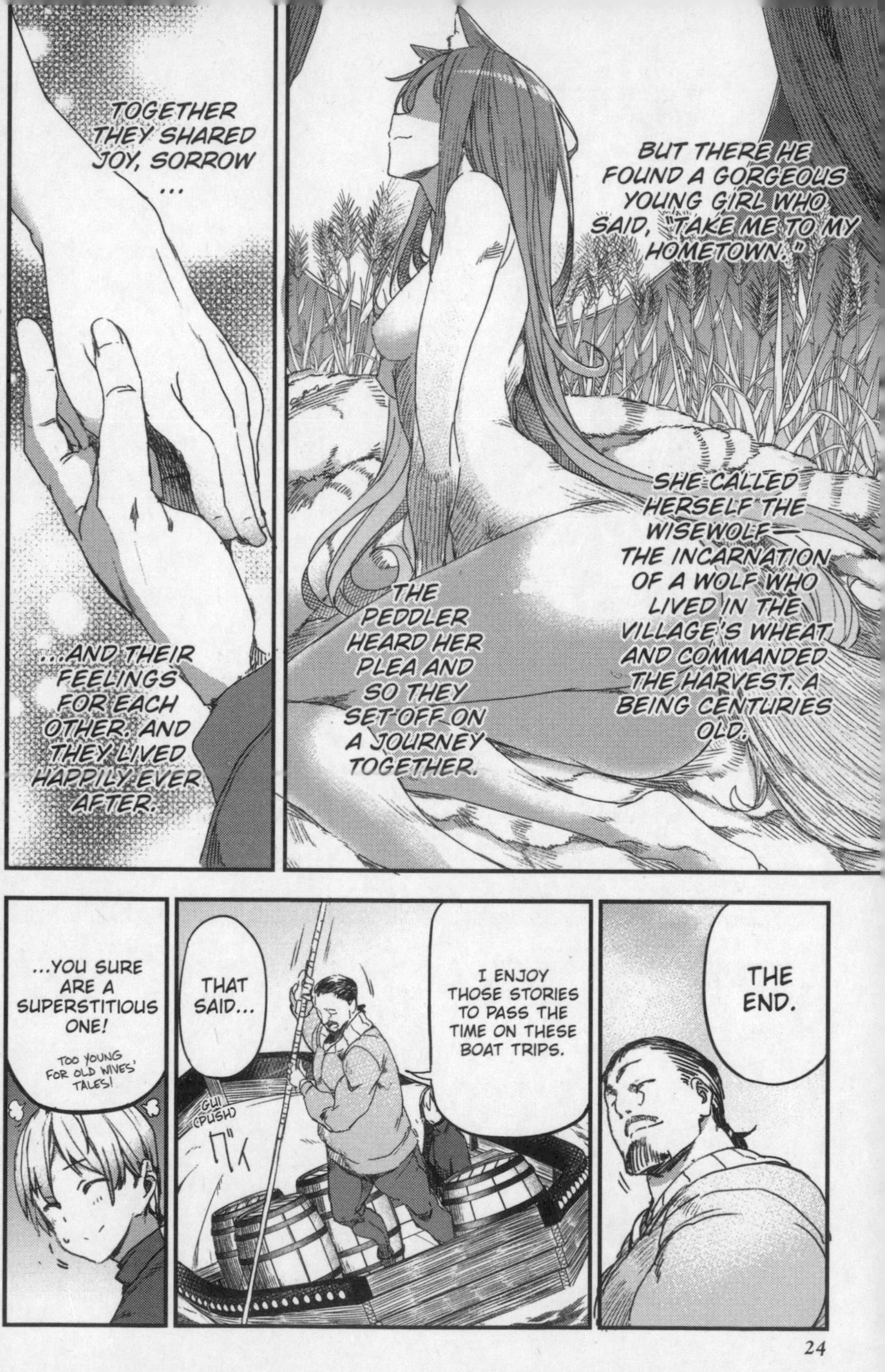
BUT THERE HE FOUND A GORGEOUS YOUNG GIRL WHO SAID, "TAKE ME TO MY HOMETOWN."
SHE CALLED HERSELF THE WISEWOLF— THE INCARNATION OF A WOLF WHO LIVED IN THE VILLAGE'S WHEAT AND COMMANDED THE HARVEST. A BEING CENTURIES OLD.
THE PEDDLER HEARD HER PLEA AND SO THEY SET OFF ON A JOURNEY TOGETHER.
TOGETHER THEY SHARED JOY, SORROW ...
...AND THEIR FEELINGS FOR EACH OTHER. AND THEY LIVED HAPPILY EVER AFTER.
THE END.
I ENJOY THOSE STORIES TO PASS THE TIME ON THESE BOAT TRIPS.
THAT SAID...
GUI (PUSH)
...YOU SURE ARE A SUPERSTITIOUS ONE!
TOO YOUNG FOR OLD WIVES' TALES!

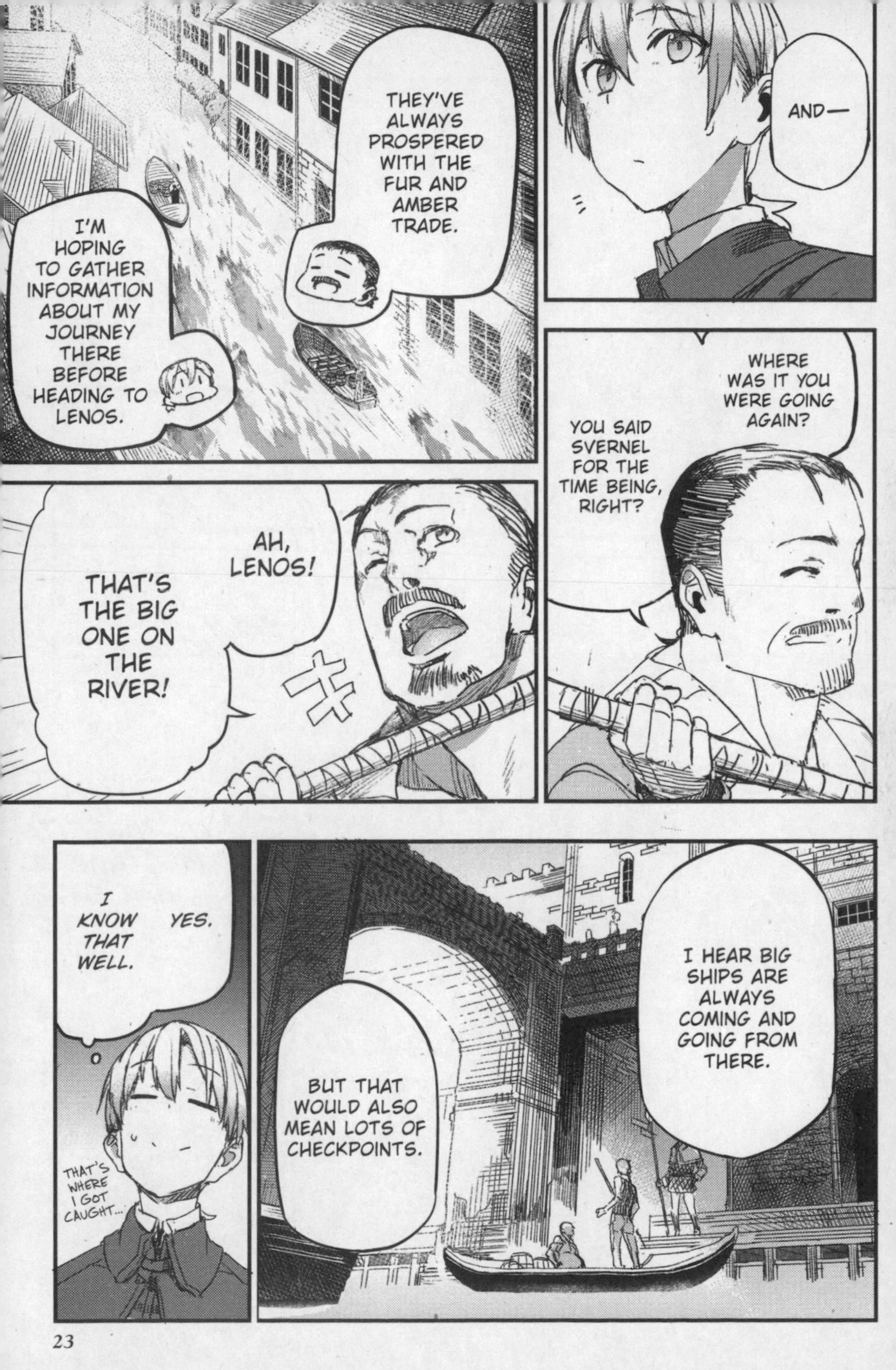
AND—
THEY'VE ALWAYS PROSPERED WITH THE FUR AND AMBER TRADE.
I'M HOPING TO GATHER INFORMATION ABOUT MY JOURNEY THERE BEFORE HEADING TO LENOS.
WHERE WAS IT YOU WERE GOING AGAIN?
YOU SAID SVERNEL FOR THE TIME BEING, RIGHT?
AH, LENOS!
THAT'S THE BIG ONE ON THE RIVER!
I HEAR BIG SHIPS ARE ALWAYS COMING AND GOING FROM THERE.
BUT THAT WOULD ALSO MEAN LOTS OF CHECKPOINTS.
YES.
I KNOW THAT WELL.
THAT'S WHERE I GOT CAUGHT...

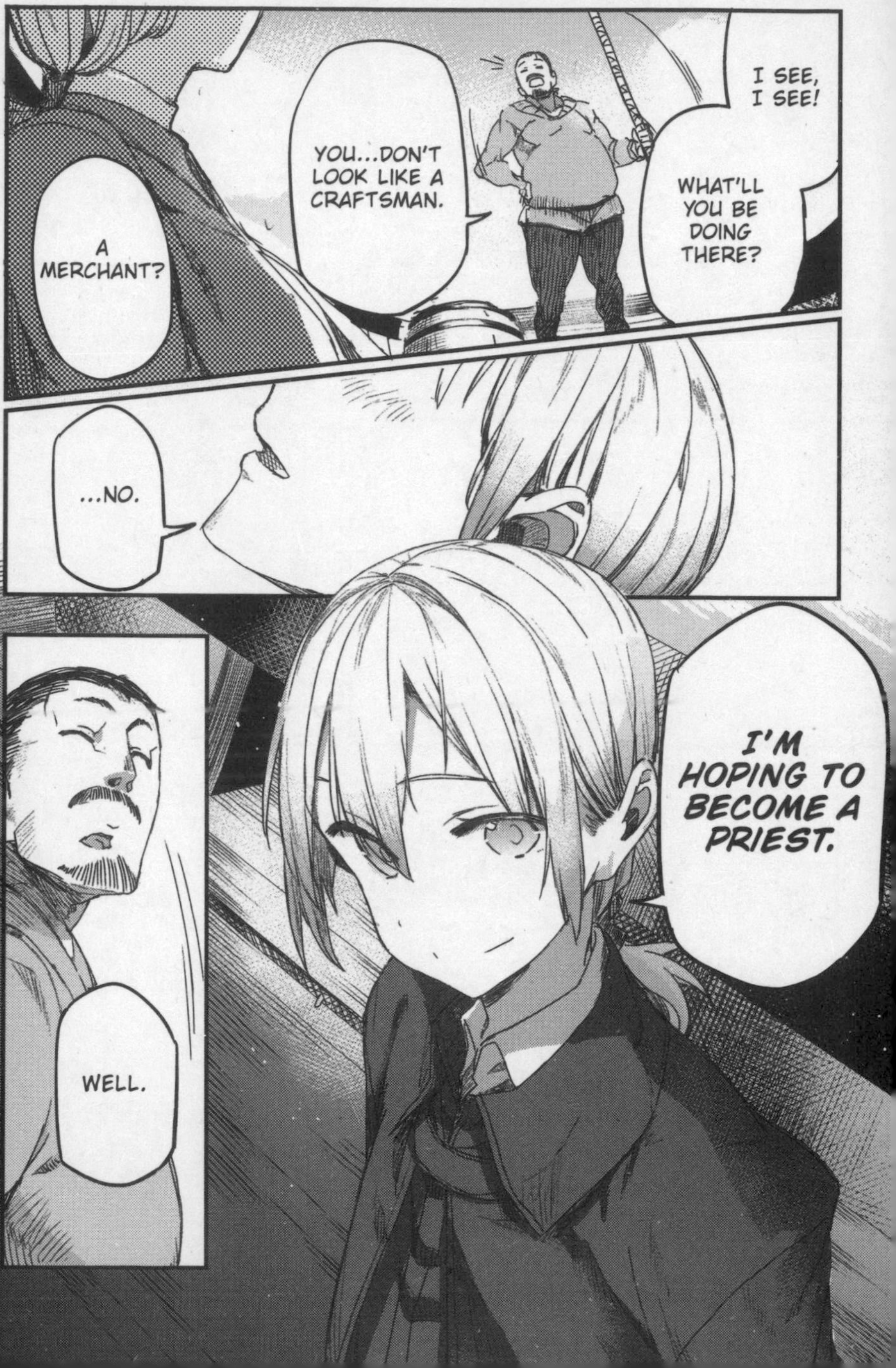
I SEE, I SEE!
WHAT'LL YOU BE DOING THERE?
YOU...DON'T LOOK LIKE A CRAFTSMAN.
A MERCHANT?
...NO.
I'M HOPING TO BECOME A PRIEST.
WELL.

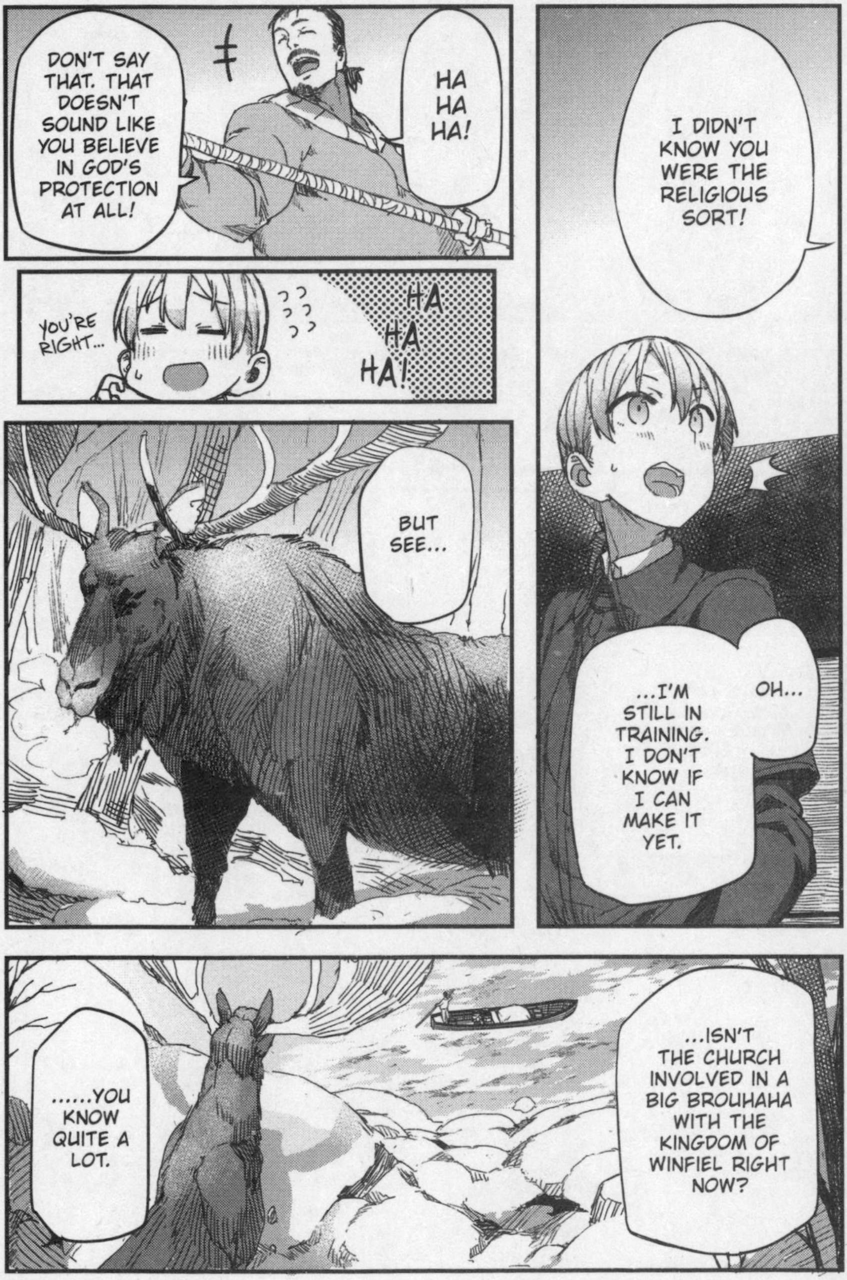
I DIDN'T KNOW YOU WERE THE RELIGIOUS SORT!
OH...
...I'M STILL IN TRAINING. I DON'T KNOW IF I CAN MAKE IT YET.
HA HA HA!
DON'T SAY THAT. THAT DOESN'T SOUND LIKE YOU BELIEVE IN GOD'S PROTECTION AT ALL!
HA HA HA!
YOU'RE RIGHT...
BUT SEE...
...ISN'T THE CHURCH INVOLVED IN A BIG BROUHAHA WITH THE KINGDOM OF WINFIEL RIGHT NOW?
......YOU KNOW QUITE A LOT.

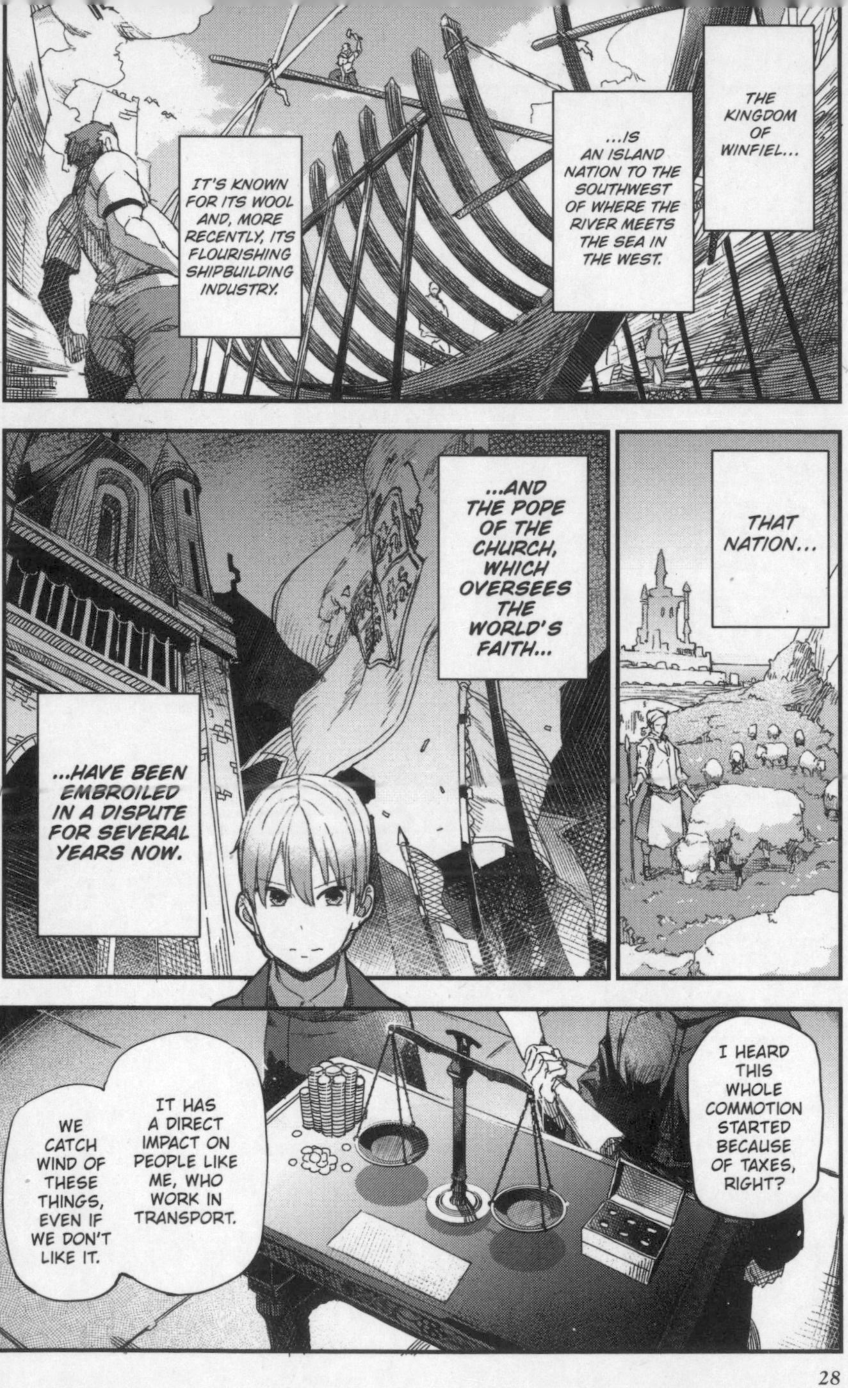
THE KINGDOM OF WINFIEL...
...IS AN ISLAND NATION TO THE SOUTHWEST OF WHERE THE RIVER MEETS THE SEA IN THE WEST.
IT'S KNOWN FOR ITS WOOL AND, MORE RECENTLY, ITS FLOURISHING SHIPBUILDING INDUSTRY.
THAT NATION...
...AND THE POPE OF THE CHURCH, WHICH OVERSEES THE WORLD'S FAITH...
...HAVE BEEN EMBROILED IN A DISPUTE FOR SEVERAL YEARS NOW.
I HEARD THIS WHOLE COMMOTION STARTED BECAUSE OF TAXES, RIGHT?
IT HAS A DIRECT IMPACT ON PEOPLE LIKE ME, WHO WORK IN TRANSPORT.
WE CATCH WIND OF THESE THINGS, EVEN IF WE DON'T LIKE IT.

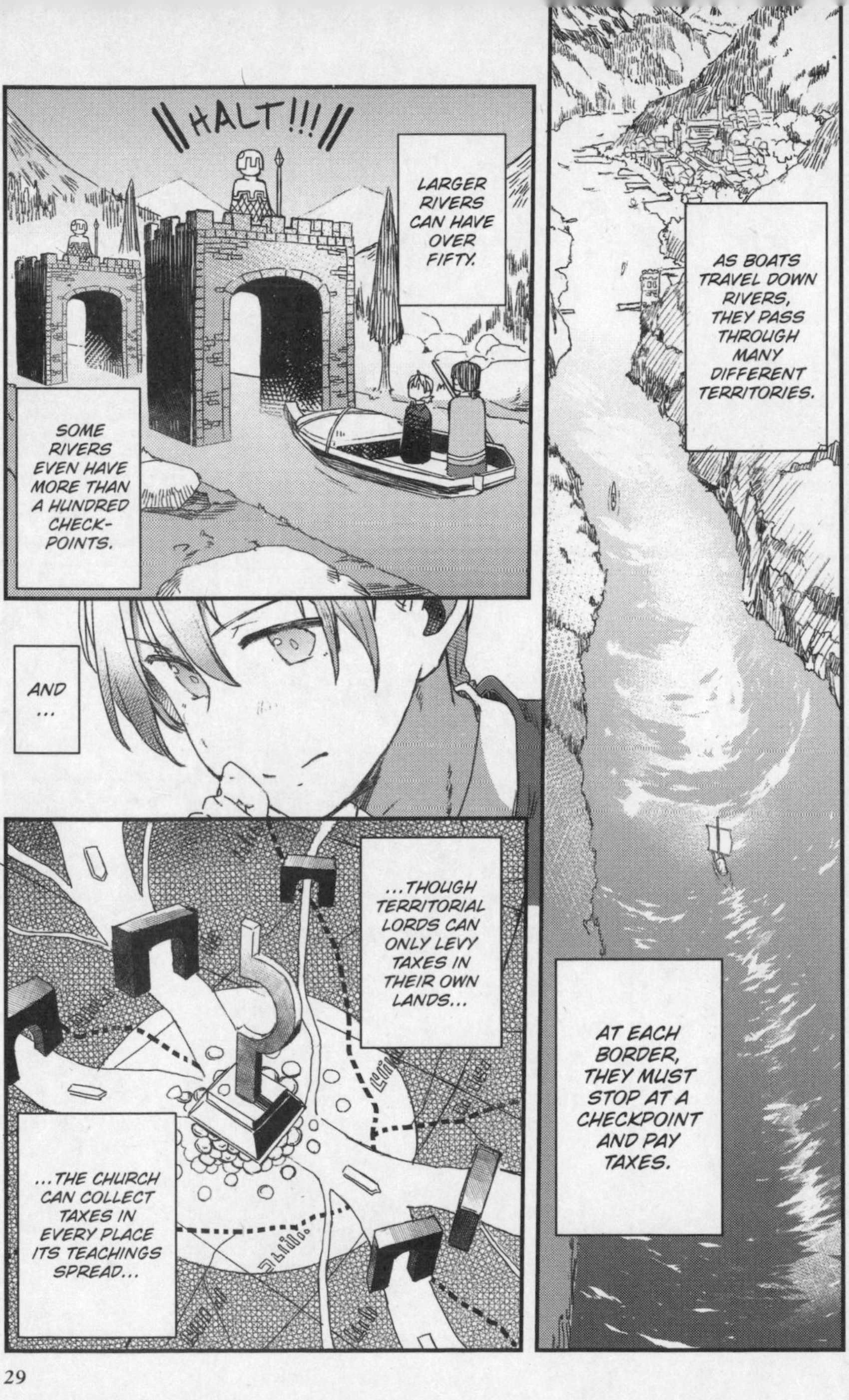
AS BOATS TRAVEL DOWN RIVERS, THEY PASS THROUGH MANY DIFFERENT TERRITORIES.
AT EACH BORDER, THEY MUST STOP AT A CHECKPOINT AND PAY TAXES.
HALT!!!
LARGER RIVERS CAN HAVE OVER FIFTY.
SOME RIVERS EVEN HAVE MORE THAN A HUNDRED CHECK-POINTS.
AND...
...THOUGH TERRITORIAL LORDS CAN ONLY LEVY TAXES IN THEIR OWN LANDS...
...THE CHURCH CAN COLLECT TAXES IN EVERY PLACE ITS TEACHINGS SPREAD...

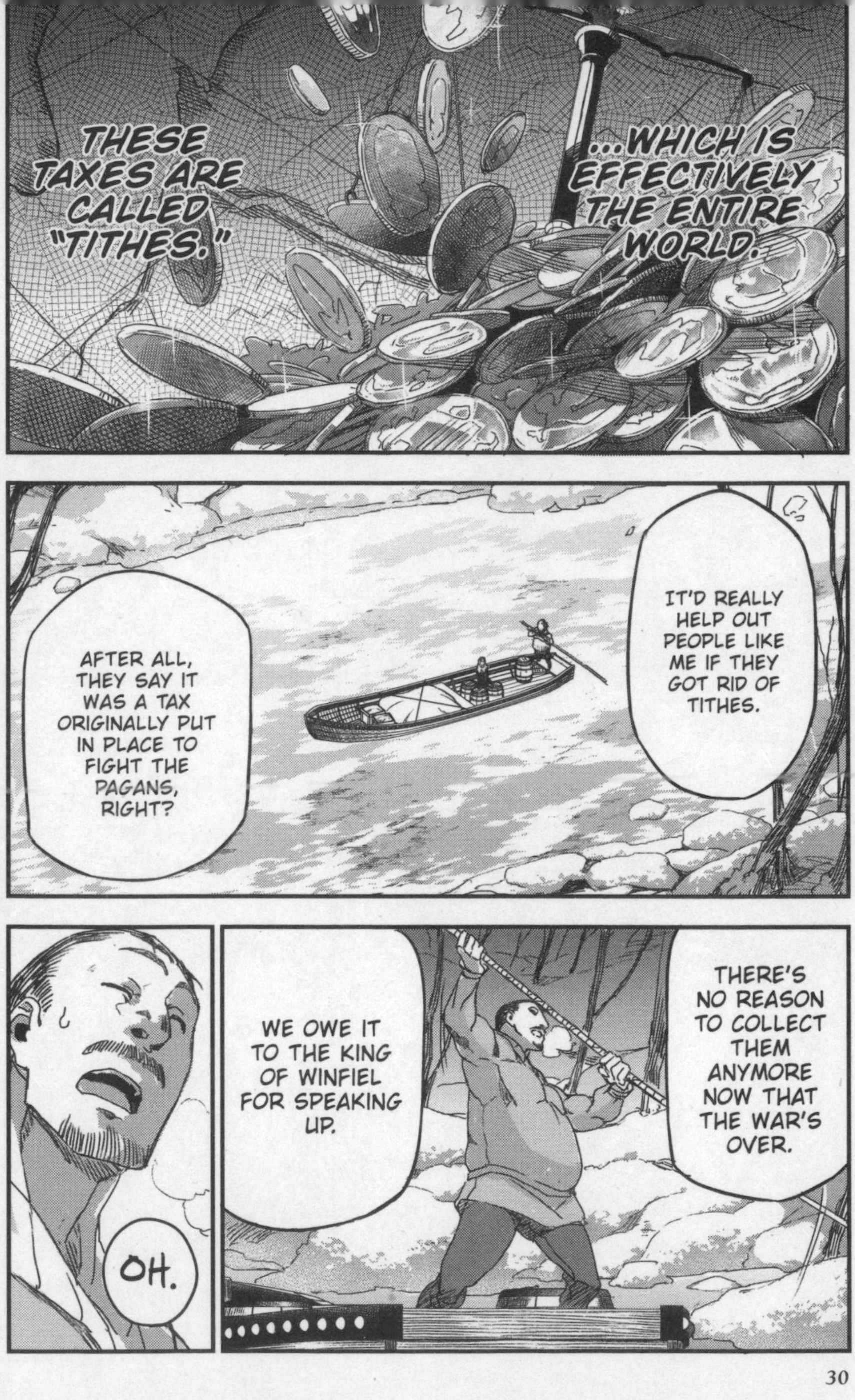
...WHICH IS EFFECTIVELY THE ENTIRE WORLD.
THESE TAXES ARE CALLED "TITHES."
IT'D REALLY HELP OUT PEOPLE LIKE ME IF THEY GOT RID OF TITHES.
AFTER ALL, THEY SAY IT WAS A TAX ORIGINALLY PUT IN PLACE TO FIGHT THE PAGANS, RIGHT?
THERE'S NO REASON TO COLLECT THEM ANYMORE NOW THAT THE WAR'S OVER.
WE OWE IT TO THE KING OF WINFIEL FOR SPEAKING UP.
OH.

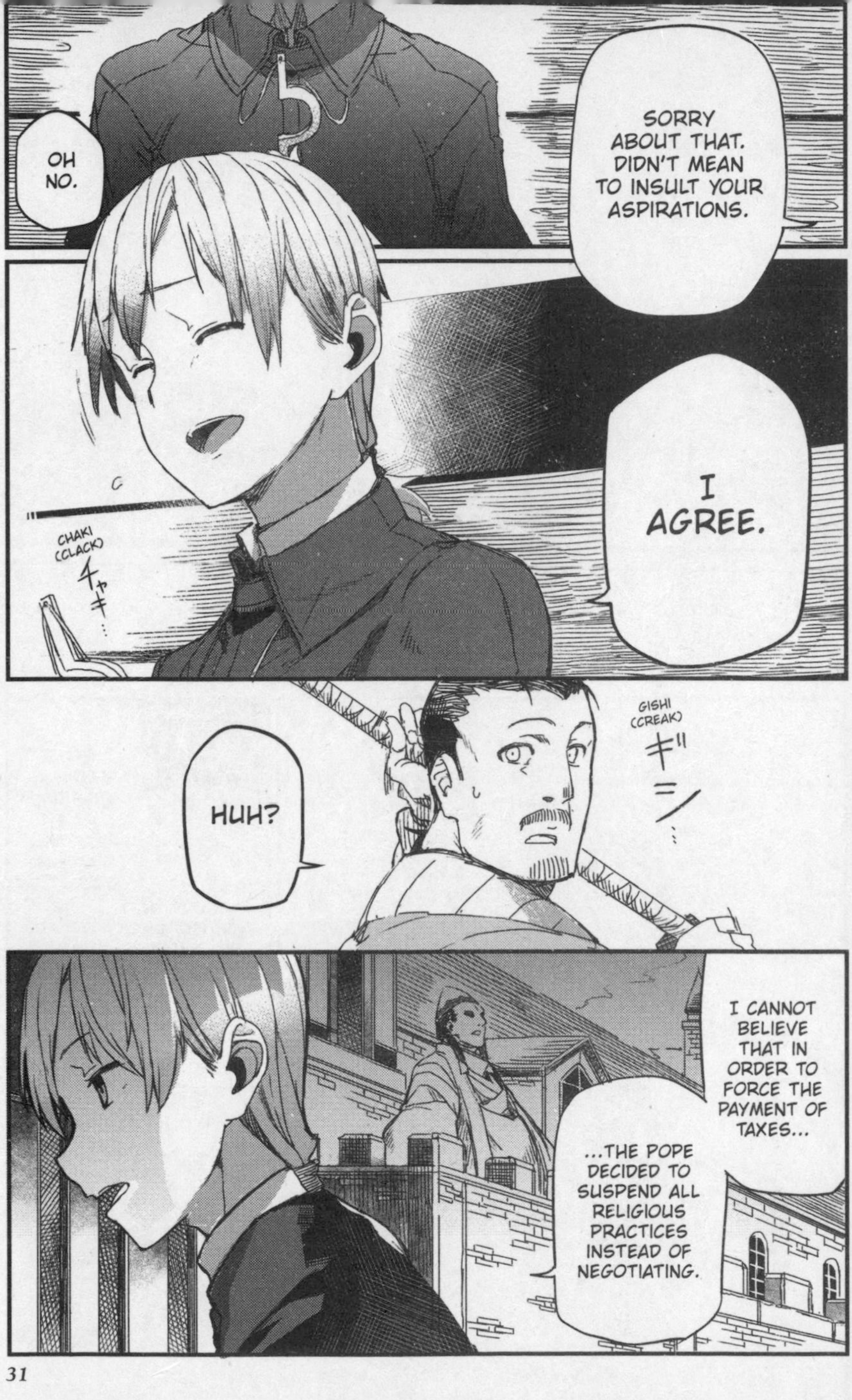
SORRY ABOUT THAT. DIDN'T MEAN TO INSULT YOUR ASPIRATIONS.
OH NO.
I AGREE.
CHAKI (CLACK)
GISHI (CREAK)
HUH?
I CANNOT BELIEVE THAT IN ORDER TO FORCE THE PAYMENT OF TAXES...
...THE POPE DECIDED TO SUSPEND ALL RELIGIOUS PRACTICES INSTEAD OF NEGOTIATING.

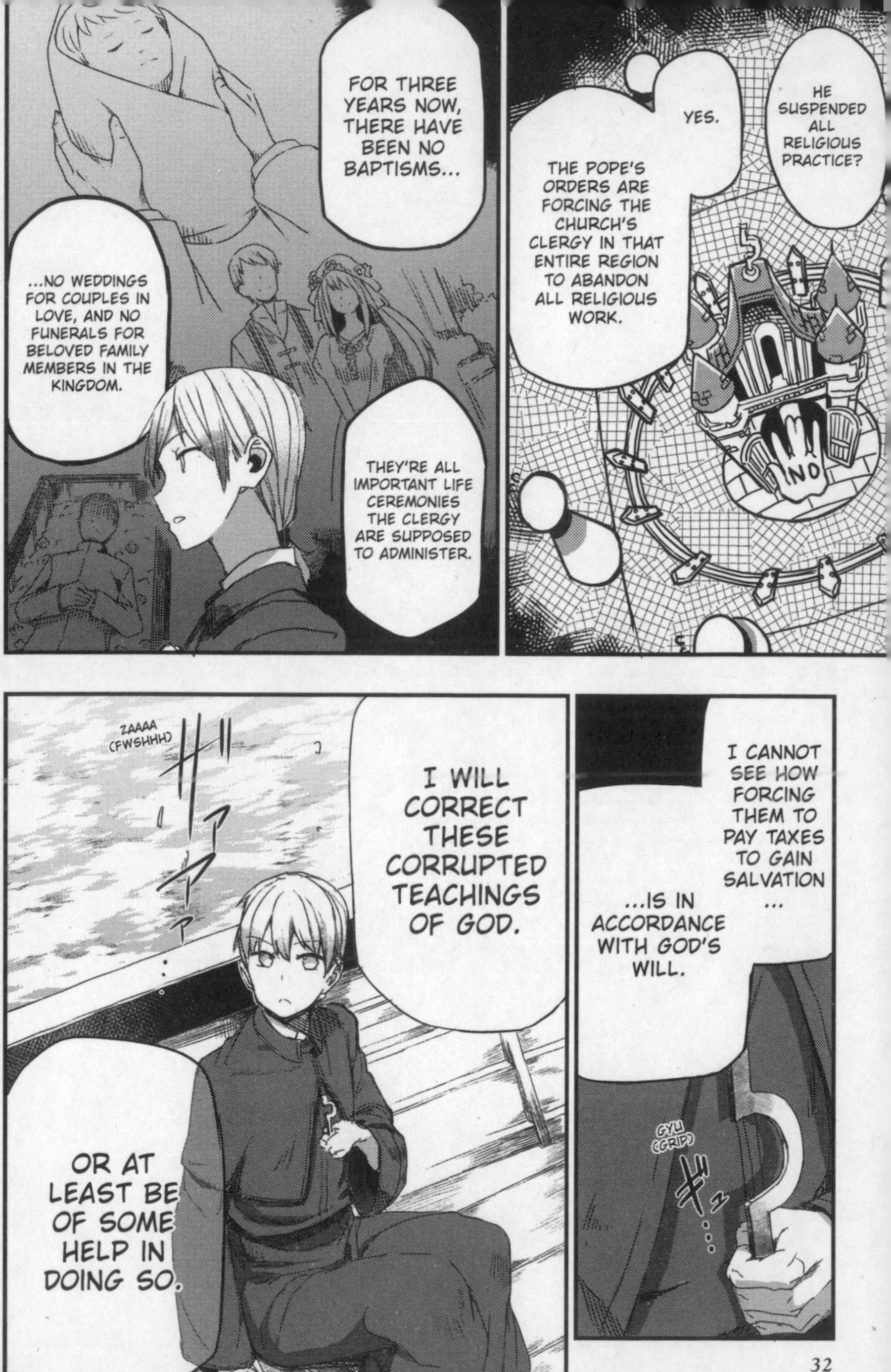
HE SUSPENDED ALL RELIGIOUS PRACTICE?
YES.
THE POPE'S ORDERS ARE FORCING THE CHURCH'S CLERGY IN THAT ENTIRE REGION TO ABANDON ALL RELIGIOUS WORK.
NO
FOR THREE YEARS NOW, THERE HAVE BEEN NO BAPTISMS...
...NO WEDDINGS FOR COUPLES IN LOVE, AND NO FUNERALS FOR BELOVED FAMILY MEMBERS IN THE KINGDOM.
THEY'RE ALL IMPORTANT LIFE CEREMONIES THE CLERGY ARE SUPPOSED TO ADMINISTER.
I CANNOT SEE HOW FORCING THEM TO PAY TAXES TO GAIN SALVATION ...
...IS IN ACCORDANCE WITH GOD'S WILL.
GYU (GRIP)
ZAAAA (FWSHHH)
I WILL CORRECT THESE CORRUPTED TEACHINGS OF GOD.
OR AT LEAST BE OF SOME HELP IN DOING SO.

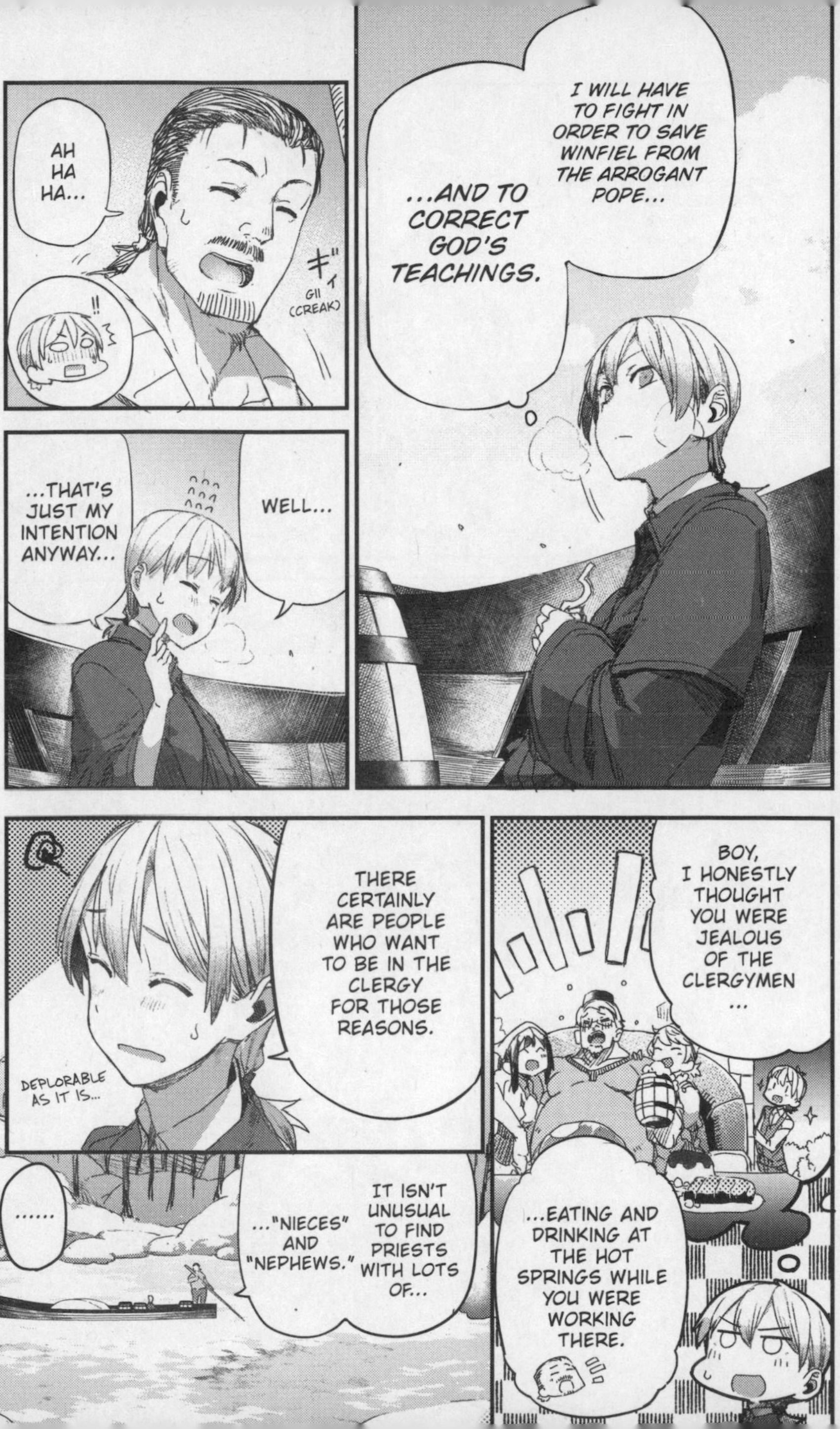
I WILL HAVE TO FIGHT IN ORDER TO SAVE WINFIEL FROM THE ARROGANT POPE...
...AND TO CORRECT GOD'S TEACHINGS.
AH HA HA...
ギイ
GII (CREAK)
!!
WELL...
...THAT'S JUST MY INTENTION ANYWAY...
BOY, I HONESTLY THOUGHT YOU WERE JEALOUS OF THE CLERGYMEN ...
...EATING AND DRINKING AT THE HOT SPRINGS WHILE YOU WERE WORKING THERE.
THERE CERTAINLY ARE PEOPLE WHO WANT TO BE IN THE CLERGY FOR THOSE REASONS.
DEPLORABLE AS IT IS...
IT ISN'T UNUSUAL TO FIND PRIESTS WITH LOTS OF...
..."NIECES" AND "NEPHEWS."
......

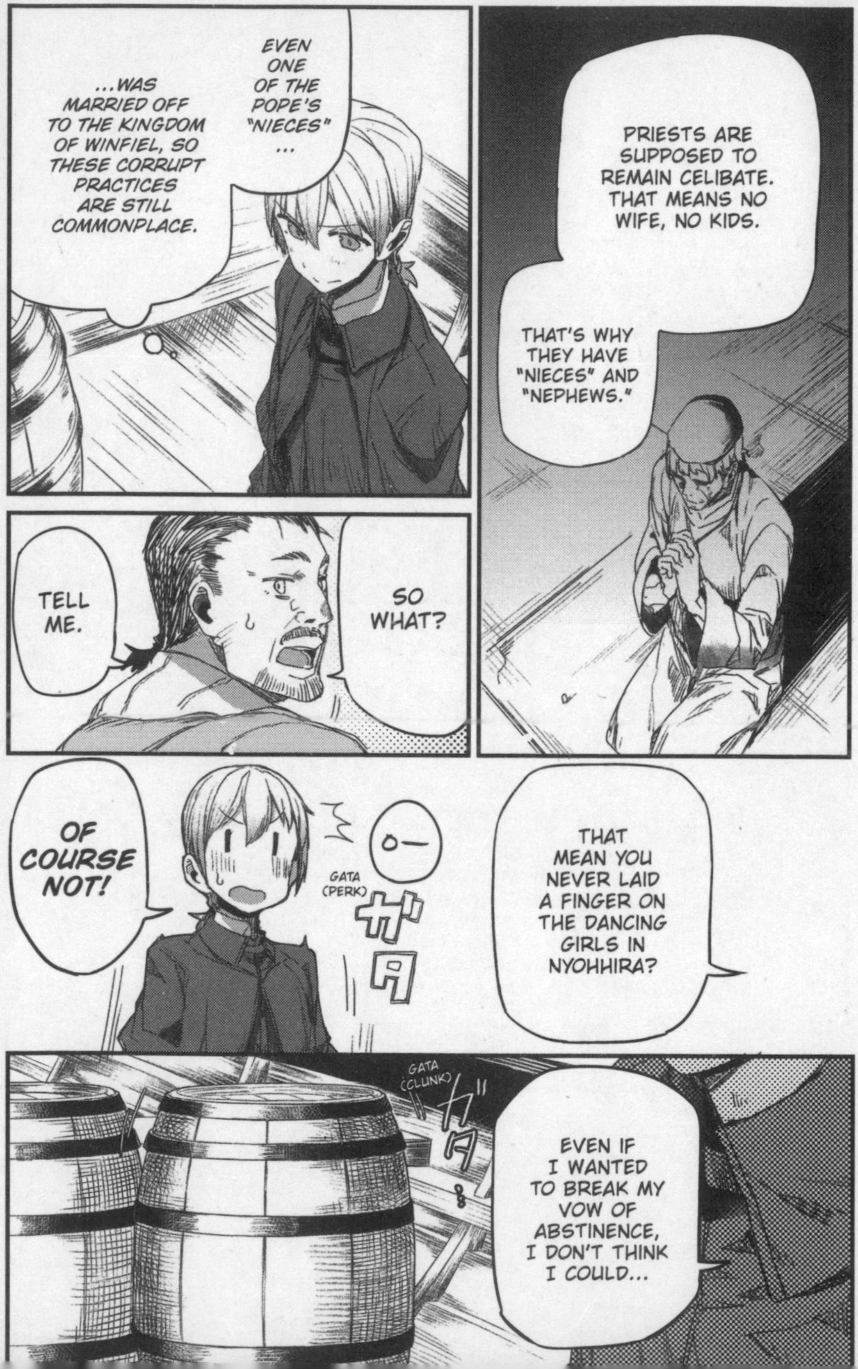
PRIESTS ARE SUPPOSED TO REMAIN CELIBATE. THAT MEANS NO WIFE, NO KIDS.
THAT'S WHY THEY HAVE "NIECES" AND "NEPHEWS."
EVEN ONE OF THE POPE'S "NIECES" ...
...WAS MARRIED OFF TO THE KINGDOM OF WINFIEL, SO THESE CORRUPT PRACTICES ARE STILL COMMONPLACE.
SO WHAT?
TELL ME.
THAT MEAN YOU NEVER LAID A FINGER ON THE DANCING GIRLS IN NYOHHIRA?
O—
GATA (PERK)
OF COURSE NOT!
EVEN IF I WANTED TO BREAK MY VOW OF ABSTINENCE, I DON'T THINK I COULD...
GATA (CLUNK)

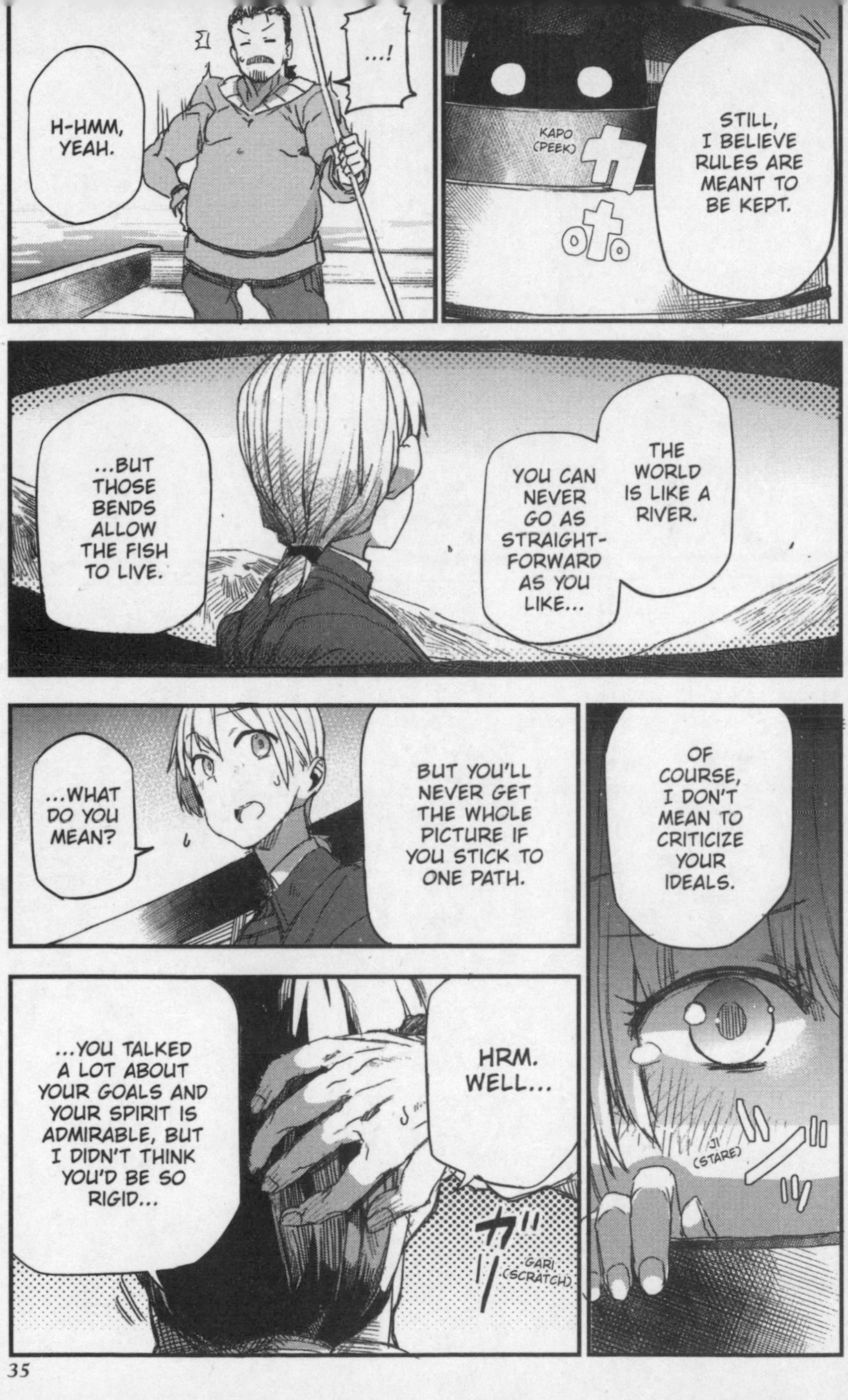
STILL, I BELIEVE RULES ARE MEANT TO BE KEPT.
KAPO (PEEK)
...!
H-HMM, YEAH.
THE WORLD IS LIKE A RIVER.
YOU CAN NEVER GO AS STRAIGHT-FORWARD AS YOU LIKE...
...BUT THOSE BENDS ALLOW THE FISH TO LIVE.
OF COURSE, I DON'T MEAN TO CRITICIZE YOUR IDEALS.
JI (STARE)
BUT YOU'LL NEVER GET THE WHOLE PICTURE IF YOU STICK TO ONE PATH.
...WHAT DO YOU MEAN?
HRM. WELL...
...YOU TALKED A LOT ABOUT YOUR GOALS AND YOUR SPIRIT IS ADMIRABLE, BUT I DIDN'T THINK YOU'D BE SO RIGID...
GARI (SCRATCH)

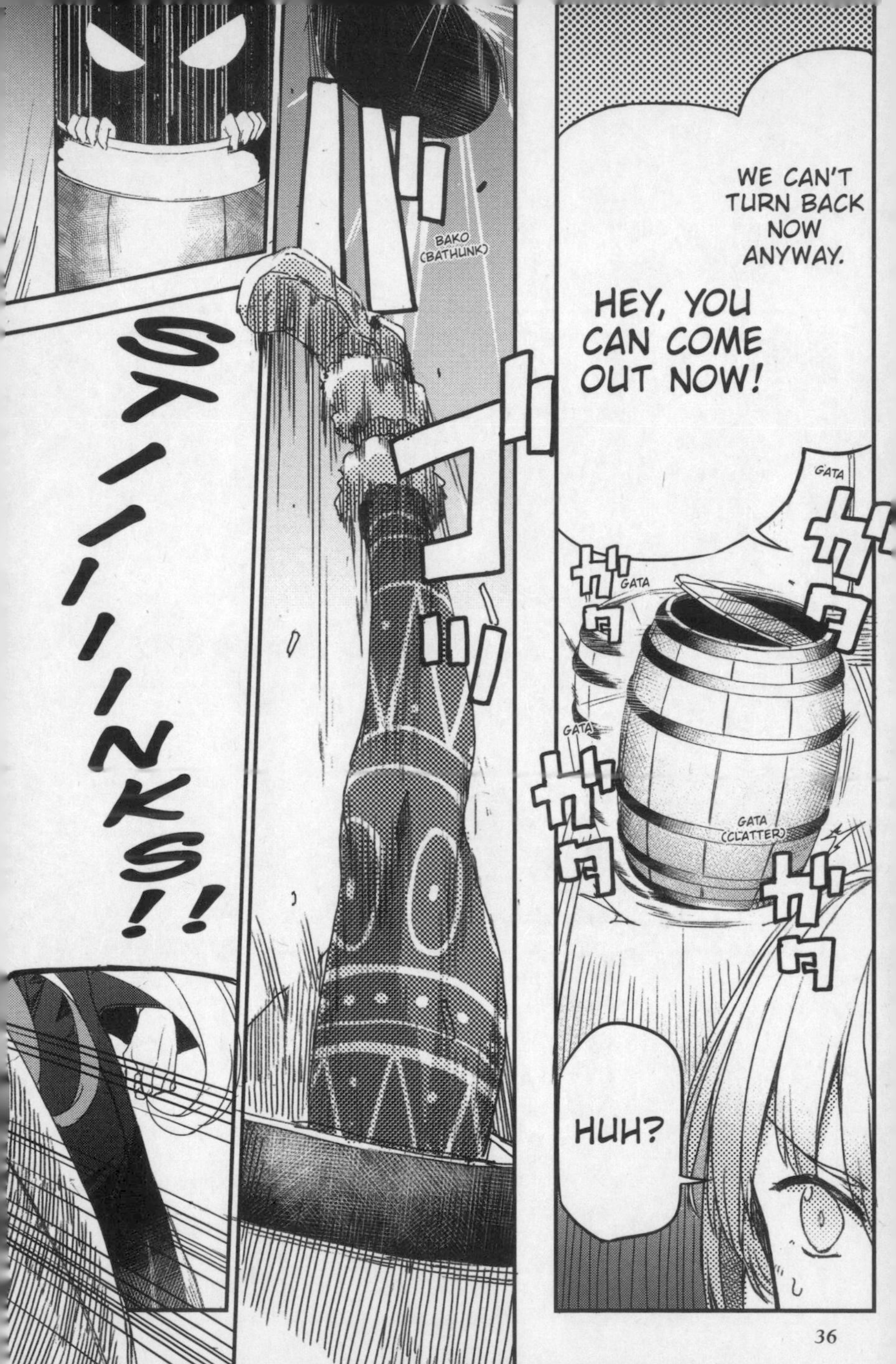
WE CAN'T TURN BACK NOW ANYWAY.
HEY, YOU CAN COME OUT NOW!
GATA
GATA
GATA
GATA (CLATTER)
HUH?
BAKO (BATHUNK)
STIIIINKS!!

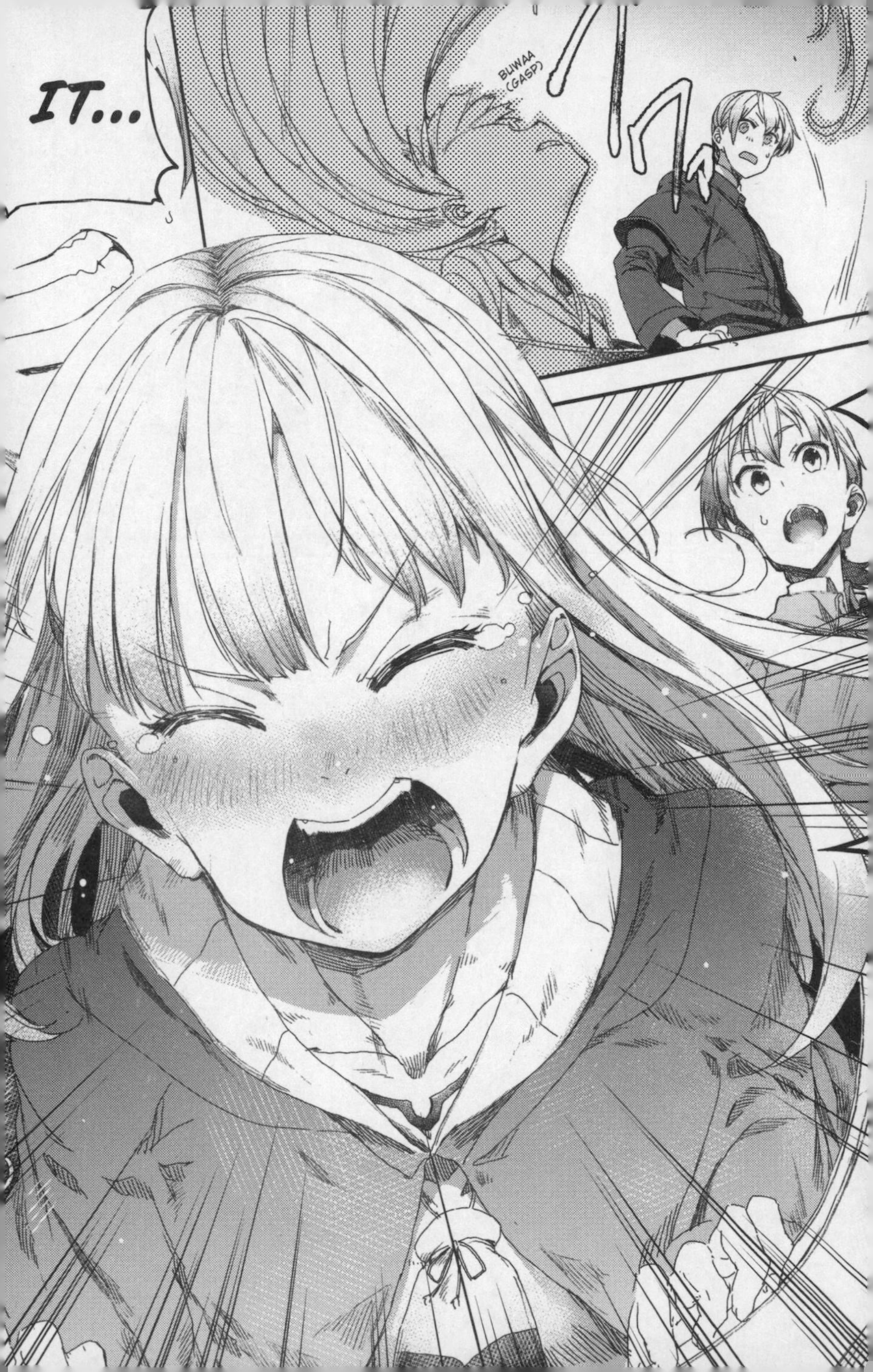
BUWAA (GASP)
IT...

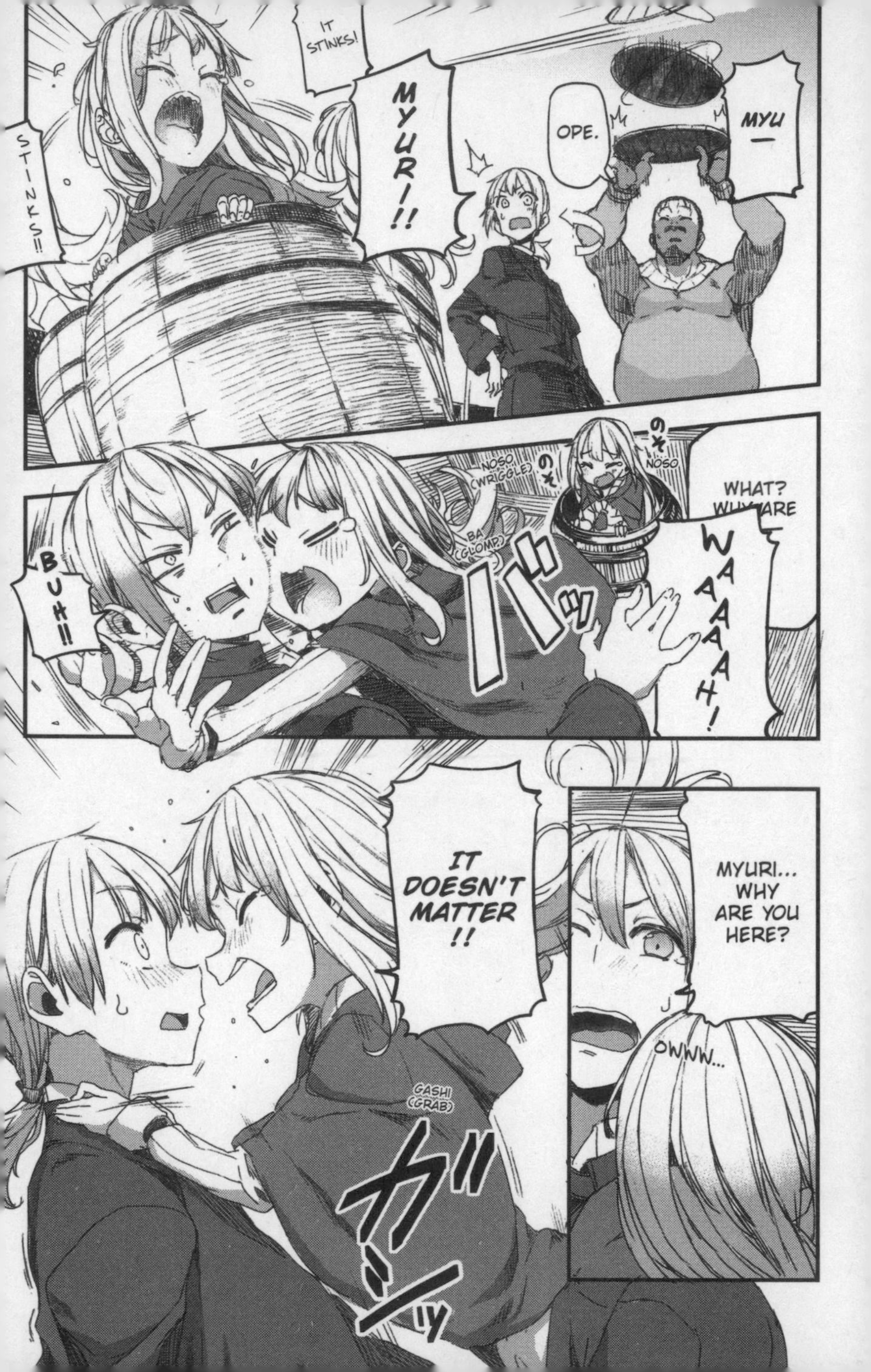
MYU—
OPE.
MYURI!!
IT STINKS!
STINKS!!
のそ
NOSO
のそ
NOSO (WRIGGLE)
WHAT? WHY ARE
WAAAAAH!
BA (GLOMP)
BUH!!
MYURI... WHY ARE YOU HERE?
OWWW...
IT DOESN'T MATTER!!
GASHI (GRAB)

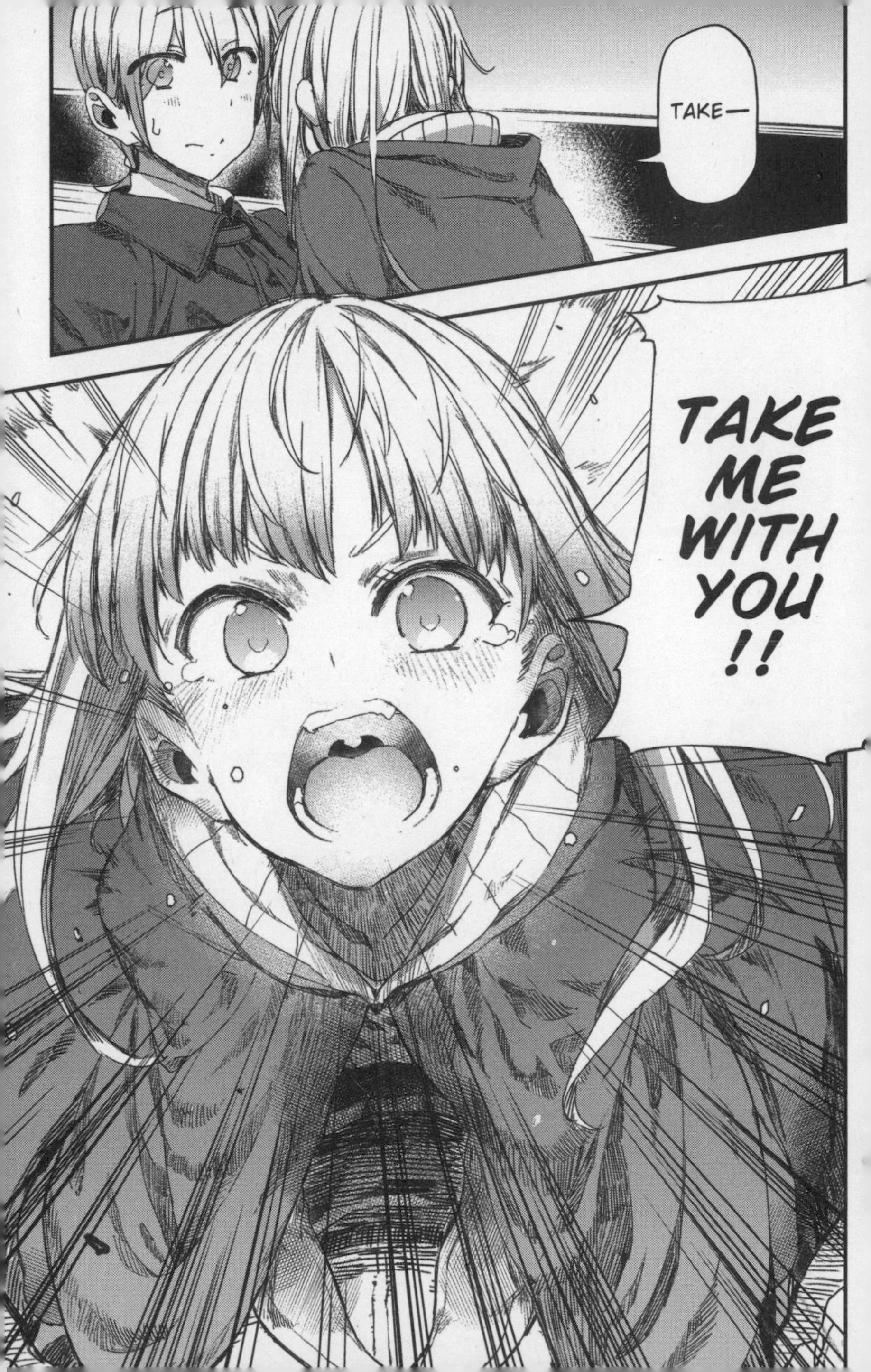
TAKE—
TAKE ME WITH YOU!!

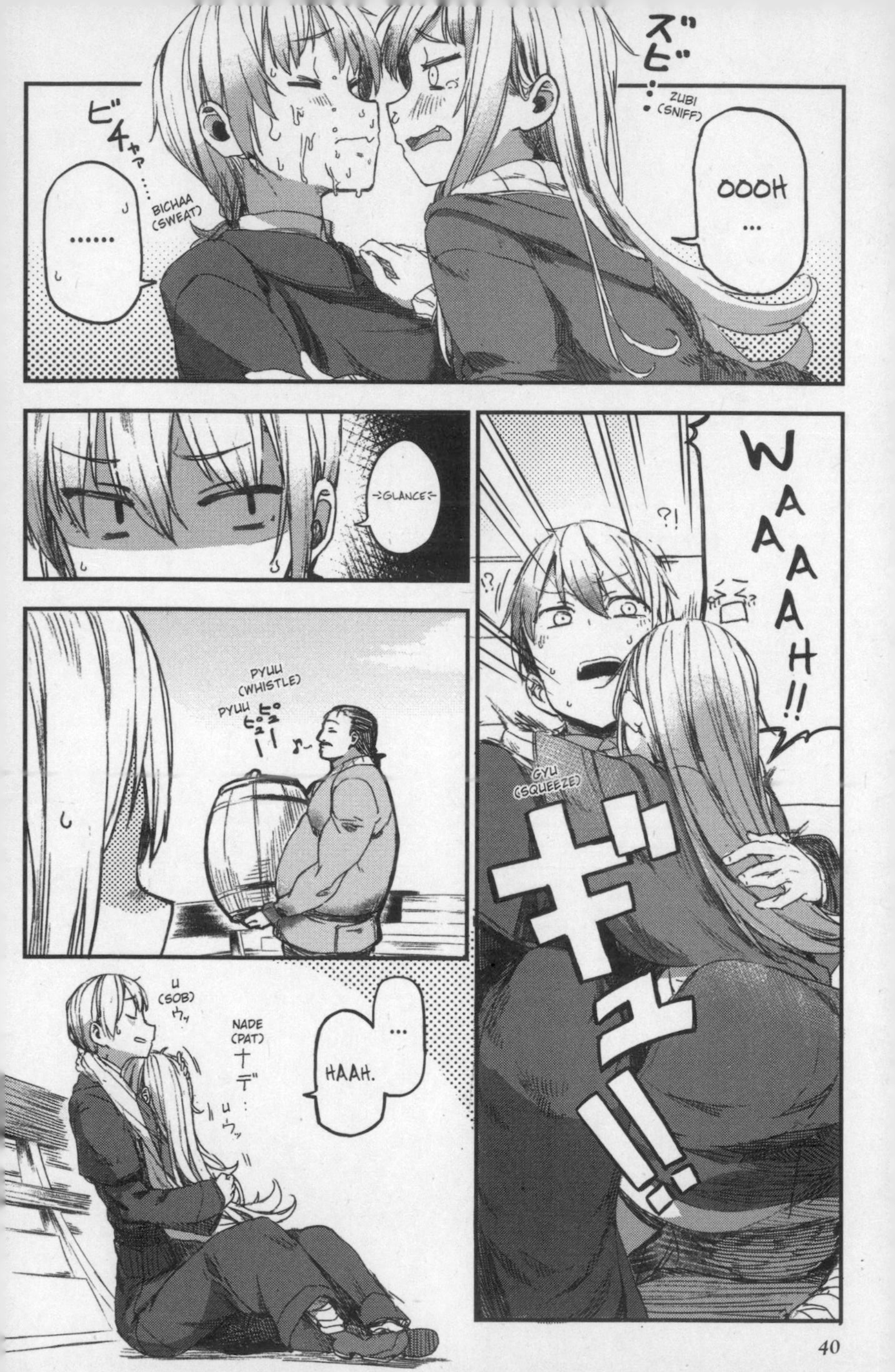
ズビ
ZUBI (SNIFF)
OOOH ...
ビチャァ
BICHAA (SWEAT)
......
WAAAAAH!!
?!
ギュ!!
GYU (SQUEEZE)
GLANCE
PYUU (WHISTLE)
PYUU
ピュ ピュー
... HAAH.
ナデ
NADE (PAT)
ウッ
U (SOB)

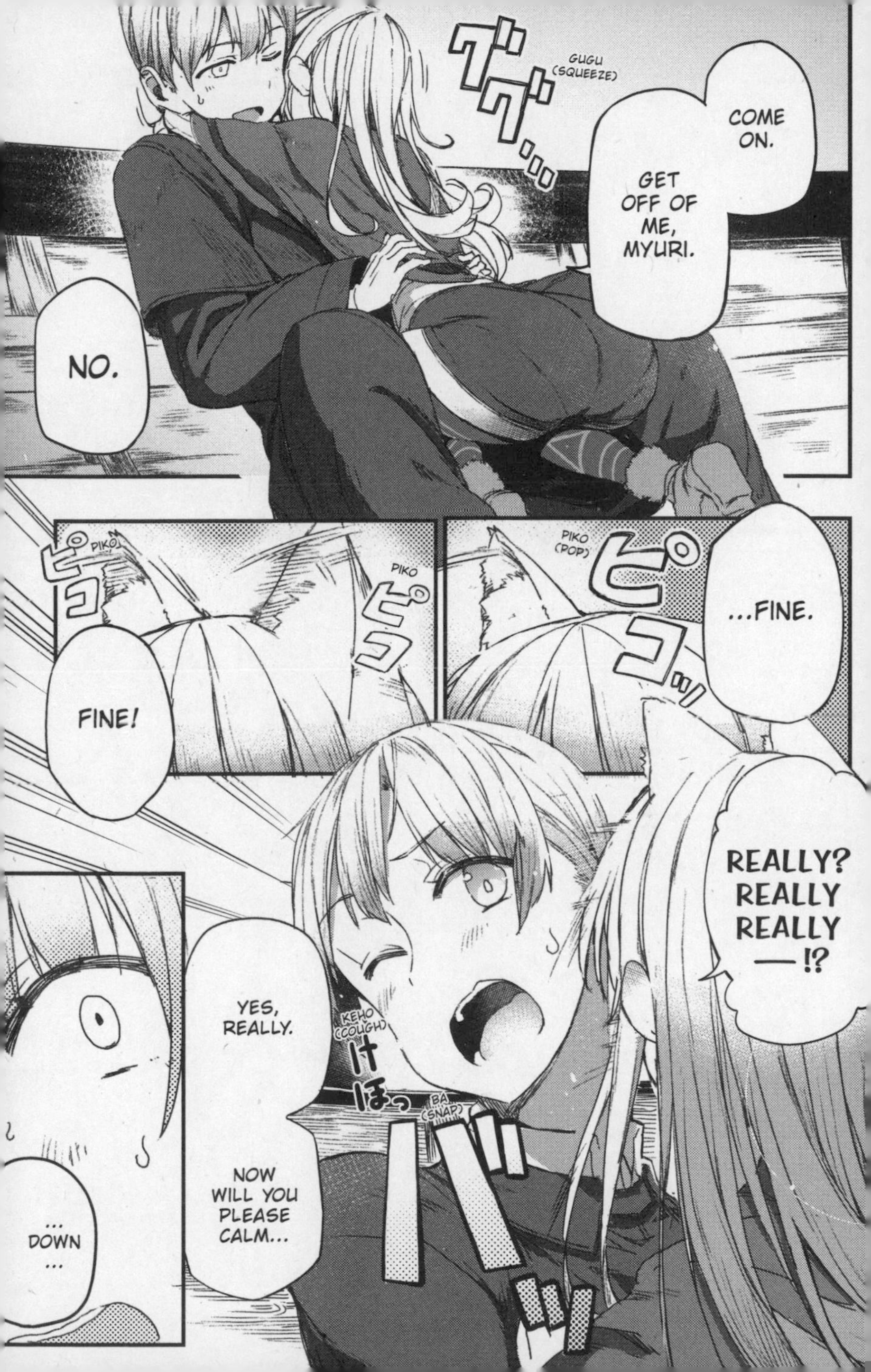
ググ…
GUGU (SQUEEZE)
COME ON.
GET OFF OF ME, MYURI.
NO.
ピコッ
PIKO (POP)
...FINE.
ピコ
PIKO
ピコ
PIKO
FINE!
REALLY? REALLY REALLY —!?
バッ
BA (SNAP)
けほっ
KEHO (COUGH)
YES, REALLY.
NOW WILL YOU PLEASE CALM...
... DOWN ...

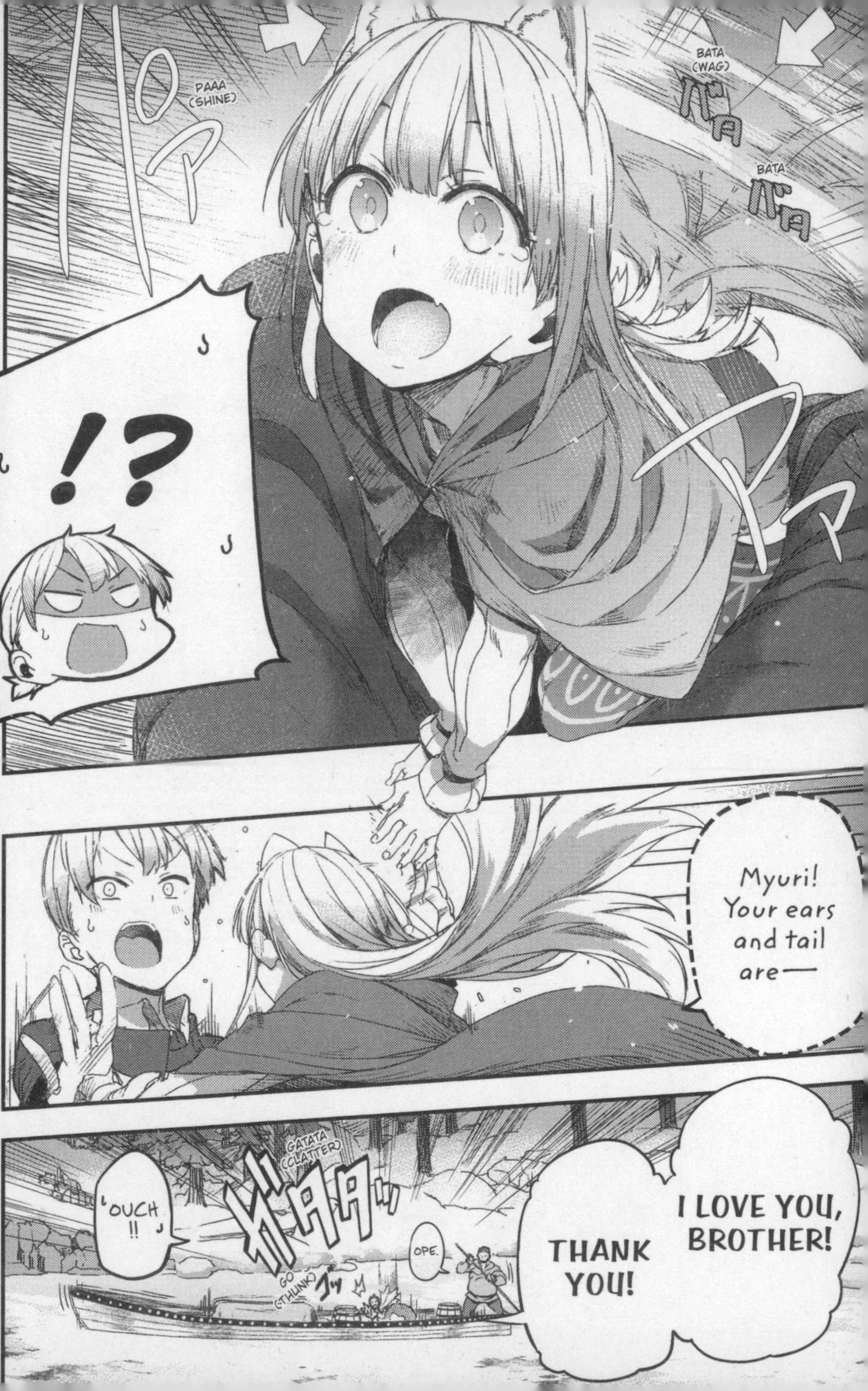
BATA (WAG)
BATA
PAAA (SHINE)
!?
Myuri! Your ears and tail are—
I LOVE YOU, BROTHER!
THANK YOU!
OPE.
GATATA (CLATTER)
GO (THUNK)
OUCH!!

WOLF & PARCHMENT

WOLF
&
PARCHMENT

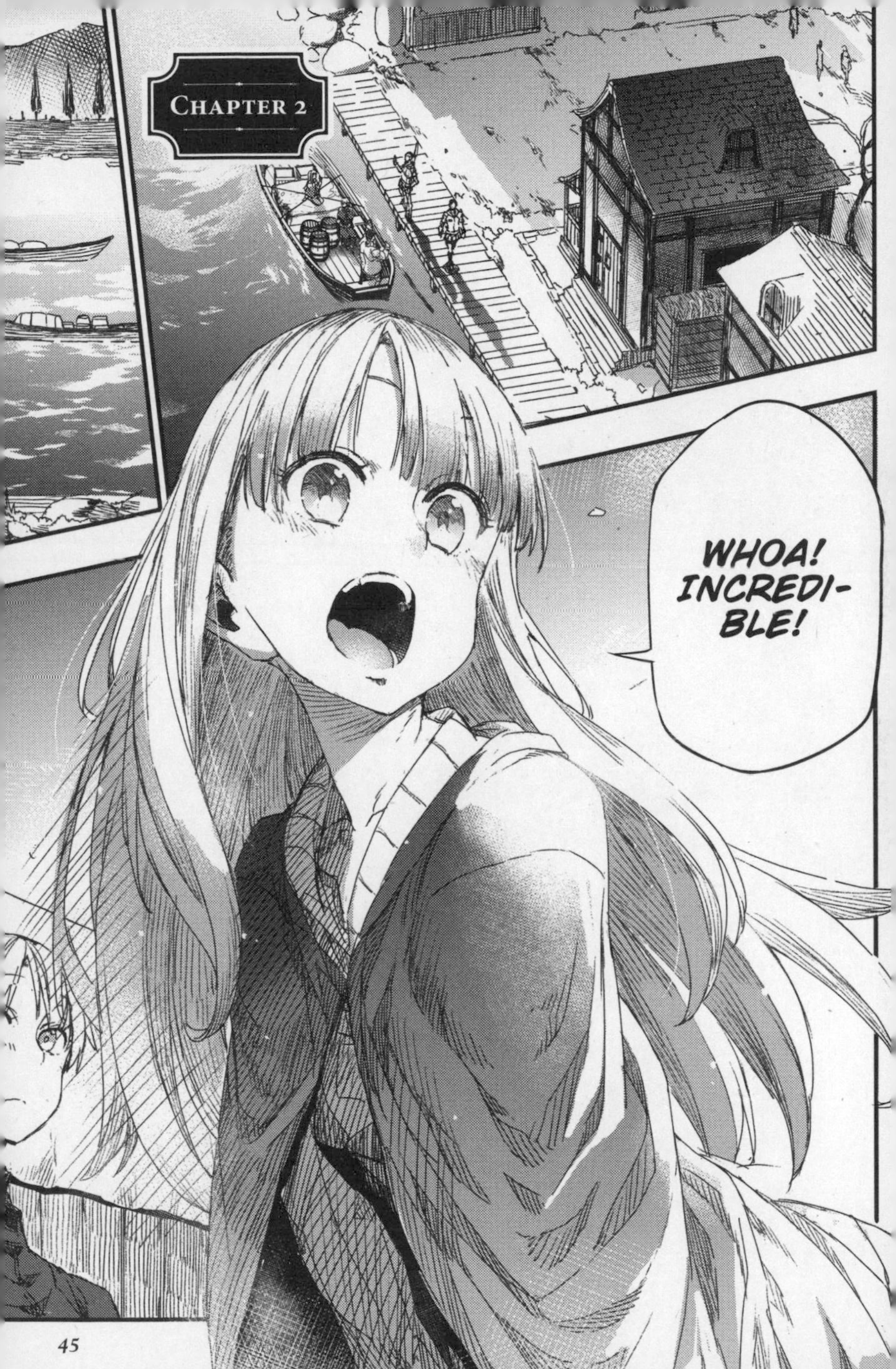
CHAPTER 2
WHOA! INCREDI-BLE!

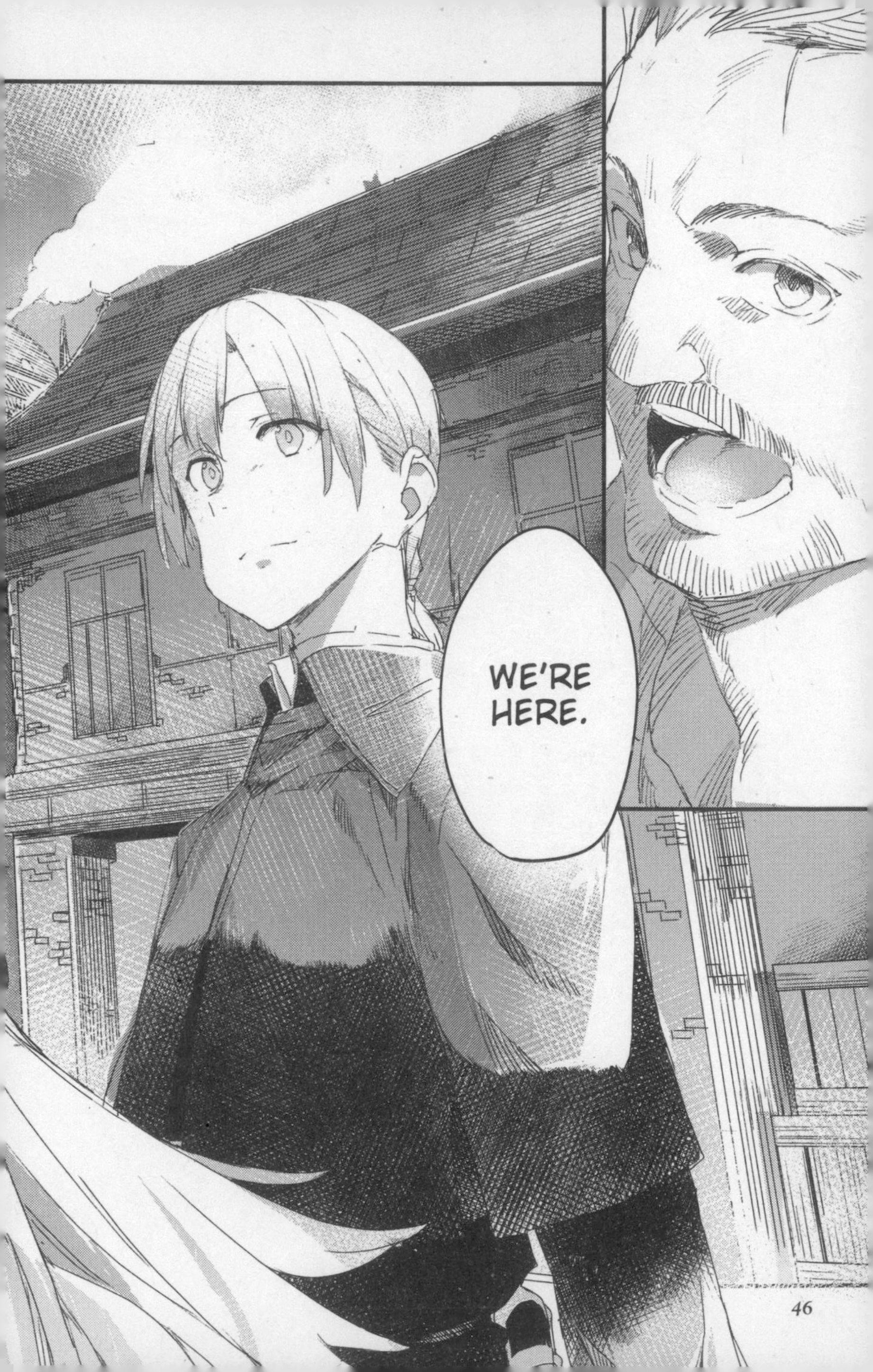
WE'RE HERE.

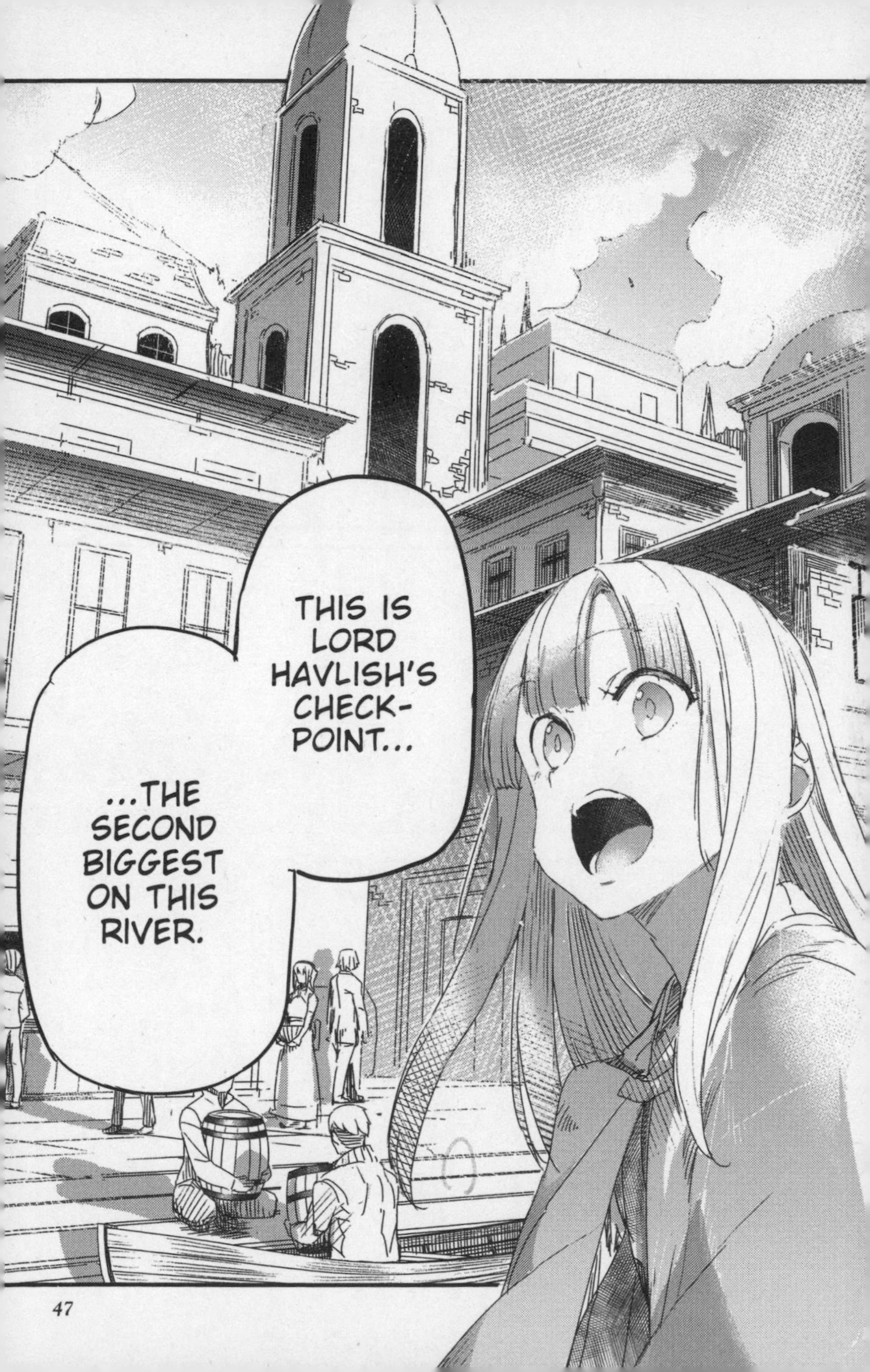
THIS IS LORD HAVLISH'S CHECK-POINT...
...THE SECOND BIGGEST ON THIS RIVER.

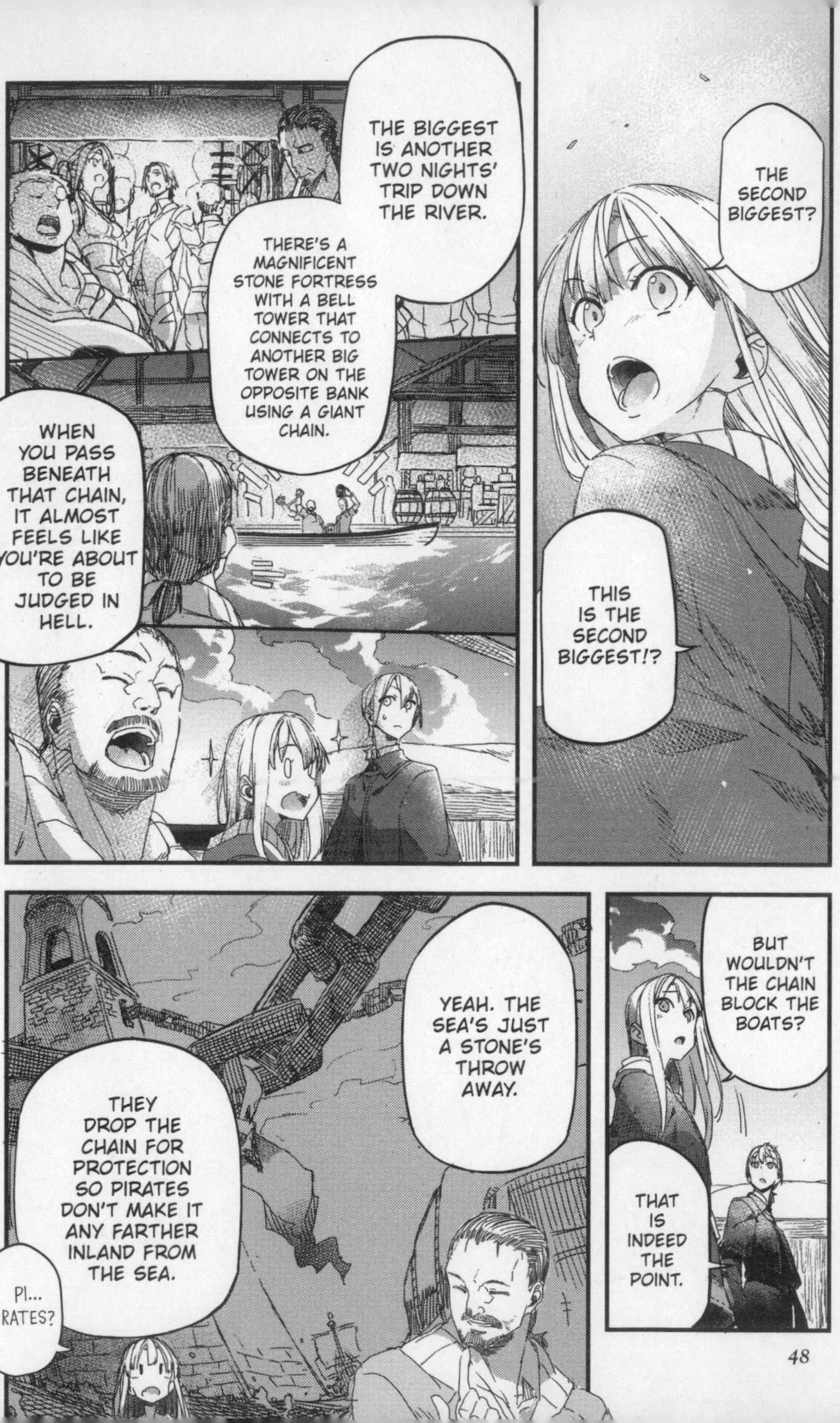
THE SECOND BIGGEST?
THIS IS THE SECOND BIGGEST!?
THE BIGGEST IS ANOTHER TWO NIGHTS' TRIP DOWN THE RIVER.
THERE'S A MAGNIFICENT STONE FORTRESS WITH A BELL TOWER THAT CONNECTS TO ANOTHER BIG TOWER ON THE OPPOSITE BANK USING A GIANT CHAIN.
WHEN YOU PASS BENEATH THAT CHAIN, IT ALMOST FEELS LIKE YOU'RE ABOUT TO BE JUDGED IN HELL.
BUT WOULDN'T THE CHAIN BLOCK THE BOATS?
THAT IS INDEED THE POINT.
YEAH. THE SEA'S JUST A STONE'S THROW AWAY.
THEY DROP THE CHAIN FOR PROTECTION SO PIRATES DON'T MAKE IT ANY FARTHER INLAND FROM THE SEA.
PI... RATES?

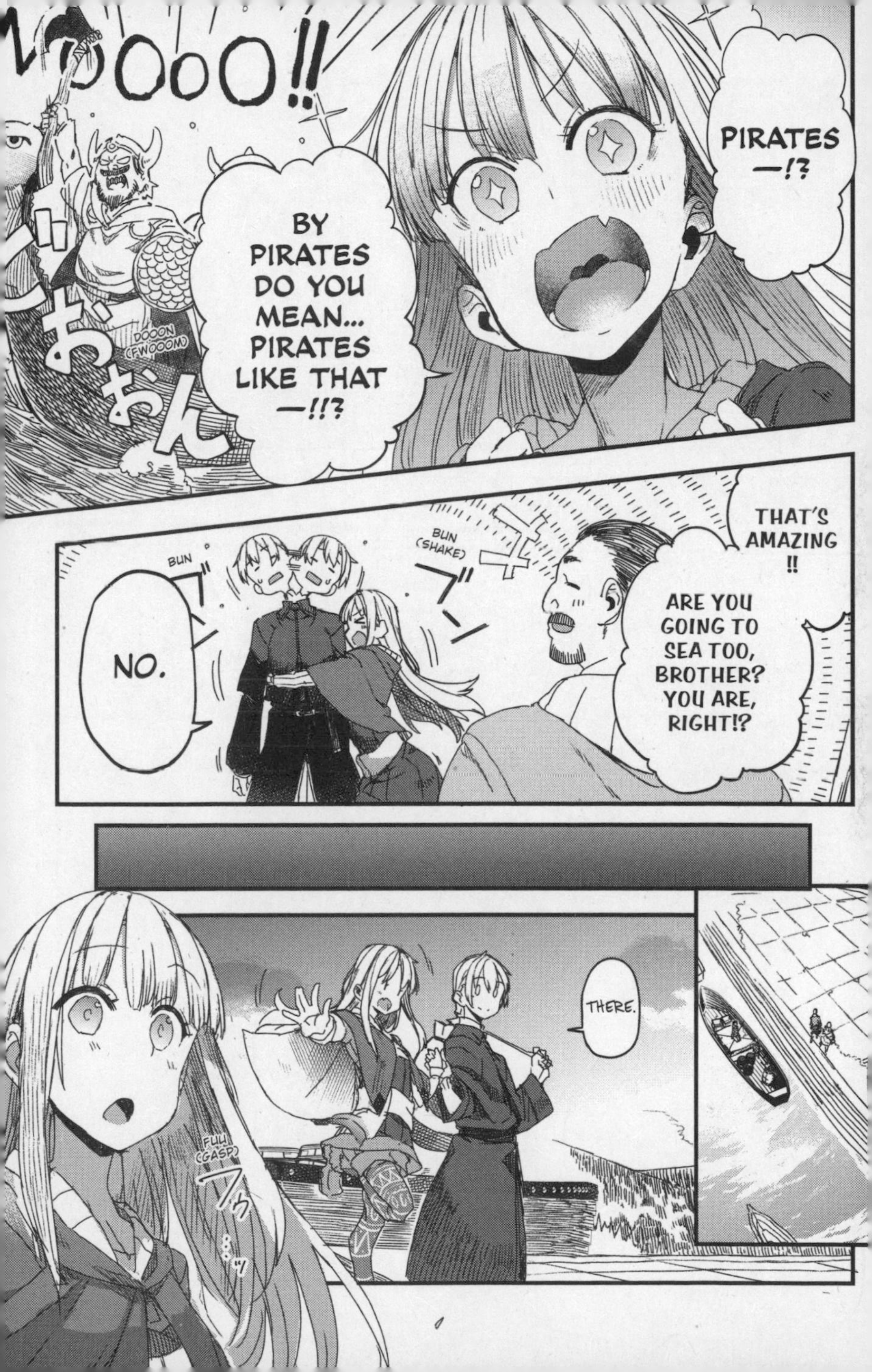

PIRATES—!?
OOOO!!
BY PIRATES DO YOU MEAN... PIRATES LIKE THAT—!!?
DOOON (FWOOOM)
THAT'S AMAZING!!
ARE YOU GOING TO SEA TOO, BROTHER? YOU ARE, RIGHT!?
BUN (SHAKE)
BUN
NO.
THERE.
FUU (GASP)

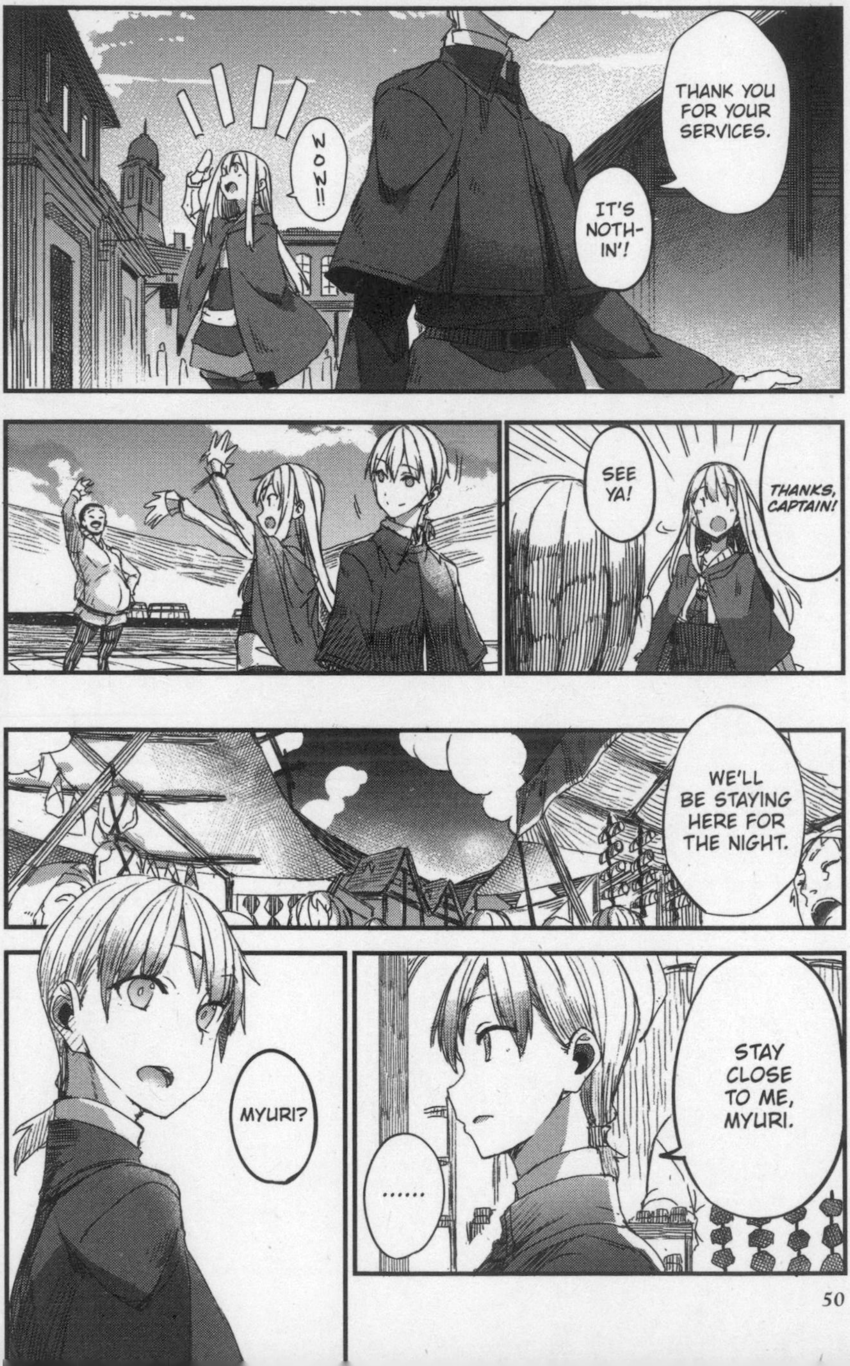
THANK YOU FOR YOUR SERVICES.
IT'S NOTH-IN'!
WOW!!
THANKS, CAPTAIN!
SEE YA!
WE'LL BE STAYING HERE FOR THE NIGHT.
STAY CLOSE TO ME, MYURI.
......
MYURI?

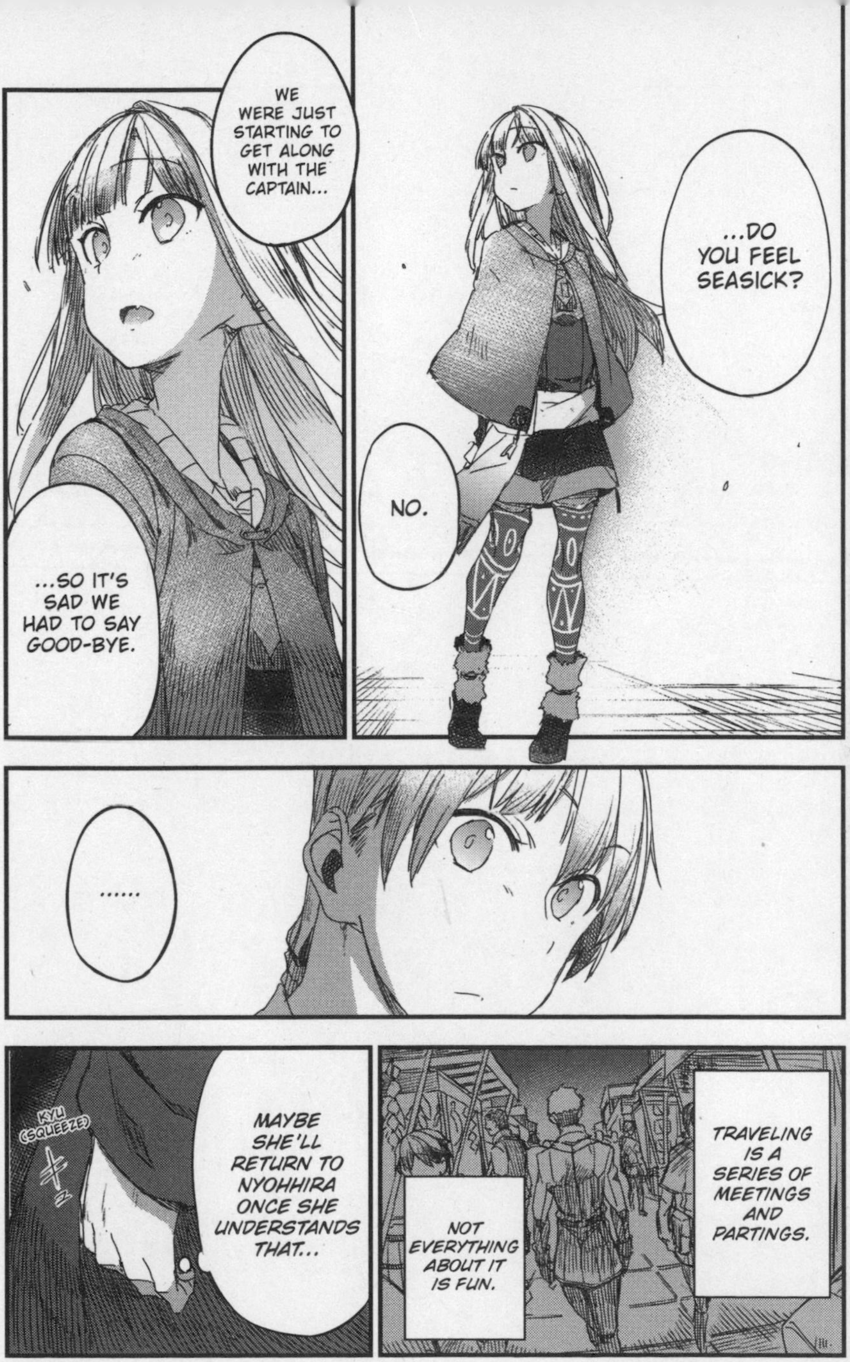
...DO YOU FEEL SEASICK?
NO.
WE WERE JUST STARTING TO GET ALONG WITH THE CAPTAIN...
...SO IT'S SAD WE HAD TO SAY GOOD-BYE.
......
TRAVELING IS A SERIES OF MEETINGS AND PARTINGS.
NOT EVERYTHING ABOUT IT IS FUN.
MAYBE SHE'LL RETURN TO NYOHHIRA ONCE SHE UNDERSTANDS THAT...
KYU (SQUEEZE)

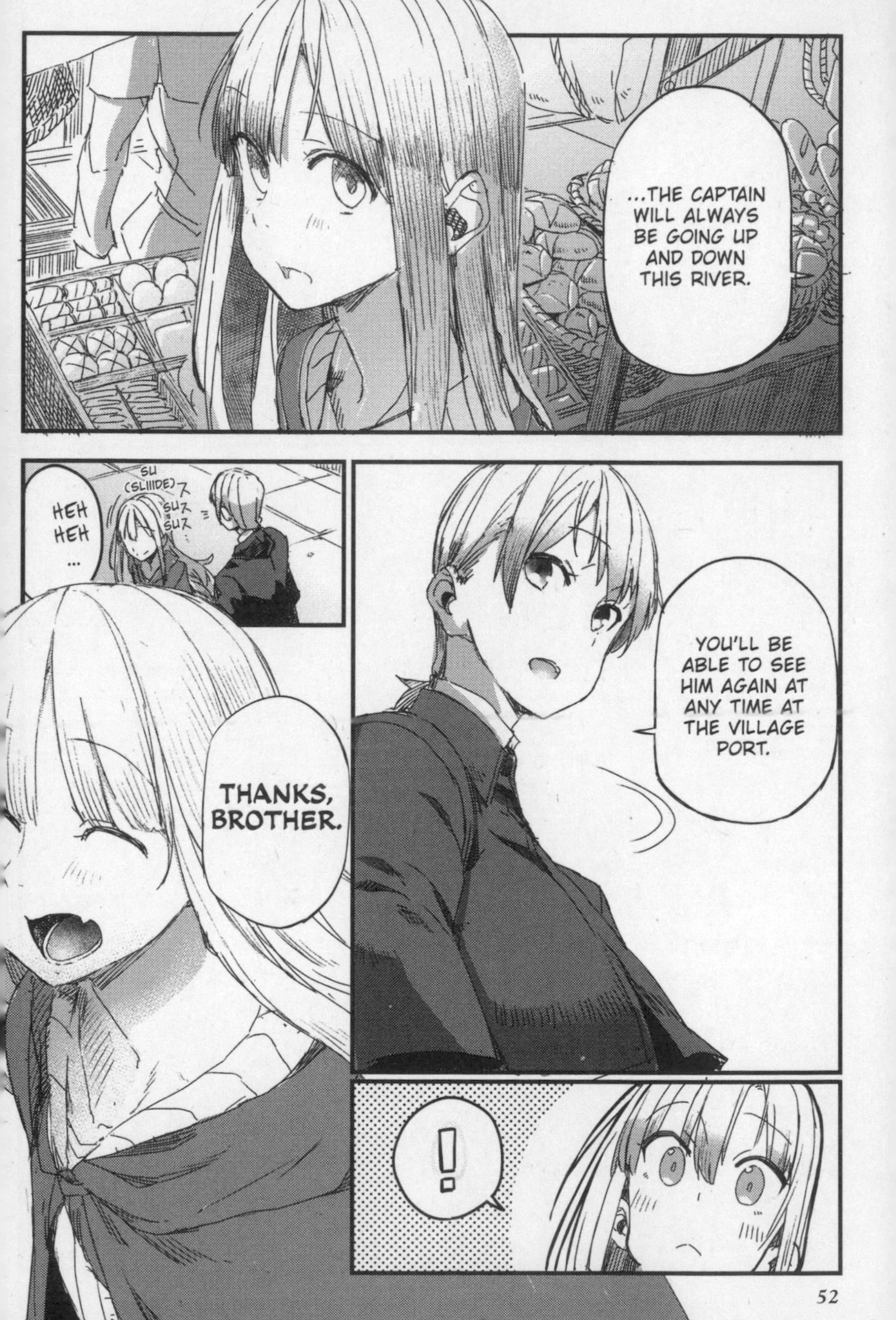
...THE CAPTAIN WILL ALWAYS BE GOING UP AND DOWN THIS RIVER.
YOU'LL BE ABLE TO SEE HIM AGAIN AT ANY TIME AT THE VILLAGE PORT.
SU (SLIIIDE) ス
SU ス SU ス
HEH HEH ...
THANKS, BROTHER.
!

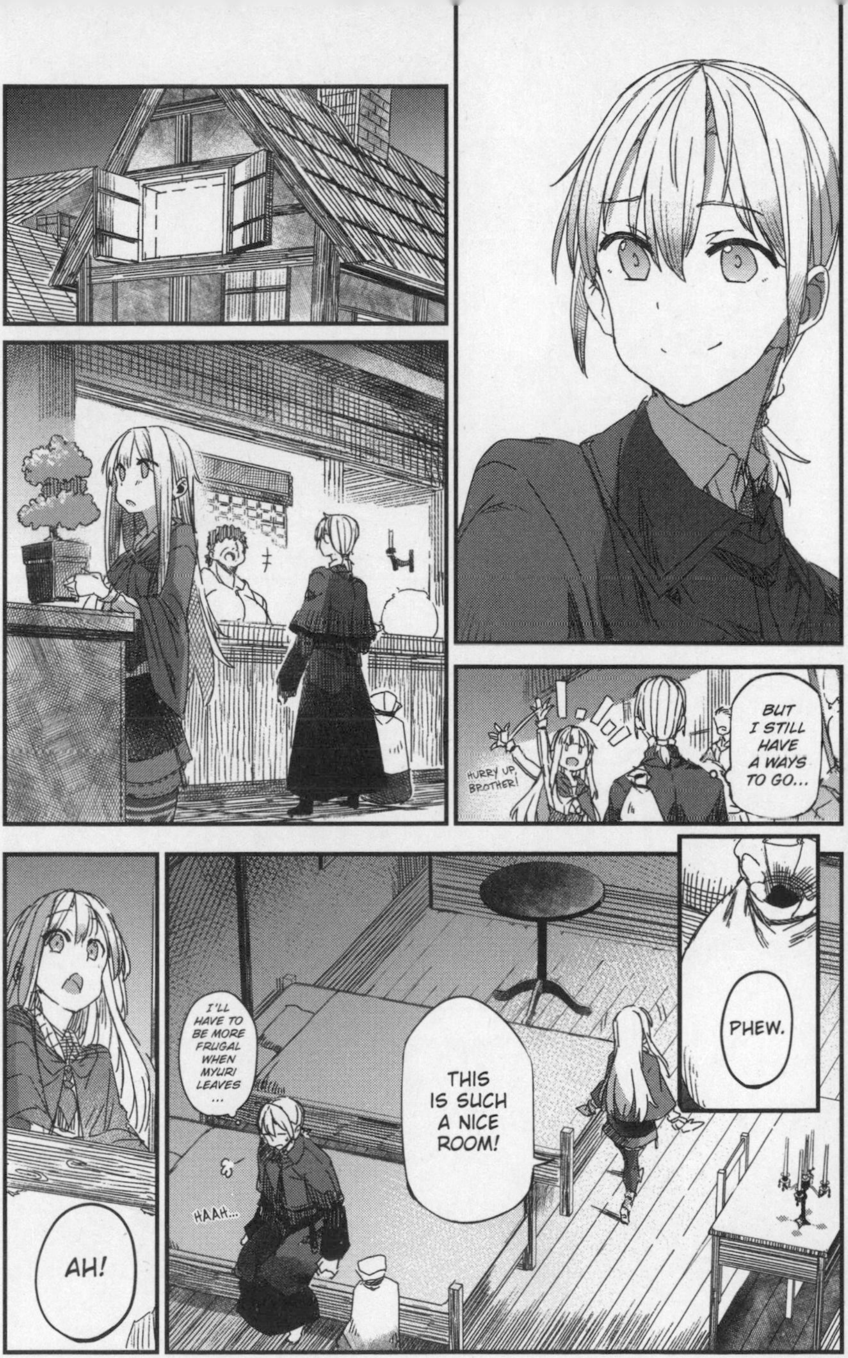
BUT I STILL HAVE A WAYS TO GO...
HURRY UP, BROTHER!
PHEW.
THIS IS SUCH A NICE ROOM!
I'LL HAVE TO BE MORE FRUGAL WHEN MYURI LEAVES ...
HAAH...
AH!

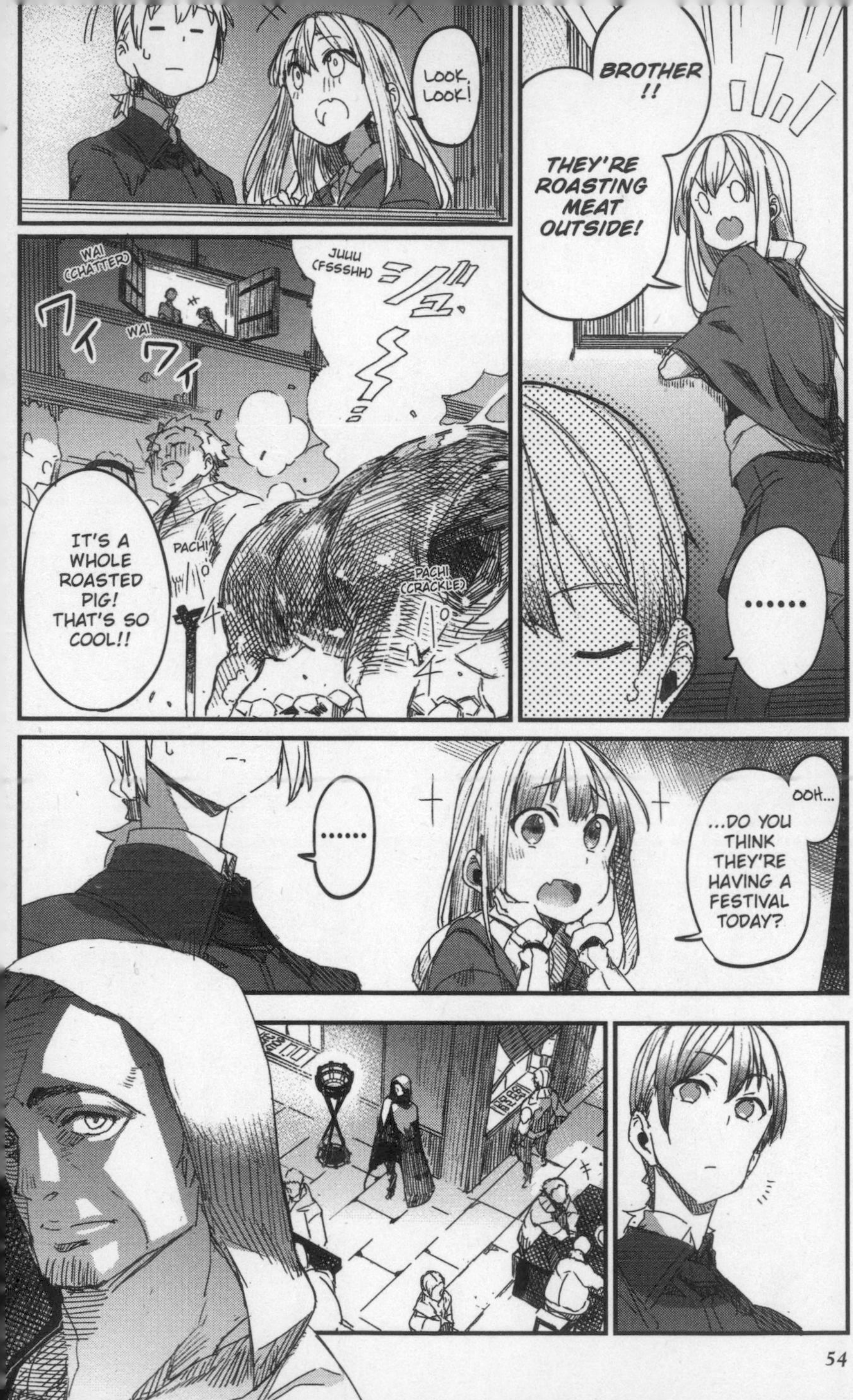
BROTHER !!
THEY'RE ROASTING MEAT OUTSIDE!
......
LOOK, LOOK!
JUUU (FSSSHH)
WAI (CHATTER)
WAI
PACHI (CRACKLE)
PACHI!
IT'S A WHOLE ROASTED PIG! THAT'S SO COOL!!
OOH...
...DO YOU THINK THEY'RE HAVING A FESTIVAL TODAY?
......

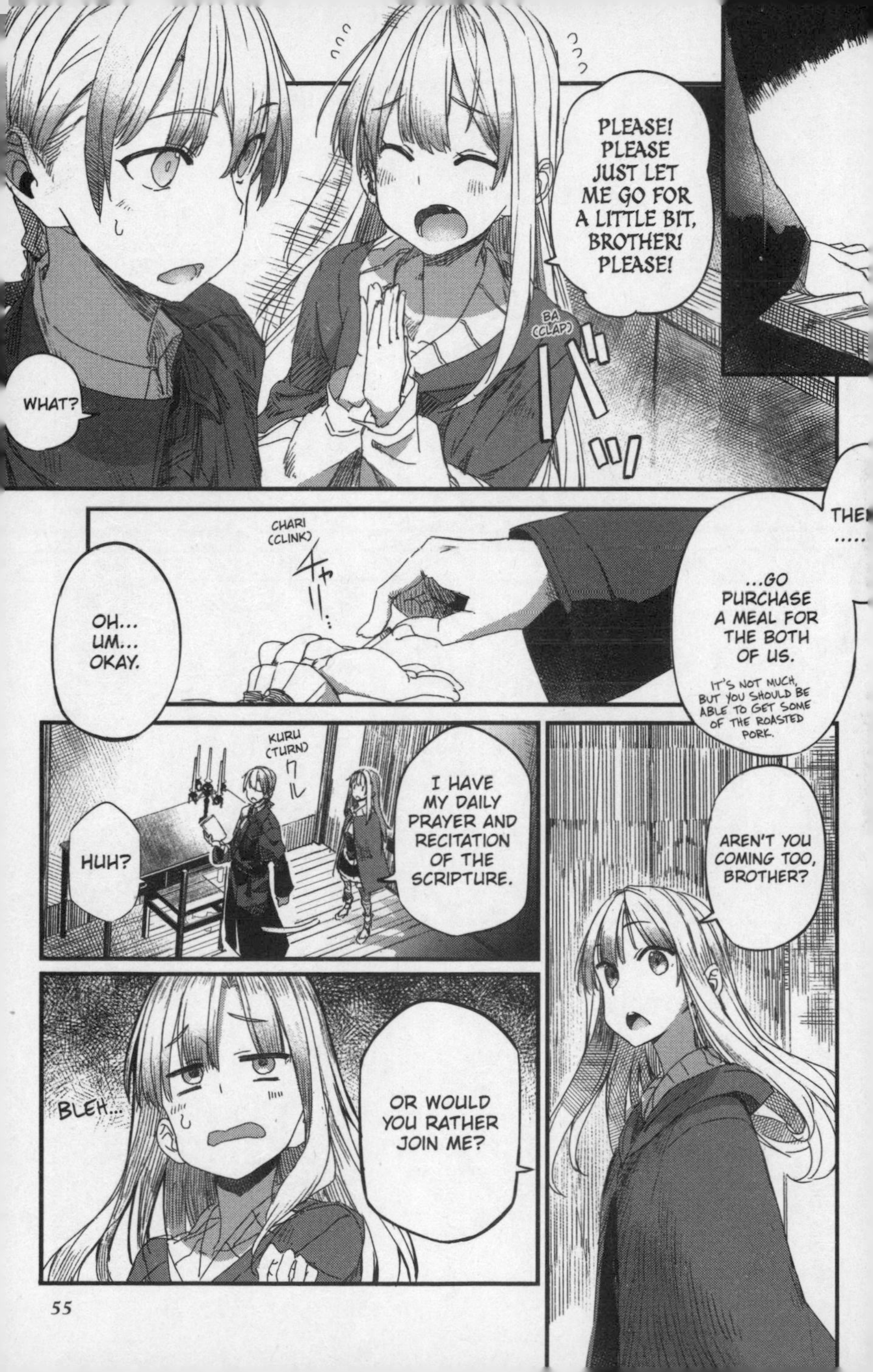
PLEASE! PLEASE JUST LET ME GO FOR A LITTLE BIT, BROTHER! PLEASE!
BA (CLAP)
WHAT?
THE .....
...GO PURCHASE A MEAL FOR THE BOTH OF US.
IT'S NOT MUCH, BUT YOU SHOULD BE ABLE TO GET SOME OF THE ROASTED PORK.
CHARI (CLINK)
OH... UM... OKAY.
AREN'T YOU COMING TOO, BROTHER?
KURU (TURN)
I HAVE MY DAILY PRAYER AND RECITATION OF THE SCRIPTURE.
HUH?
OR WOULD YOU RATHER JOIN ME?
BLEH...

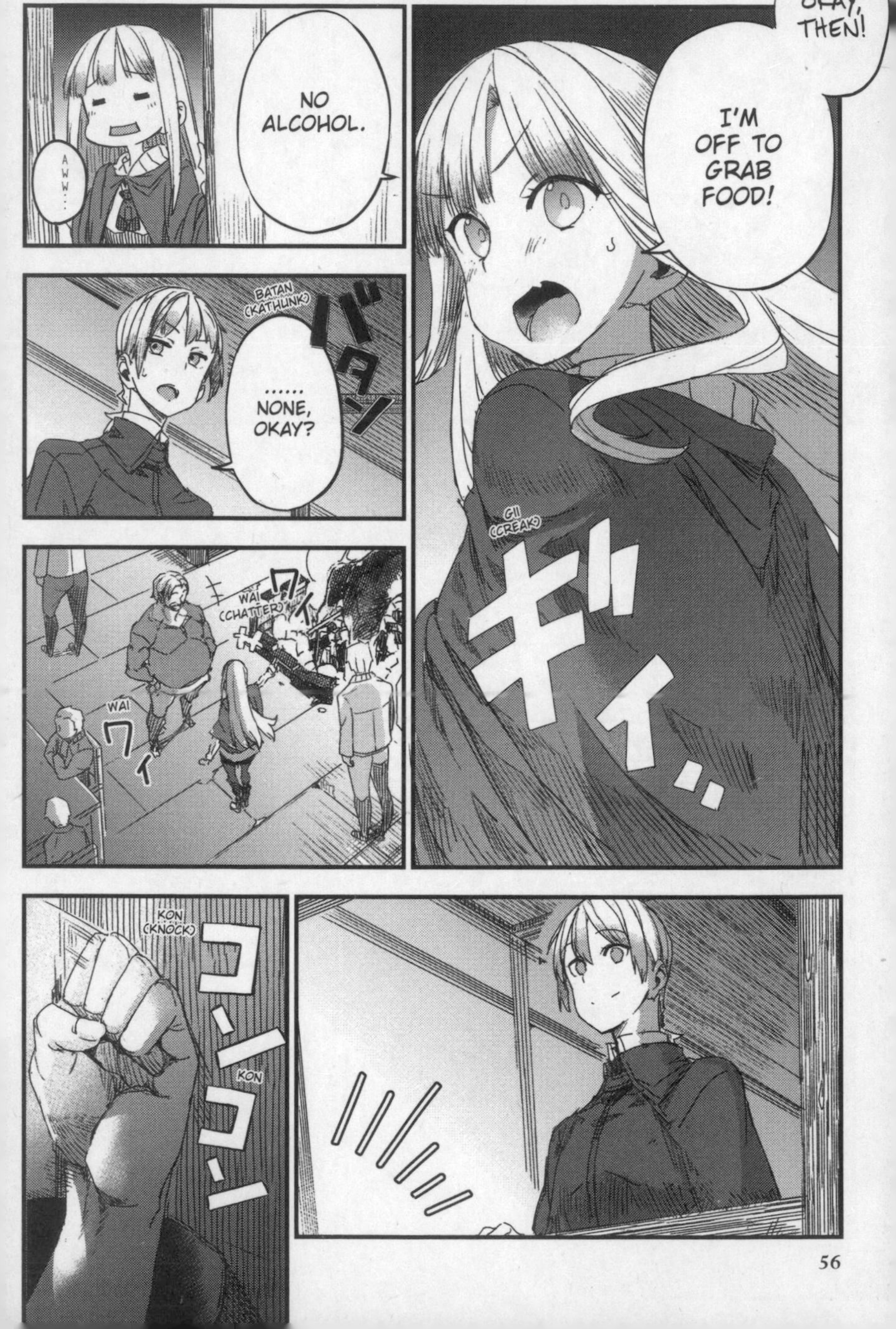
OKAY, THEN!
I'M OFF TO GRAB FOOD!
GII (CREAK)
NO ALCOHOL.
AWW...
BATAN (KATHUNK)
...... NONE, OKAY?
WAI (CHATTER)
WAI
KON (KNOCK)
KON

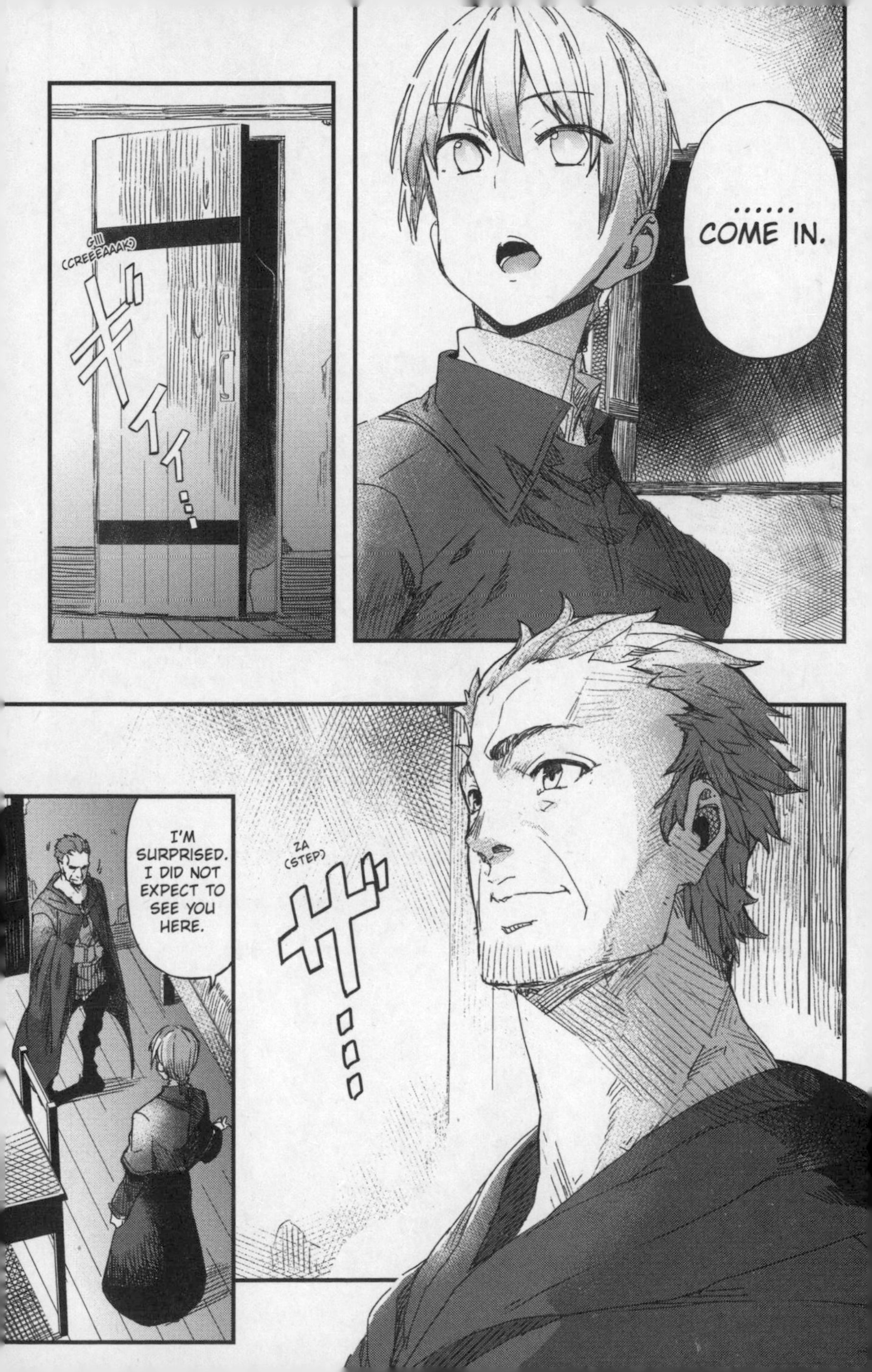

......
COME IN.
GIII (CREEEAAAK)
ギィィ…
ZA (STEP)
ザ…
I'M SURPRISED. I DID NOT EXPECT TO SEE YOU HERE.

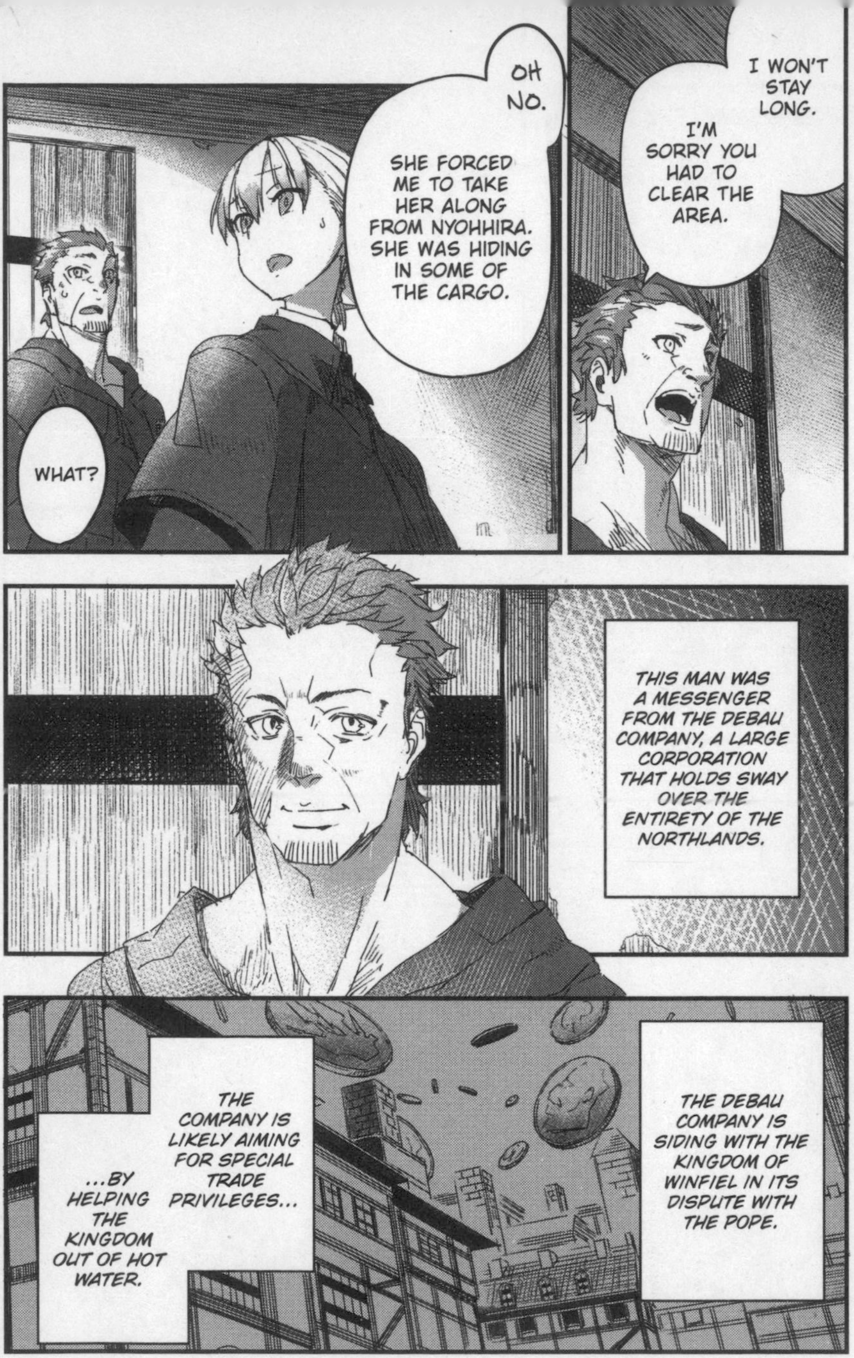
I WON'T STAY LONG.
I'M SORRY YOU HAD TO CLEAR THE AREA.
OH NO.
SHE FORCED ME TO TAKE HER ALONG FROM NYOHHIRA. SHE WAS HIDING IN SOME OF THE CARGO.
WHAT?
THIS MAN WAS A MESSENGER FROM THE DEBAU COMPANY, A LARGE CORPORATION THAT HOLDS SWAY OVER THE ENTIRETY OF THE NORTHLANDS.
THE DEBAU COMPANY IS SIDING WITH THE KINGDOM OF WINFIEL IN ITS DISPUTE WITH THE POPE.
THE COMPANY IS LIKELY AIMING FOR SPECIAL TRADE PRIVILEGES...
...BY HELPING THE KINGDOM OUT OF HOT WATER.

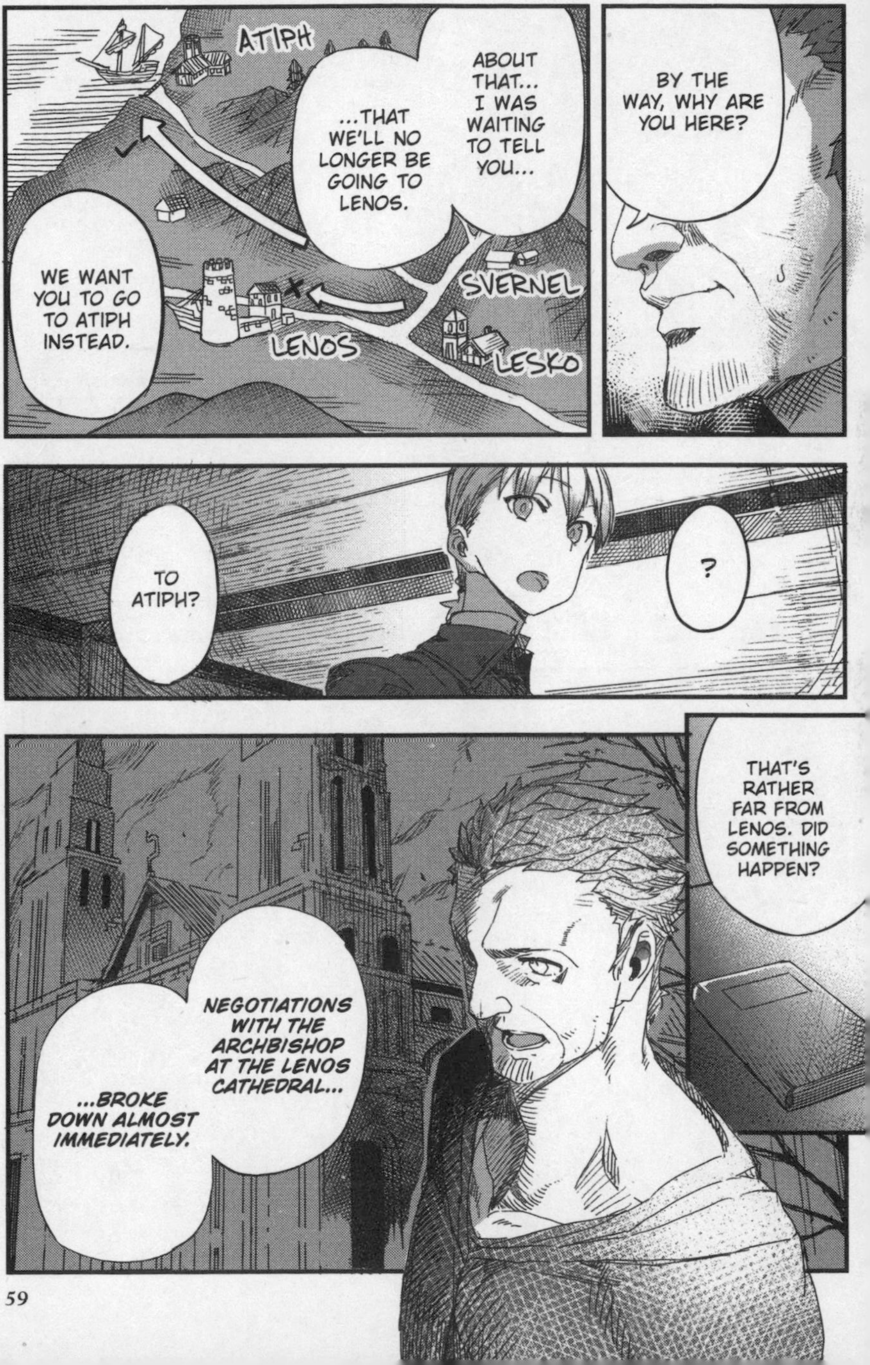

BY THE WAY, WHY ARE YOU HERE?
ATIPH
ABOUT THAT... I WAS WAITING TO TELL YOU...
...THAT WE'LL NO LONGER BE GOING TO LENOS.
SVERNEL
LENOS
LESKO
WE WANT YOU TO GO TO ATIPH INSTEAD.
?
TO ATIPH?
THAT'S RATHER FAR FROM LENOS. DID SOMETHING HAPPEN?
NEGOTIATIONS WITH THE ARCHBISHOP AT THE LENOS CATHEDRAL...
...BROKE DOWN ALMOST IMMEDIATELY.

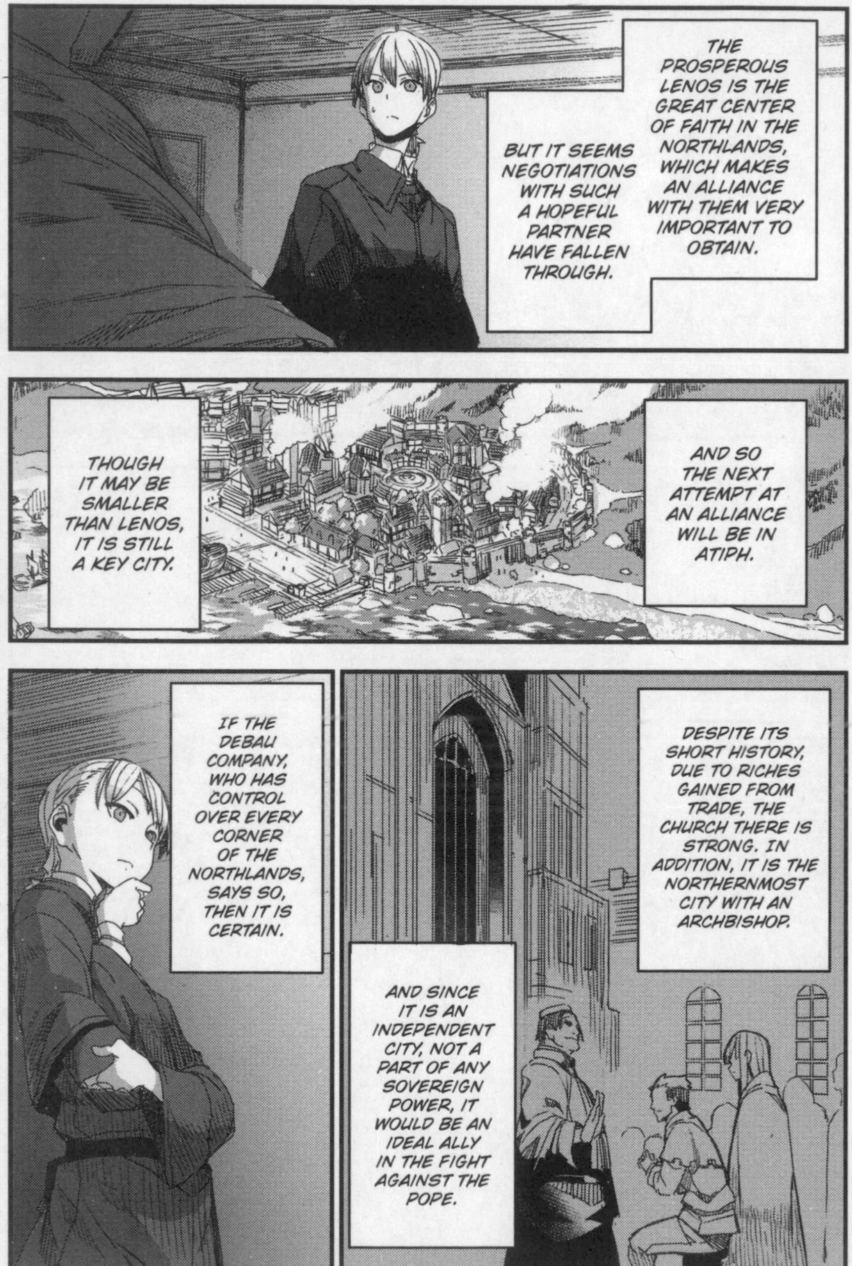
THE PROSPEROUS LENOS IS THE GREAT CENTER OF FAITH IN THE NORTHLANDS, WHICH MAKES AN ALLIANCE WITH THEM VERY IMPORTANT TO OBTAIN.
BUT IT SEEMS NEGOTIATIONS WITH SUCH A HOPEFUL PARTNER HAVE FALLEN THROUGH.
AND SO THE NEXT ATTEMPT AT AN ALLIANCE WILL BE IN ATIPH.
THOUGH IT MAY BE SMALLER THAN LENOS, IT IS STILL A KEY CITY.
DESPITE ITS SHORT HISTORY, DUE TO RICHES GAINED FROM TRADE, THE CHURCH THERE IS STRONG. IN ADDITION, IT IS THE NORTHERNMOST CITY WITH AN ARCHBISHOP.
AND SINCE IT IS AN INDEPENDENT CITY, NOT A PART OF ANY SOVEREIGN POWER, IT WOULD BE AN IDEAL ALLY IN THE FIGHT AGAINST THE POPE.
IF THE DEBAU COMPANY, WHO HAS CONTROL OVER EVERY CORNER OF THE NORTHLANDS, SAYS SO, THEN IT IS CERTAIN.

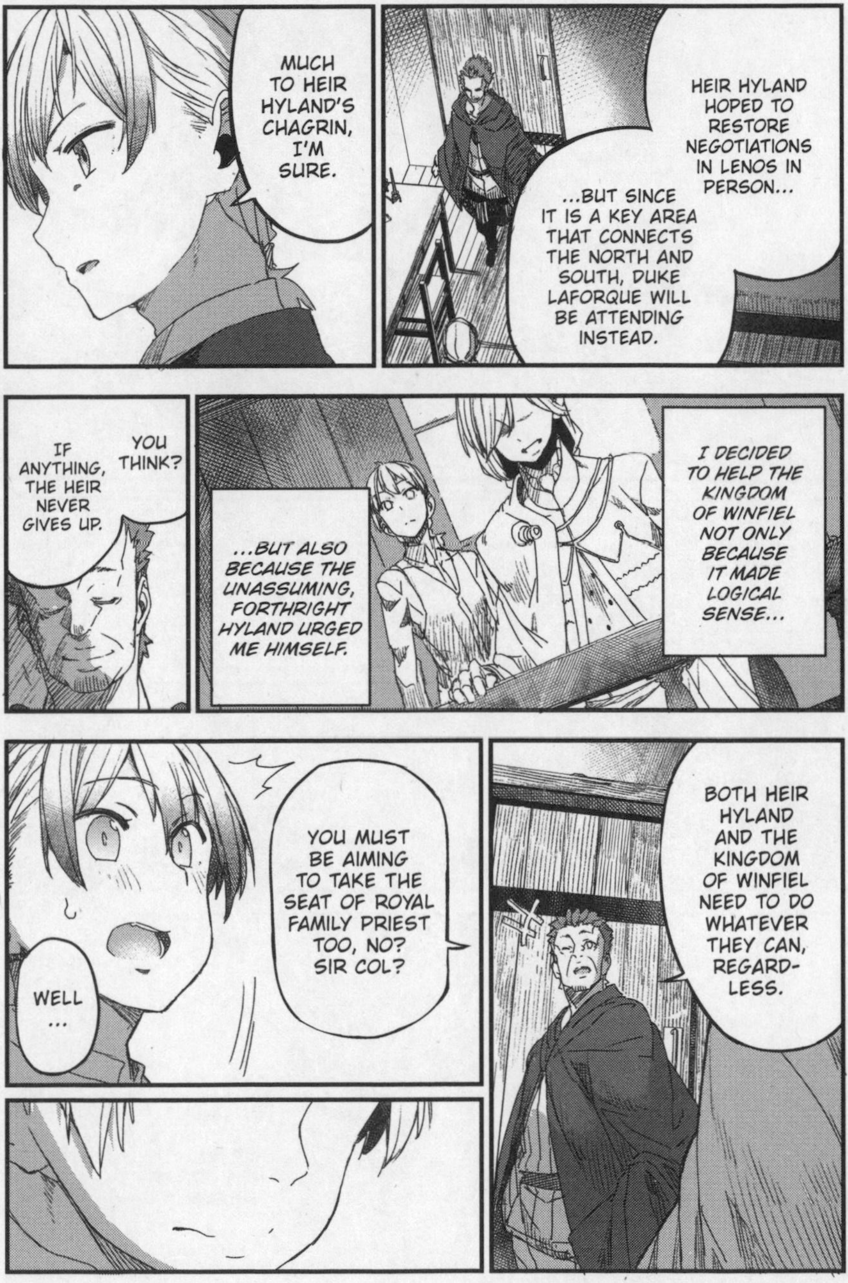
HEIR HYLAND HOPED TO RESTORE NEGOTIATIONS IN LENOS IN PERSON...
...BUT SINCE IT IS A KEY AREA THAT CONNECTS THE NORTH AND SOUTH, DUKE LAFORQUE WILL BE ATTENDING INSTEAD.
MUCH TO HEIR HYLAND'S CHAGRIN, I'M SURE.
I DECIDED TO HELP THE KINGDOM OF WINFIEL NOT ONLY BECAUSE IT MADE LOGICAL SENSE...
...BUT ALSO BECAUSE THE UNASSUMING, FORTHRIGHT HYLAND URGED ME HIMSELF.
YOU THINK?
IF ANYTHING, THE HEIR NEVER GIVES UP.
BOTH HEIR HYLAND AND THE KINGDOM OF WINFIEL NEED TO DO WHATEVER THEY CAN, REGARDLESS.
YOU MUST BE AIMING TO TAKE THE SEAT OF ROYAL FAMILY PRIEST TOO, NO? SIR COL?
WELL...

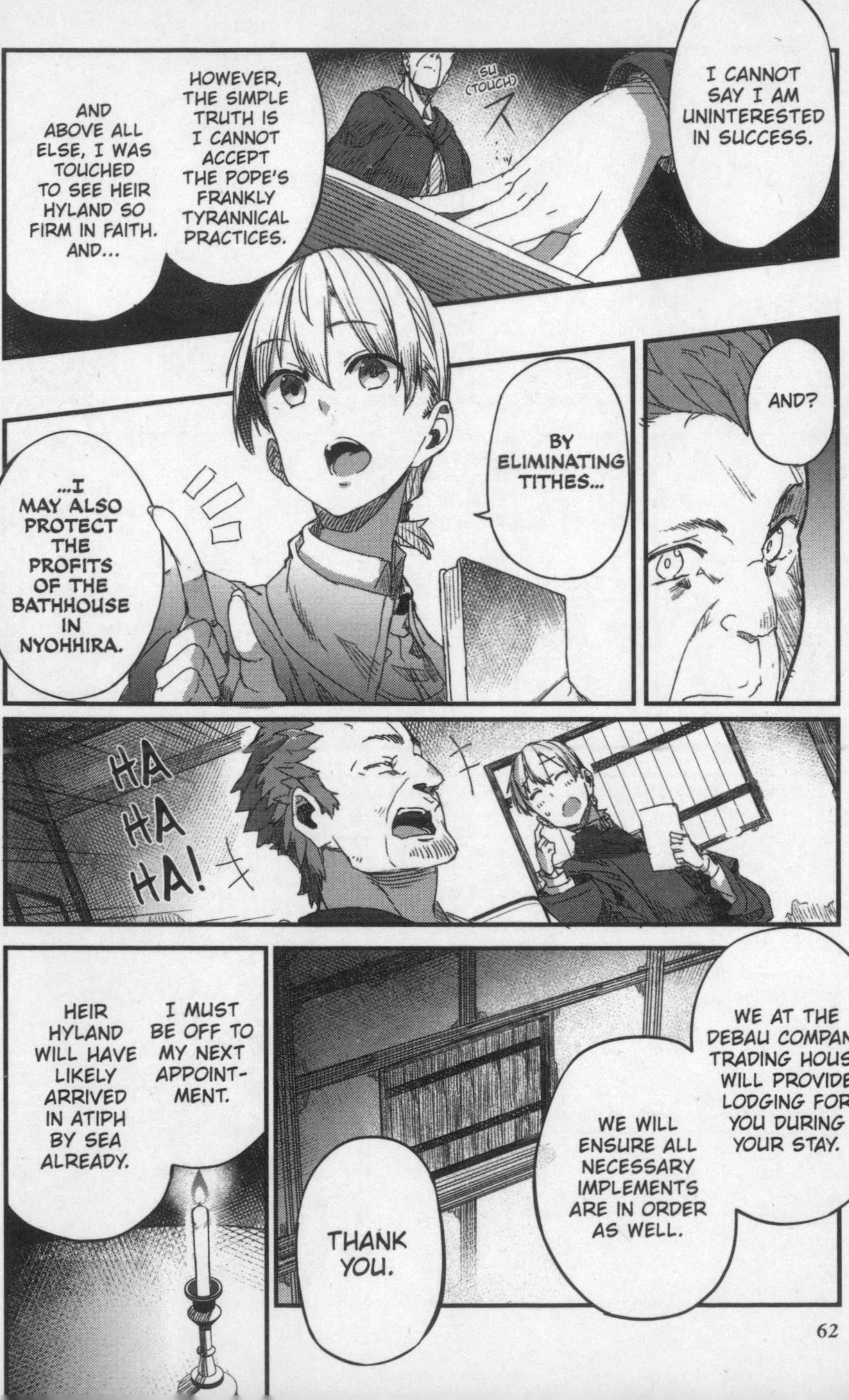
I CANNOT SAY I AM UNINTERESTED IN SUCCESS.
SU (TOUCH)
HOWEVER, THE SIMPLE TRUTH IS I CANNOT ACCEPT THE POPE'S FRANKLY TYRANNICAL PRACTICES.
AND ABOVE ALL ELSE, I WAS TOUCHED TO SEE HEIR HYLAND SO FIRM IN FAITH. AND...
AND?
BY ELIMINATING TITHES...
...I MAY ALSO PROTECT THE PROFITS OF THE BATHHOUSE IN NYOHHIRA.
HA HA HA!
WE AT THE DEBAU COMPANY TRADING HOUSE WILL PROVIDE LODGING FOR YOU DURING YOUR STAY.
WE WILL ENSURE ALL NECESSARY IMPLEMENTS ARE IN ORDER AS WELL.
THANK YOU.
I MUST BE OFF TO MY NEXT APPOINT-MENT.
HEIR HYLAND WILL HAVE LIKELY ARRIVED IN ATIPH BY SEA ALREADY.

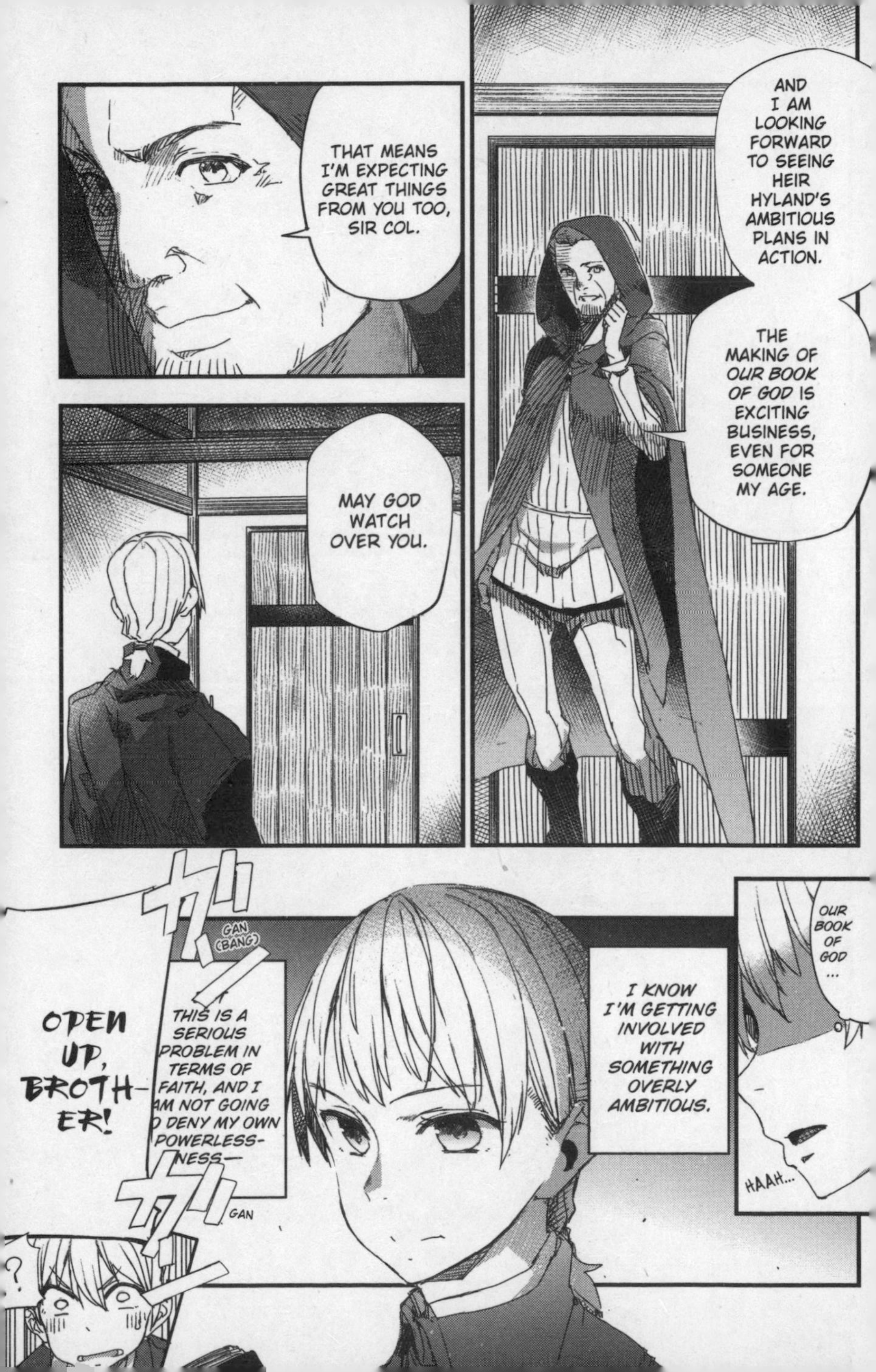
AND I AM LOOKING FORWARD TO SEEING HEIR HYLAND'S AMBITIOUS PLANS IN ACTION.
THE MAKING OF OUR BOOK OF GOD IS EXCITING BUSINESS, EVEN FOR SOMEONE MY AGE.
THAT MEANS I'M EXPECTING GREAT THINGS FROM YOU TOO, SIR COL.
MAY GOD WATCH OVER YOU.
OUR BOOK OF GOD ...
HAAH...
I KNOW I'M GETTING INVOLVED WITH SOMETHING OVERLY AMBITIOUS.
THIS IS A SERIOUS PROBLEM IN TERMS OF FAITH, AND I AM NOT GOING TO DENY MY OWN POWERLESS-NESS—
GAN (BANG)
OPEN UP, BROTH-ER!
GAN
?

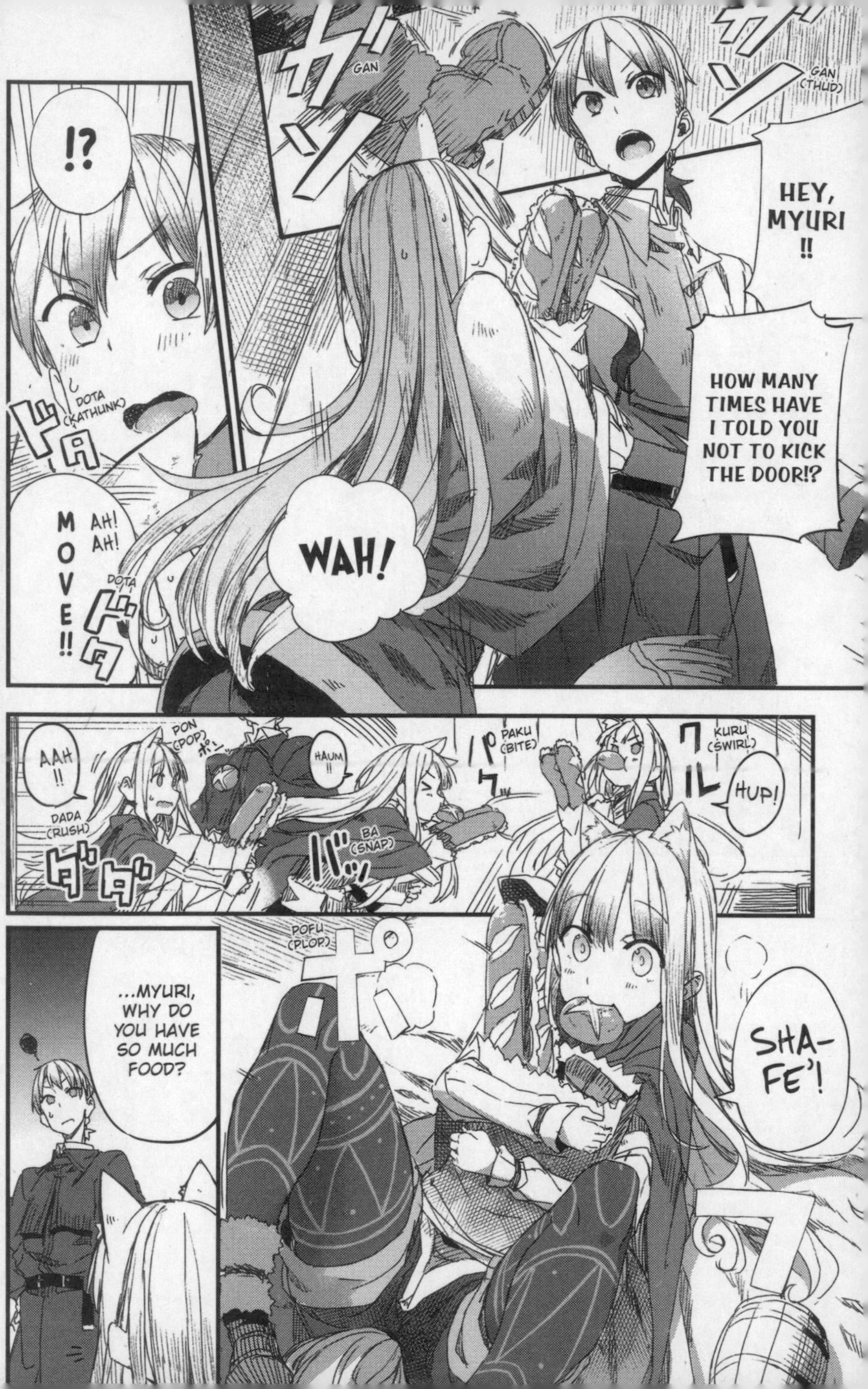
GAN (THUD)
GAN
HEY, MYURI !!
HOW MANY TIMES HAVE I TOLD YOU NOT TO KICK THE DOOR!?
WAH!
!?
DOTA (KATHUNK)
AH! AH!
MOVE!!
DOTA
KURU (SWIRL)
HUP!
PAKU (BITE)
HAUM !!
BA (SNAP)
PON (POP)
AAH !!
DADA (RUSH)
SHA-FE'!
POFU (PLOP)
...MYURI, WHY DO YOU HAVE SO MUCH FOOD?

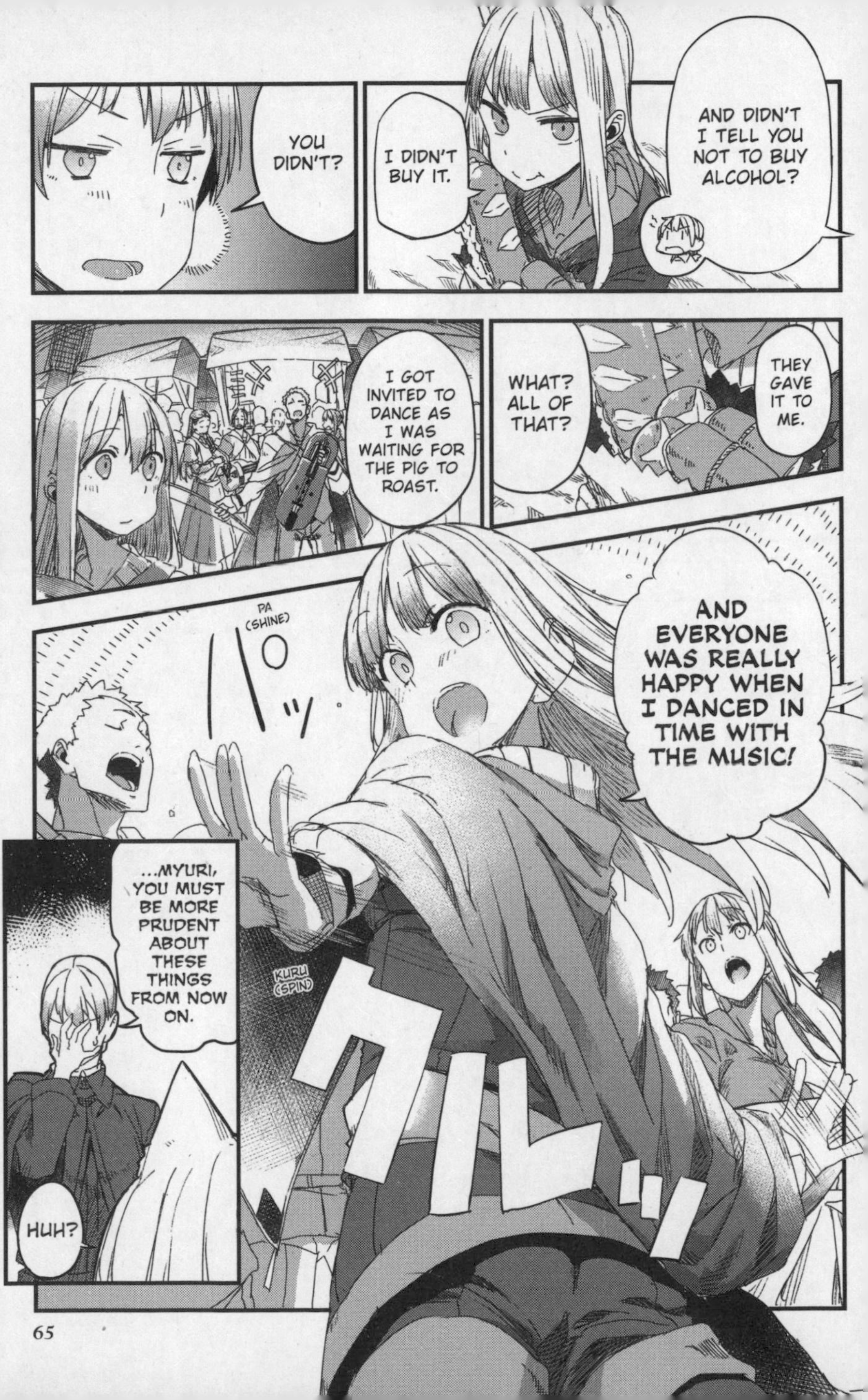
AND DIDN'T I TELL YOU NOT TO BUY ALCOHOL?
I DIDN'T BUY IT.
YOU DIDN'T?
THEY GAVE IT TO ME.
WHAT? ALL OF THAT?
I GOT INVITED TO DANCE AS I WAS WAITING FOR THE PIG TO ROAST.
AND EVERYONE WAS REALLY HAPPY WHEN I DANCED IN TIME WITH THE MUSIC!
PA (SHINE)
KURU (SPIN)
...MYURI, YOU MUST BE MORE PRUDENT ABOUT THESE THINGS FROM NOW ON.
HUH?

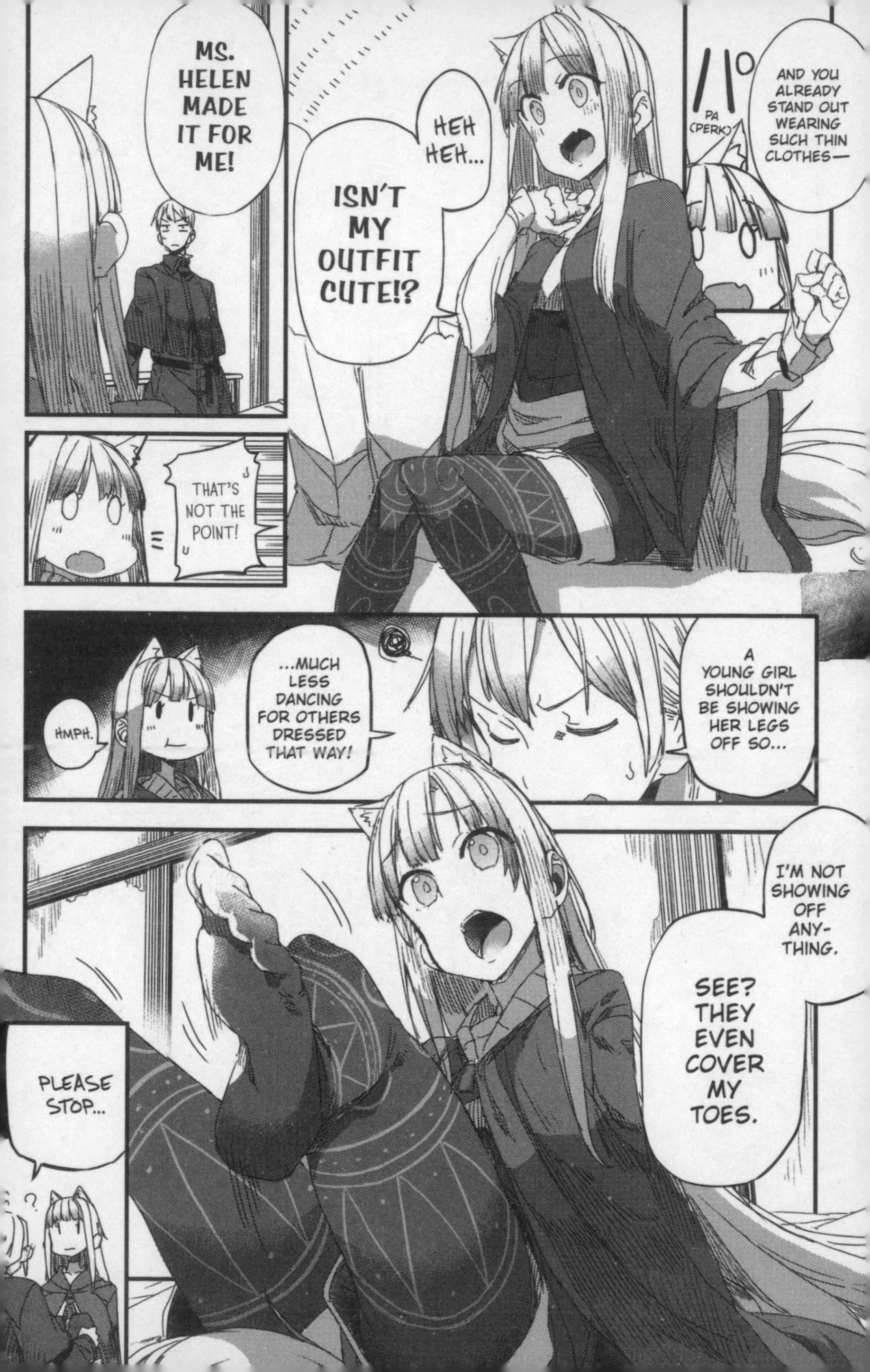
PA (PERK)
AND YOU ALREADY STAND OUT WEARING SUCH THIN CLOTHES—
HEH HEH...
ISN'T MY OUTFIT CUTE!?
MS. HELEN MADE IT FOR ME!
THAT'S NOT THE POINT!
A YOUNG GIRL SHOULDN'T BE SHOWING HER LEGS OFF SO...
...MUCH LESS DANCING FOR OTHERS DRESSED THAT WAY!
HMPH.
I'M NOT SHOWING OFF ANYTHING.
SEE? THEY EVEN COVER MY TOES.
PLEASE STOP...

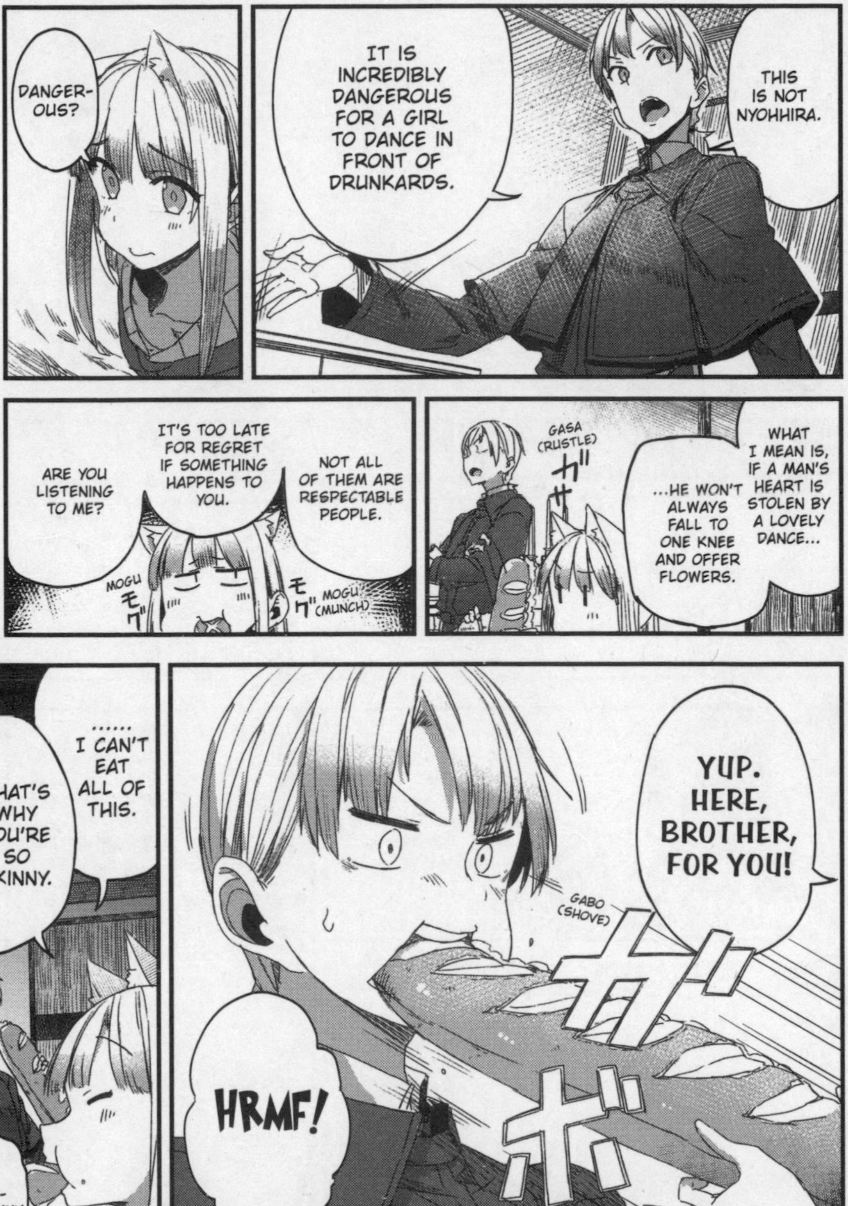
THIS IS NOT NYOHHIRA.
IT IS INCREDIBLY DANGEROUS FOR A GIRL TO DANCE IN FRONT OF DRUNKARDS.
DANGER-OUS?
WHAT I MEAN IS, IF A MAN'S HEART IS STOLEN BY A LOVELY DANCE...
...HE WON'T ALWAYS FALL TO ONE KNEE AND OFFER FLOWERS.
ガサ
GASA (RUSTLE)
NOT ALL OF THEM ARE RESPECTABLE PEOPLE.
IT'S TOO LATE FOR REGRET IF SOMETHING HAPPENS TO YOU.
ARE YOU LISTENING TO ME?
モグ
MOGU (MUNCH)
モグ
MOGU
YUP. HERE, BROTHER, FOR YOU!
GABO (SHOVE)
ガボッ
HRMF!
...... I CAN'T EAT ALL OF THIS.
THAT'S WHY YOU'RE SO SKINNY.
S-SKINNY ...?

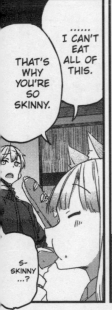

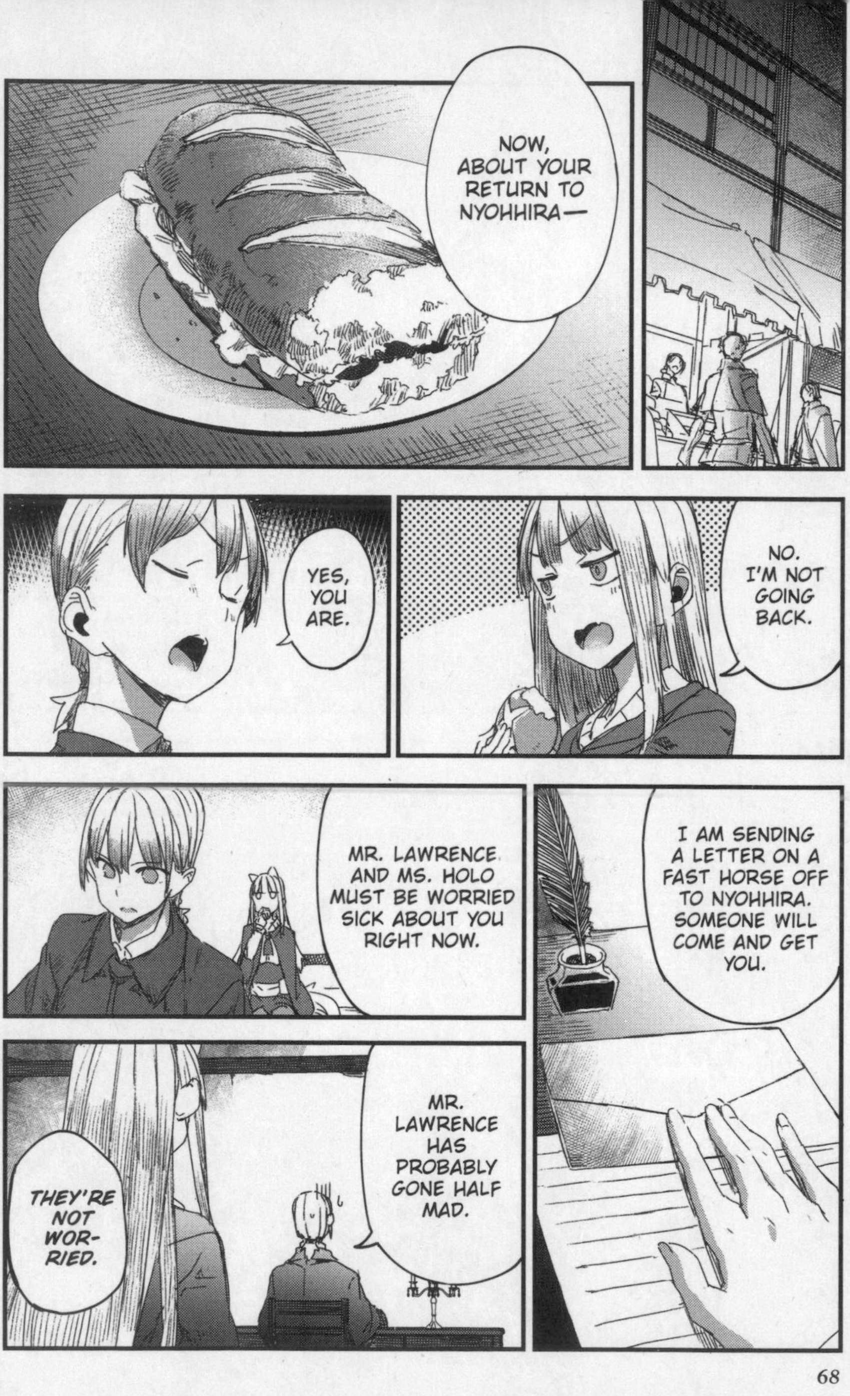
NOW, ABOUT YOUR RETURN TO NYOHHIRA—
NO. I'M NOT GOING BACK.
YES, YOU ARE.
I AM SENDING A LETTER ON A FAST HORSE OFF TO NYOHHIRA. SOMEONE WILL COME AND GET YOU.
MR. LAWRENCE AND MS. HOLO MUST BE WORRIED SICK ABOUT YOU RIGHT NOW.
MR. LAWRENCE HAS PROBABLY GONE HALF MAD.
THEY'RE NOT WOR-RIED.

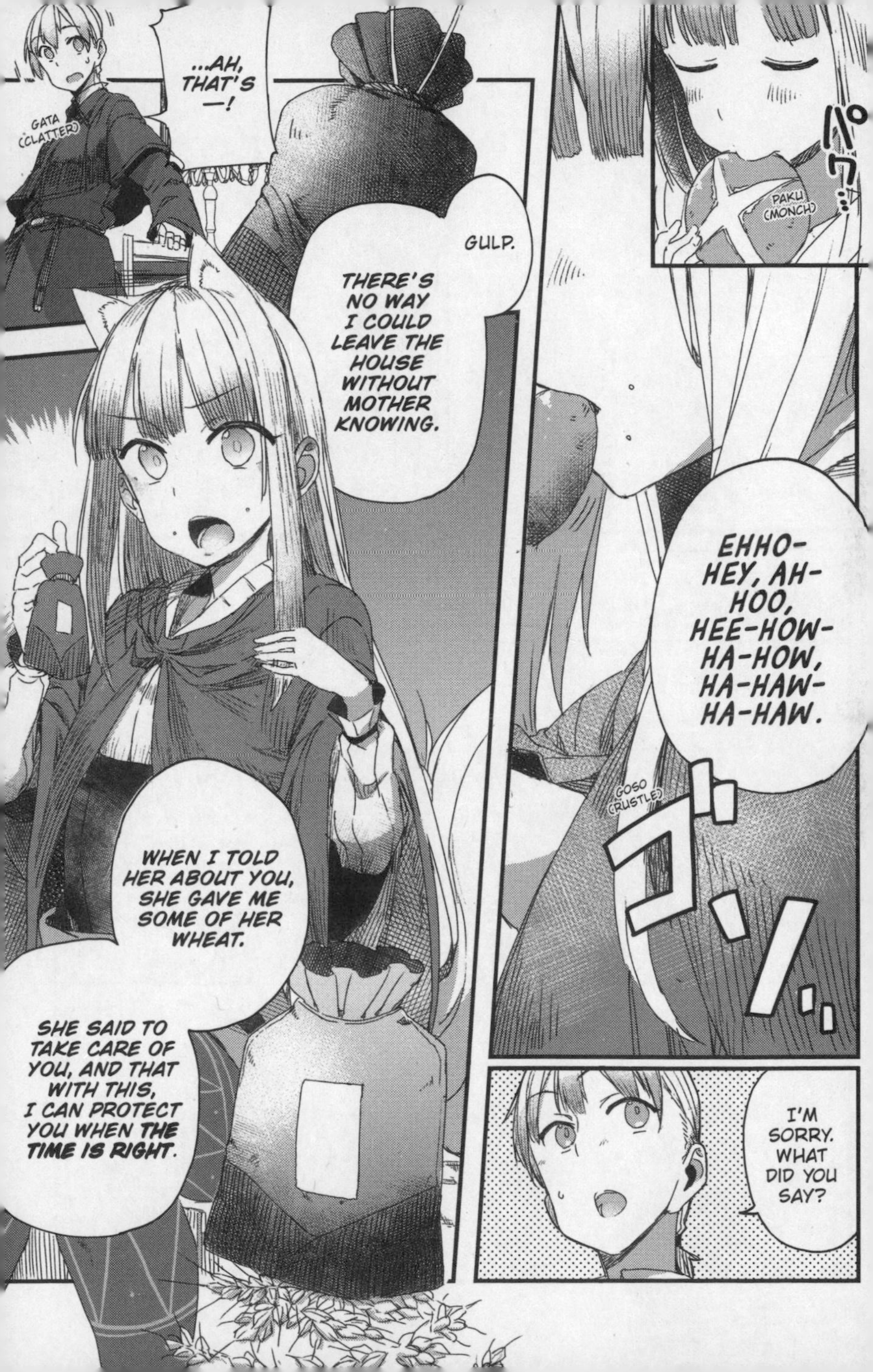
PAKU (MONCH)
EHHO-HEY, AH-HOO, HEE-HOW-HA-HOW, HA-HAW-HA-HAW.
GOSO (RUSTLE)
I'M SORRY. WHAT DID YOU SAY?
...AH, THAT'S—!
GATA (CLATTER)
GULP.
THERE'S NO WAY I COULD LEAVE THE HOUSE WITHOUT MOTHER KNOWING.
WHEN I TOLD HER ABOUT YOU, SHE GAVE ME SOME OF HER WHEAT.
SHE SAID TO TAKE CARE OF YOU, AND THAT WITH THIS, I CAN PROTECT YOU WHEN THE TIME IS RIGHT.

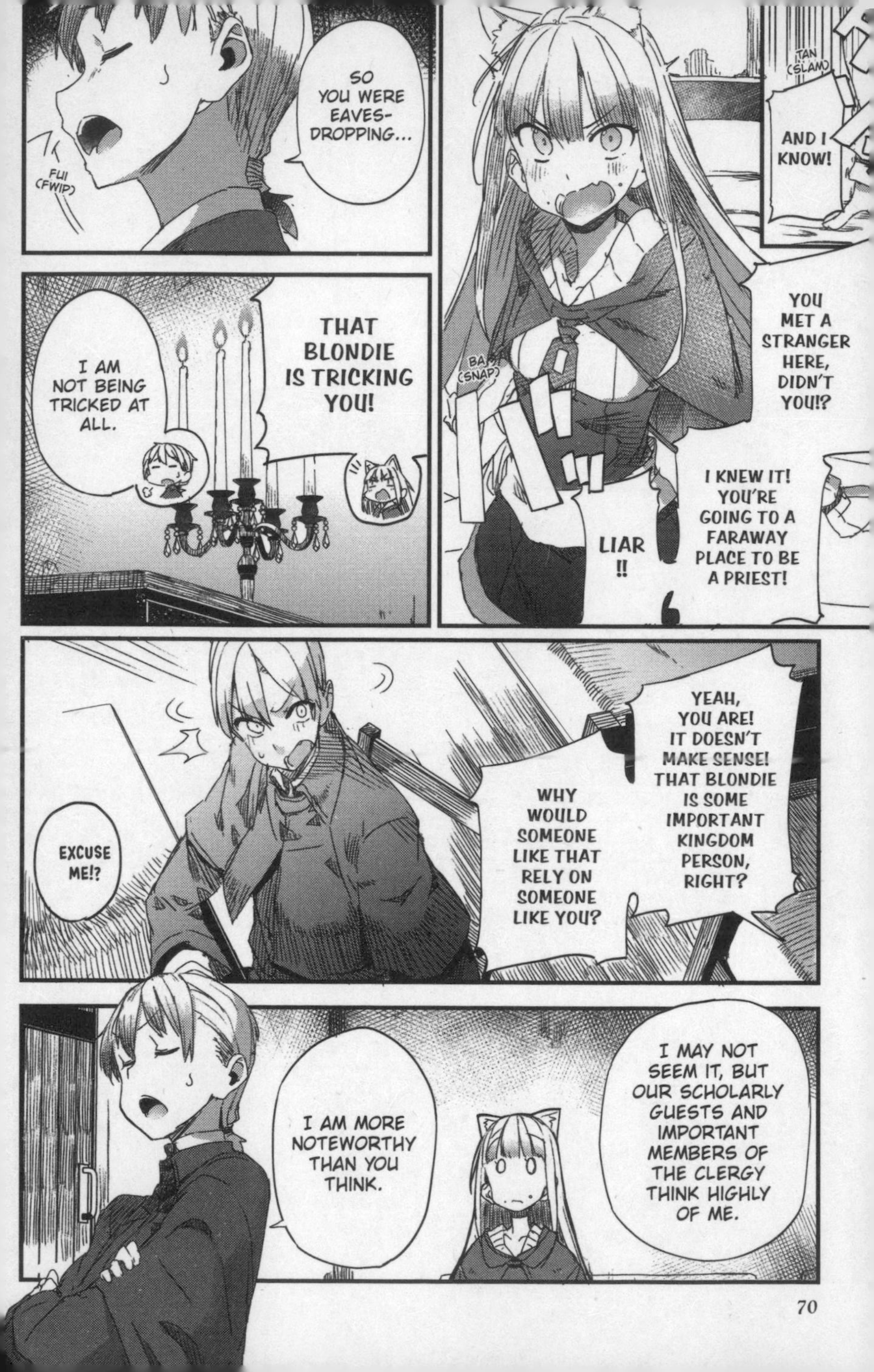
TAN (SLAM)
AND I KNOW!
YOU MET A STRANGER HERE, DIDN'T YOU!?
BA (SNAP)
I KNEW IT! YOU'RE GOING TO A FARAWAY PLACE TO BE A PRIEST!
LIAR!!
SO YOU WERE EAVES-DROPPING...
FUI (FWIP)
THAT BLONDIE IS TRICKING YOU!
I AM NOT BEING TRICKED AT ALL.
YEAH, YOU ARE! IT DOESN'T MAKE SENSE! THAT BLONDIE IS SOME IMPORTANT KINGDOM PERSON, RIGHT?
WHY WOULD SOMEONE LIKE THAT RELY ON SOMEONE LIKE YOU?
EXCUSE ME!?
I MAY NOT SEEM IT, BUT OUR SCHOLARLY GUESTS AND IMPORTANT MEMBERS OF THE CLERGY THINK HIGHLY OF ME.
I AM MORE NOTEWORTHY THAN YOU THINK.

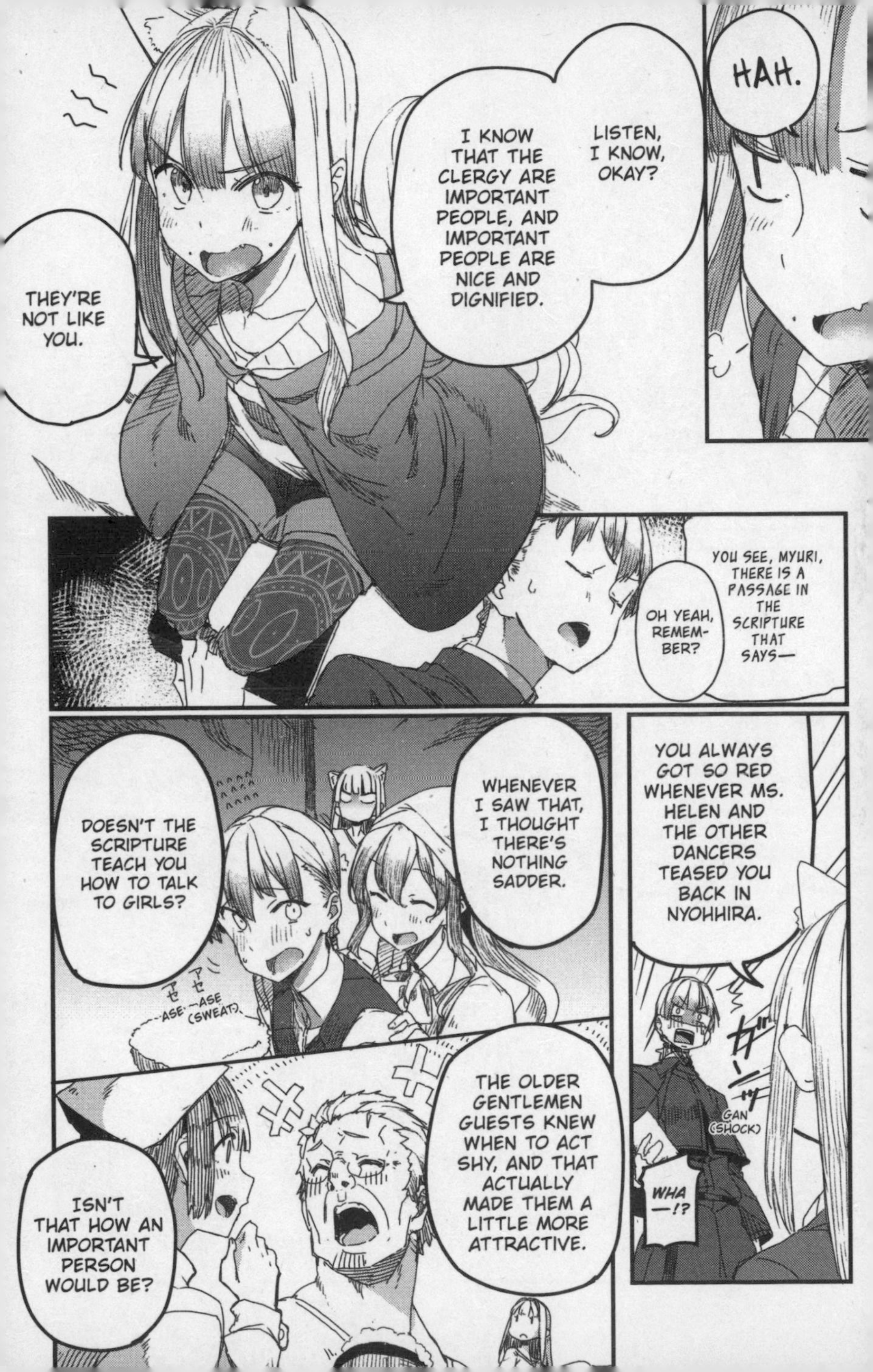
HAH.
LISTEN, I KNOW, OKAY?
I KNOW THAT THE CLERGY ARE IMPORTANT PEOPLE, AND IMPORTANT PEOPLE ARE NICE AND DIGNIFIED.
THEY'RE NOT LIKE YOU.
YOU SEE, MYURI, THERE IS A PASSAGE IN THE SCRIPTURE THAT SAYS—
OH YEAH, REMEMBER?
YOU ALWAYS GOT SO RED WHENEVER MS. HELEN AND THE OTHER DANCERS TEASED YOU BACK IN NYOHHIRA.
GAN (SHOCK)
WHA—!?
WHENEVER I SAW THAT, I THOUGHT THERE'S NOTHING SADDER.
DOESN'T THE SCRIPTURE TEACH YOU HOW TO TALK TO GIRLS?
アセ アセ
ASE—ASE (SWEAT)
THE OLDER GENTLEMEN GUESTS KNEW WHEN TO ACT SHY, AND THAT ACTUALLY MADE THEM A LITTLE MORE ATTRACTIVE.
ISN'T THAT HOW AN IMPORTANT PERSON WOULD BE?

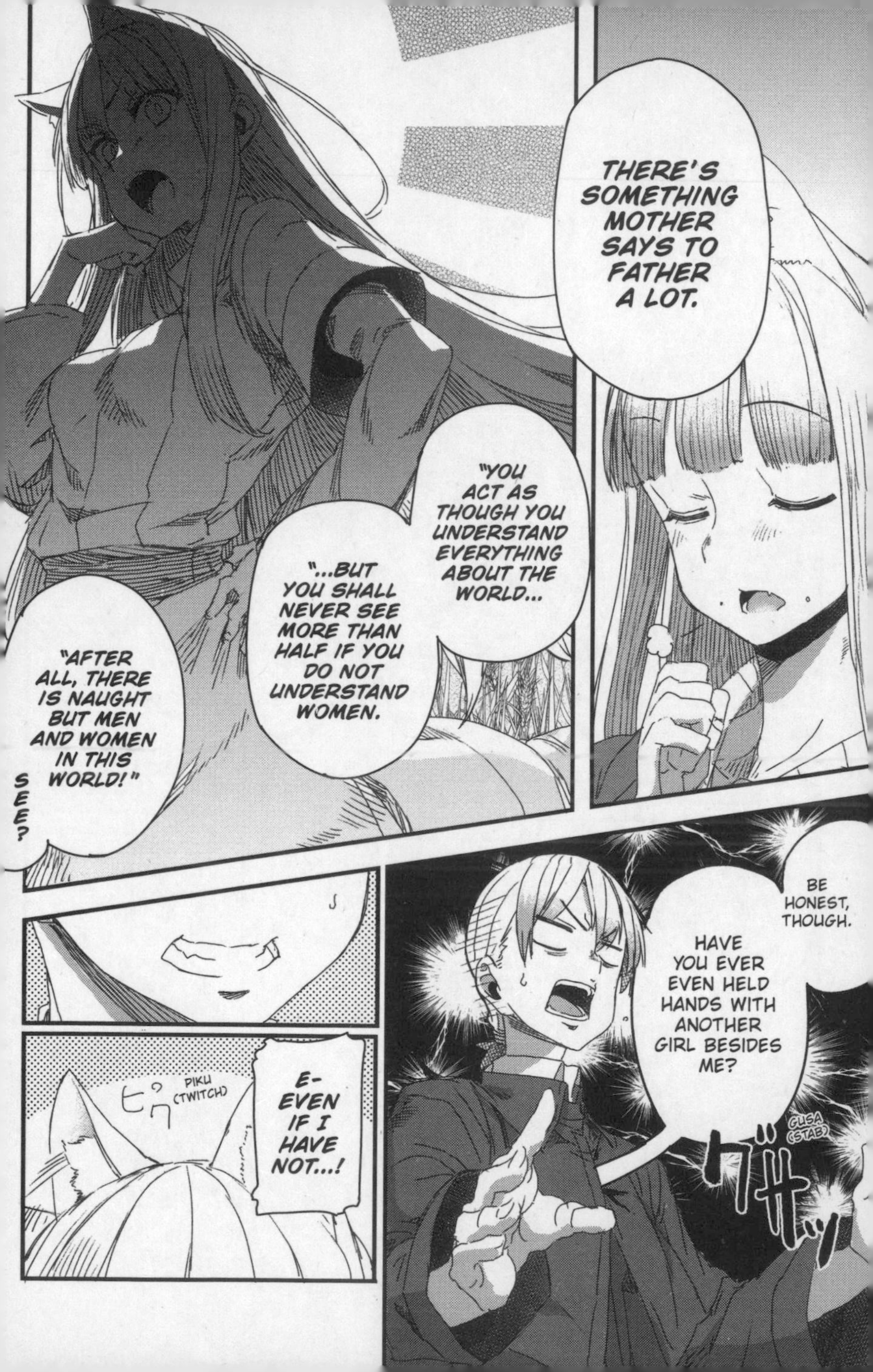
THERE'S SOMETHING MOTHER SAYS TO FATHER A LOT.
"YOU ACT AS THOUGH YOU UNDERSTAND EVERYTHING ABOUT THE WORLD...
"...BUT YOU SHALL NEVER SEE MORE THAN HALF IF YOU DO NOT UNDERSTAND WOMEN.
"AFTER ALL, THERE IS NAUGHT BUT MEN AND WOMEN IN THIS WORLD!"
SEE?
BE HONEST, THOUGH.
HAVE YOU EVER EVEN HELD HANDS WITH ANOTHER GIRL BESIDES ME?
GUSA (STAB)
E-EVEN IF I HAVE NOT...!
PIKU (TWITCH)

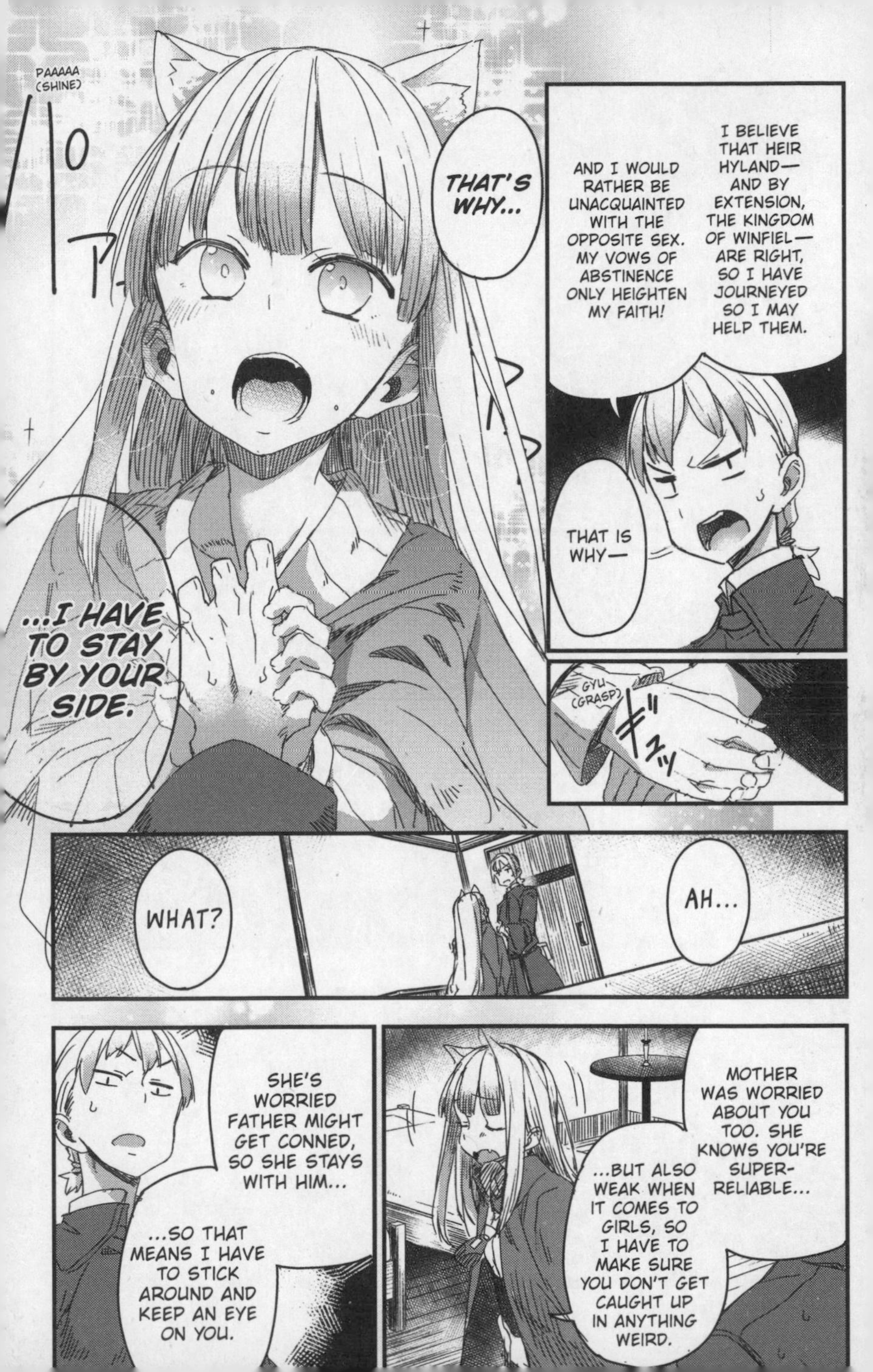
I BELIEVE THAT HEIR HYLAND—AND BY EXTENSION, THE KINGDOM OF WINFIEL—ARE RIGHT, SO I HAVE JOURNEYED SO I MAY HELP THEM.
AND I WOULD RATHER BE UNACQUAINTED WITH THE OPPOSITE SEX. MY VOWS OF ABSTINENCE ONLY HEIGHTEN MY FAITH!
THAT IS WHY—
GYU (GRASP)
THAT'S WHY...
PAAAAA (SHINE)
...I HAVE TO STAY BY YOUR SIDE.
AH...
WHAT?
MOTHER WAS WORRIED ABOUT YOU TOO. SHE KNOWS YOU'RE SUPER-RELIABLE...
...BUT ALSO WEAK WHEN IT COMES TO GIRLS, SO I HAVE TO MAKE SURE YOU DON'T GET CAUGHT UP IN ANYTHING WEIRD.
SHE'S WORRIED FATHER MIGHT GET CONNED, SO SHE STAYS WITH HIM...
...SO THAT MEANS I HAVE TO STICK AROUND AND KEEP AN EYE ON YOU.

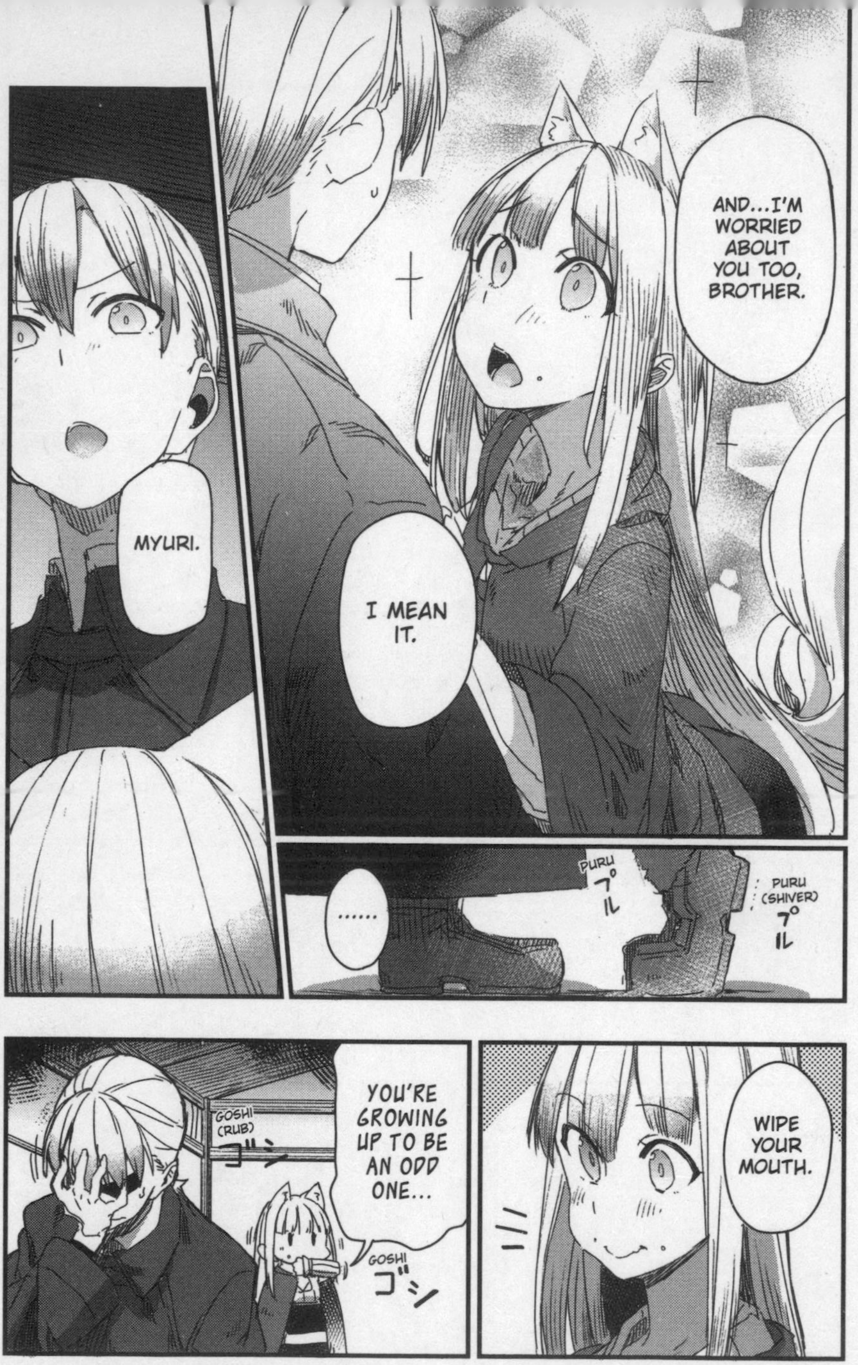

AND...I'M WORRIED ABOUT YOU TOO, BROTHER.
I MEAN IT.
......
PURU
プル
PURU (SHIVER)
プル
MYURI.
WIPE YOUR MOUTH.
YOU'RE GROWING UP TO BE AN ODD ONE...
GOSHI (RUB)
ゴシ
GOSHI
ゴシ

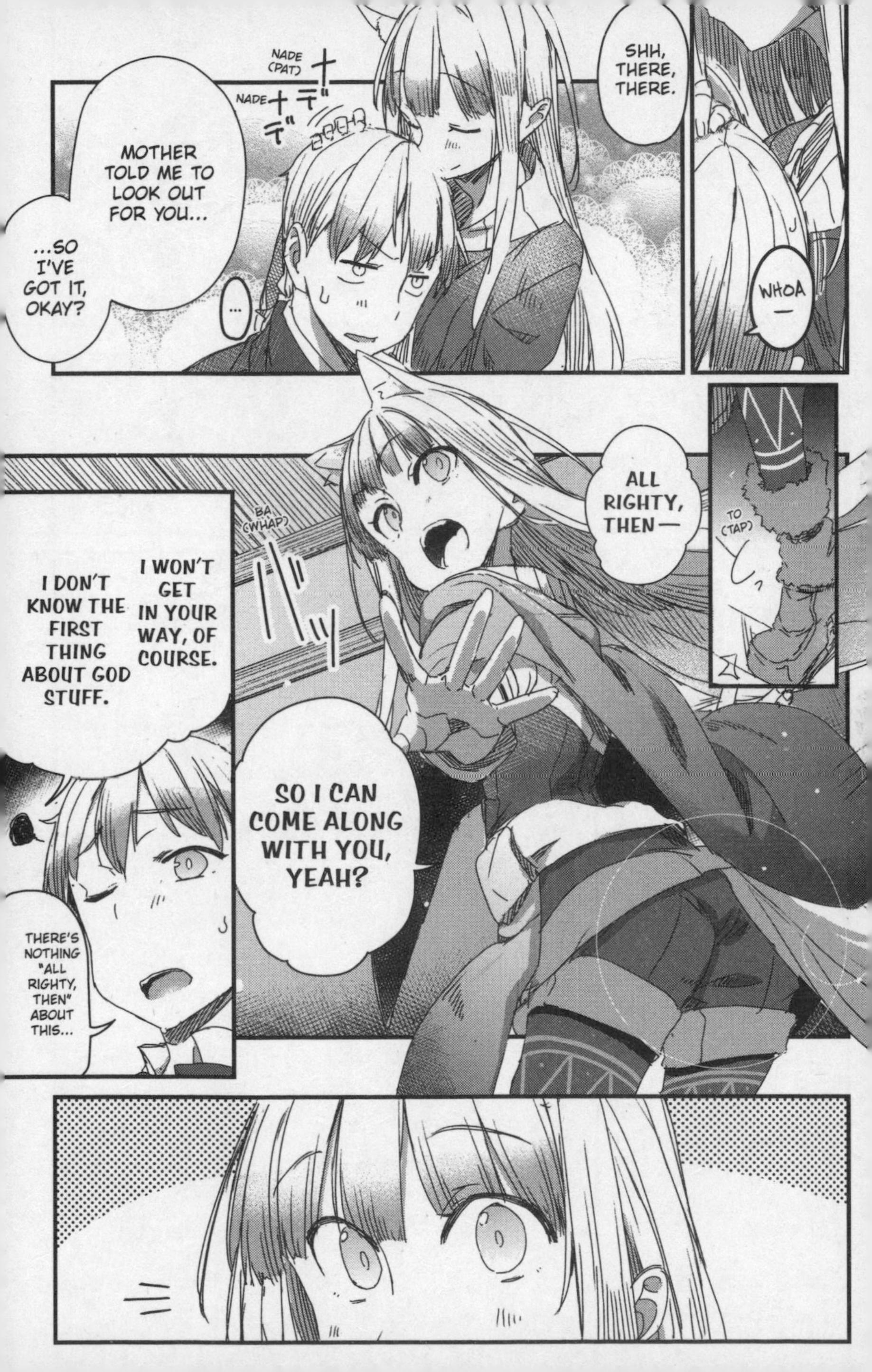
WHOA —
SHH, THERE, THERE.
NADE (PAT)
NADE
MOTHER TOLD ME TO LOOK OUT FOR YOU...
...SO I'VE GOT IT, OKAY?
...
TO (TAP)
ALL RIGHTY, THEN —
BA (WHAP)
I WON'T GET IN YOUR WAY, OF COURSE.
I DON'T KNOW THE FIRST THING ABOUT GOD STUFF.
SO I CAN COME ALONG WITH YOU, YEAH?
THERE'S NOTHING "ALL RIGHTY, THEN" ABOUT THIS...

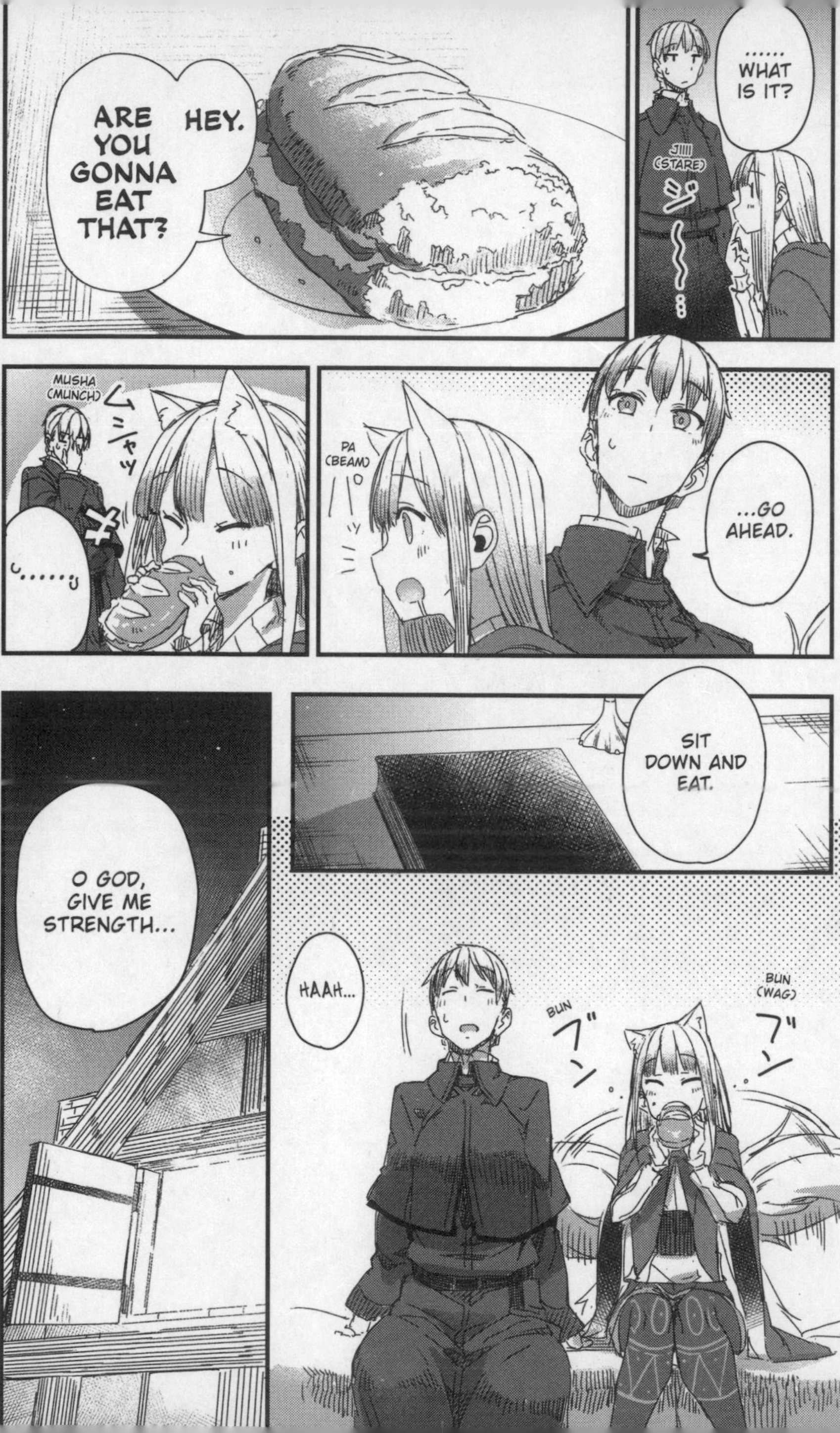

……
WHAT IS IT?
JIII (STARE)
HEY.
ARE YOU GONNA EAT THAT?
PA (BEAM)
...GO AHEAD.
MUSHA (MUNCH)
「……」
SIT DOWN AND EAT.
HAAH...
BUN (WAG)
BUN
O GOD, GIVE ME STRENGTH...

WOLF & PARCHMENT

WOLF & PARCHMENT

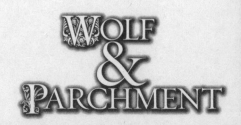

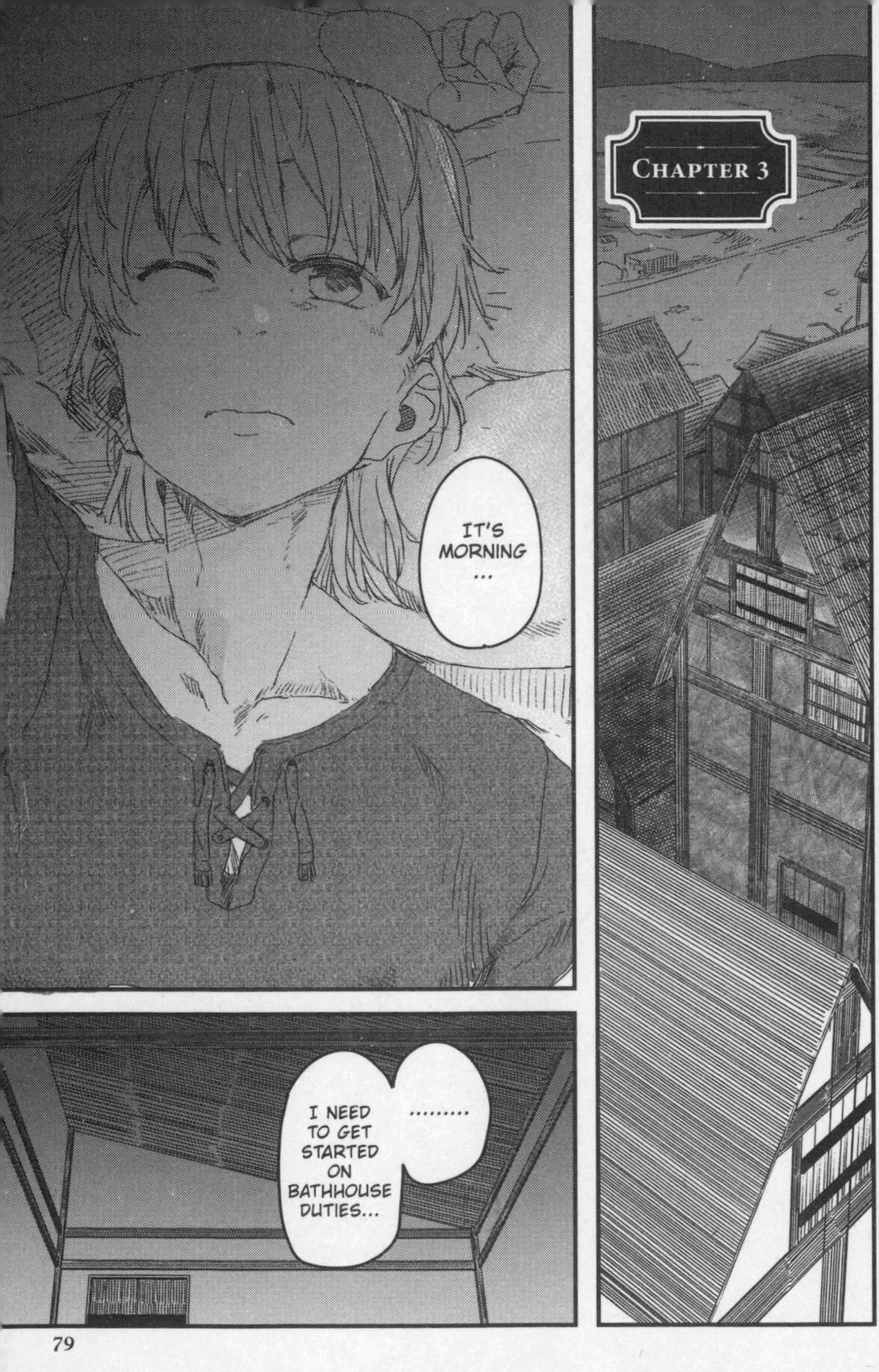
CHAPTER 3
IT'S MORNING ...
....
I NEED TO GET STARTED ON BATHHOUSE DUTIES...

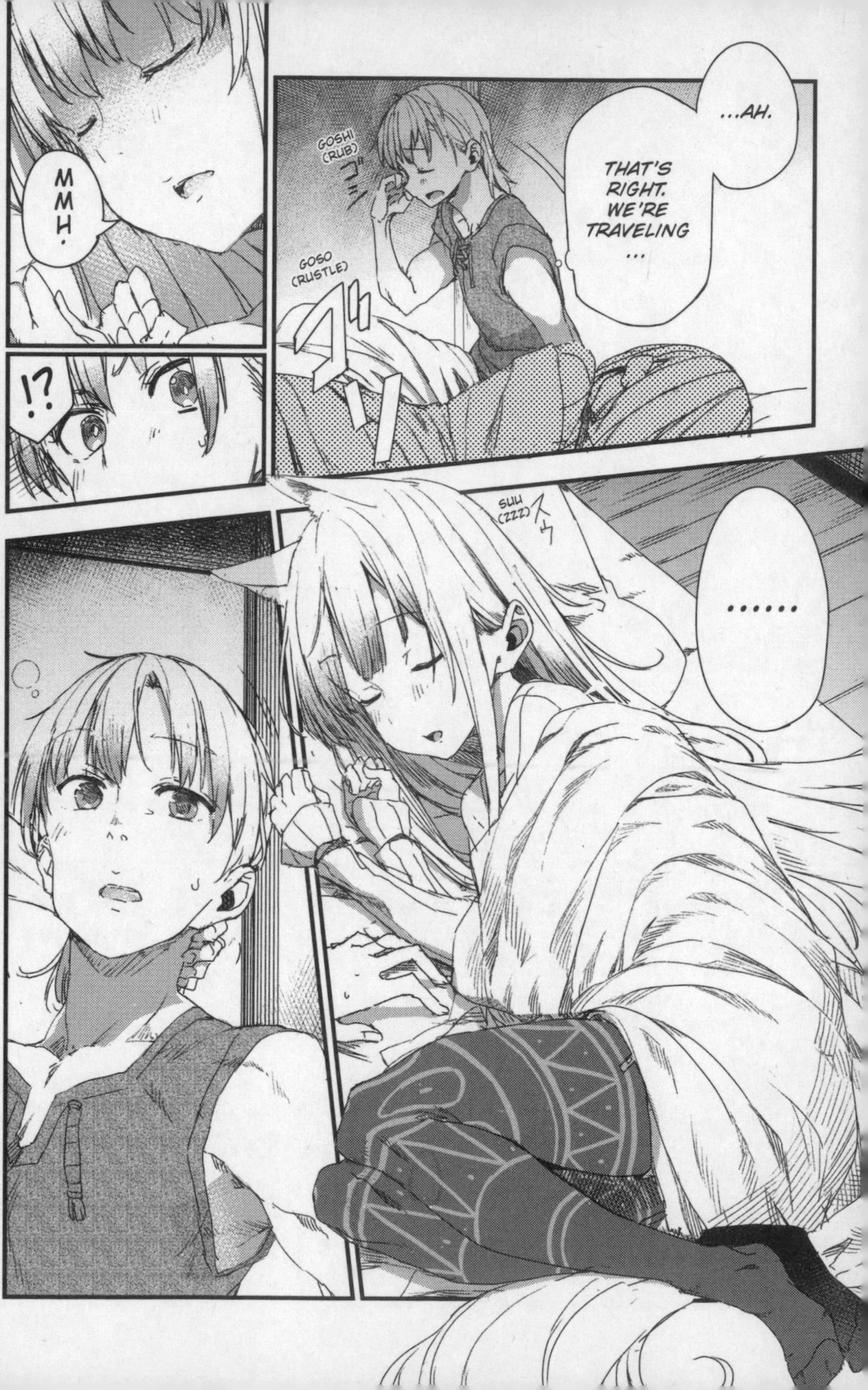
...AH.
THAT'S RIGHT. WE'RE TRAVELING ...
GOSHI (RUB)
GOSO (RUSTLE)
MMH.
!?
SUU (ZZZZ)
......

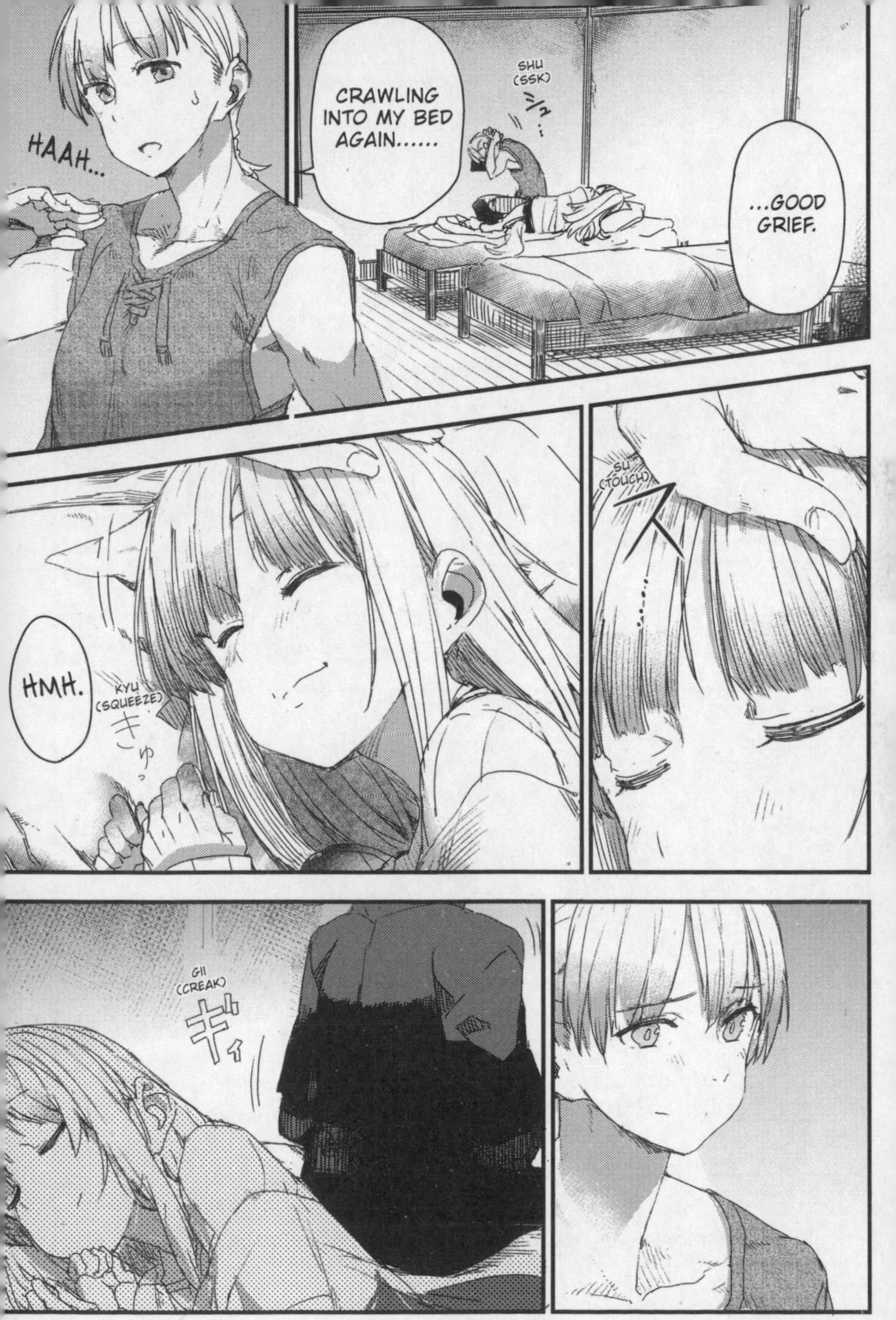
SHU
(SSK)
シュ
...GOOD GRIEF.
CRAWLING INTO MY BED AGAIN......
HAAH...
SU
(TOUCH)
ス
HMH.
KYU
(SQUEEZE)
きゅっ
GII
(CREAK)
ギィ

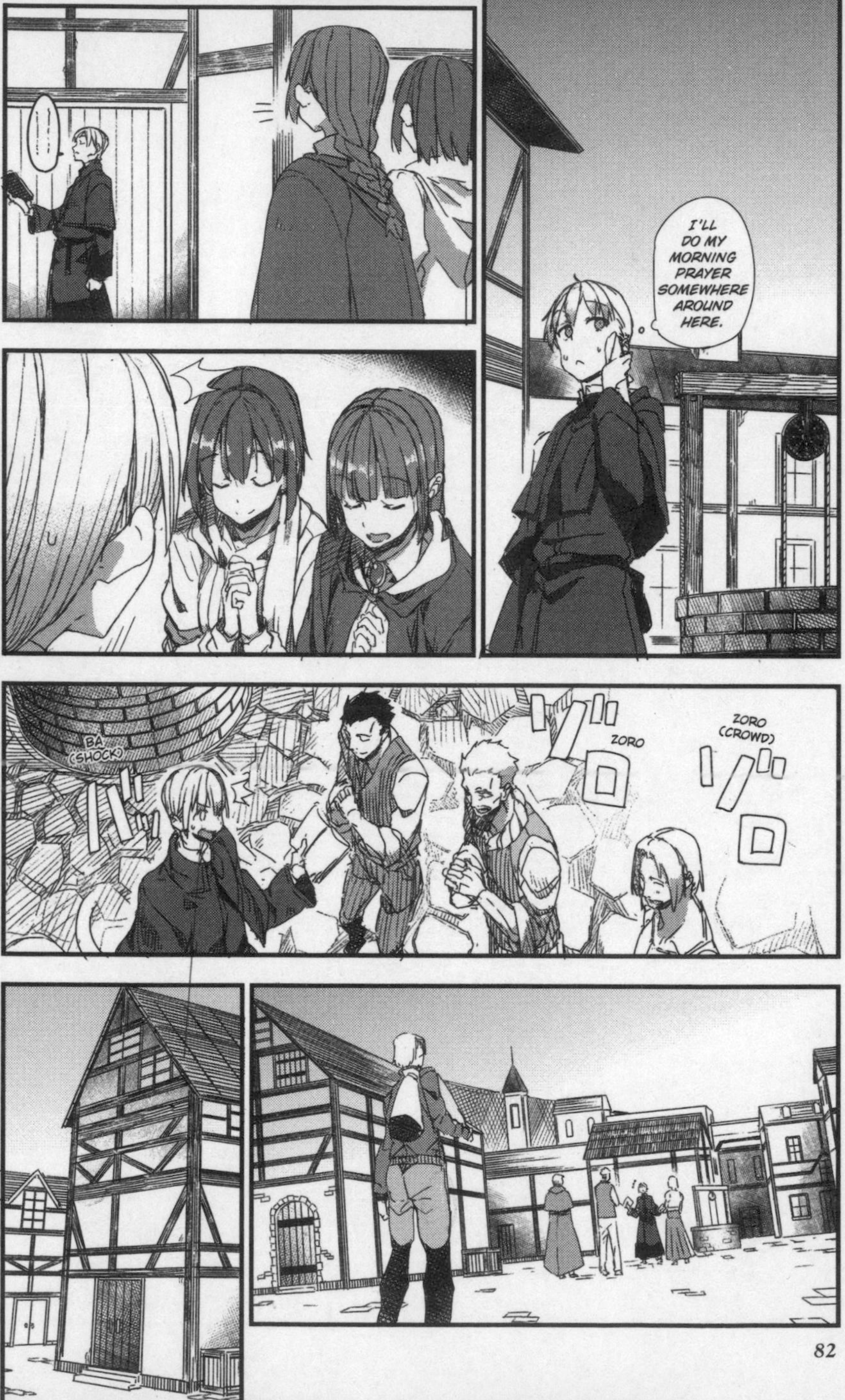
I'LL DO MY MORNING PRAYER SOMEWHERE AROUND HERE.
...!
ZORO (CROWD)
ZORO
BA (SHOCK)

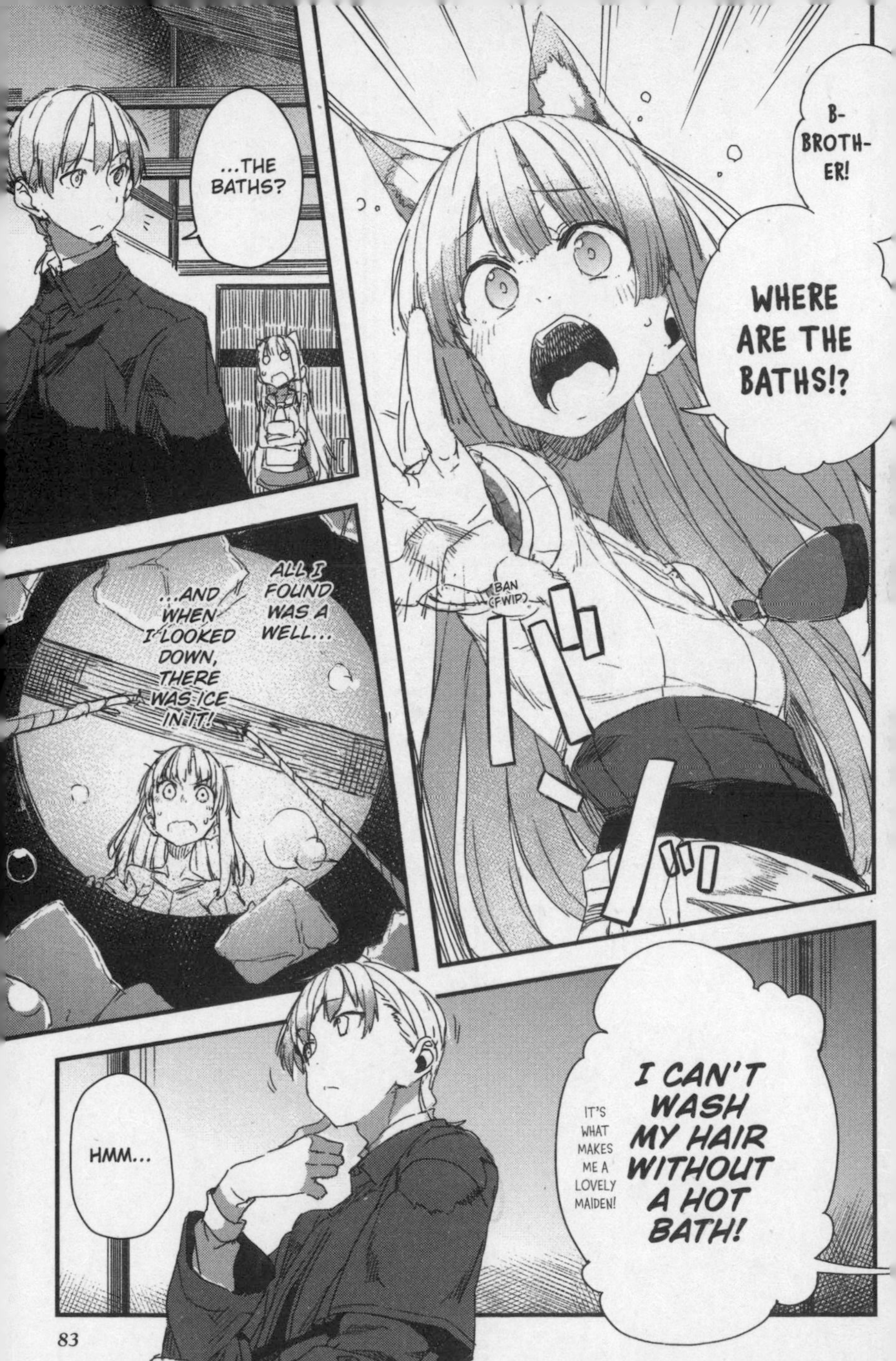
B-BROTHER!
WHERE ARE THE BATHS!?
BAN (FWIP)
...THE BATHS?
ALL I FOUND WAS A WELL...
...AND WHEN I LOOKED DOWN, THERE WAS ICE IN IT!
I CAN'T WASH MY HAIR WITHOUT A HOT BATH!
IT'S WHAT MAKES ME A LOVELY MAIDEN!
HMM...

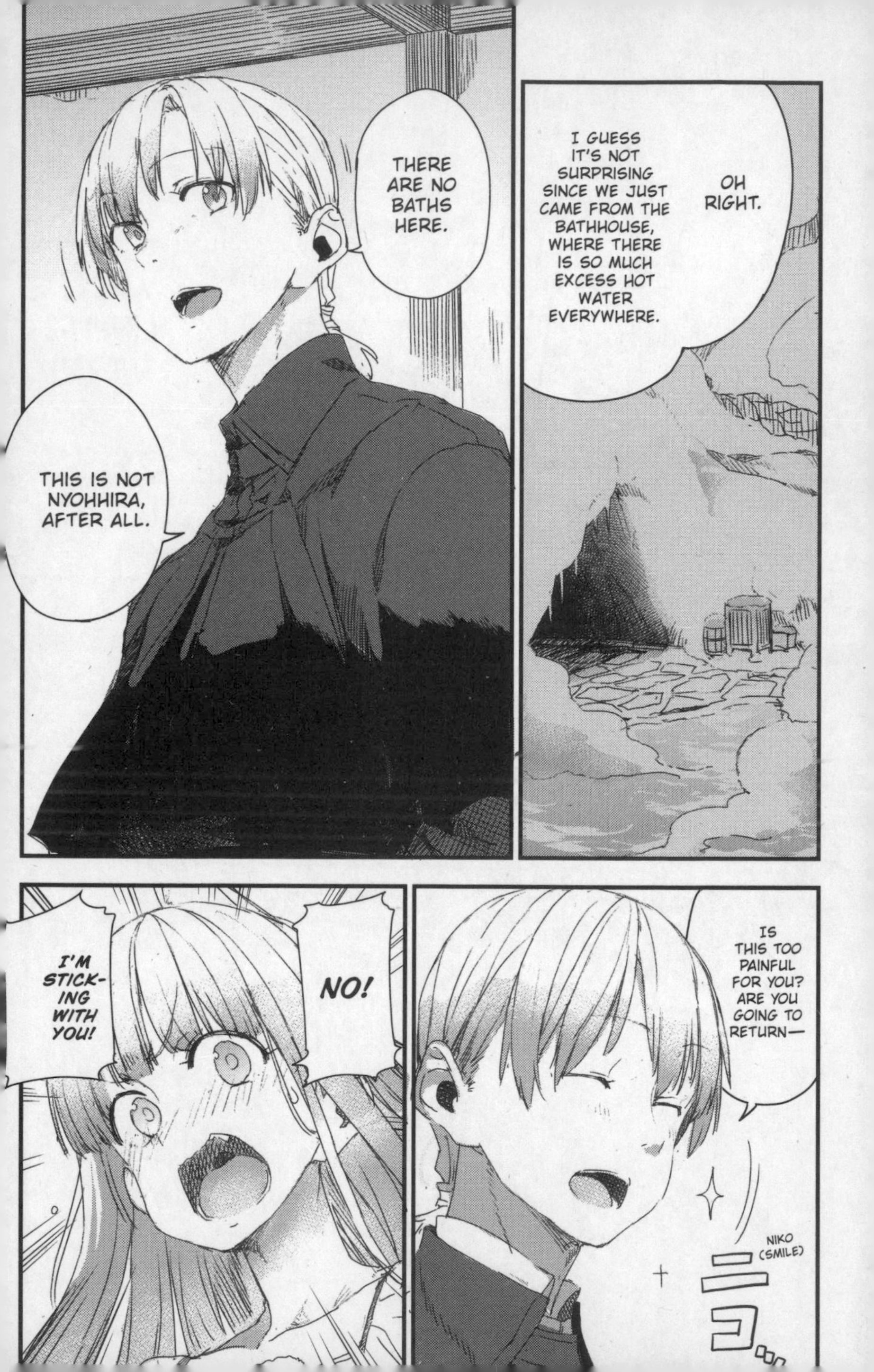

OH RIGHT.
I GUESS IT'S NOT SURPRISING SINCE WE JUST CAME FROM THE BATHHOUSE, WHERE THERE IS SO MUCH EXCESS HOT WATER EVERYWHERE.
THERE ARE NO BATHS HERE.
THIS IS NOT NYOHHIRA, AFTER ALL.
IS THIS TOO PAINFUL FOR YOU? ARE YOU GOING TO RETURN—
NIKO (SMILE)
NO!
I'M STICK-ING WITH YOU!

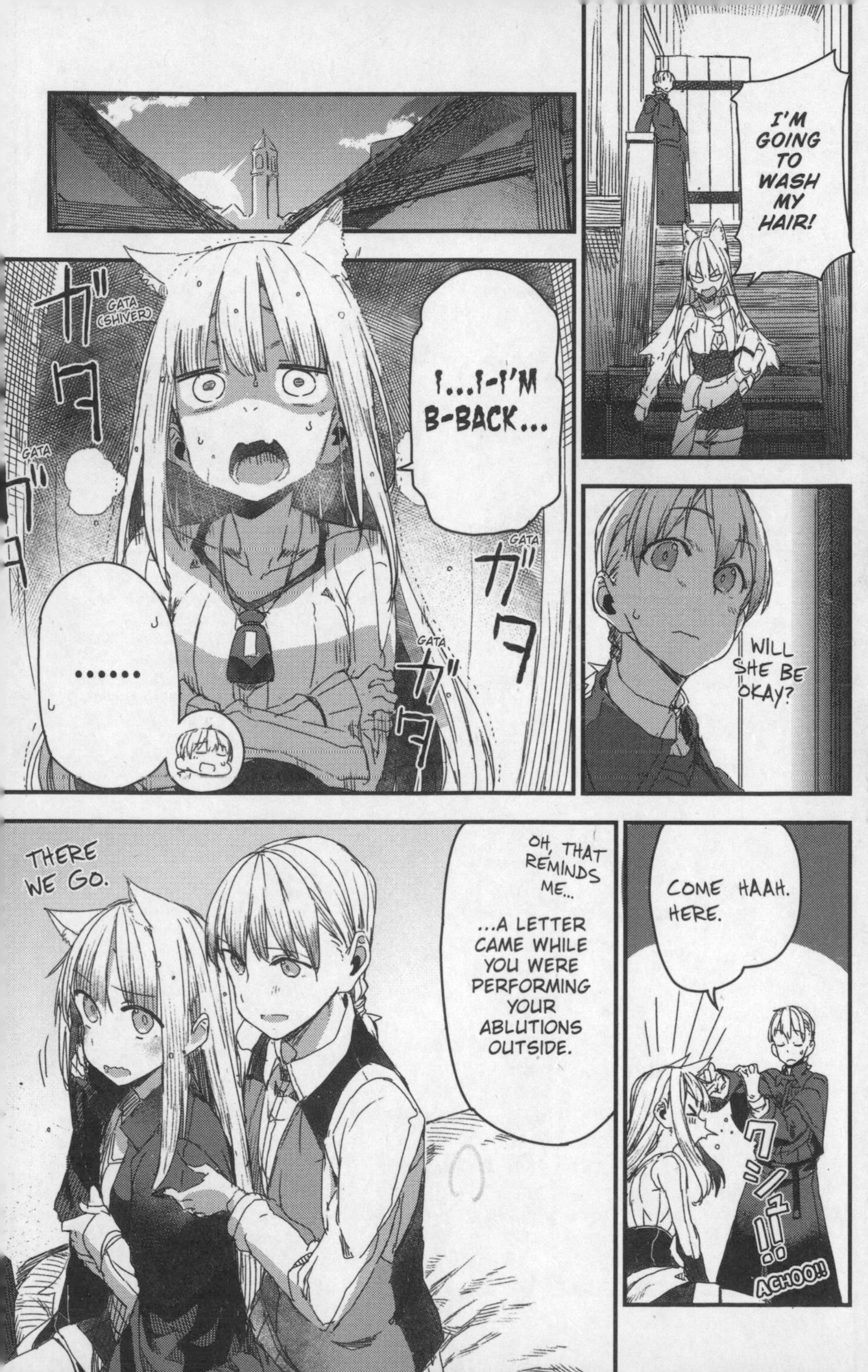
I'M GOING TO WASH MY HAIR!
GATA (SHIVER)
GATA
I...I-I'M B-BACK...
GATA
GATA
......
WILL SHE BE OKAY?
COME HERE.
HAAH.
ACHOO!!
OH, THAT REMINDS ME...
...A LETTER CAME WHILE YOU WERE PERFORMING YOUR ABLUTIONS OUTSIDE.
THERE WE GO.

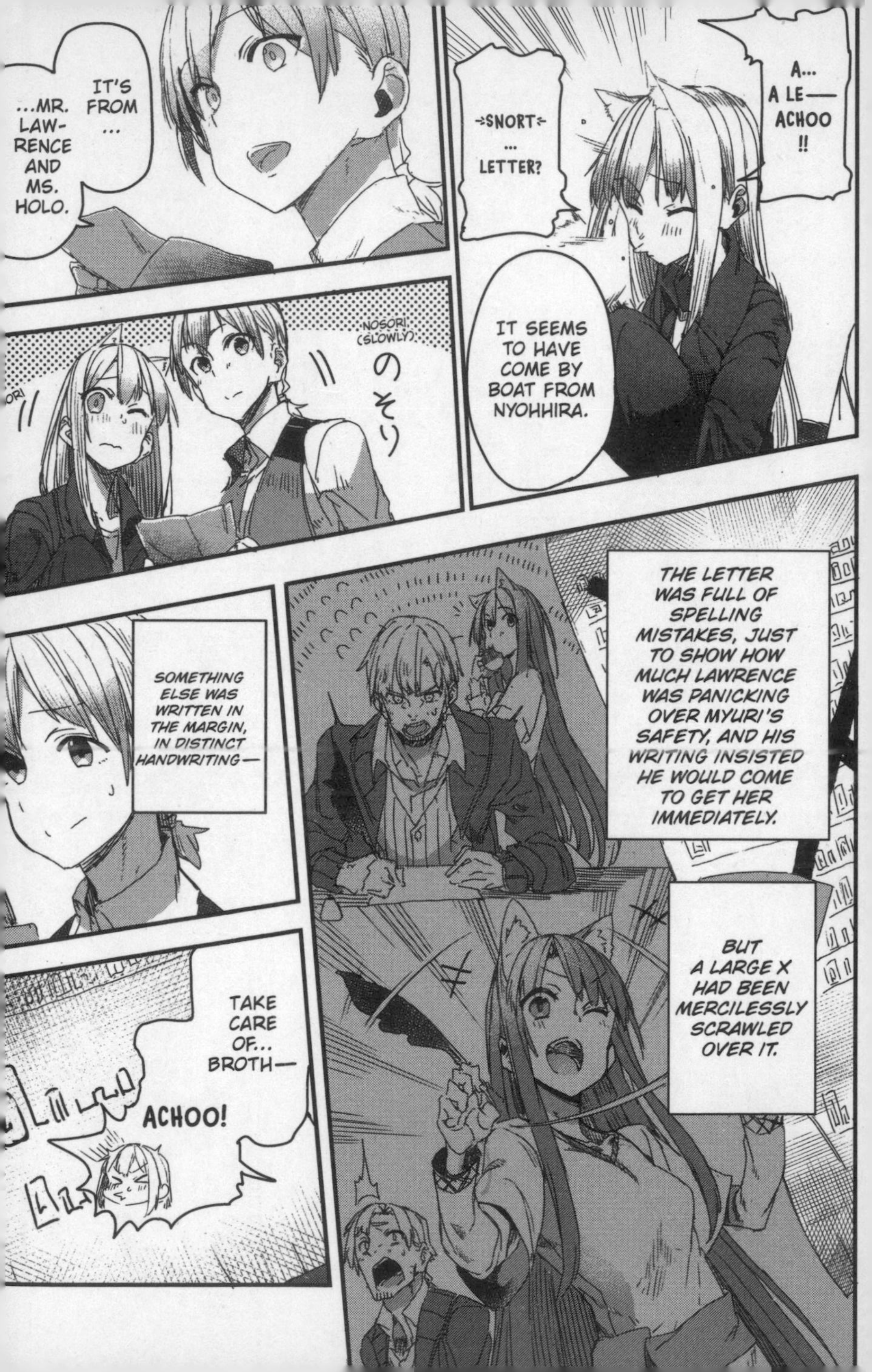
A... A LE— ACHOO!!
≈SNORT≈ ... LETTER?
IT SEEMS TO HAVE COME BY BOAT FROM NYOHHIRA.
IT'S FROM ... ...MR. LAWRENCE AND MS. HOLO.
NOSORI (SLOWLY)
のそり
THE LETTER WAS FULL OF SPELLING MISTAKES, JUST TO SHOW HOW MUCH LAWRENCE WAS PANICKING OVER MYURI'S SAFETY, AND HIS WRITING INSISTED HE WOULD COME TO GET HER IMMEDIATELY.
BUT A LARGE X HAD BEEN MERCILESSLY SCRAWLED OVER IT.
SOMETHING ELSE WAS WRITTEN IN THE MARGIN, IN DISTINCT HANDWRITING—
TAKE CARE OF... BROTH—
ACHOO!

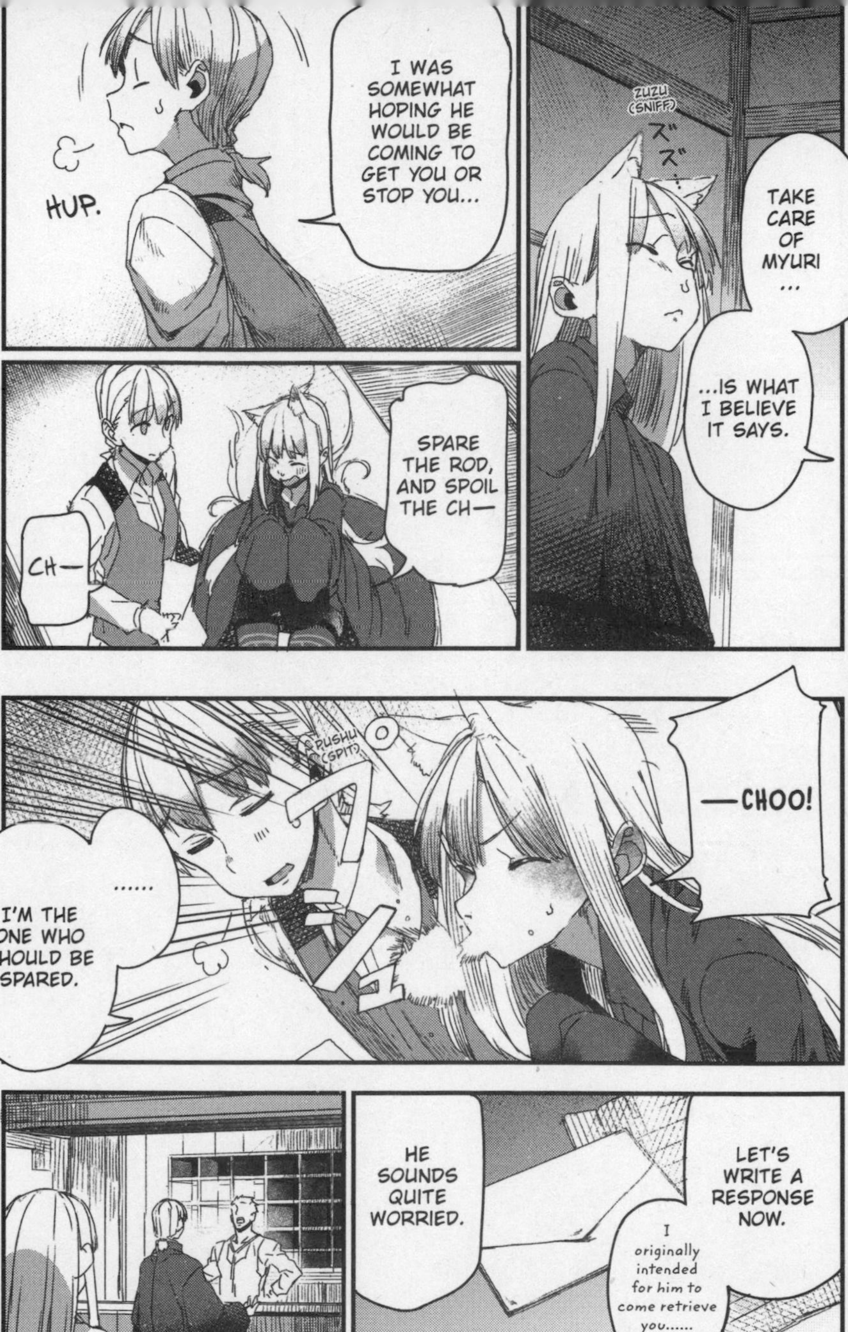
ZUZU (SNIFF)
TAKE CARE OF MYURI ...
...IS WHAT I BELIEVE IT SAYS.
I WAS SOMEWHAT HOPING HE WOULD BE COMING TO GET YOU OR STOP YOU...
HUP.
SPARE THE ROD, AND SPOIL THE CH—
CH—
—CHOO!
PUSHU (SPIT)
......
I'M THE ONE WHO SHOULD BE SPARED.
LET'S WRITE A RESPONSE NOW.
I originally intended for him to come retrieve you......
HE SOUNDS QUITE WORRIED.

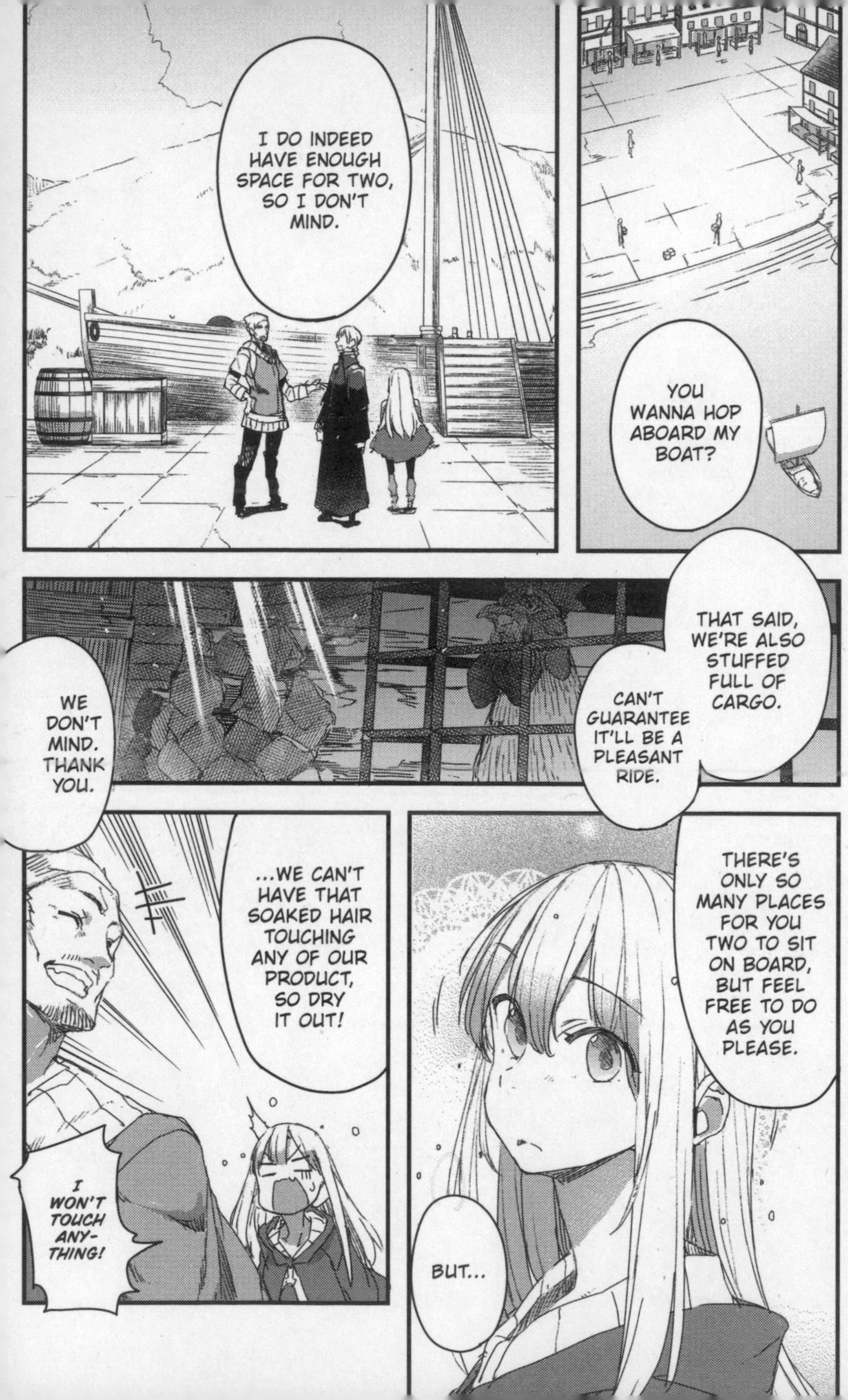
YOU WANNA HOP ABOARD MY BOAT?
I DO INDEED HAVE ENOUGH SPACE FOR TWO, SO I DON'T MIND.
THAT SAID, WE'RE ALSO STUFFED FULL OF CARGO.
CAN'T GUARANTEE IT'LL BE A PLEASANT RIDE.
WE DON'T MIND. THANK YOU.
THERE'S ONLY SO MANY PLACES FOR YOU TWO TO SIT ON BOARD, BUT FEEL FREE TO DO AS YOU PLEASE.
BUT...
...WE CAN'T HAVE THAT SOAKED HAIR TOUCHING ANY OF OUR PRODUCT, SO DRY IT OUT!
I WON'T TOUCH ANYTHING!

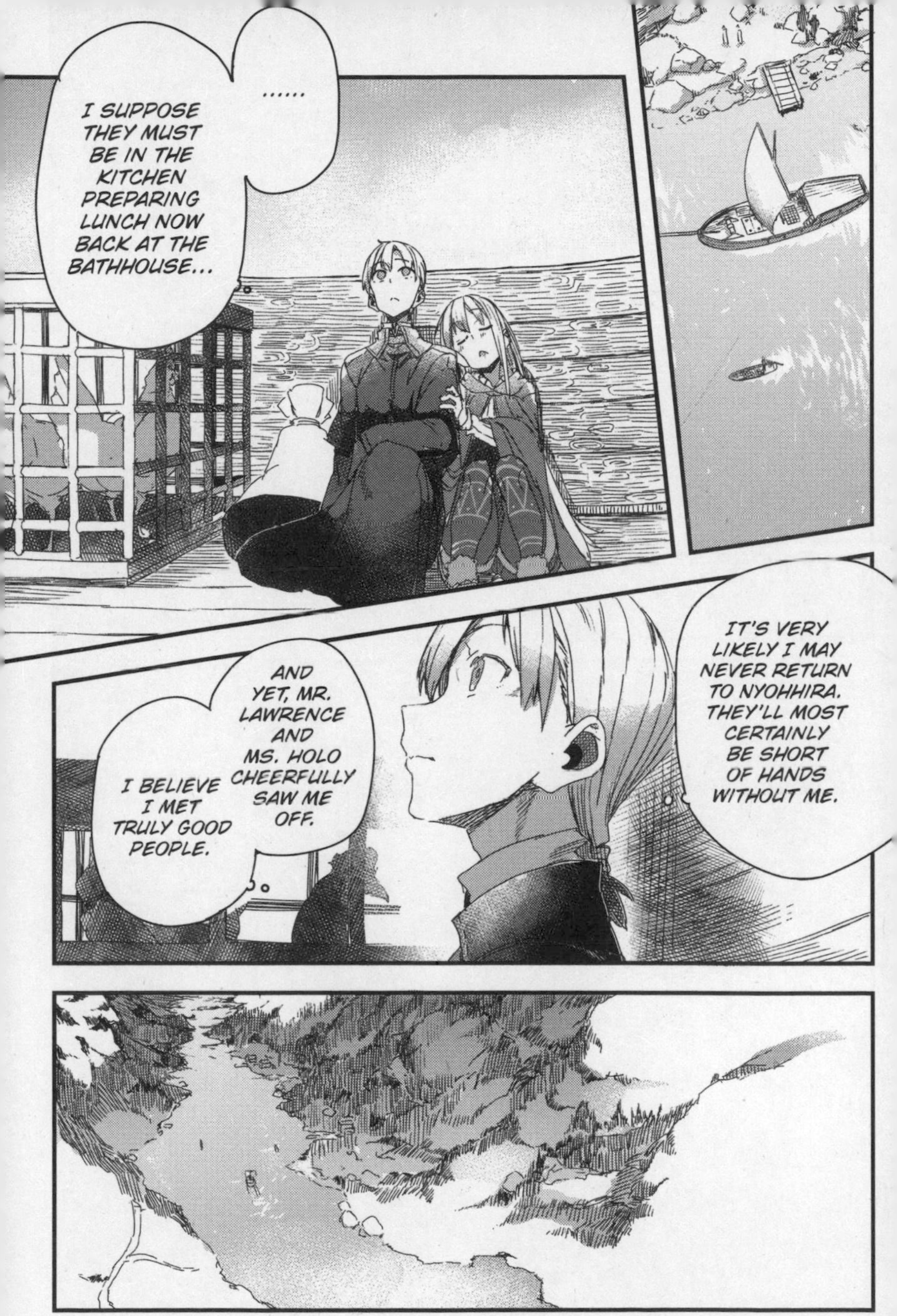
......
I SUPPOSE THEY MUST BE IN THE KITCHEN PREPARING LUNCH NOW BACK AT THE BATHHOUSE...
IT'S VERY LIKELY I MAY NEVER RETURN TO NYOHHIRA. THEY'LL MOST CERTAINLY BE SHORT OF HANDS WITHOUT ME.
AND YET, MR. LAWRENCE AND MS. HOLO CHEERFULLY SAW ME OFF.
I BELIEVE I MET TRULY GOOD PEOPLE.

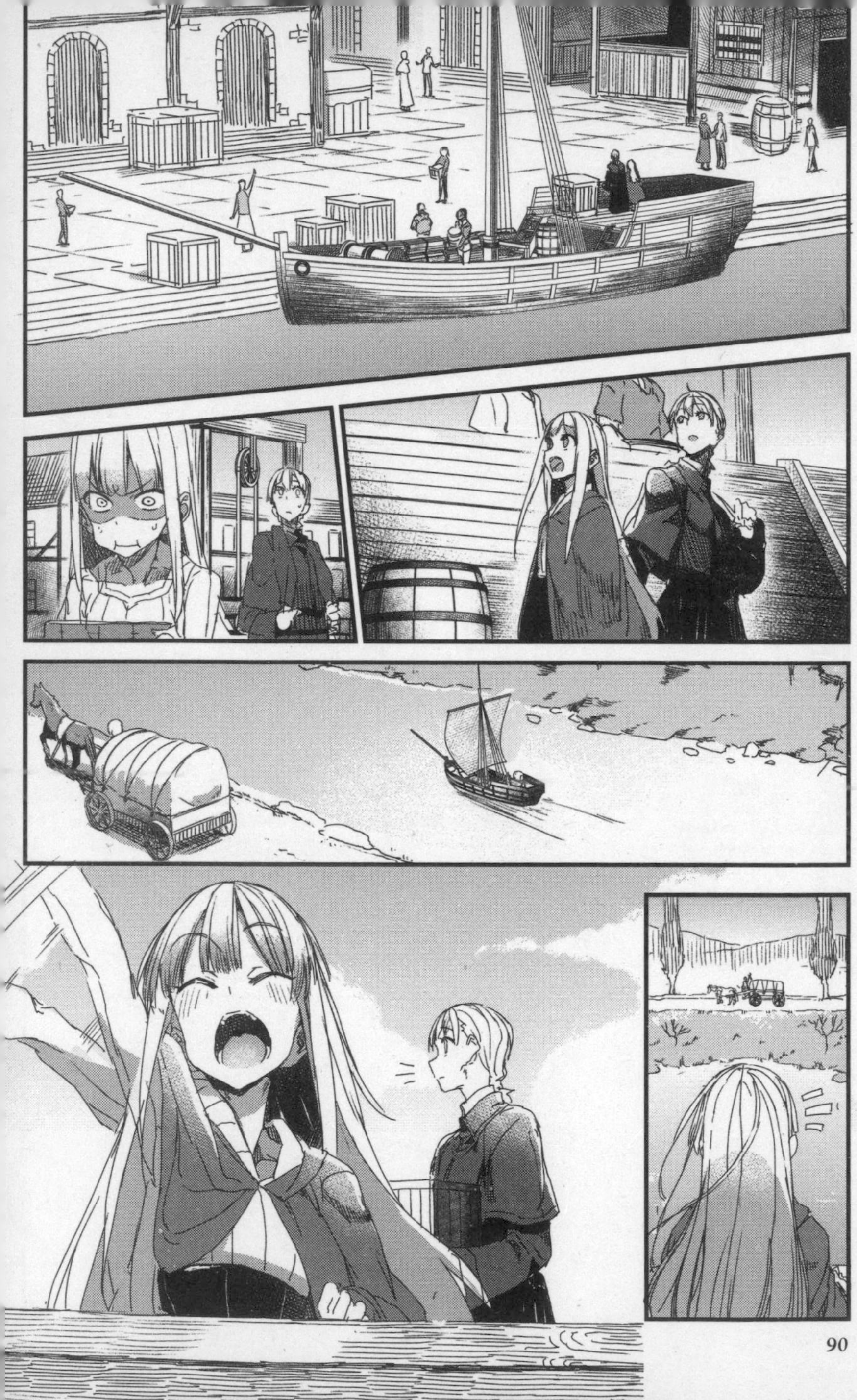

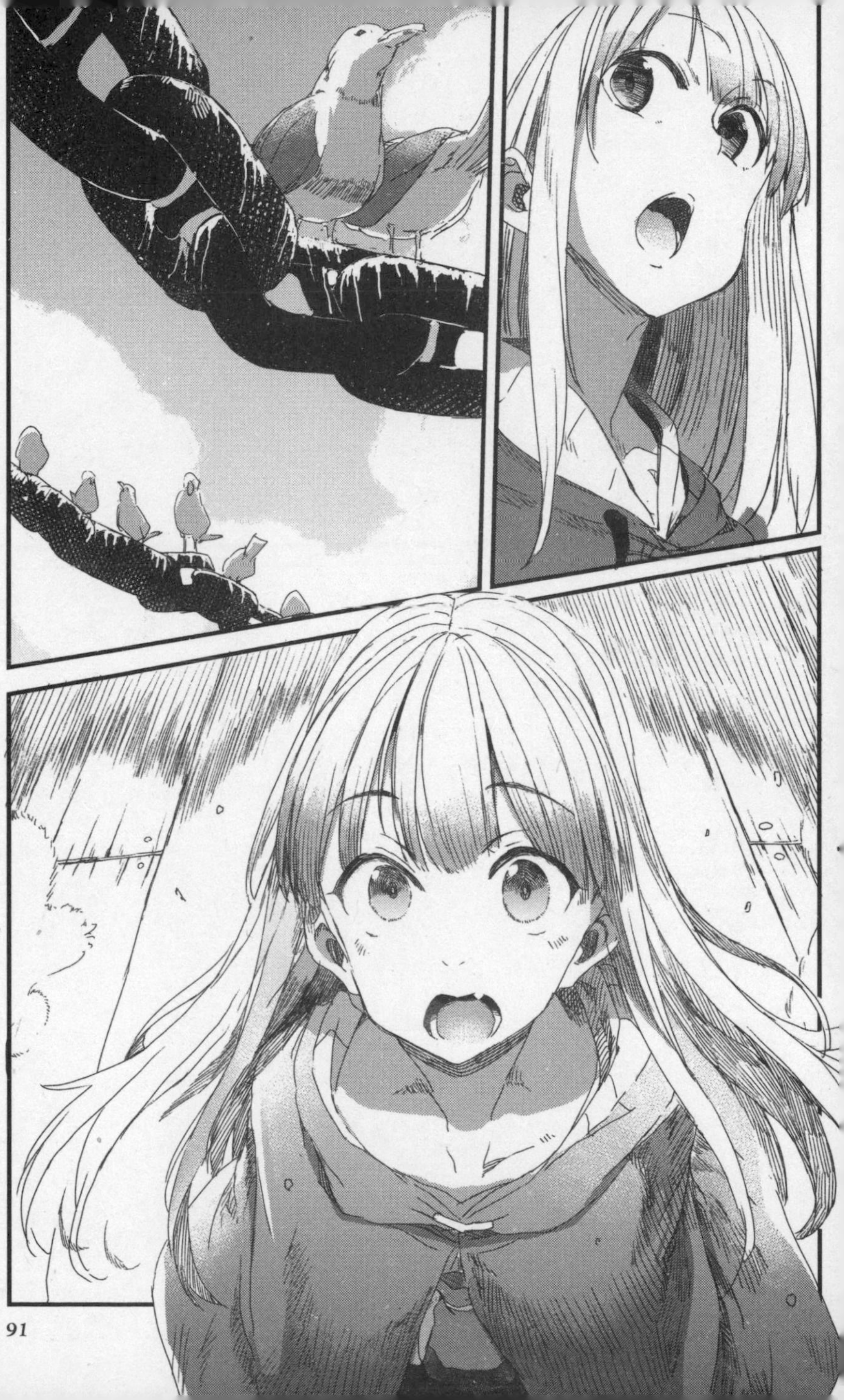

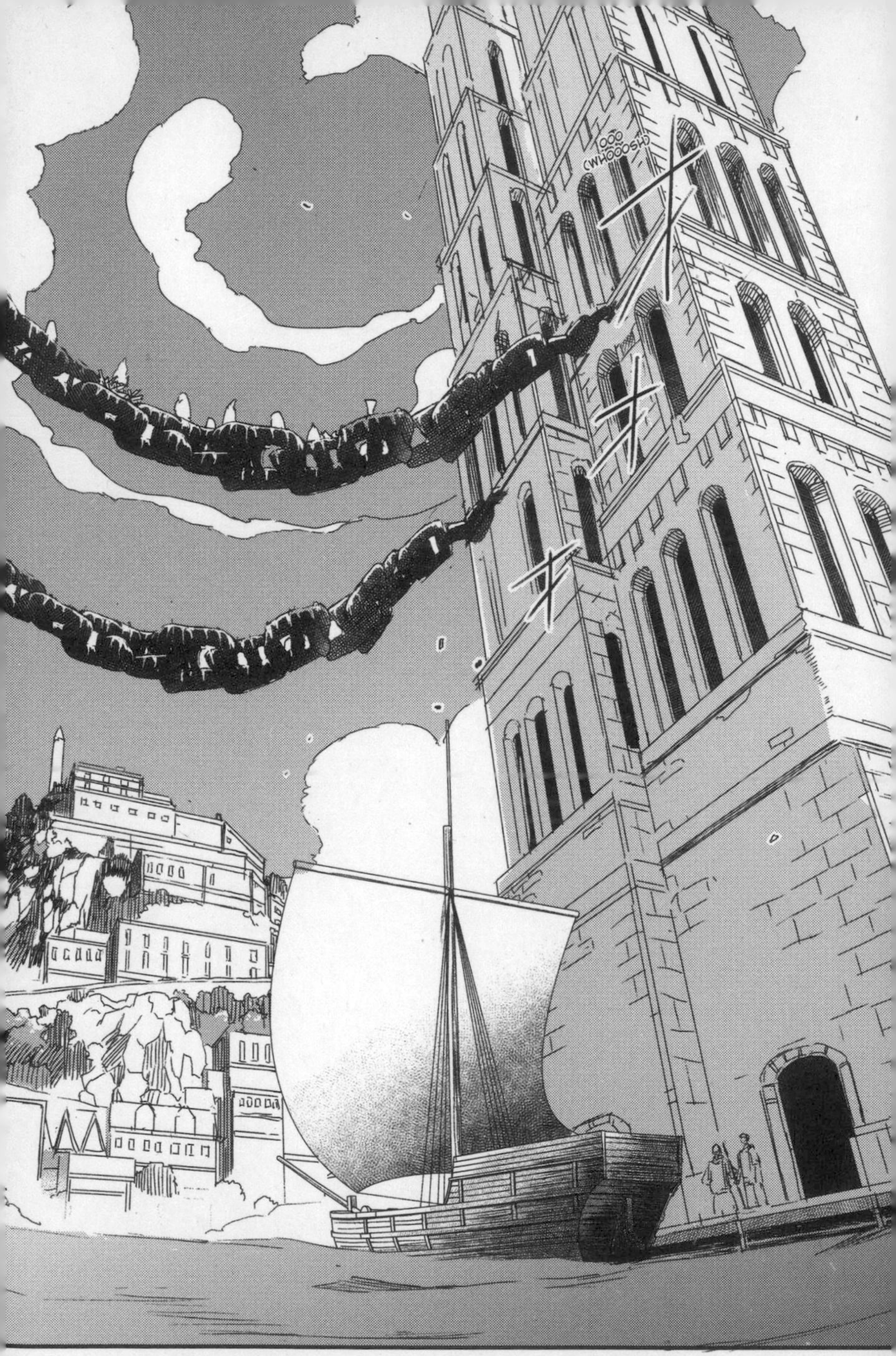
ŌŌŌ
(WHŌŌŌSH)

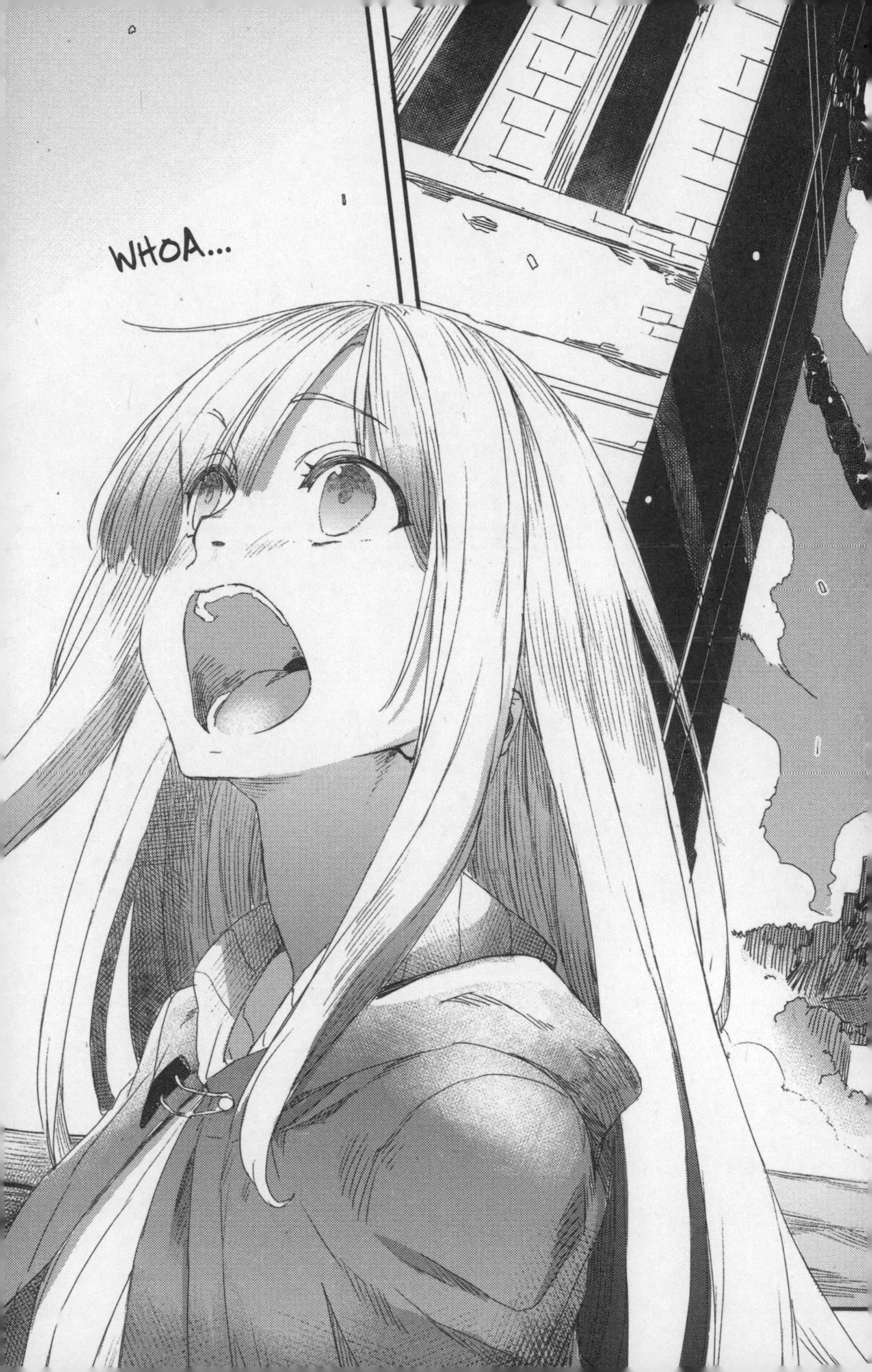
WHOA...

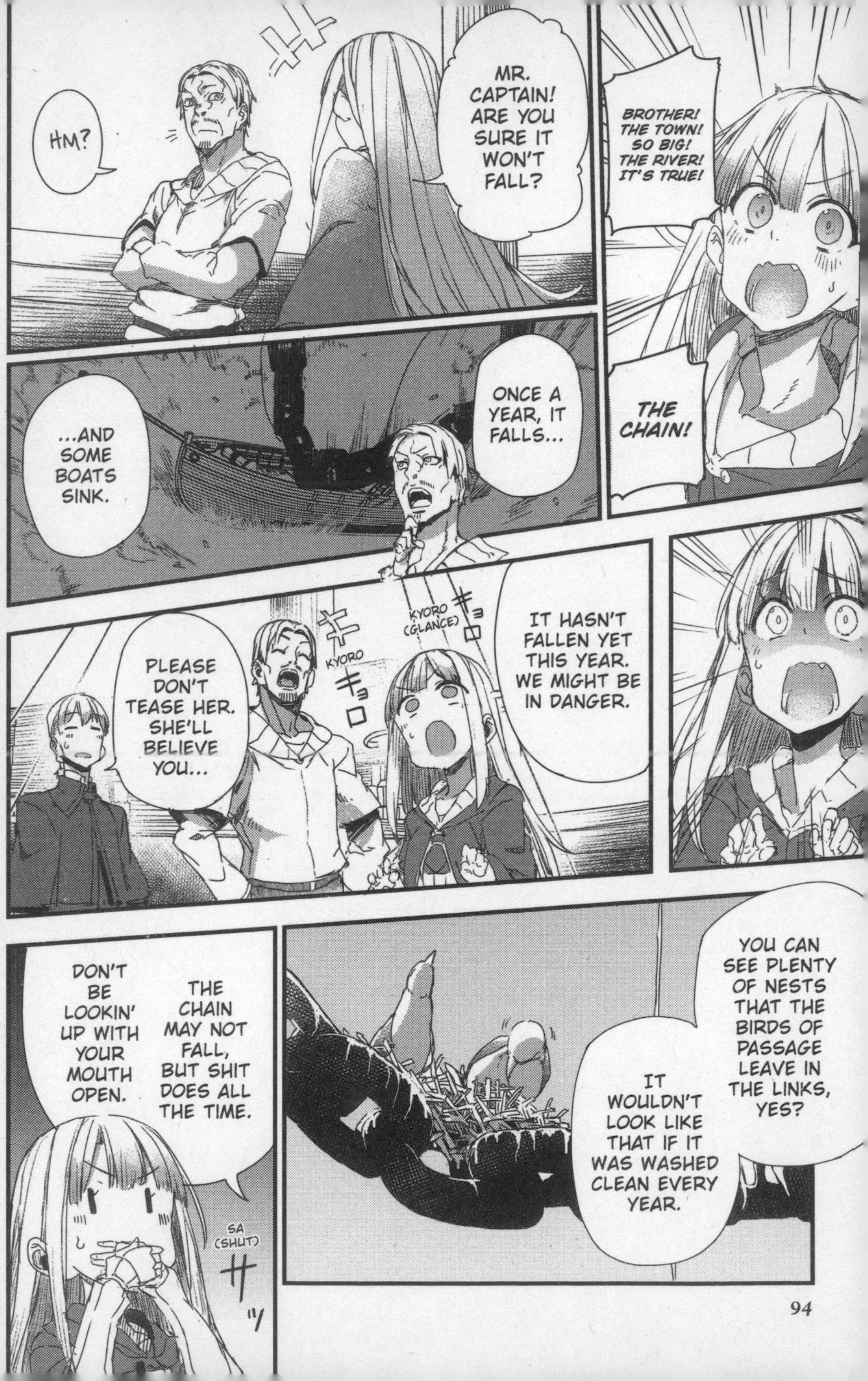
BROTHER! THE TOWN! SO BIG! THE RIVER! IT'S TRUE!
THE CHAIN!
MR. CAPTAIN! ARE YOU SURE IT WON'T FALL?
HM?
ONCE A YEAR, IT FALLS...
...AND SOME BOATS SINK.
IT HASN'T FALLEN YET THIS YEAR. WE MIGHT BE IN DANGER.
KYORO (GLANCE)
KYORO
PLEASE DON'T TEASE HER. SHE'LL BELIEVE YOU...
YOU CAN SEE PLENTY OF NESTS THAT THE BIRDS OF PASSAGE LEAVE IN THE LINKS, YES?
IT WOULDN'T LOOK LIKE THAT IF IT WAS WASHED CLEAN EVERY YEAR.
THE CHAIN MAY NOT FALL, BUT SHIT DOES ALL THE TIME.
DON'T BE LOOKIN' UP WITH YOUR MOUTH OPEN.
SA (SHUT)

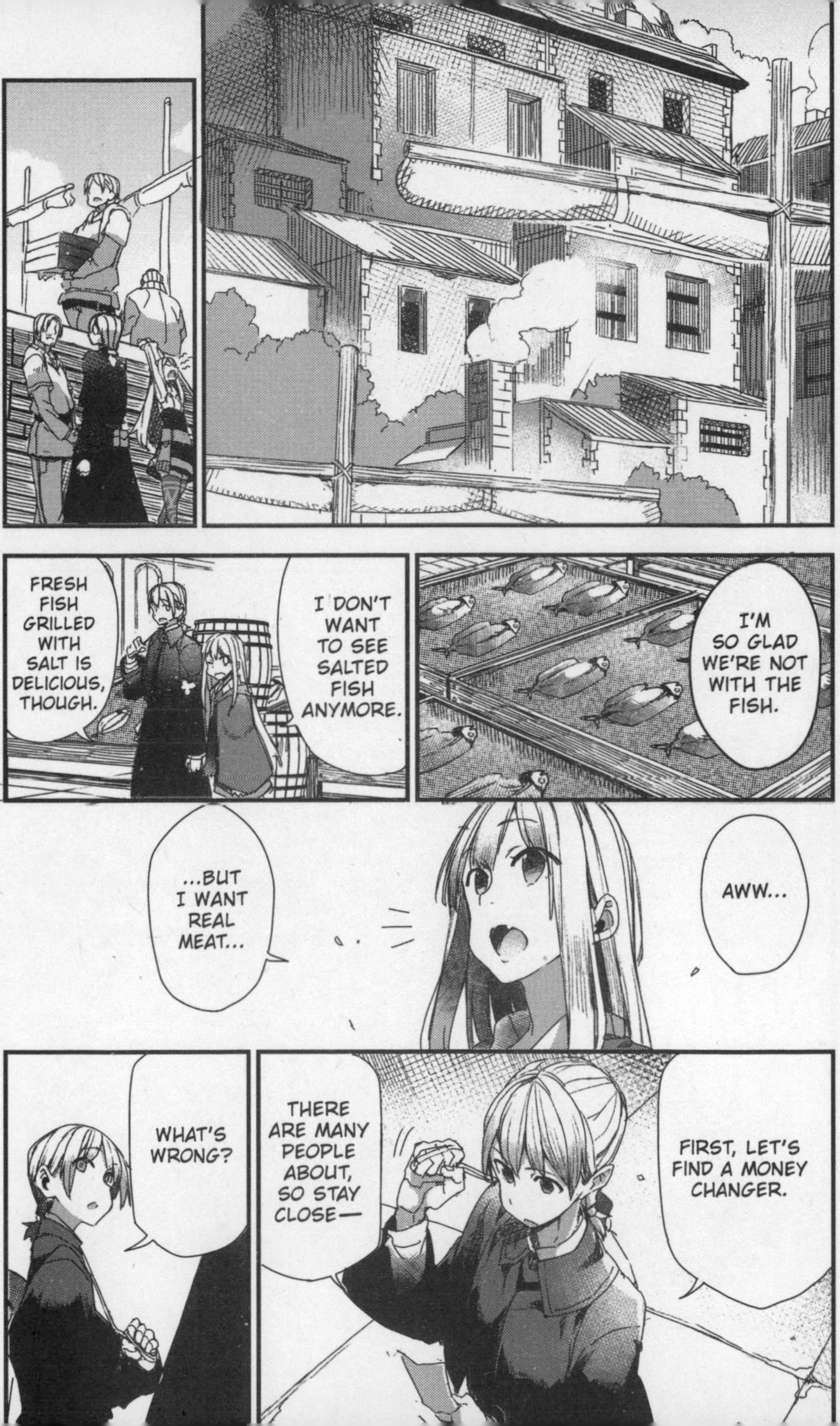
I'M SO GLAD WE'RE NOT WITH THE FISH.
I DON'T WANT TO SEE SALTED FISH ANYMORE.
FRESH FISH GRILLED WITH SALT IS DELICIOUS, THOUGH.
AWW...
...BUT I WANT REAL MEAT...
FIRST, LET'S FIND A MONEY CHANGER.
THERE ARE MANY PEOPLE ABOUT, SO STAY CLOSE—
WHAT'S WRONG?

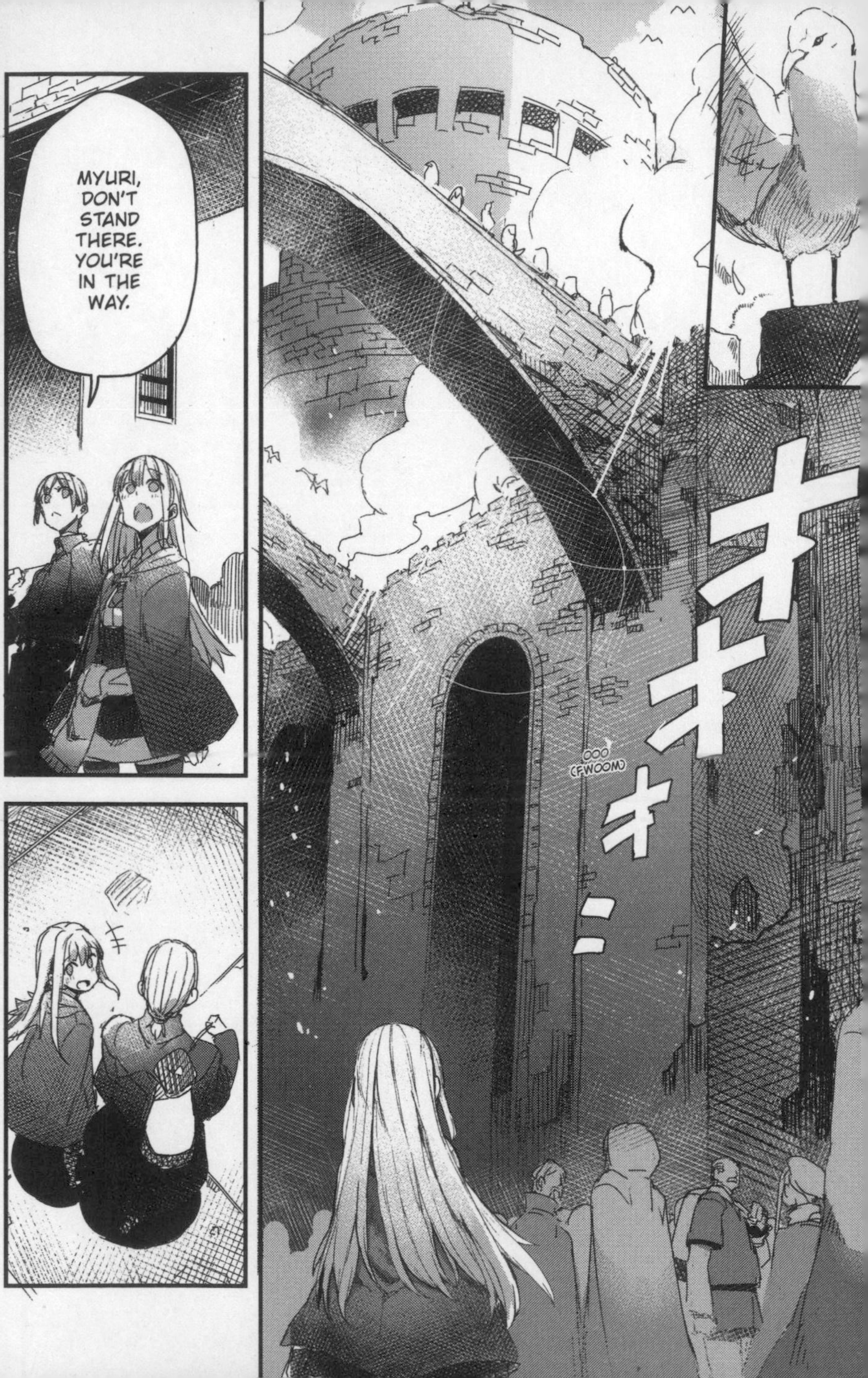
オオォ
OOO (FWOOM)
MYURI, DON'T STAND THERE. YOU'RE IN THE WAY.

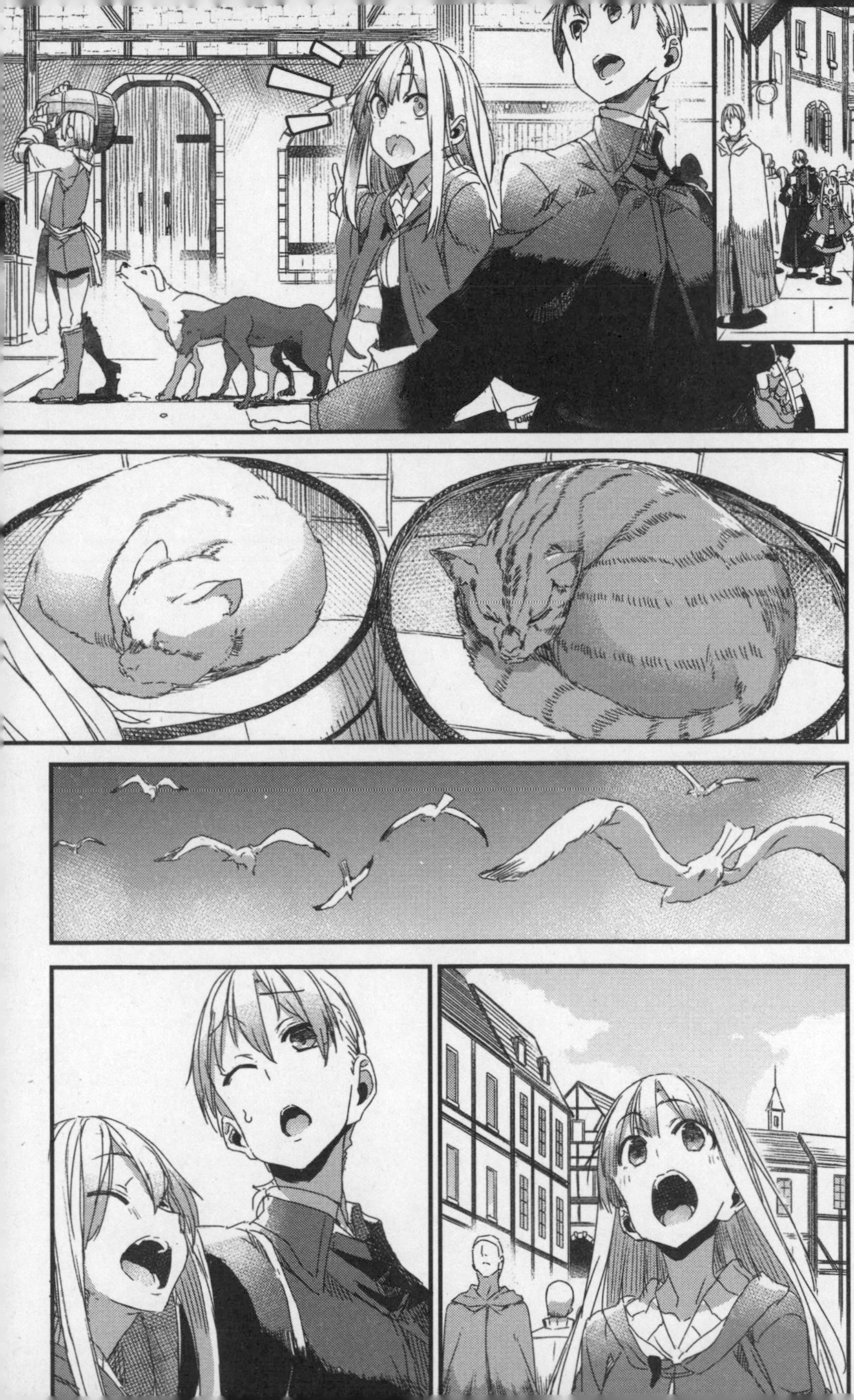

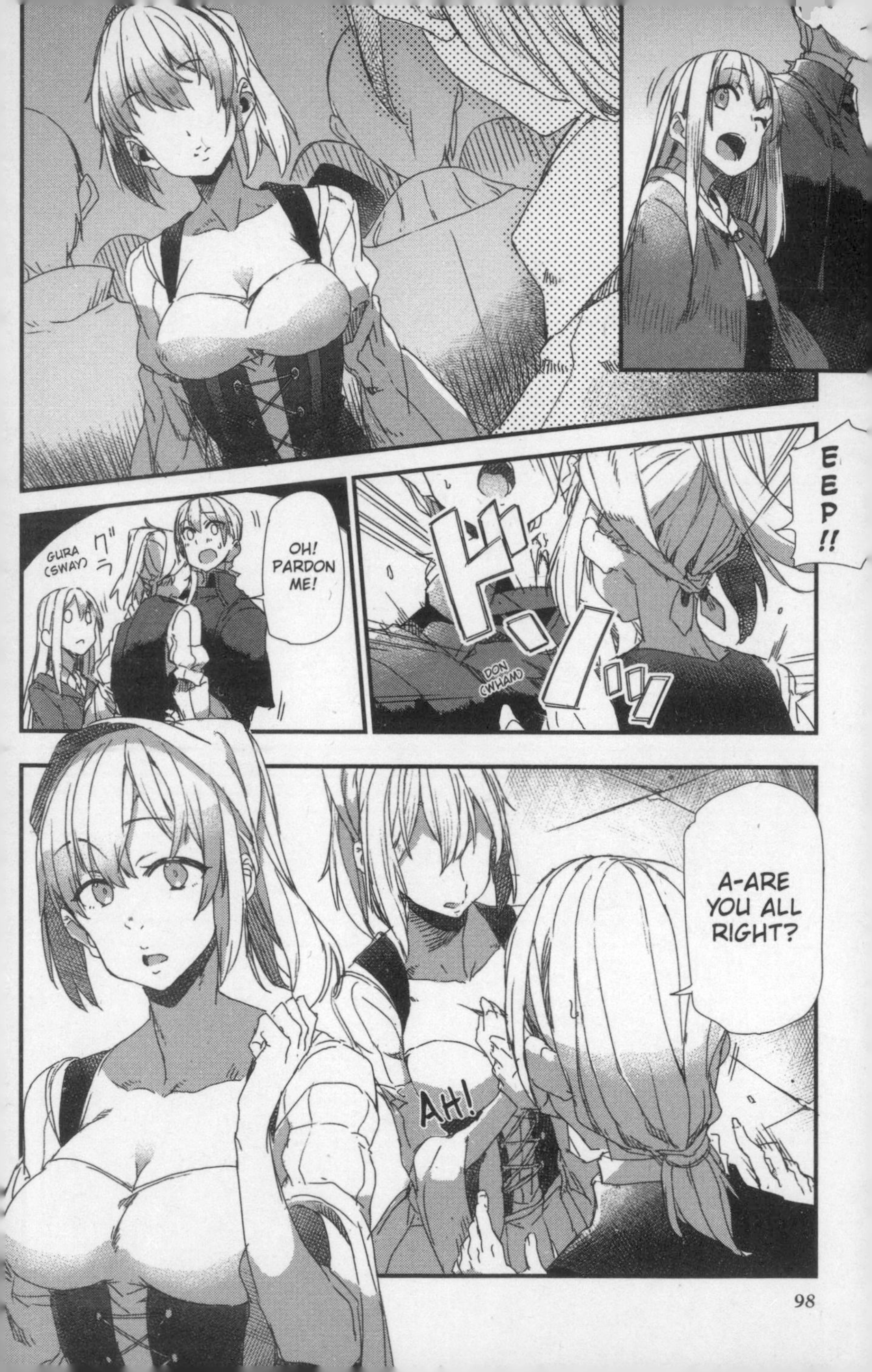
EEP!!
DON (WHAM)
OH! PARDON ME!
GURA (SWAY)
A-ARE YOU ALL RIGHT?
AH!

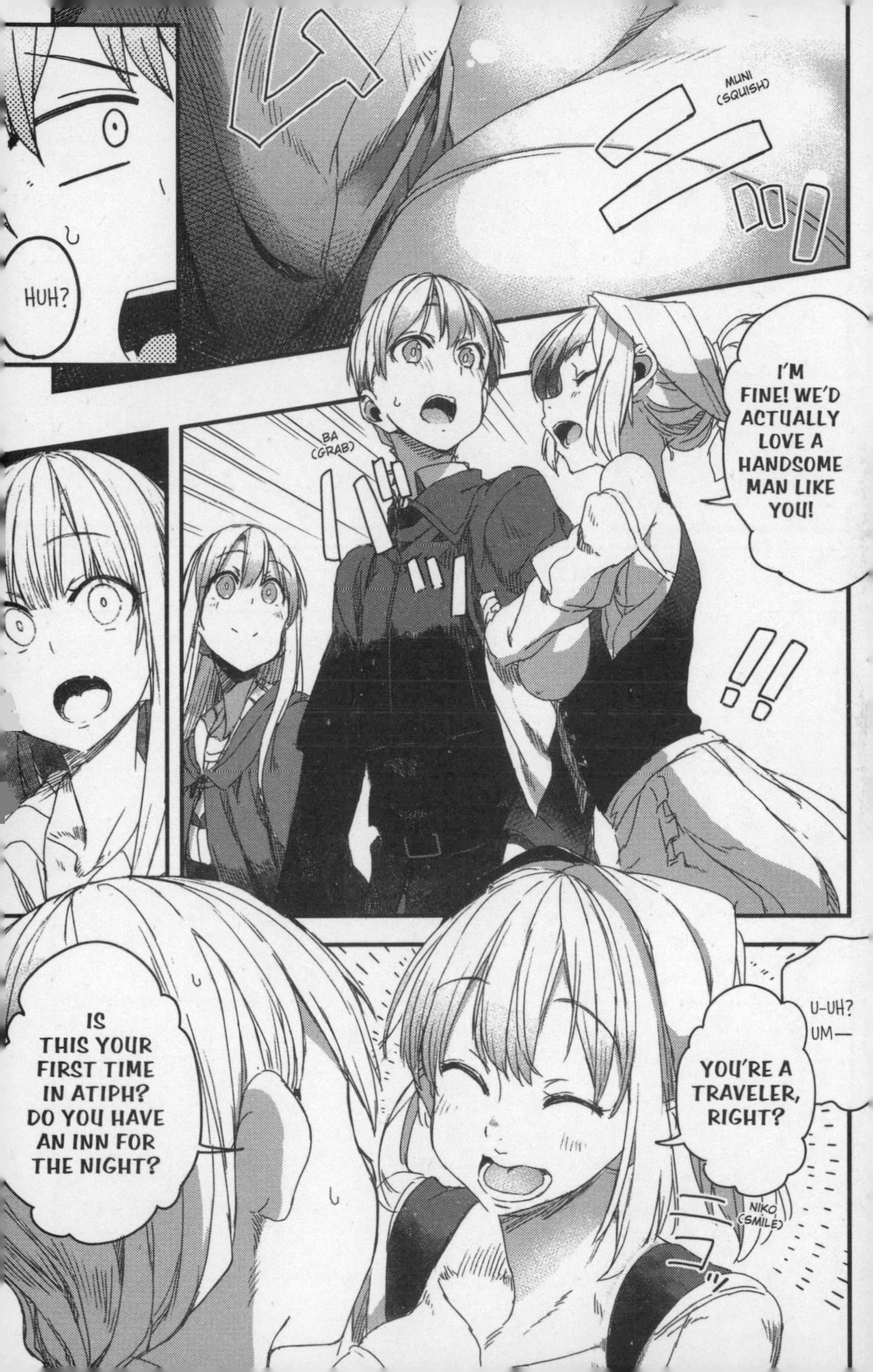
MUNI (SQUISH)
HUH?
I'M FINE! WE'D ACTUALLY LOVE A HANDSOME MAN LIKE YOU!
BA (GRAB)
!!
U-UH? UM—
YOU'RE A TRAVELER, RIGHT?
NIKO (SMILE)
IS THIS YOUR FIRST TIME IN ATIPH? DO YOU HAVE AN INN FOR THE NIGHT?

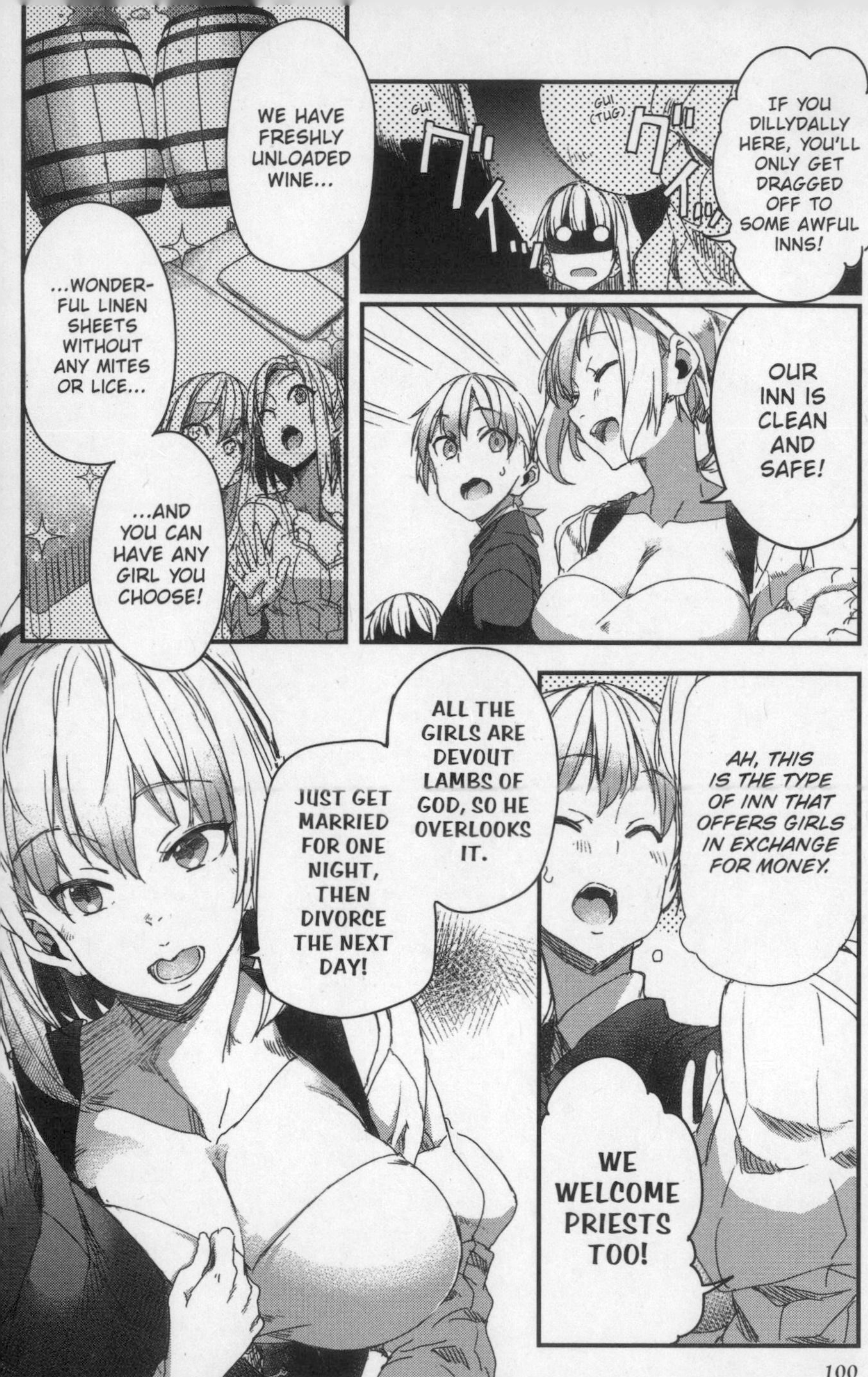
GUI
GUI (TUG)
IF YOU DILLYDALLY HERE, YOU'LL ONLY GET DRAGGED OFF TO SOME AWFUL INNS!
OUR INN IS CLEAN AND SAFE!
WE HAVE FRESHLY UNLOADED WINE...
...WONDERFUL LINEN SHEETS WITHOUT ANY MITES OR LICE...
...AND YOU CAN HAVE ANY GIRL YOU CHOOSE!
AH, THIS IS THE TYPE OF INN THAT OFFERS GIRLS IN EXCHANGE FOR MONEY.
WE WELCOME PRIESTS TOO!
ALL THE GIRLS ARE DEVOUT LAMBS OF GOD, SO HE OVERLOOKS IT.
JUST GET MARRIED FOR ONE NIGHT, THEN DIVORCE THE NEXT DAY!

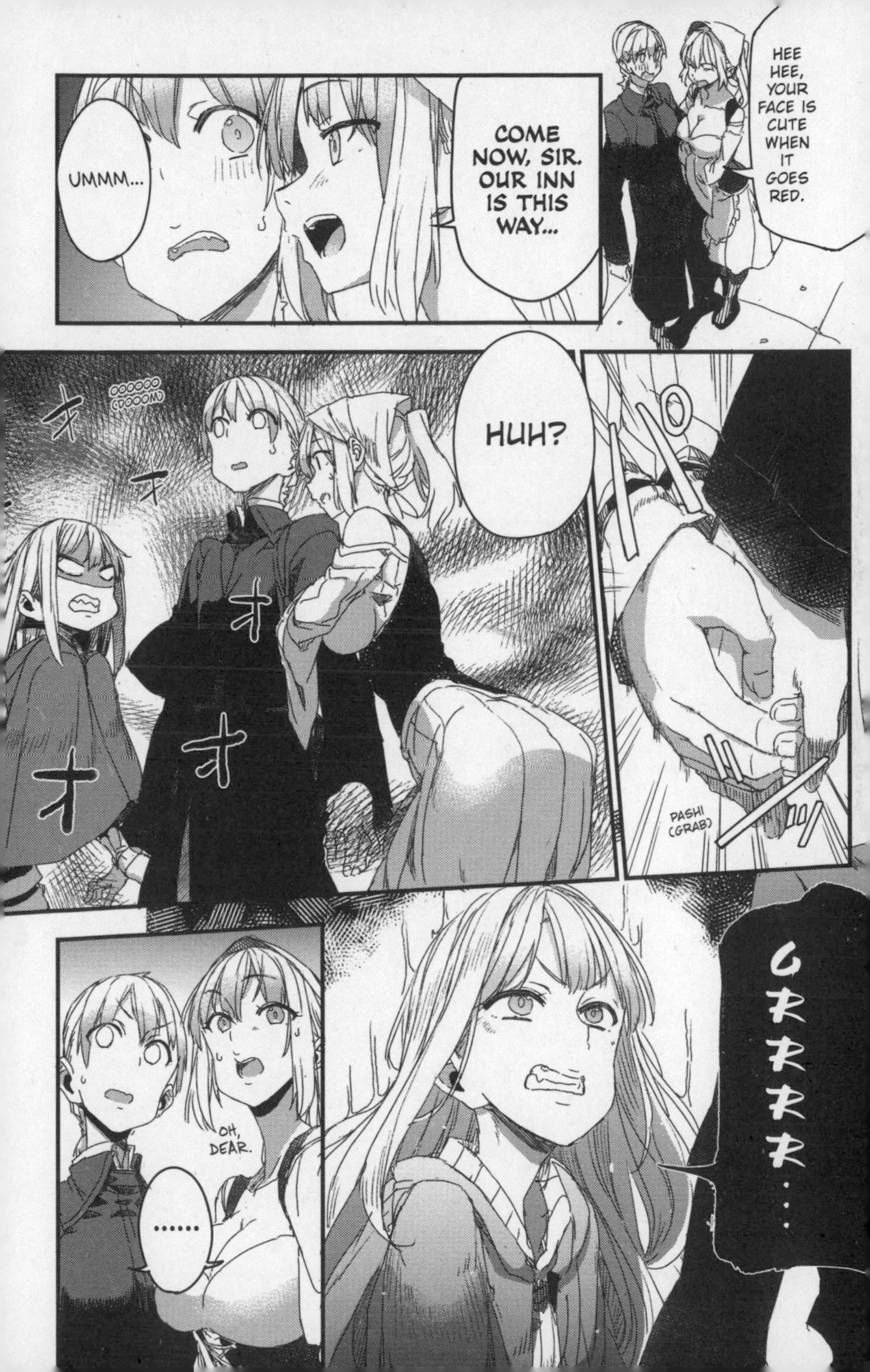
HEE HEE, YOUR FACE IS CUTE WHEN IT GOES RED.
COME NOW, SIR. OUR INN IS THIS WAY...
UMMM...
PASHI (GRAB)
HUH?
OOOOOO (DOOOM)
GRRRR...
OH, DEAR.
......

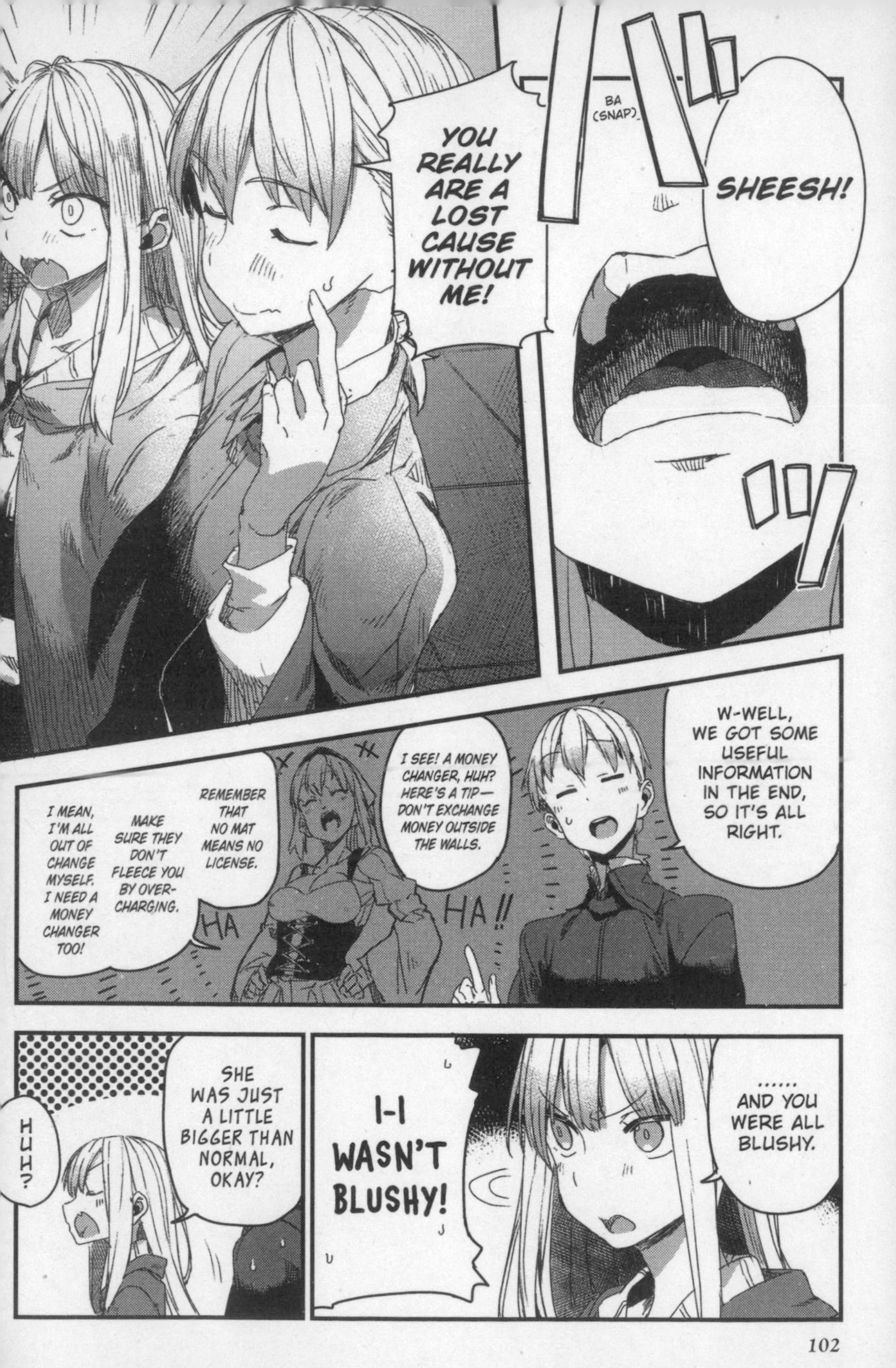
BA (SNAP)
SHEESH!
YOU REALLY ARE A LOST CAUSE WITHOUT ME!
W-WELL, WE GOT SOME USEFUL INFORMATION IN THE END, SO IT'S ALL RIGHT.
I SEE! A MONEY CHANGER, HUH? HERE'S A TIP— DON'T EXCHANGE MONEY OUTSIDE THE WALLS.
HA HA!!
REMEMBER THAT NO MAT MEANS NO LICENSE.
MAKE SURE THEY DON'T FLEECE YOU BY OVER-CHARGING.
I MEAN, I'M ALL OUT OF CHANGE MYSELF. I NEED A MONEY CHANGER TOO!
...... AND YOU WERE ALL BLUSHY.
I-I WASN'T BLUSHY!
SHE WAS JUST A LITTLE BIGGER THAN NORMAL, OKAY?
HUH?

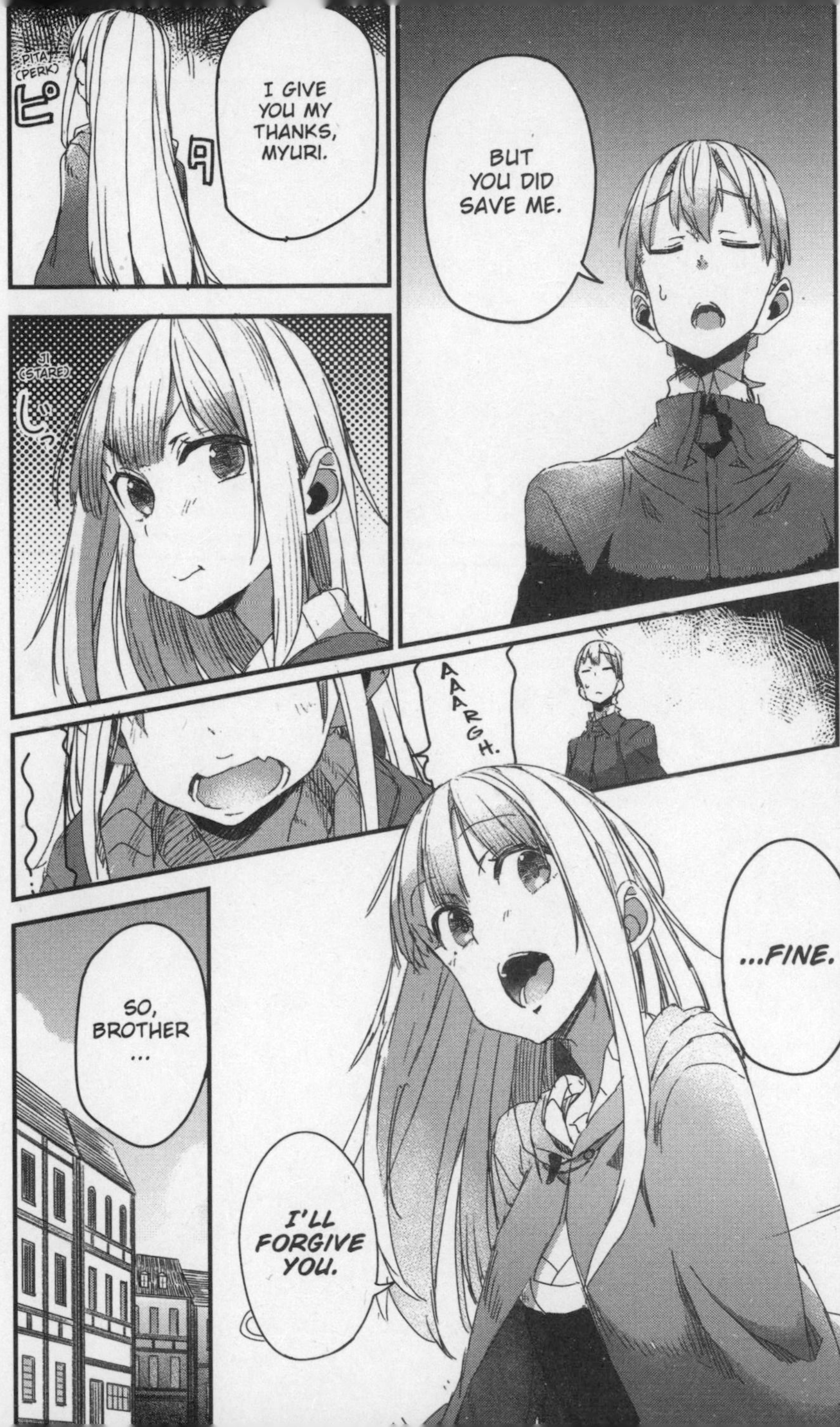
BUT YOU DID SAVE ME.
I GIVE YOU MY THANKS, MYURI.
PITA (PERK)
JI (STARE)
AAARGH.
...FINE.
SO, BROTHER ...
I'LL FORGIVE YOU.

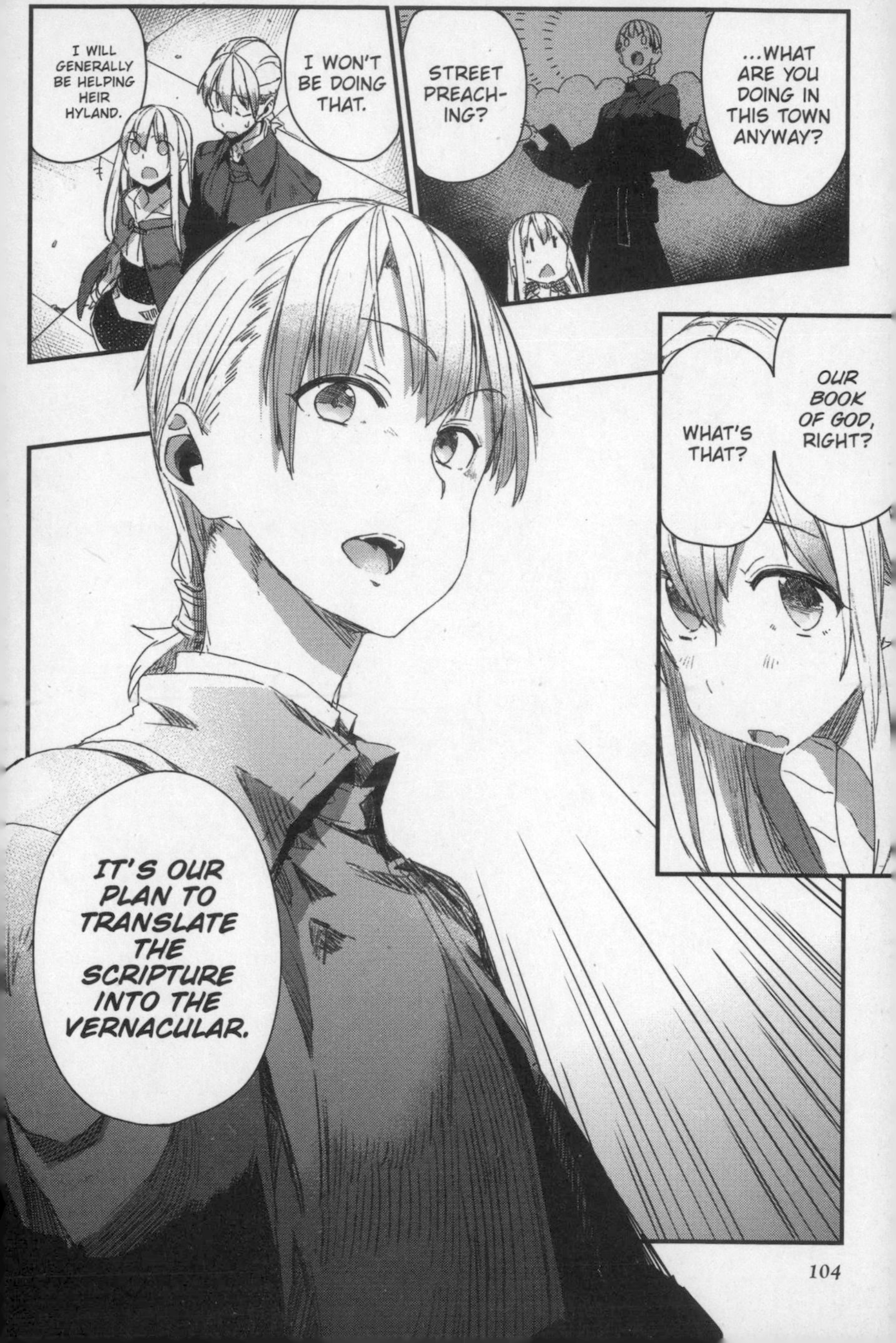
...WHAT ARE YOU DOING IN THIS TOWN ANYWAY?
STREET PREACHING?
I WON'T BE DOING THAT.
I WILL GENERALLY BE HELPING HEIR HYLAND.
OUR BOOK OF GOD, RIGHT?
WHAT'S THAT?
IT'S OUR PLAN TO TRANSLATE THE SCRIPTURE INTO THE VERNACULAR.

WOLF & PARCHMENT

WOLF
&
PARCHMENT

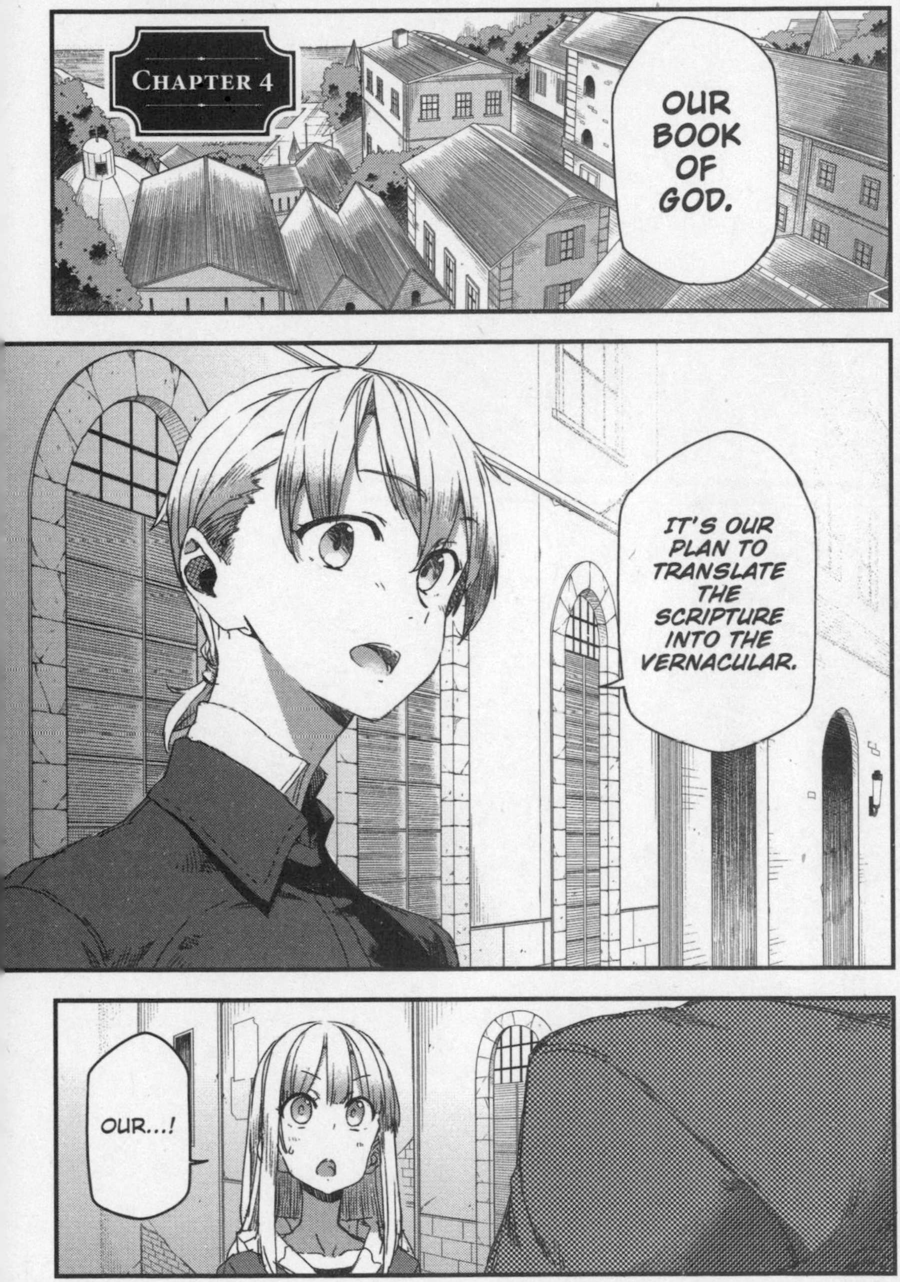
Chapter 4
OUR BOOK OF GOD.
IT'S OUR PLAN TO TRANSLATE THE SCRIPTURE INTO THE VERNACULAR.
OUR...!

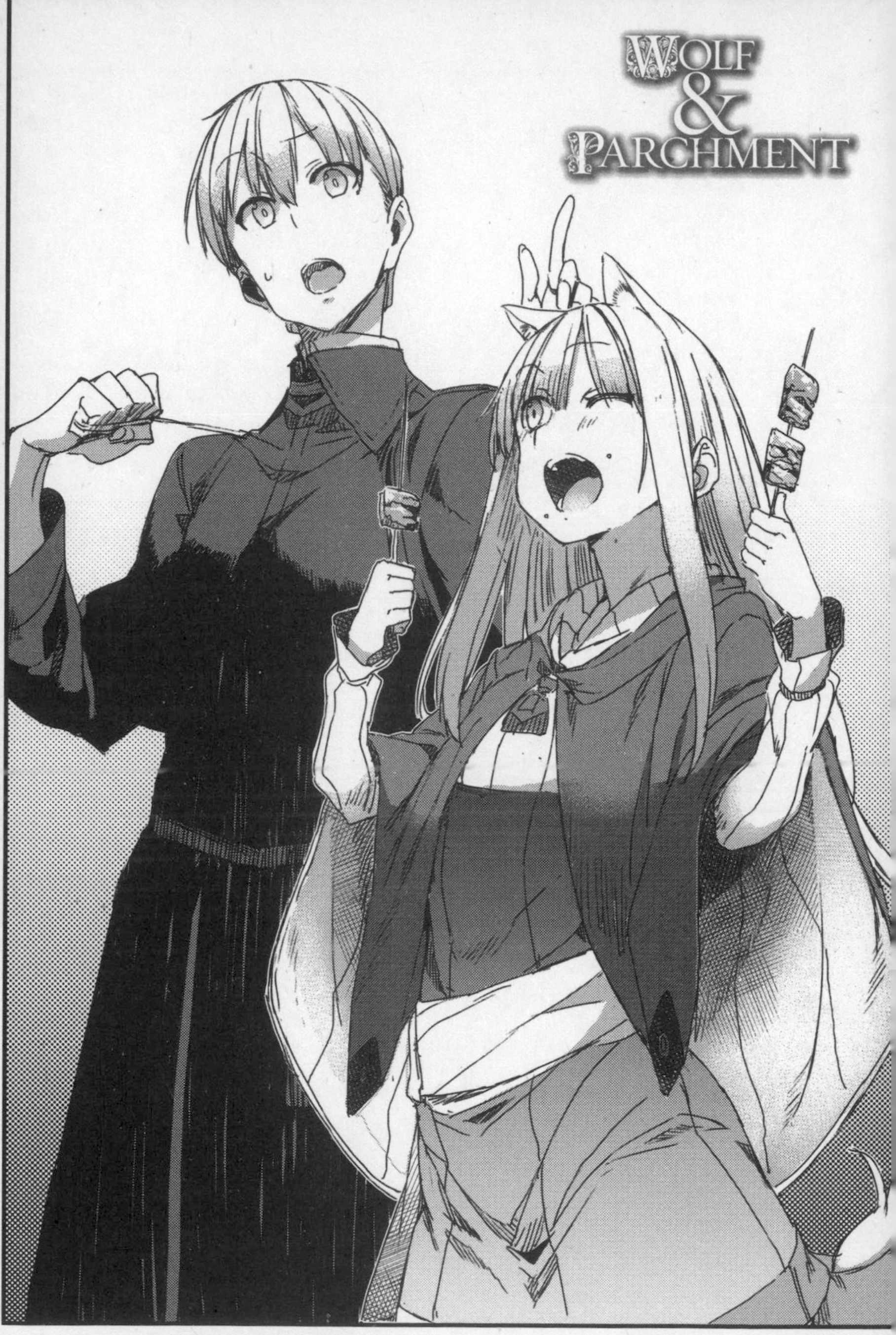
WOLF & PARCHMENT

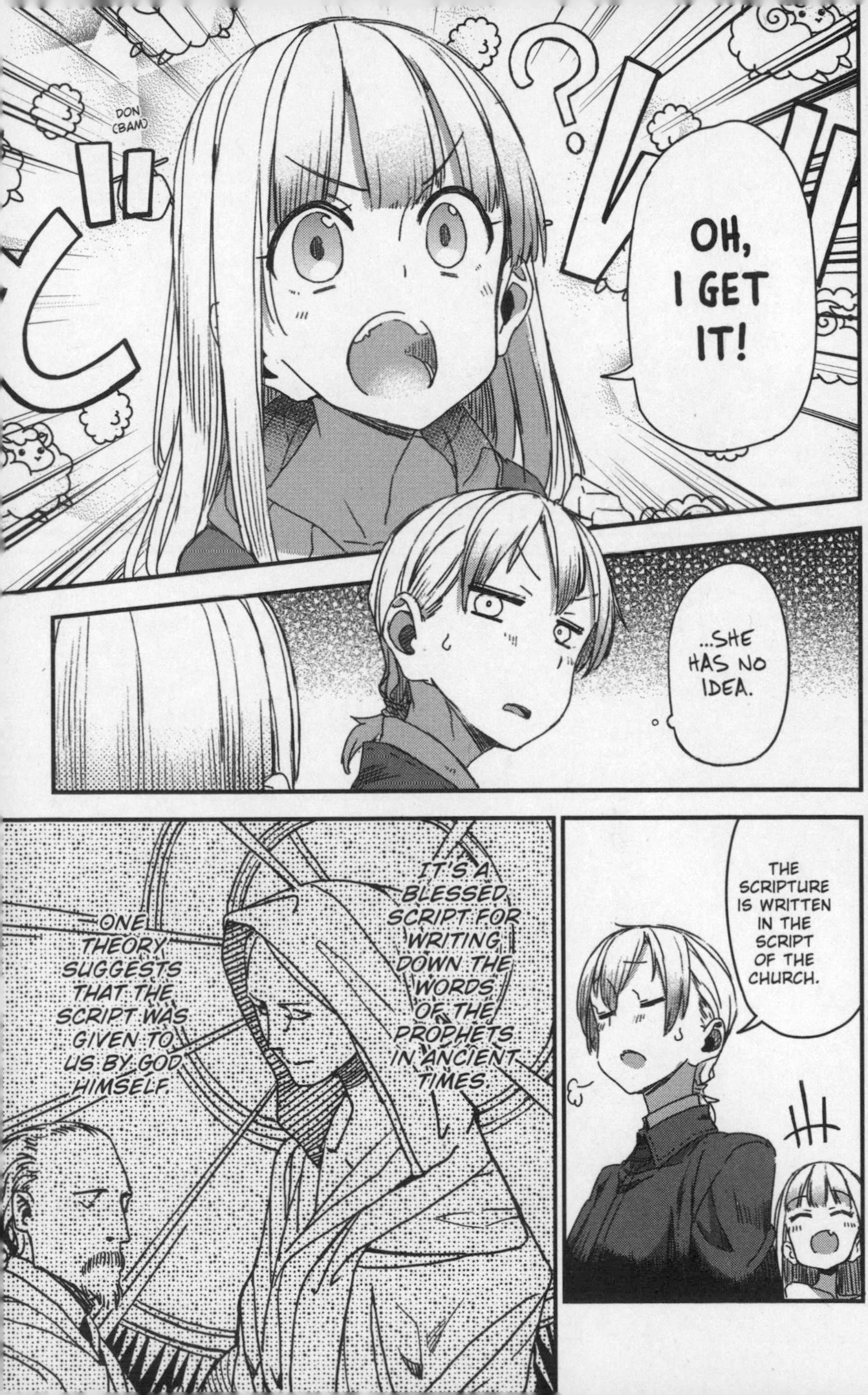
OH, I GET IT!
DON (BAM)
...SHE HAS NO IDEA.
THE SCRIPTURE IS WRITTEN IN THE SCRIPT OF THE CHURCH.
IT'S A BLESSED SCRIPT FOR WRITING DOWN THE WORDS OF THE PROPHETS IN ANCIENT TIMES.
ONE THEORY SUGGESTS THAT THE SCRIPT WAS GIVEN TO US BY GOD HIMSELF.

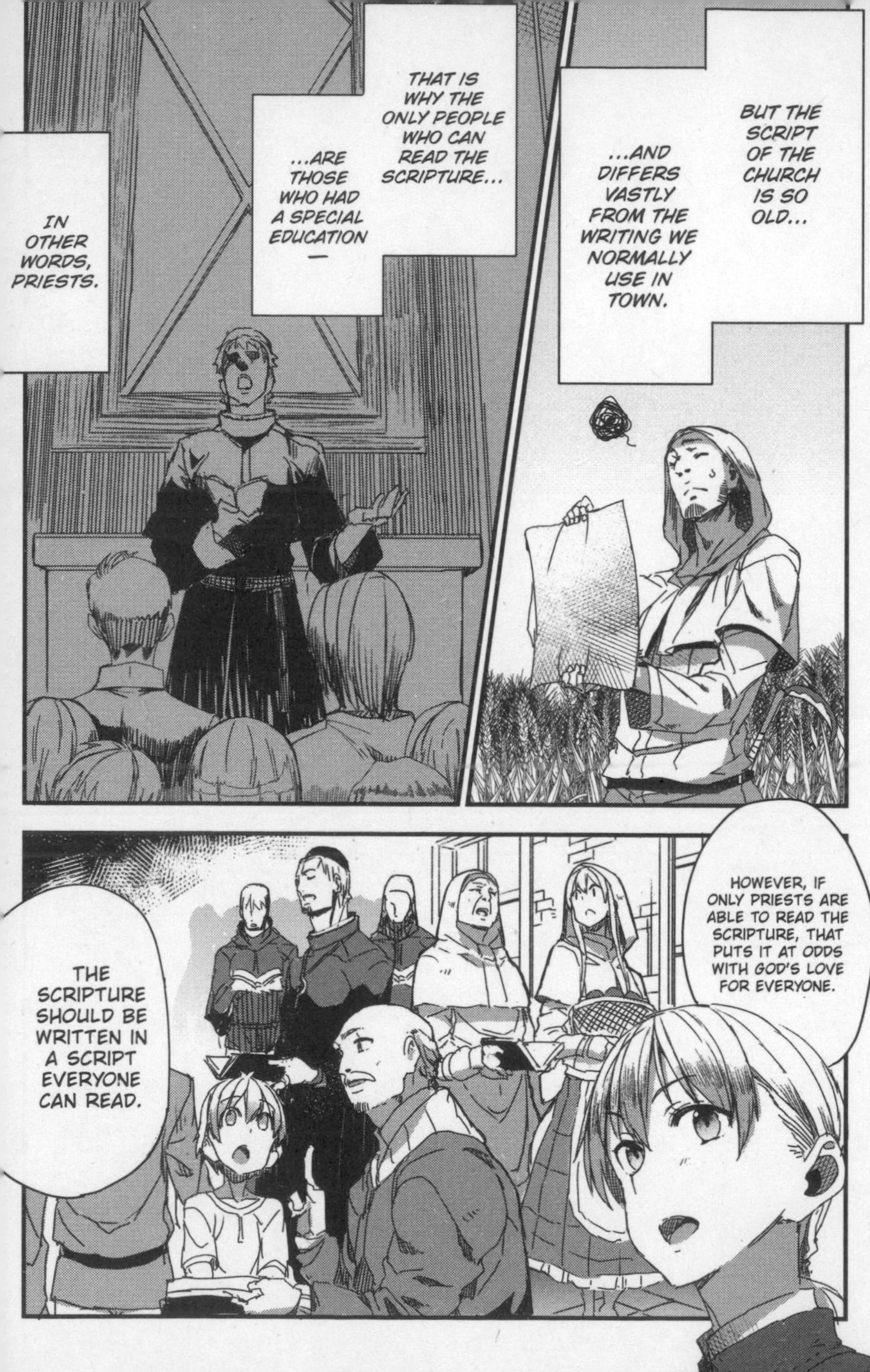
BUT THE SCRIPT OF THE CHURCH IS SO OLD...
...AND DIFFERS VASTLY FROM THE WRITING WE NORMALLY USE IN TOWN.
THAT IS WHY THE ONLY PEOPLE WHO CAN READ THE SCRIPTURE...
...ARE THOSE WHO HAD A SPECIAL EDUCATION —
IN OTHER WORDS, PRIESTS.
HOWEVER, IF ONLY PRIESTS ARE ABLE TO READ THE SCRIPTURE, THAT PUTS IT AT ODDS WITH GOD'S LOVE FOR EVERYONE.
THE SCRIPTURE SHOULD BE WRITTEN IN A SCRIPT EVERYONE CAN READ.

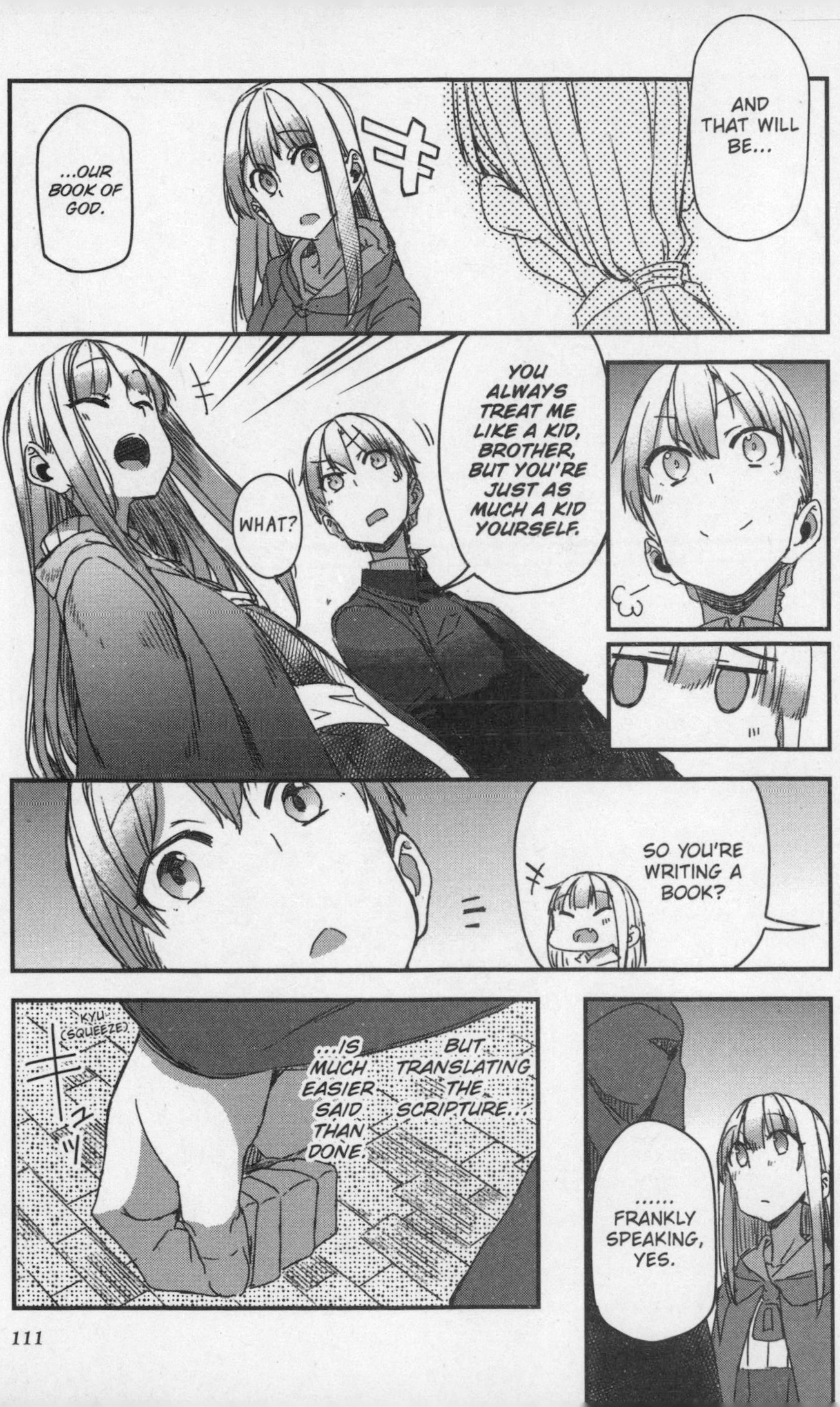
AND THAT WILL BE...
...OUR BOOK OF GOD.
YOU ALWAYS TREAT ME LIKE A KID, BROTHER, BUT YOU'RE JUST AS MUCH A KID YOURSELF.
WHAT?
SO YOU'RE WRITING A BOOK?
......FRANKLY SPEAKING, YES.
BUT TRANSLATING THE SCRIPTURE...
...IS MUCH EASIER SAID THAN DONE.
KYU (SQUEEZE)

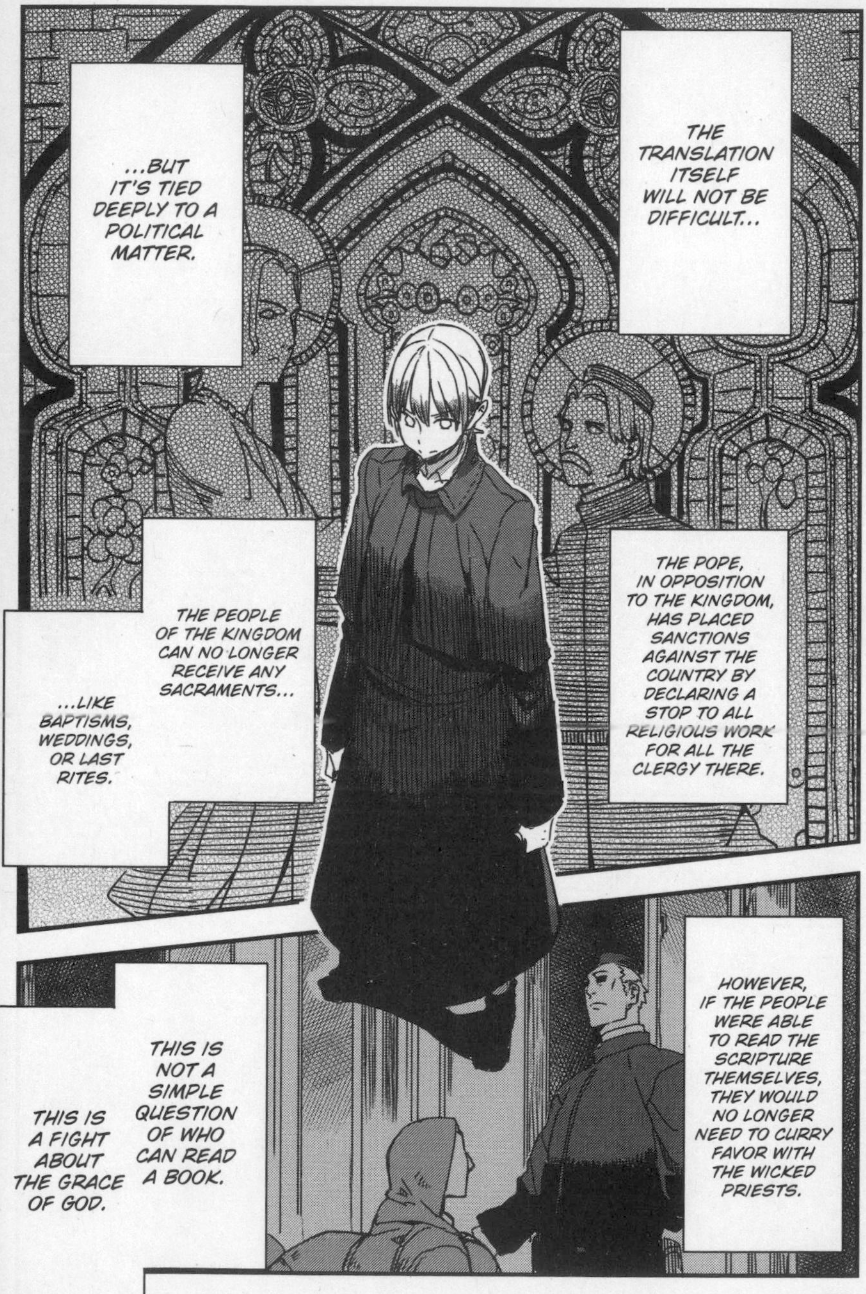
THE TRANSLATION ITSELF WILL NOT BE DIFFICULT...
...BUT IT'S TIED DEEPLY TO A POLITICAL MATTER.
THE POPE, IN OPPOSITION TO THE KINGDOM, HAS PLACED SANCTIONS AGAINST THE COUNTRY BY DECLARING A STOP TO ALL RELIGIOUS WORK FOR ALL THE CLERGY THERE.
THE PEOPLE OF THE KINGDOM CAN NO LONGER RECEIVE ANY SACRAMENTS...
...LIKE BAPTISMS, WEDDINGS, OR LAST RITES.
HOWEVER, IF THE PEOPLE WERE ABLE TO READ THE SCRIPTURE THEMSELVES, THEY WOULD NO LONGER NEED TO CURRY FAVOR WITH THE WICKED PRIESTS.
THIS IS NOT A SIMPLE QUESTION OF WHO CAN READ A BOOK.
THIS IS A FIGHT ABOUT THE GRACE OF GOD.

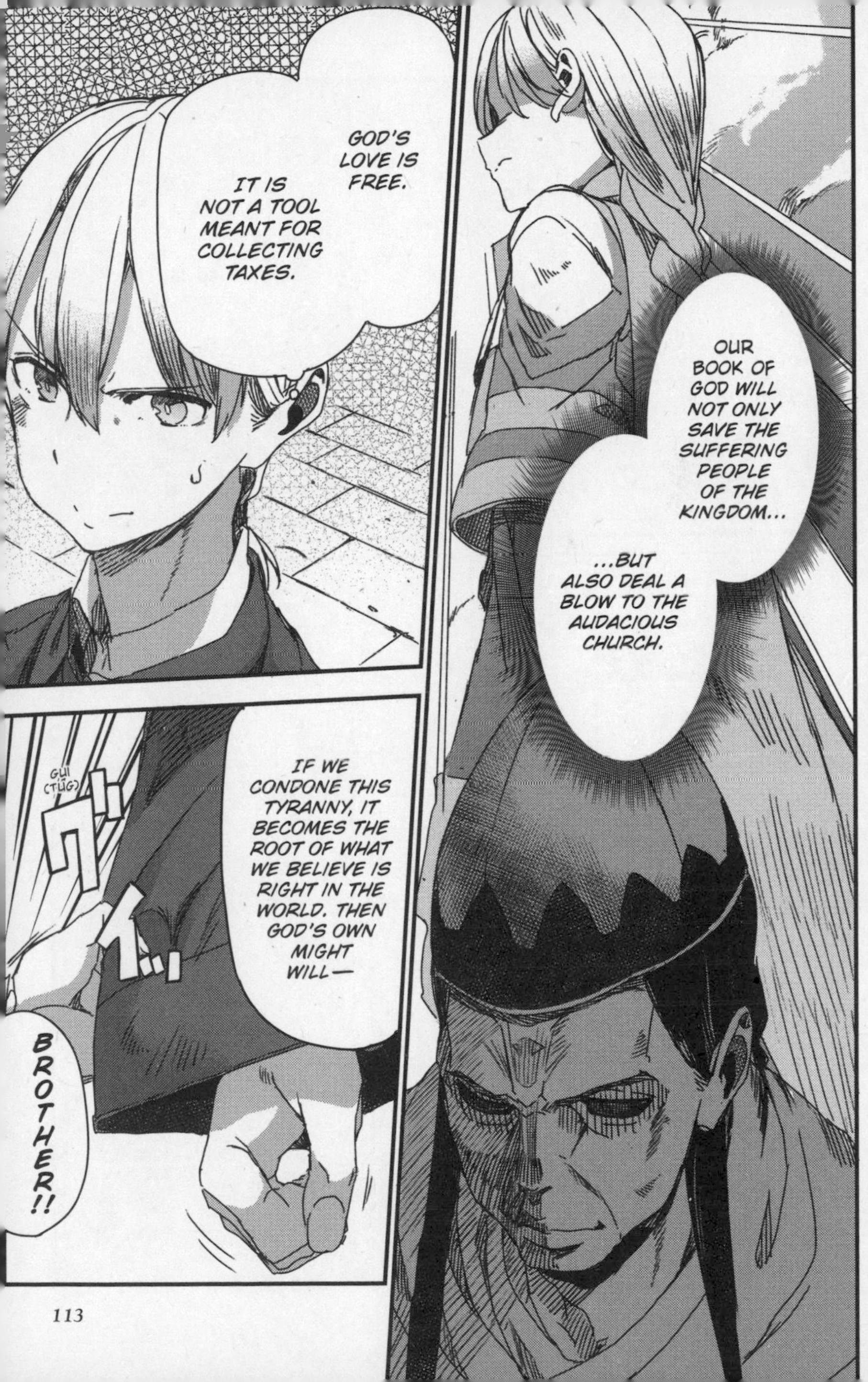
OUR BOOK OF GOD WILL NOT ONLY SAVE THE SUFFERING PEOPLE OF THE KINGDOM...
...BUT ALSO DEAL A BLOW TO THE AUDACIOUS CHURCH.
GOD'S LOVE IS FREE.
IT IS NOT A TOOL MEANT FOR COLLECTING TAXES.
IF WE CONDONE THIS TYRANNY, IT BECOMES THE ROOT OF WHAT WE BELIEVE IS RIGHT IN THE WORLD. THEN GOD'S OWN MIGHT WILL—
GUI (TUG)
BROTHER!!

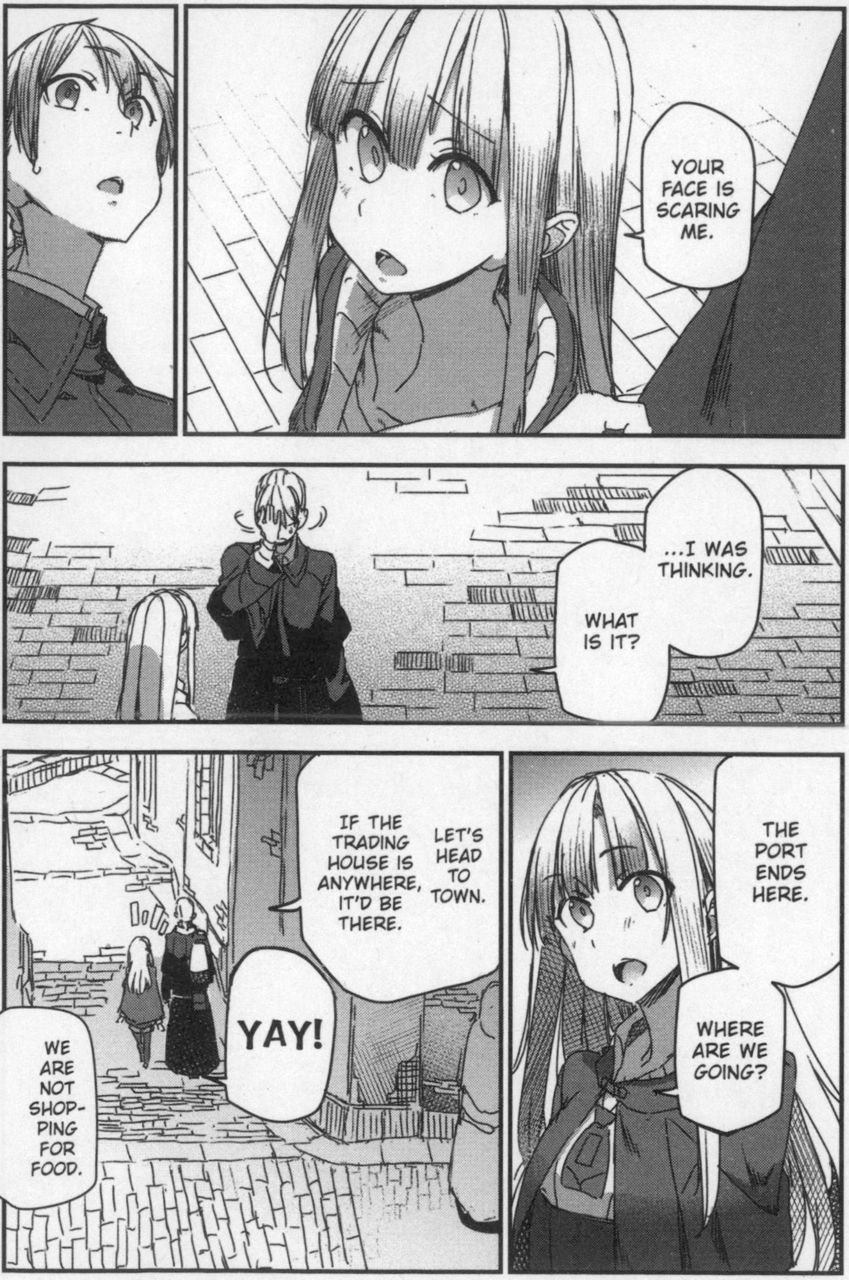
YOUR FACE IS SCARING ME.
...I WAS THINKING.
WHAT IS IT?
THE PORT ENDS HERE.
WHERE ARE WE GOING?
LET'S HEAD TO TOWN.
IF THE TRADING HOUSE IS ANYWHERE, IT'D BE THERE.
YAY!
WE ARE NOT SHOP-PING FOR FOOD.

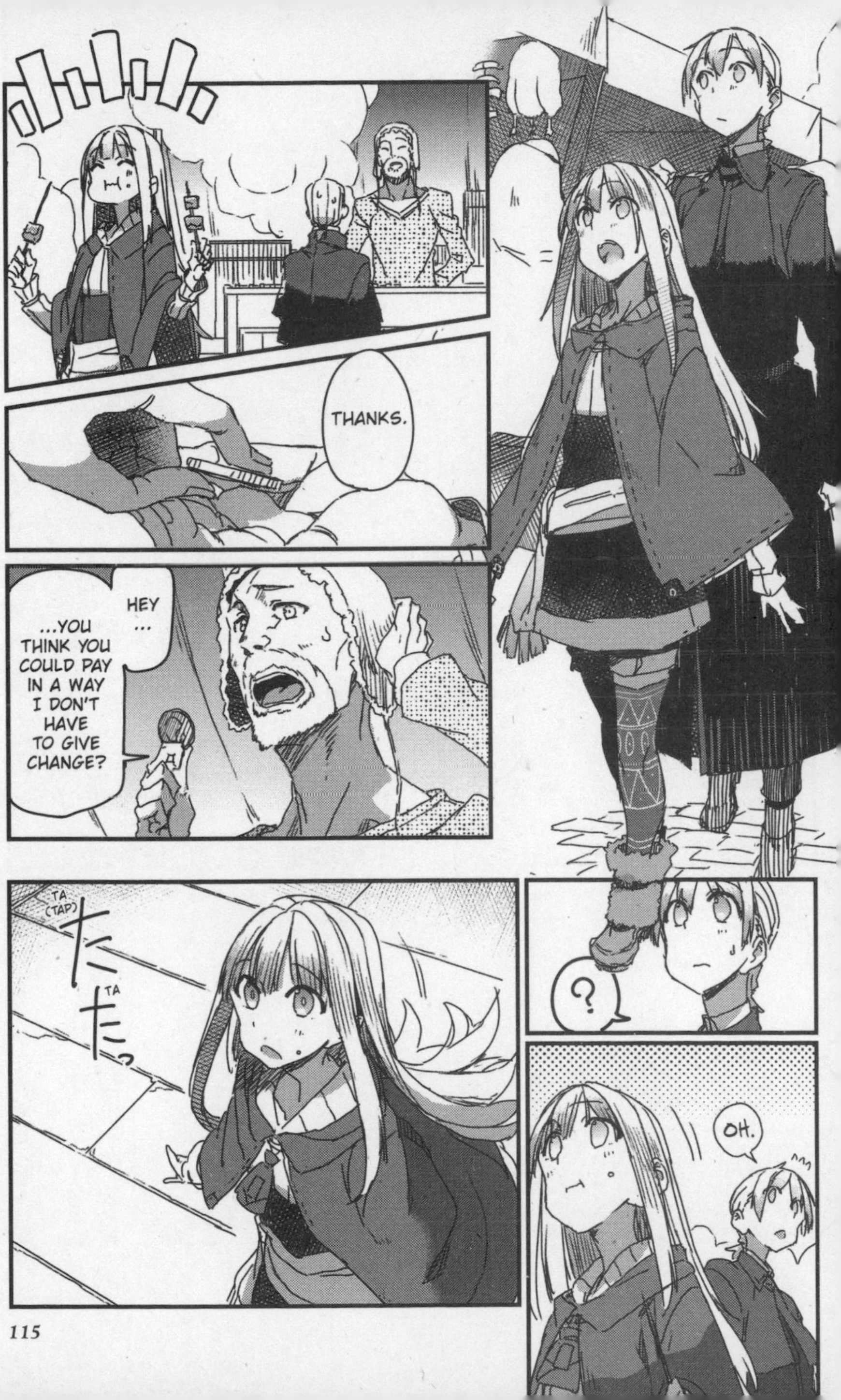
THANKS.
HEY ...
...YOU THINK YOU COULD PAY IN A WAY I DON'T HAVE TO GIVE CHANGE?
?
OH.
TA (TAP)
た
TA
たっ

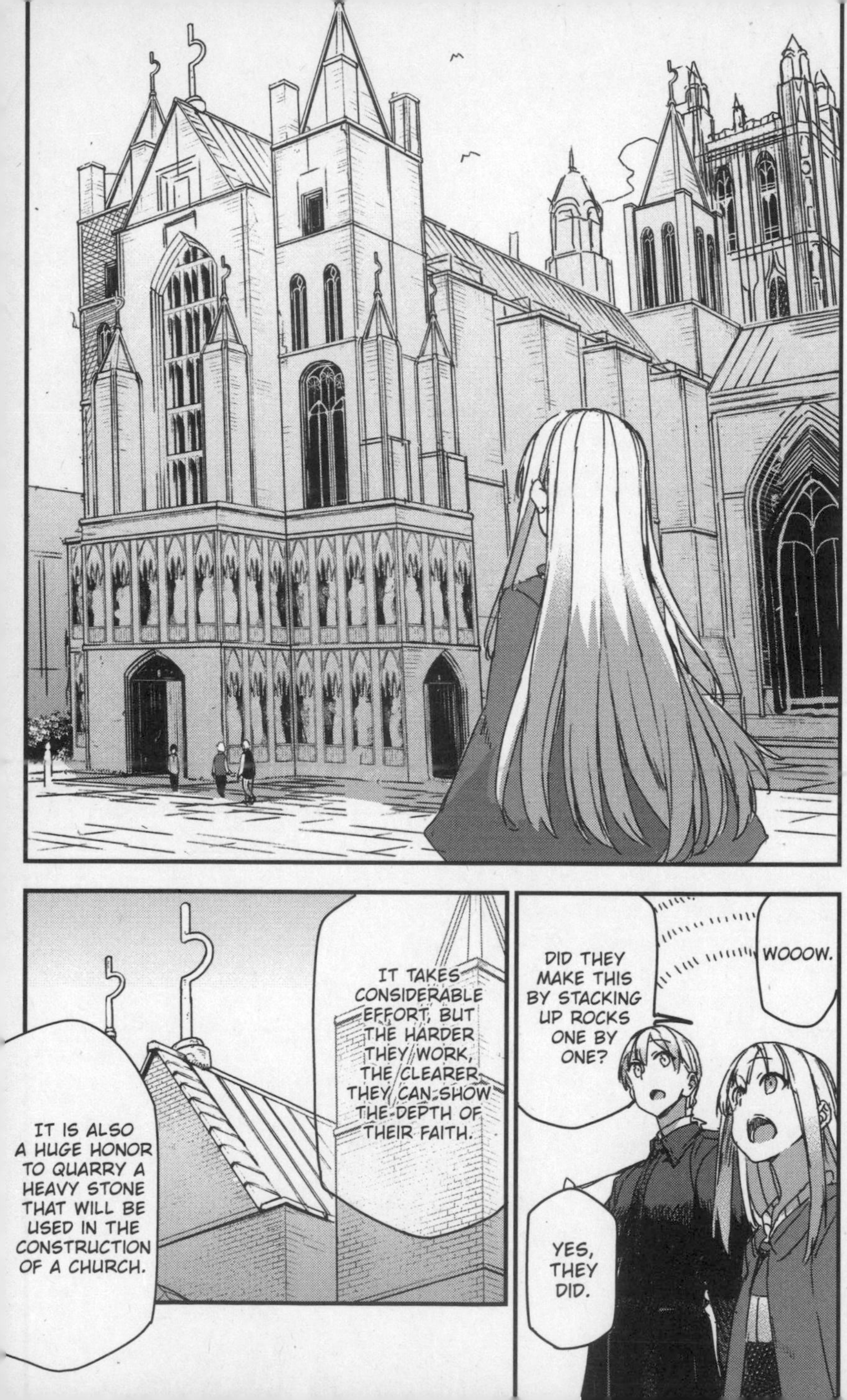
WOOOW.
DID THEY MAKE THIS BY STACKING UP ROCKS ONE BY ONE?
YES, THEY DID.
IT TAKES CONSIDERABLE EFFORT, BUT THE HARDER THEY WORK, THE CLEARER THEY CAN SHOW THE DEPTH OF THEIR FAITH.
IT IS ALSO A HUGE HONOR TO QUARRY A HEAVY STONE THAT WILL BE USED IN THE CONSTRUCTION OF A CHURCH.

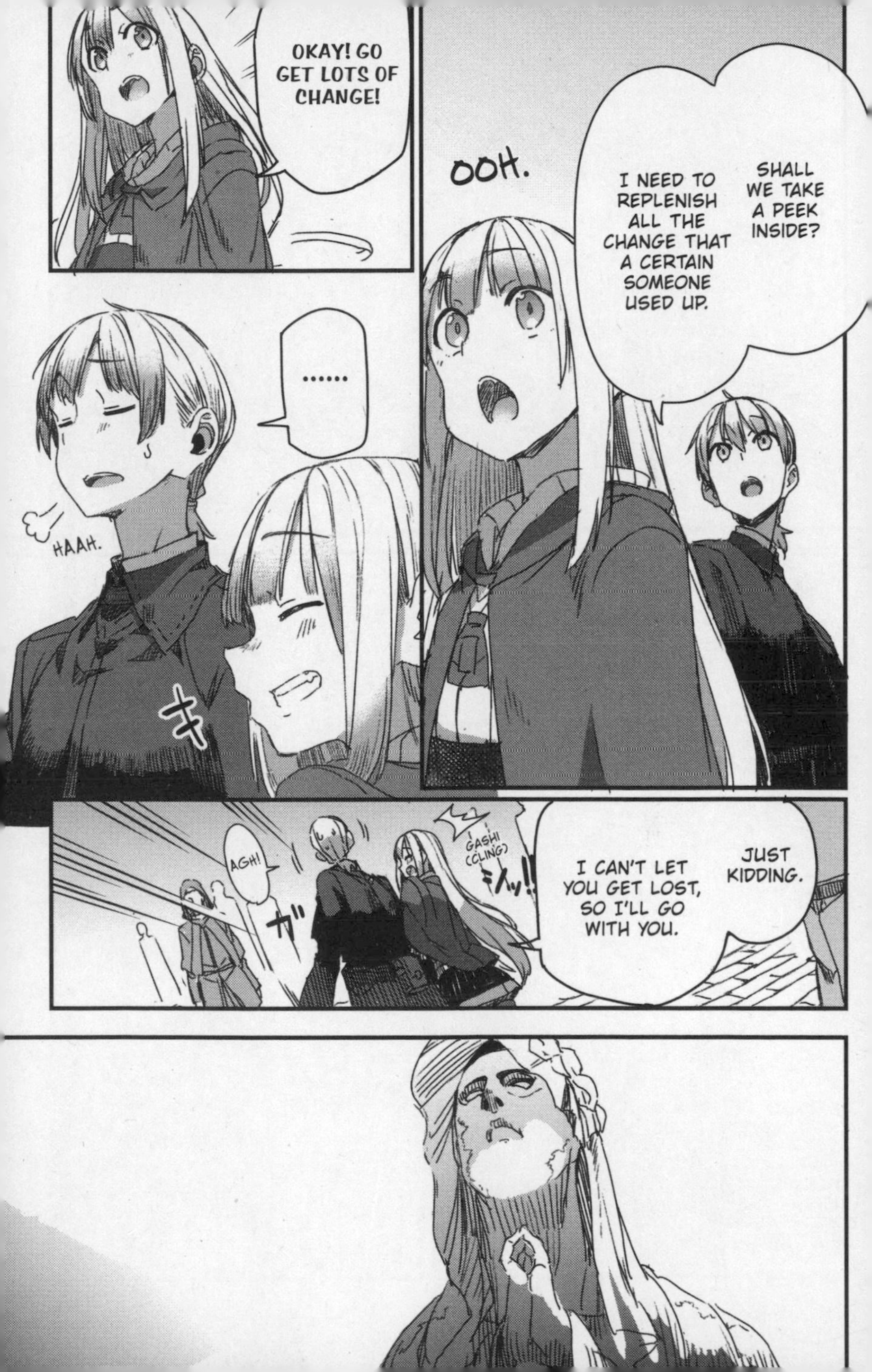
SHALL WE TAKE A PEEK INSIDE?
I NEED TO REPLENISH ALL THE CHANGE THAT A CERTAIN SOMEONE USED UP.
OOH.
OKAY! GO GET LOTS OF CHANGE!
......
HAAH.
キ
JUST KIDDING.
I CAN'T LET YOU GET LOST, SO I'LL GO WITH YOU.
GASHI (CLING)
ガシッ!!
AGH!
ガ

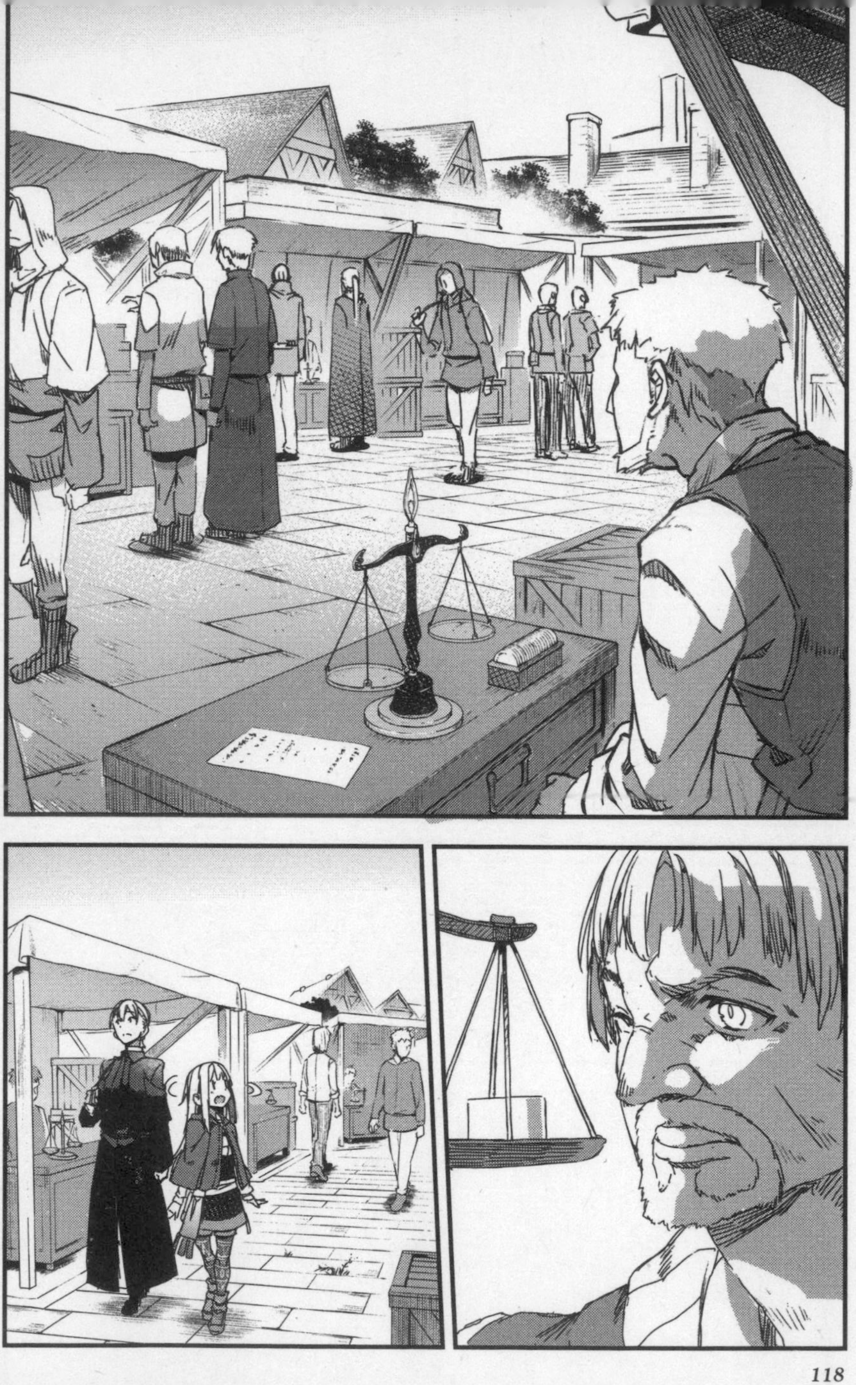

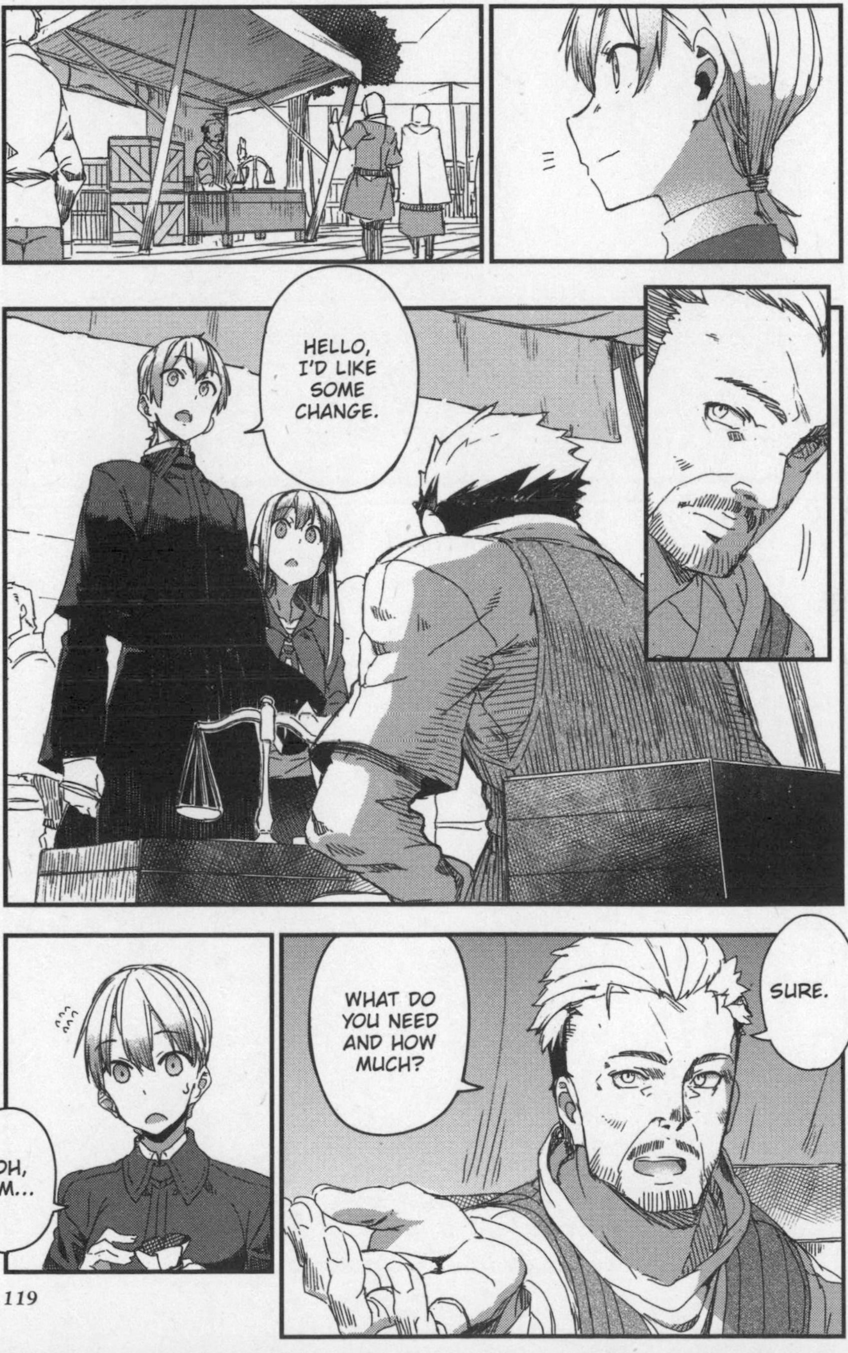
HELLO, I'D LIKE SOME CHANGE.
SURE.
WHAT DO YOU NEED AND HOW MUCH?
OH, UM...

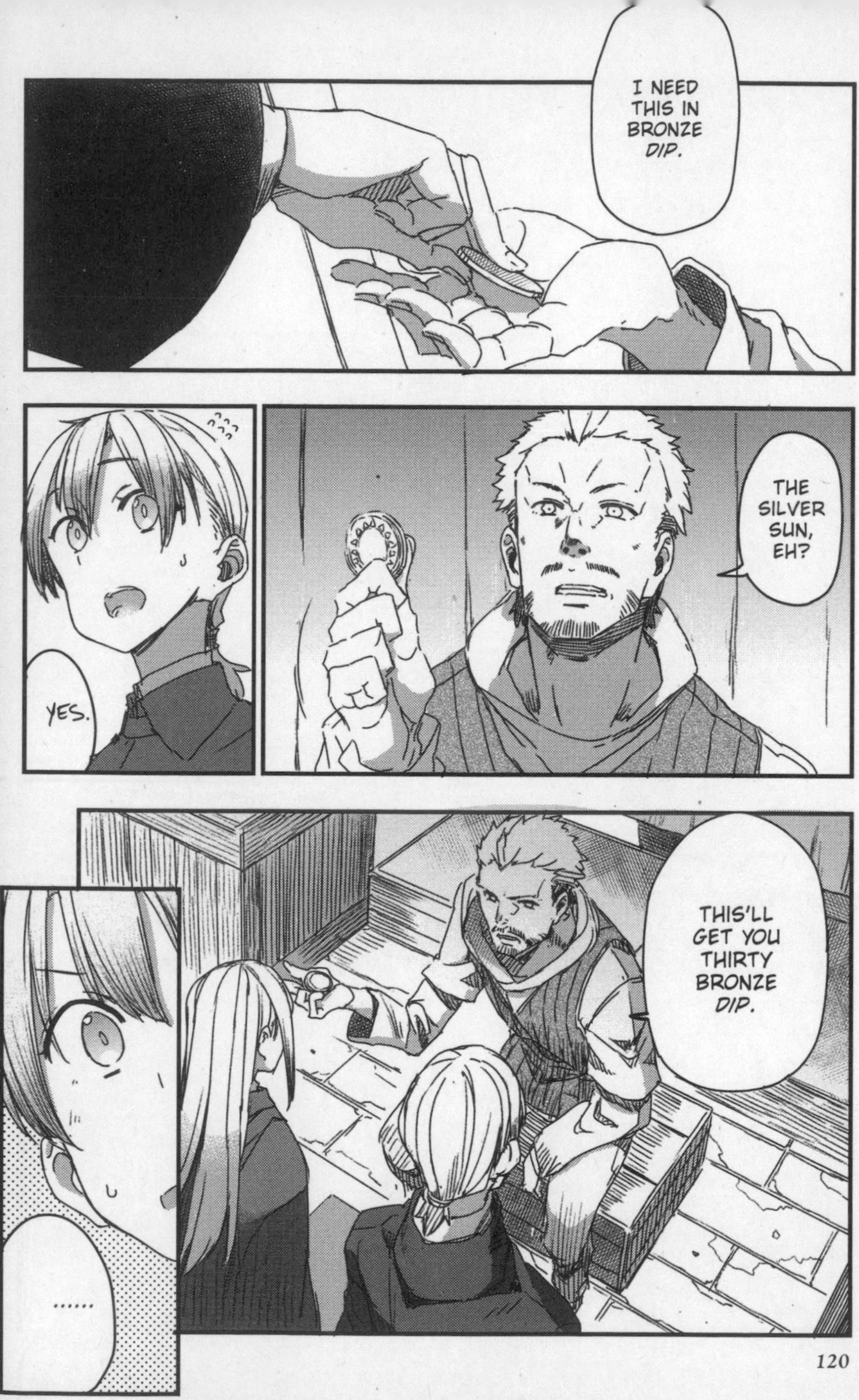
I NEED THIS IN BRONZE *DIP*.
THE SILVER SUN, EH?
YES.
THIS'LL GET YOU THIRTY BRONZE *DIP*.
......

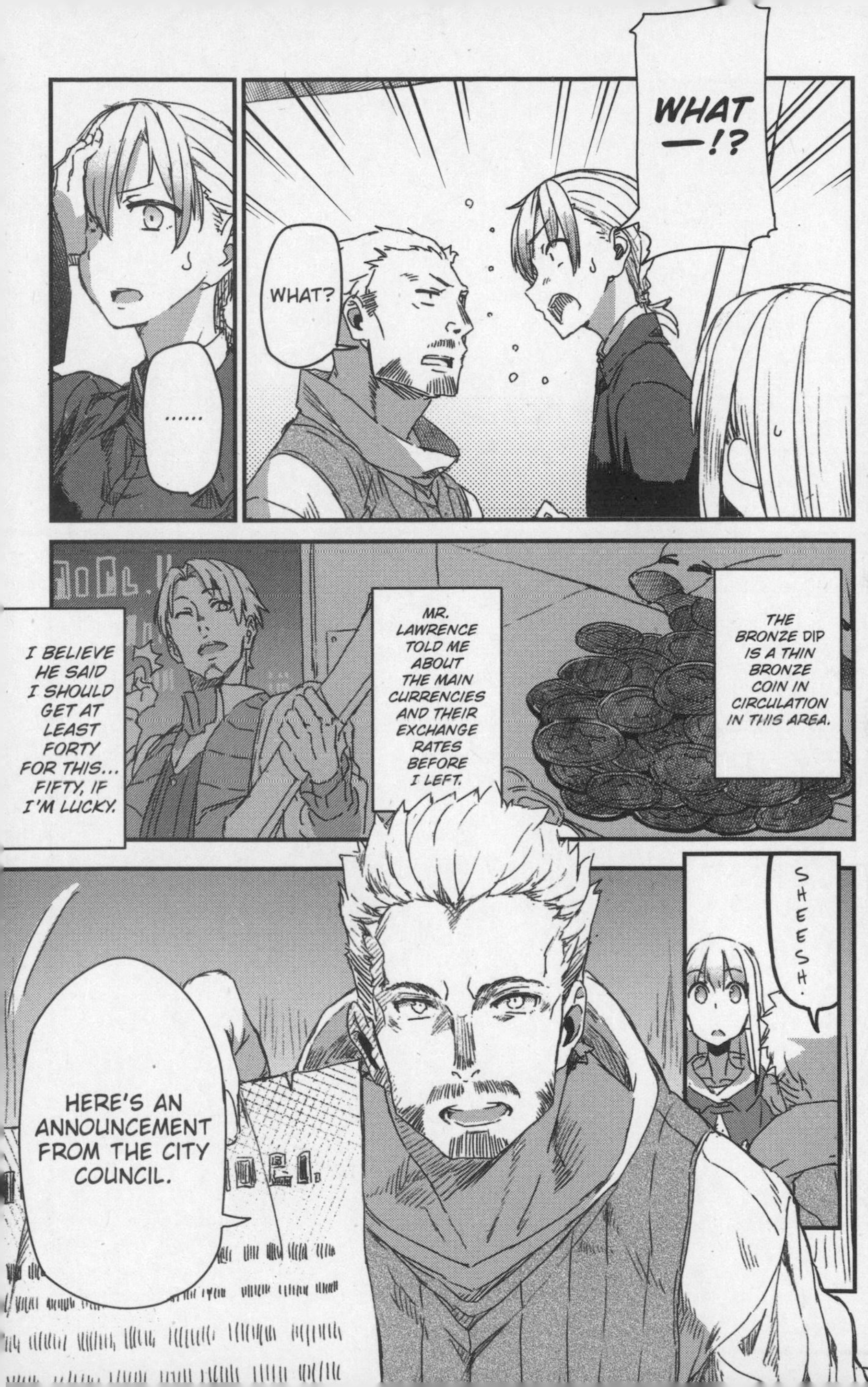
WHAT—!?
WHAT?
......
THE BRONZE DIP IS A THIN BRONZE COIN IN CIRCULATION IN THIS AREA.
MR. LAWRENCE TOLD ME ABOUT THE MAIN CURRENCIES AND THEIR EXCHANGE RATES BEFORE I LEFT.
I BELIEVE HE SAID I SHOULD GET AT LEAST FORTY FOR THIS... FIFTY, IF I'M LUCKY.
SHEESH.
HERE'S AN ANNOUNCEMENT FROM THE CITY COUNCIL.

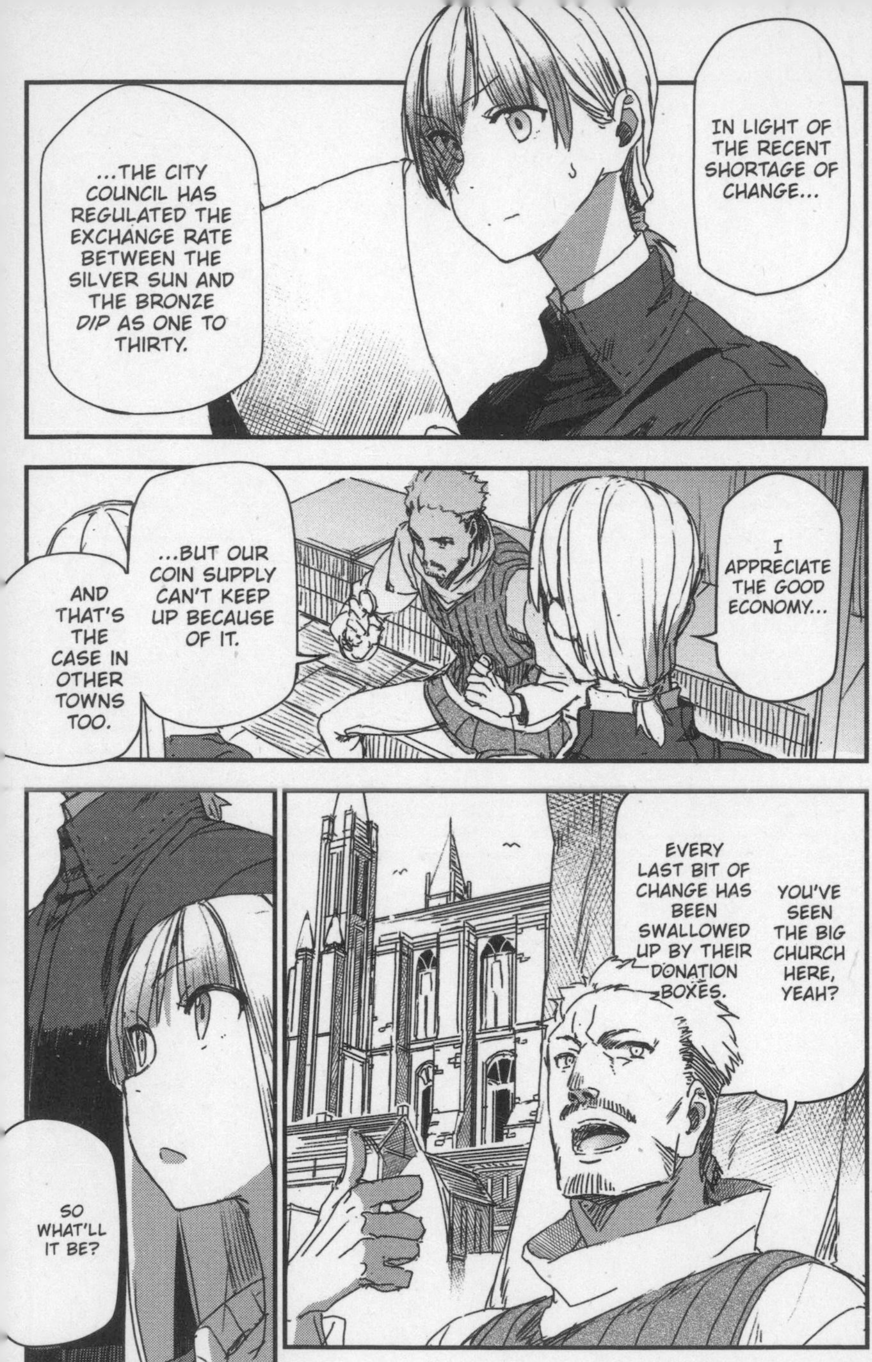
IN LIGHT OF THE RECENT SHORTAGE OF CHANGE...
...THE CITY COUNCIL HAS REGULATED THE EXCHANGE RATE BETWEEN THE SILVER SUN AND THE BRONZE *DIP* AS ONE TO THIRTY.
I APPRECIATE THE GOOD ECONOMY...
...BUT OUR COIN SUPPLY CAN'T KEEP UP BECAUSE OF IT.
AND THAT'S THE CASE IN OTHER TOWNS TOO.
YOU'VE SEEN THE BIG CHURCH HERE, YEAH?
EVERY LAST BIT OF CHANGE HAS BEEN SWALLOWED UP BY THEIR DONATION BOXES.
SO WHAT'LL IT BE?

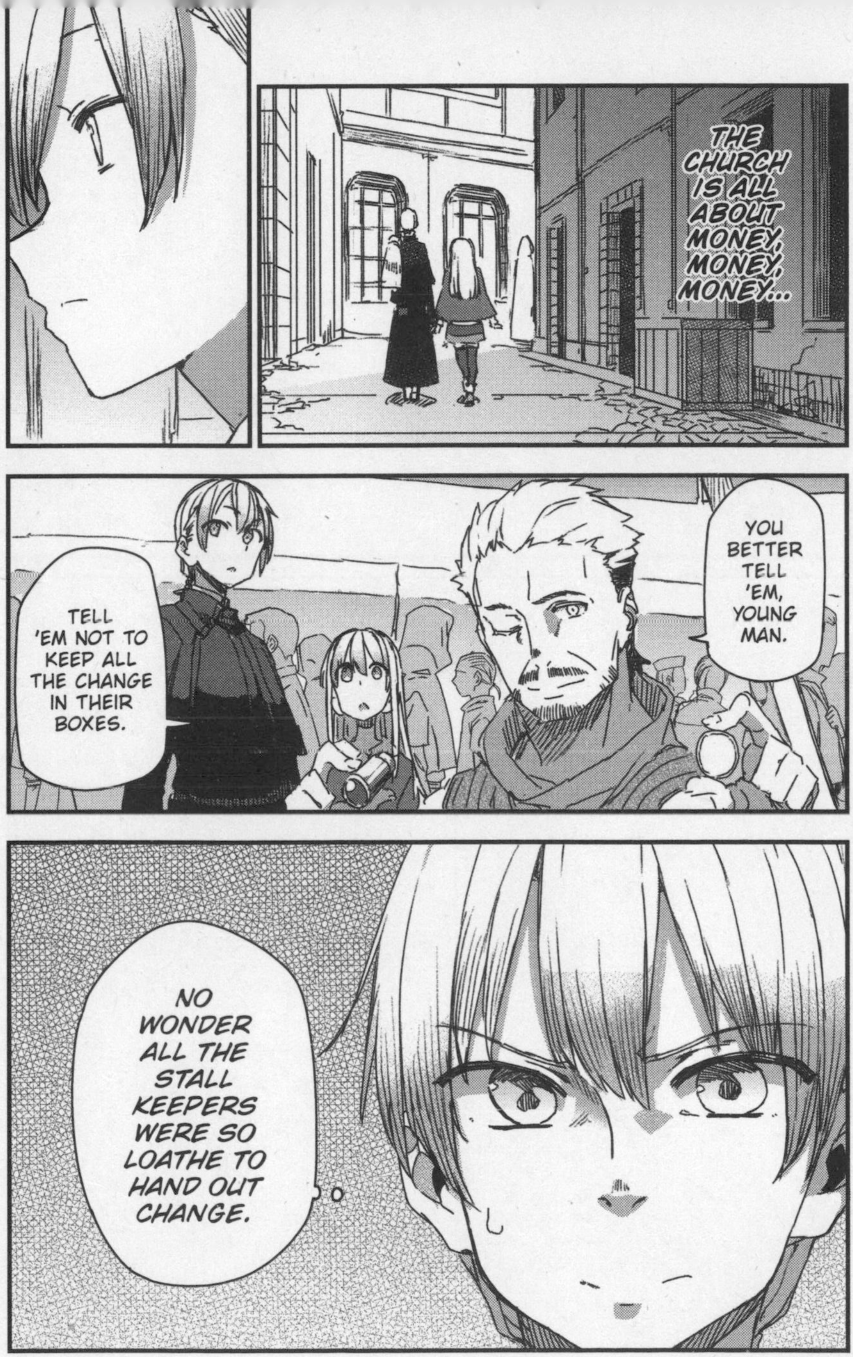
THE CHURCH IS ALL ABOUT MONEY, MONEY, MONEY...
YOU BETTER TELL 'EM, YOUNG MAN.
TELL 'EM NOT TO KEEP ALL THE CHANGE IN THEIR BOXES.
NO WONDER ALL THE STALL KEEPERS WERE SO LOATHE TO HAND OUT CHANGE.

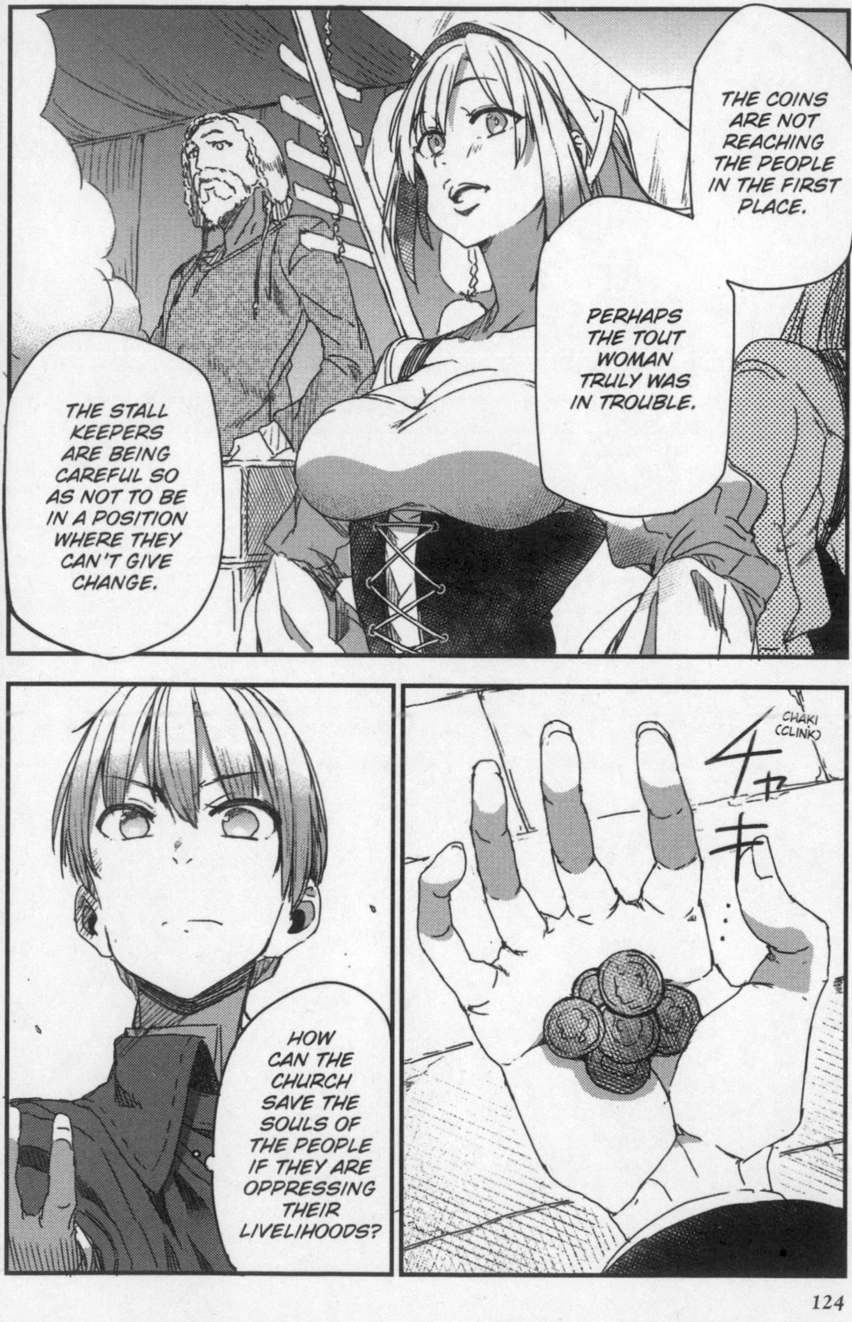
THE COINS ARE NOT REACHING THE PEOPLE IN THE FIRST PLACE.
PERHAPS THE TOUT WOMAN TRULY WAS IN TROUBLE.
THE STALL KEEPERS ARE BEING CAREFUL SO AS NOT TO BE IN A POSITION WHERE THEY CAN'T GIVE CHANGE.
CHAKI (CLINK)
HOW CAN THE CHURCH SAVE THE SOULS OF THE PEOPLE IF THEY ARE OPPRESSING THEIR LIVELIHOODS?

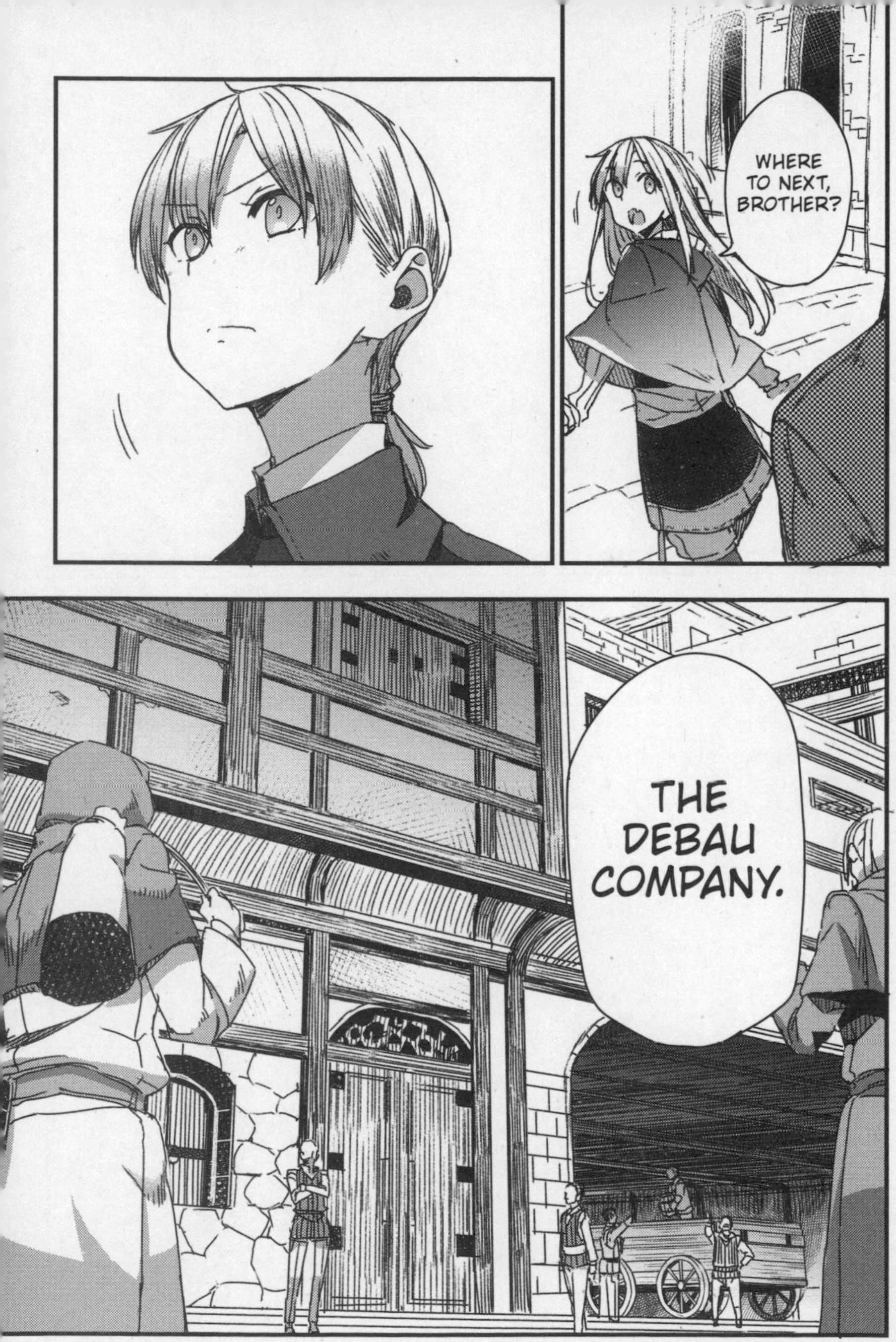
WHERE TO NEXT, BROTHER?
THE DEBAU COMPANY.

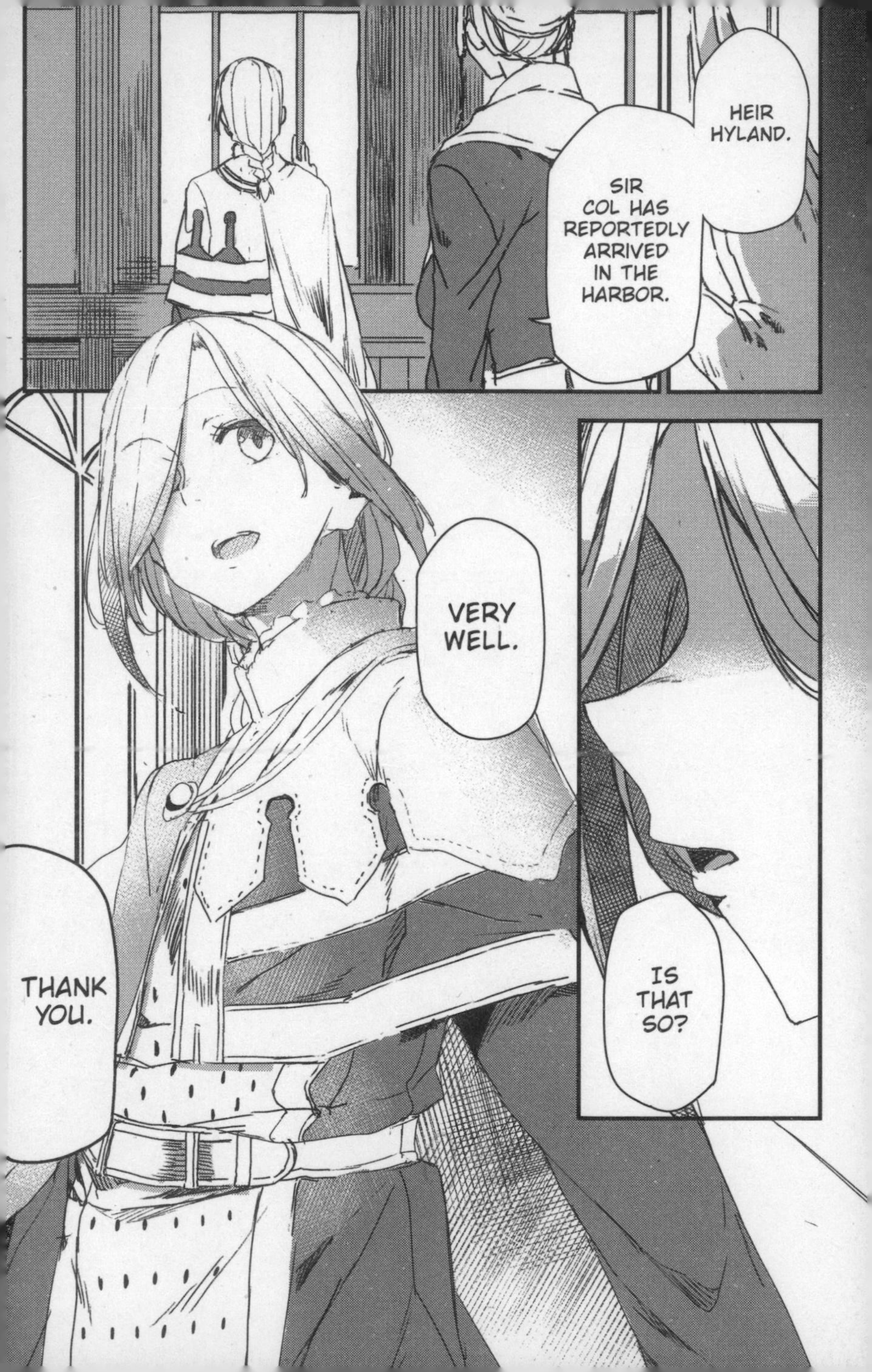
HEIR HYLAND.
SIR COL HAS REPORTEDLY ARRIVED IN THE HARBOR.
IS THAT SO?
VERY WELL.
THANK YOU.

WOLF & PARCHMENT

WOLF & PARCHMENT

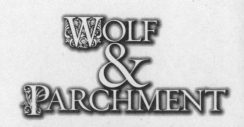

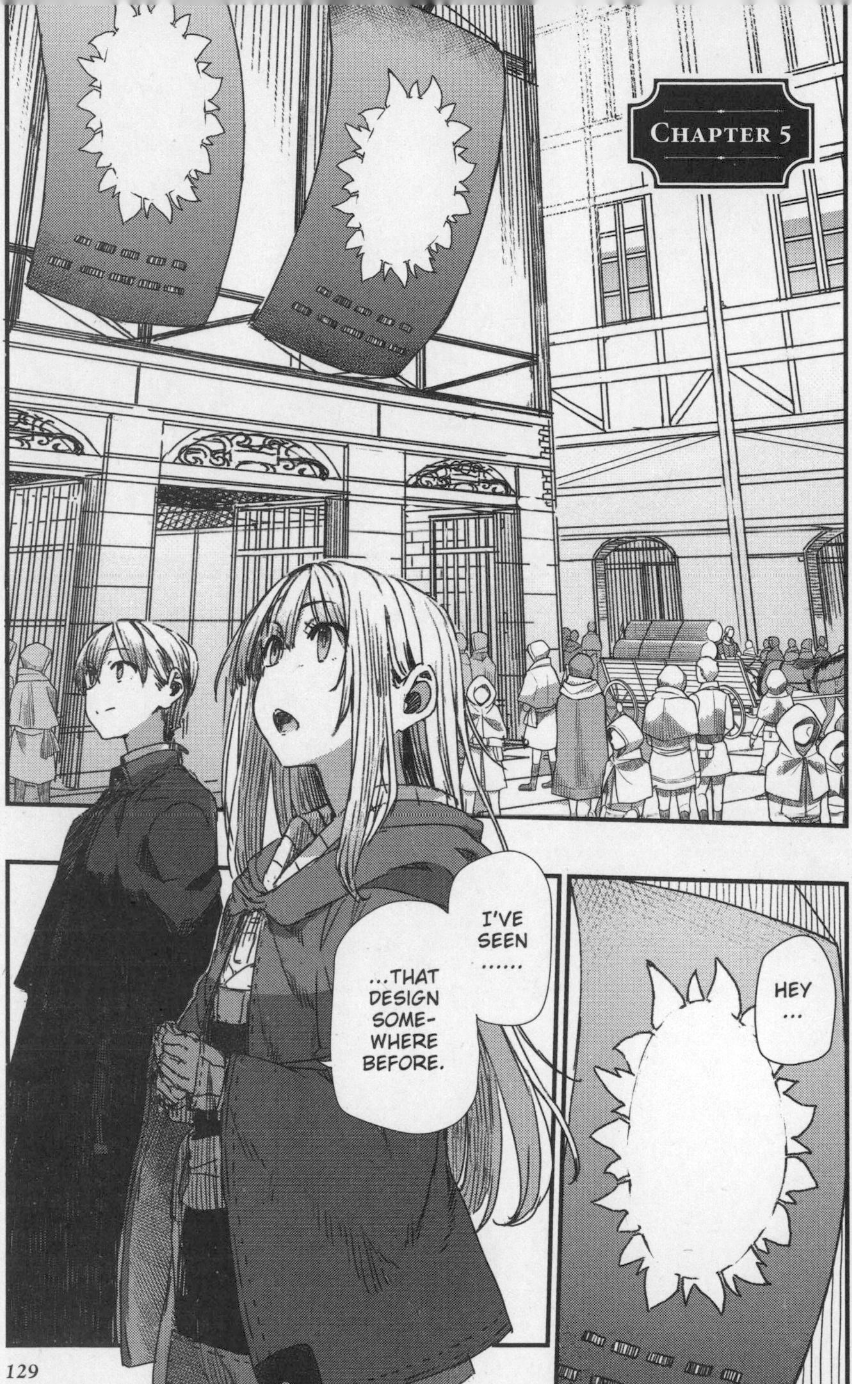
Chapter 5
HEY ...
I'VE SEEN ......
...THAT DESIGN SOMEWHERE BEFORE.

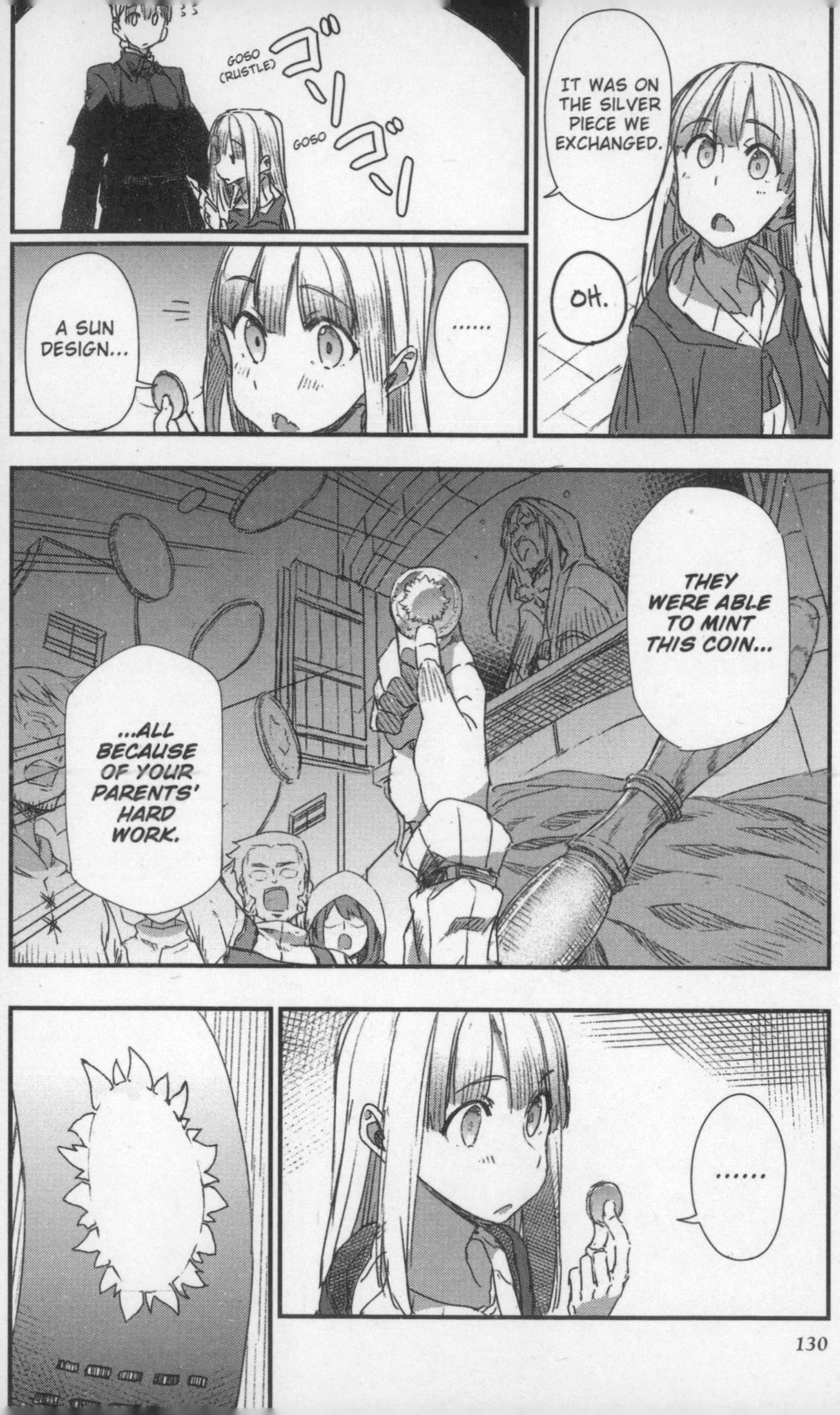
IT WAS ON THE SILVER PIECE WE EXCHANGED.
OH.
GOSO (RUSTLE)
GOSO
......
A SUN DESIGN...
THEY WERE ABLE TO MINT THIS COIN...
...ALL BECAUSE OF YOUR PARENTS' HARD WORK.
......

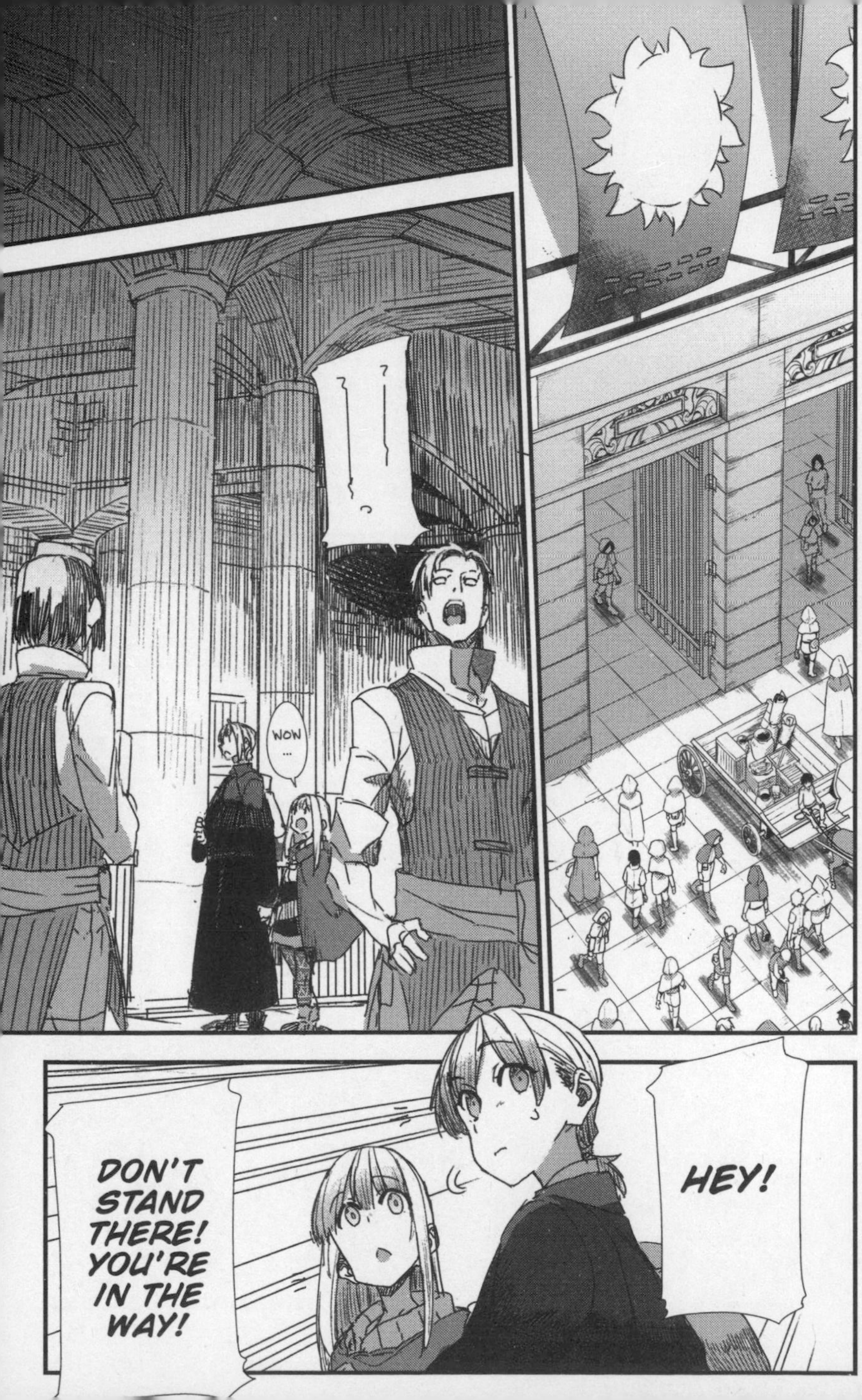
WOW...
HEY!
DON'T STAND THERE! YOU'RE IN THE WAY!

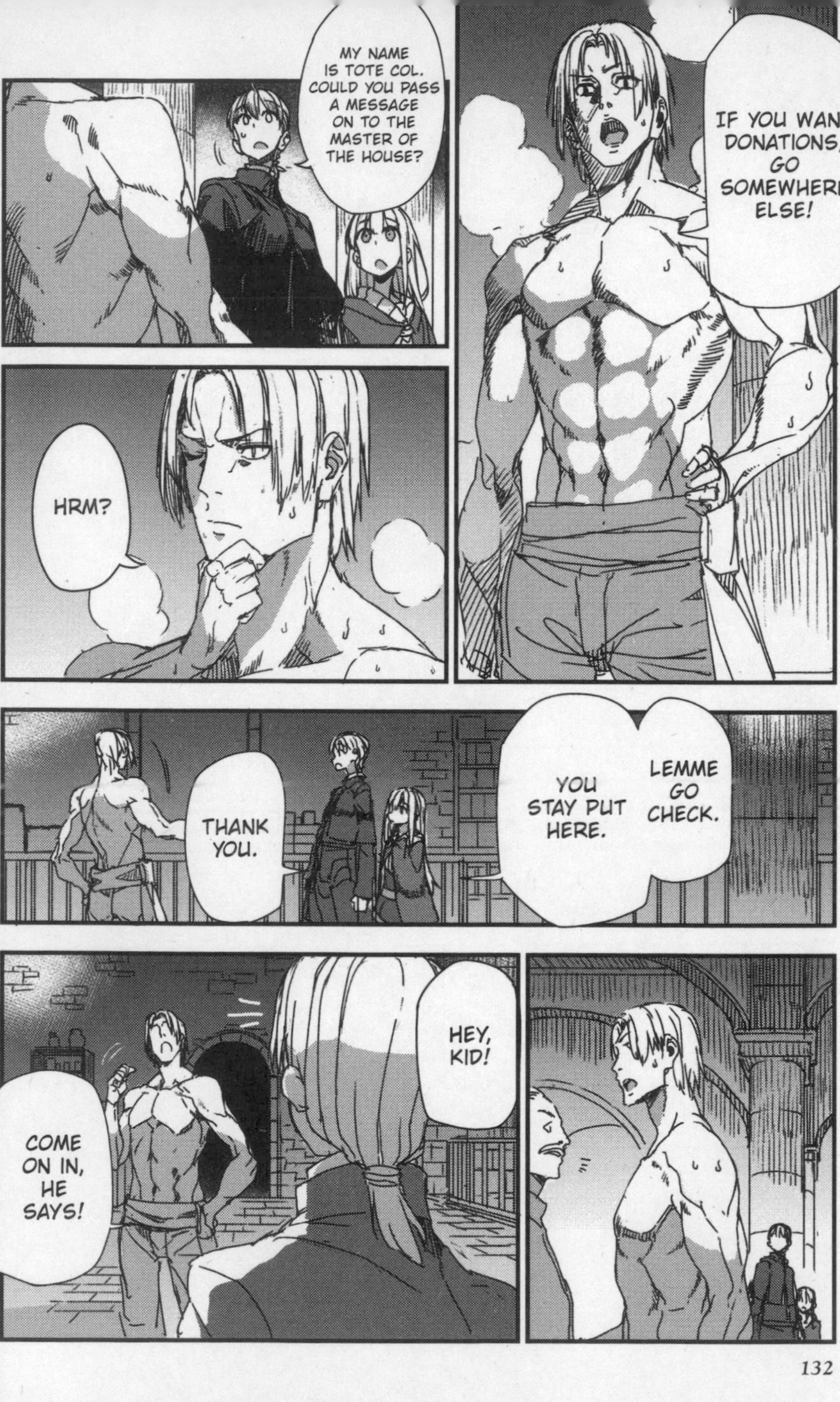
IF YOU WANT DONATIONS, GO SOMEWHERE ELSE!
MY NAME IS TOTE COL. COULD YOU PASS A MESSAGE ON TO THE MASTER OF THE HOUSE?
HRM?
LEMME GO CHECK.
YOU STAY PUT HERE.
THANK YOU.
HEY, KID!
COME ON IN, HE SAYS!

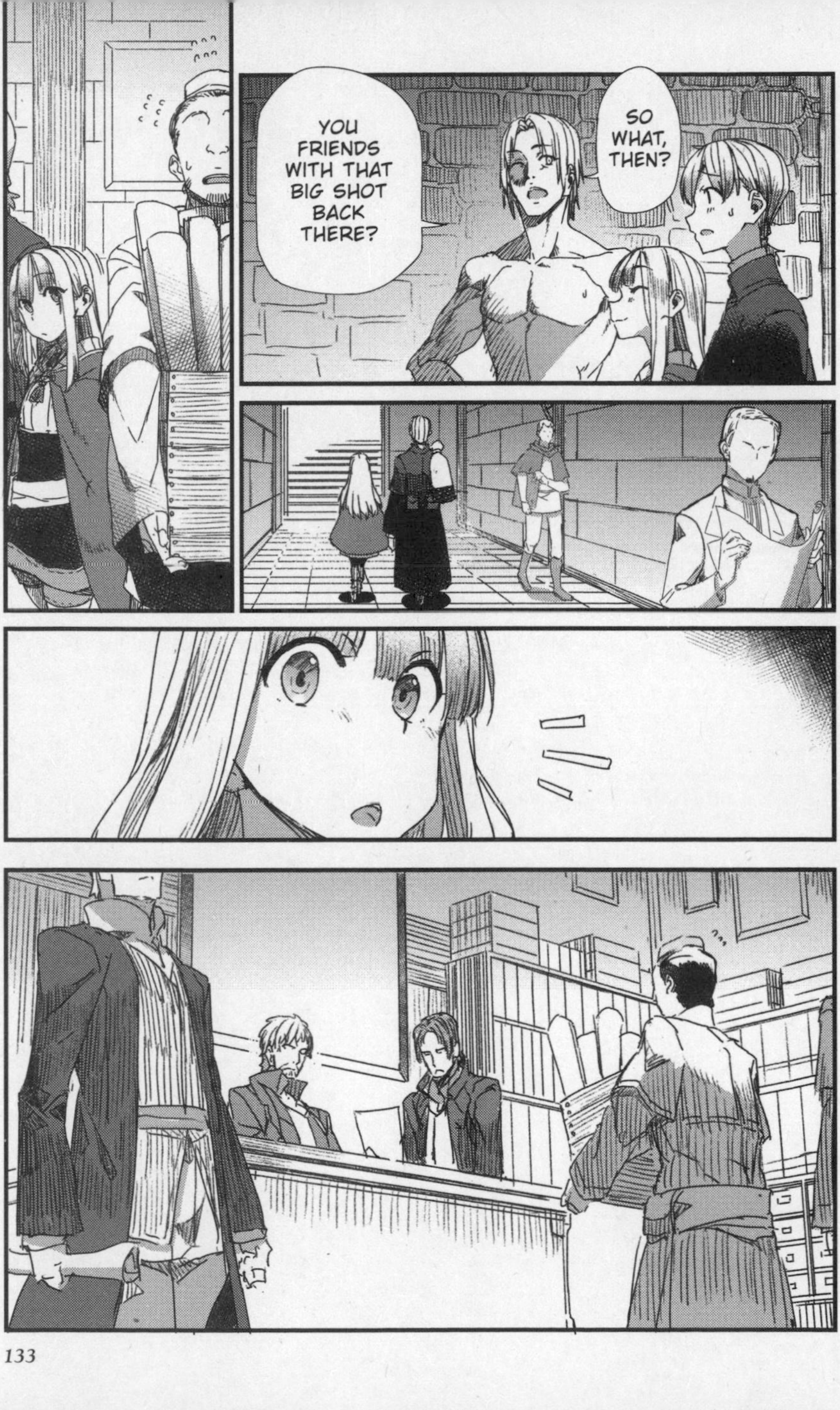
SO WHAT, THEN?
YOU FRIENDS WITH THAT BIG SHOT BACK THERE?

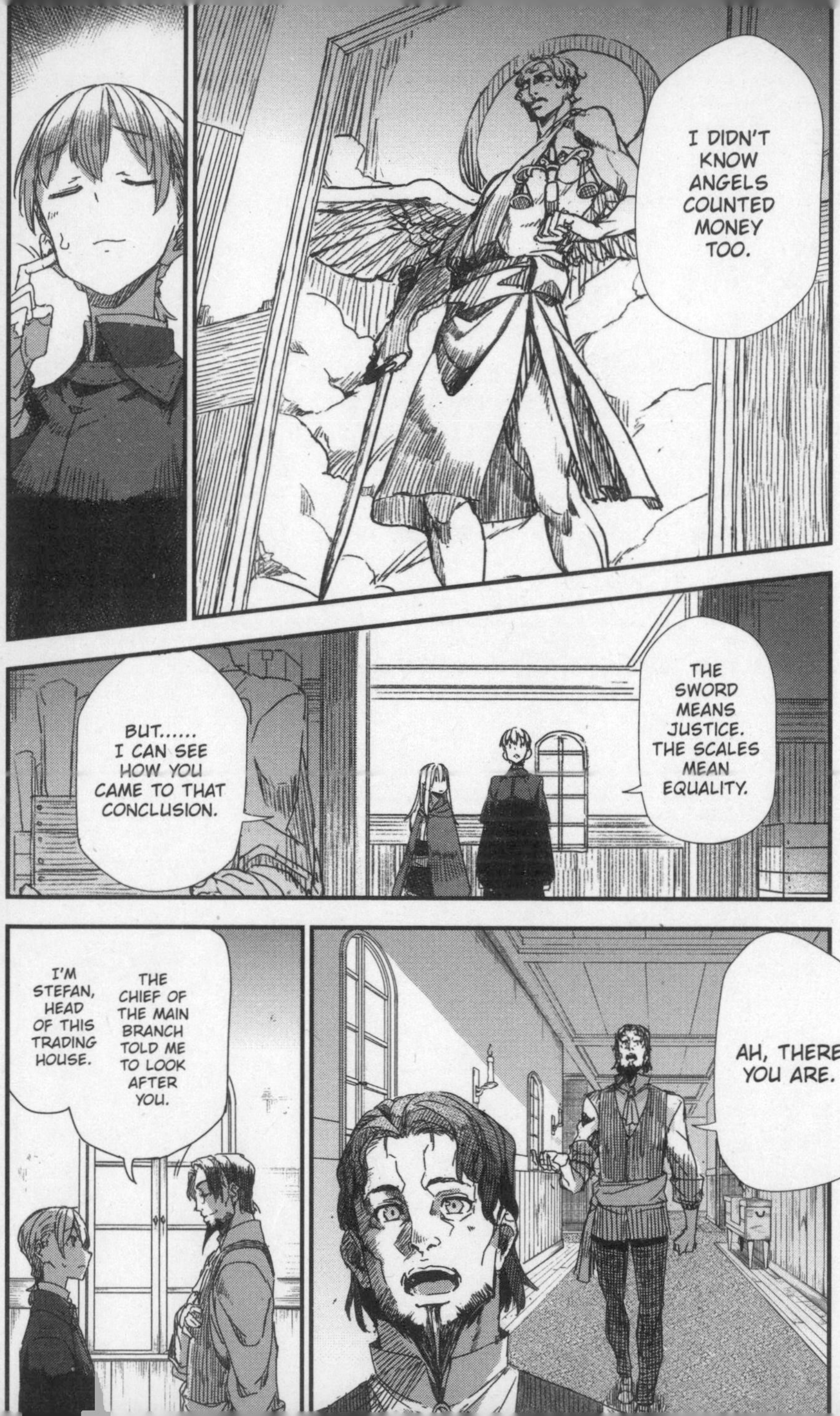
I DIDN'T KNOW ANGELS COUNTED MONEY TOO.
THE SWORD MEANS JUSTICE. THE SCALES MEAN EQUALITY.
BUT...... I CAN SEE HOW YOU CAME TO THAT CONCLUSION.
AH, THERE YOU ARE.
I'M STEFAN, HEAD OF THIS TRADING HOUSE.
THE CHIEF OF THE MAIN BRANCH TOLD ME TO LOOK AFTER YOU.

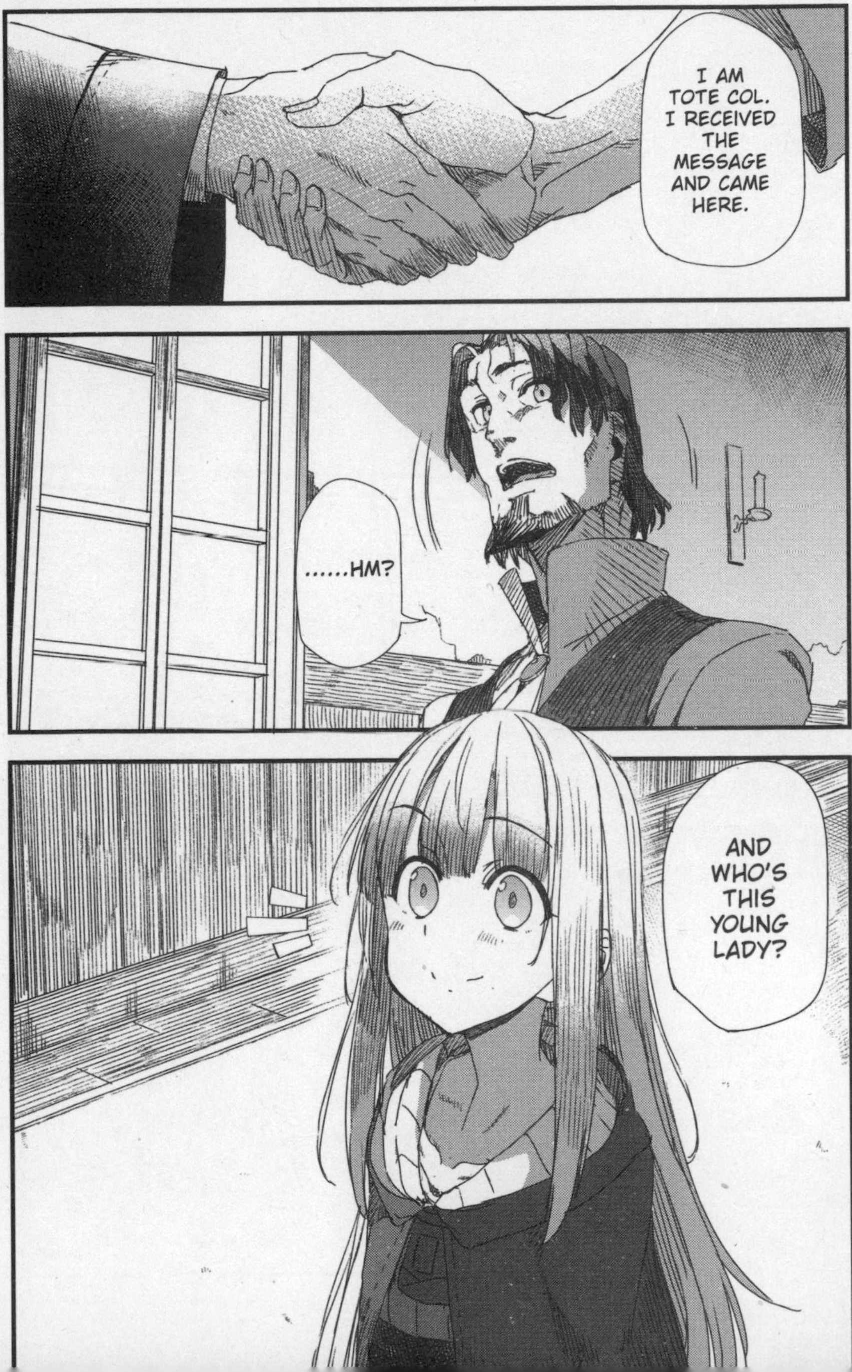
I AM TOTE COL. I RECEIVED THE MESSAGE AND CAME HERE.
......HM?
AND WHO'S THIS YOUNG LADY?

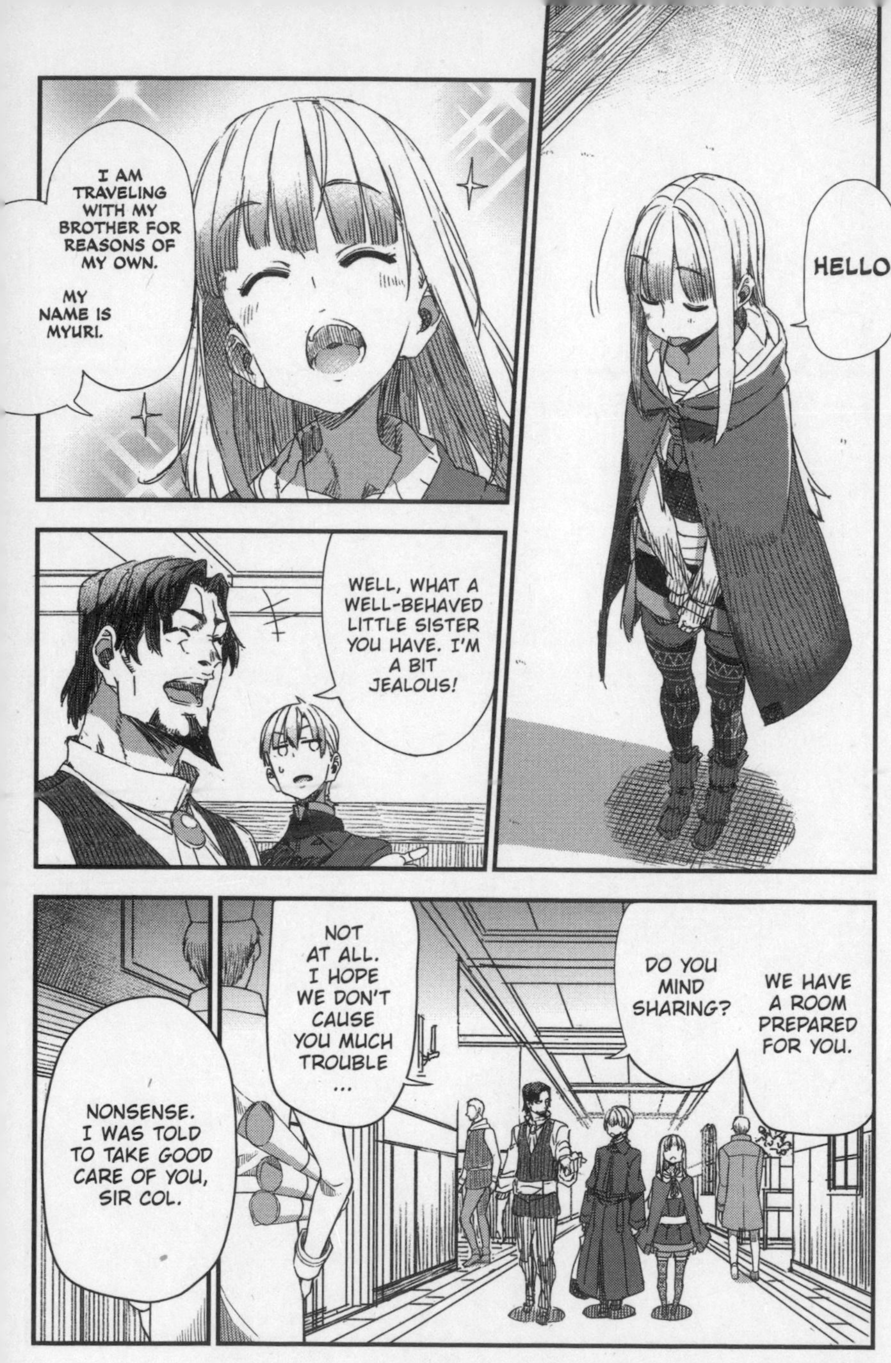
HELLO.
I AM TRAVELING WITH MY BROTHER FOR REASONS OF MY OWN.
MY NAME IS MYURI.
WELL, WHAT A WELL-BEHAVED LITTLE SISTER YOU HAVE. I'M A BIT JEALOUS!
WE HAVE A ROOM PREPARED FOR YOU.
DO YOU MIND SHARING?
NOT AT ALL. I HOPE WE DON'T CAUSE YOU MUCH TROUBLE ...
NONSENSE. I WAS TOLD TO TAKE GOOD CARE OF YOU, SIR COL.

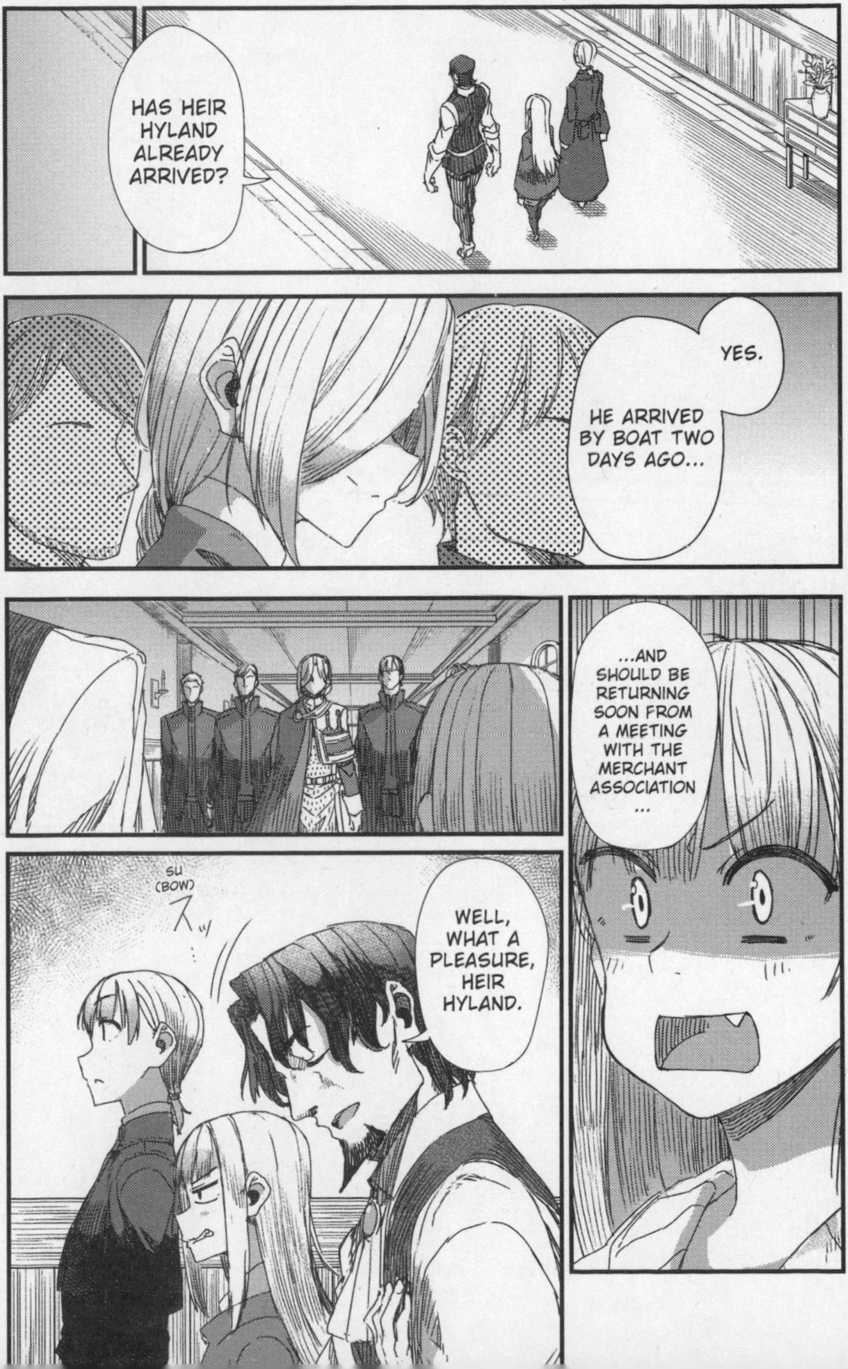
HAS HEIR HYLAND ALREADY ARRIVED?
YES.
HE ARRIVED BY BOAT TWO DAYS AGO...
...AND SHOULD BE RETURNING SOON FROM A MEETING WITH THE MERCHANT ASSOCIATION ...
WELL, WHAT A PLEASURE, HEIR HYLAND.
SU (BOW)
スッ

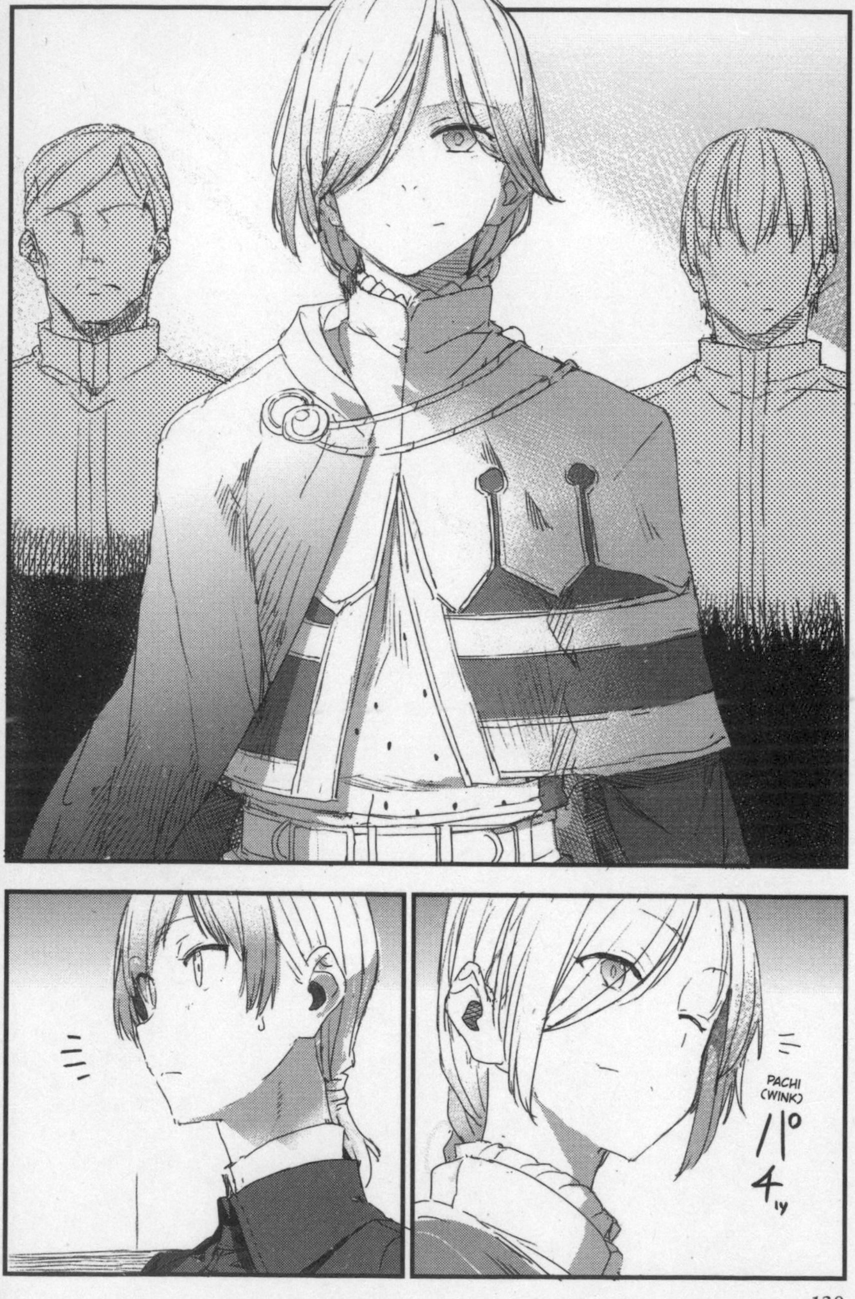
PACHI
(WINK)

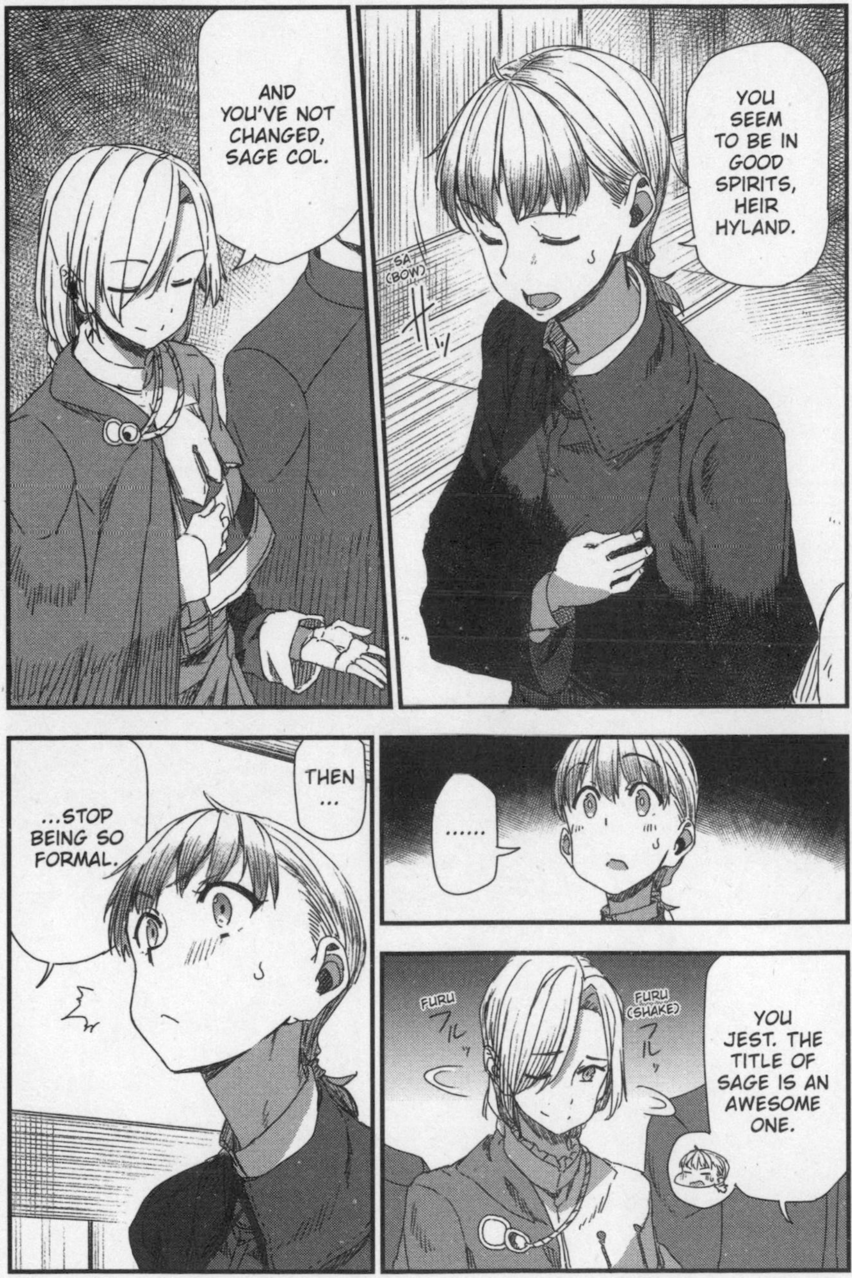

YOU SEEM TO BE IN GOOD SPIRITS, HEIR HYLAND.
SA (BOW)
AND YOU'VE NOT CHANGED, SAGE COL.
......
FURU
FURU (SHAKE)
YOU JEST. THE TITLE OF SAGE IS AN AWESOME ONE.
THEN ...
...STOP BEING SO FORMAL.

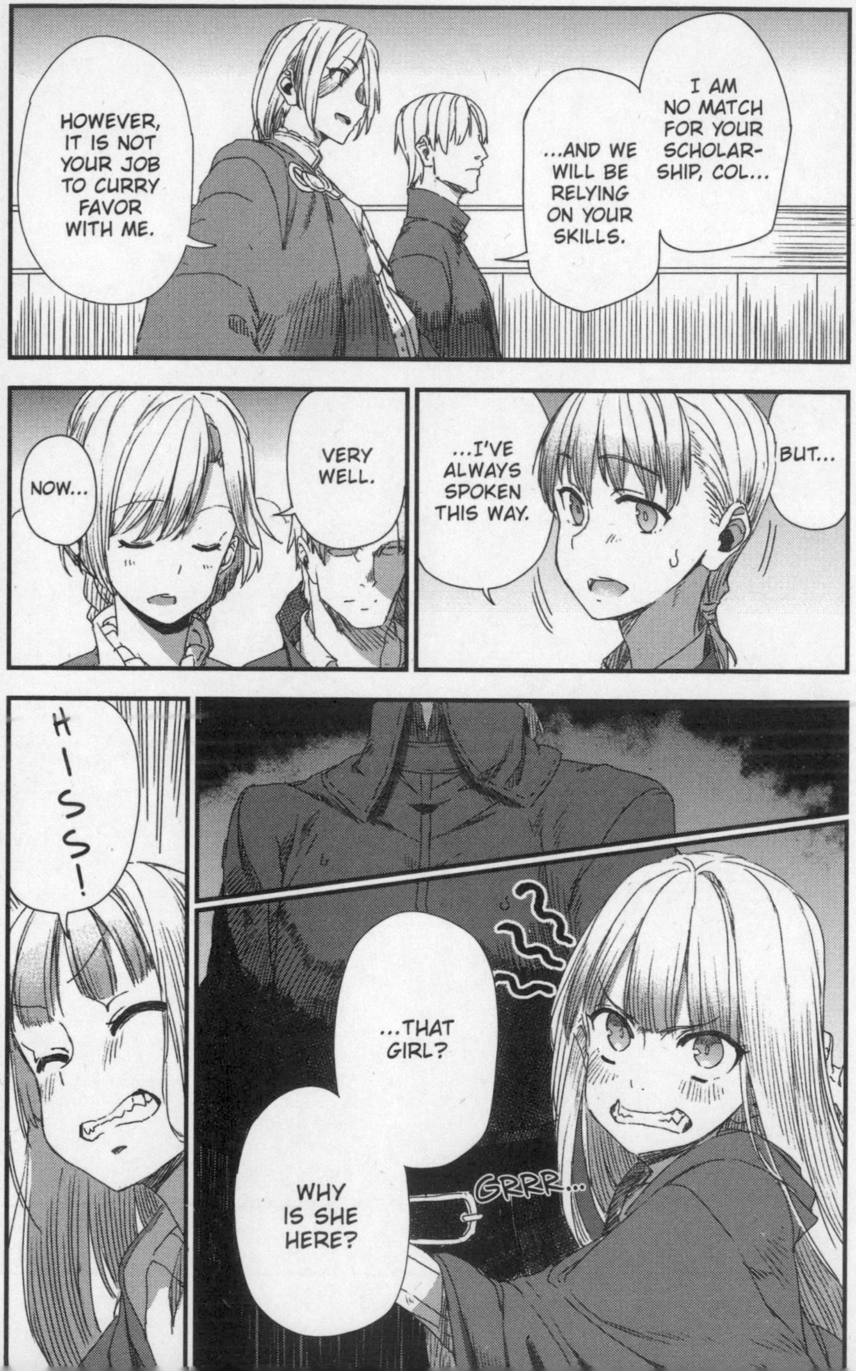
I AM NO MATCH FOR YOUR SCHOLAR-SHIP, COL...
...AND WE WILL BE RELYING ON YOUR SKILLS.
HOWEVER, IT IS NOT YOUR JOB TO CURRY FAVOR WITH ME.
BUT...
...I'VE ALWAYS SPOKEN THIS WAY.
VERY WELL.
NOW...
...THAT GIRL?
WHY IS SHE HERE?
GRRR...
HISS!

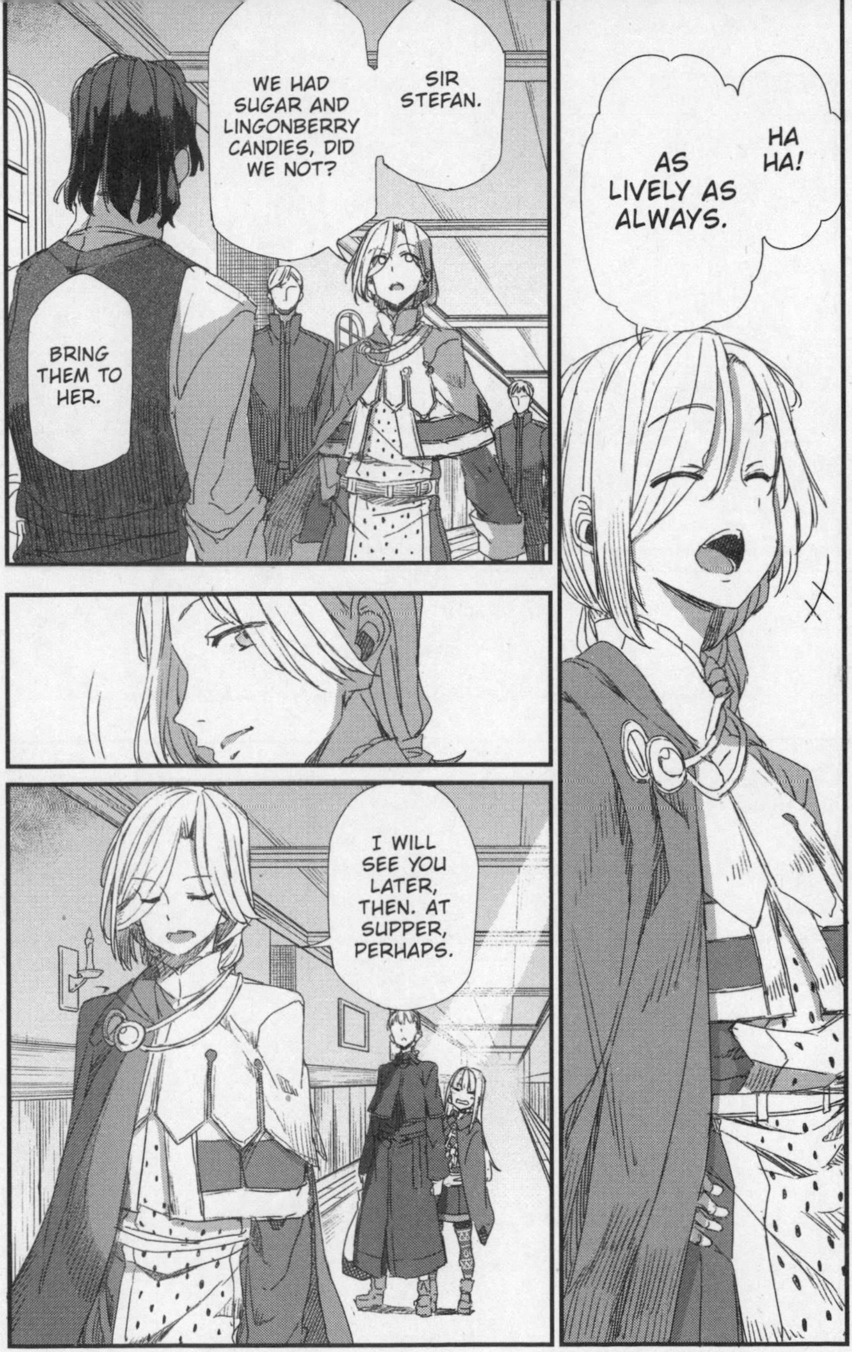
HA HA!
AS LIVELY AS ALWAYS.
SIR STEFAN.
WE HAD SUGAR AND LINGONBERRY CANDIES, DID WE NOT?
BRING THEM TO HER.
I WILL SEE YOU LATER, THEN. AT SUPPER, PERHAPS.

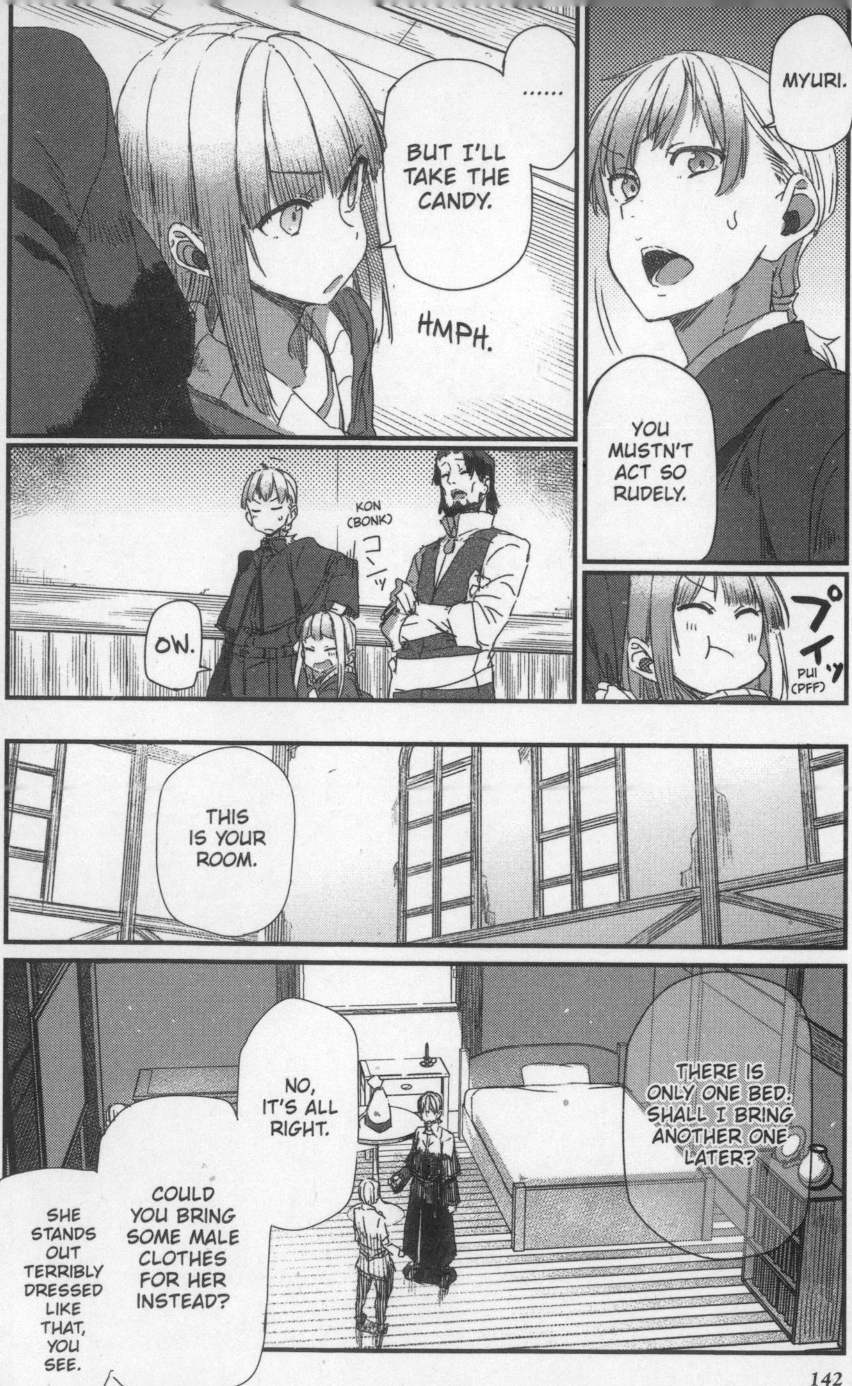
MYURI.
YOU MUSTN'T ACT SO RUDELY.
......
BUT I'LL TAKE THE CANDY.
HMPH.
プイッ
PUI (PFF)
コンッ
KON (BONK)
OW.
THIS IS YOUR ROOM.
THERE IS ONLY ONE BED. SHALL I BRING ANOTHER ONE LATER?
NO, IT'S ALL RIGHT.
COULD YOU BRING SOME MALE CLOTHES FOR HER INSTEAD?
SHE STANDS OUT TERRIBLY DRESSED LIKE THAT, YOU SEE.

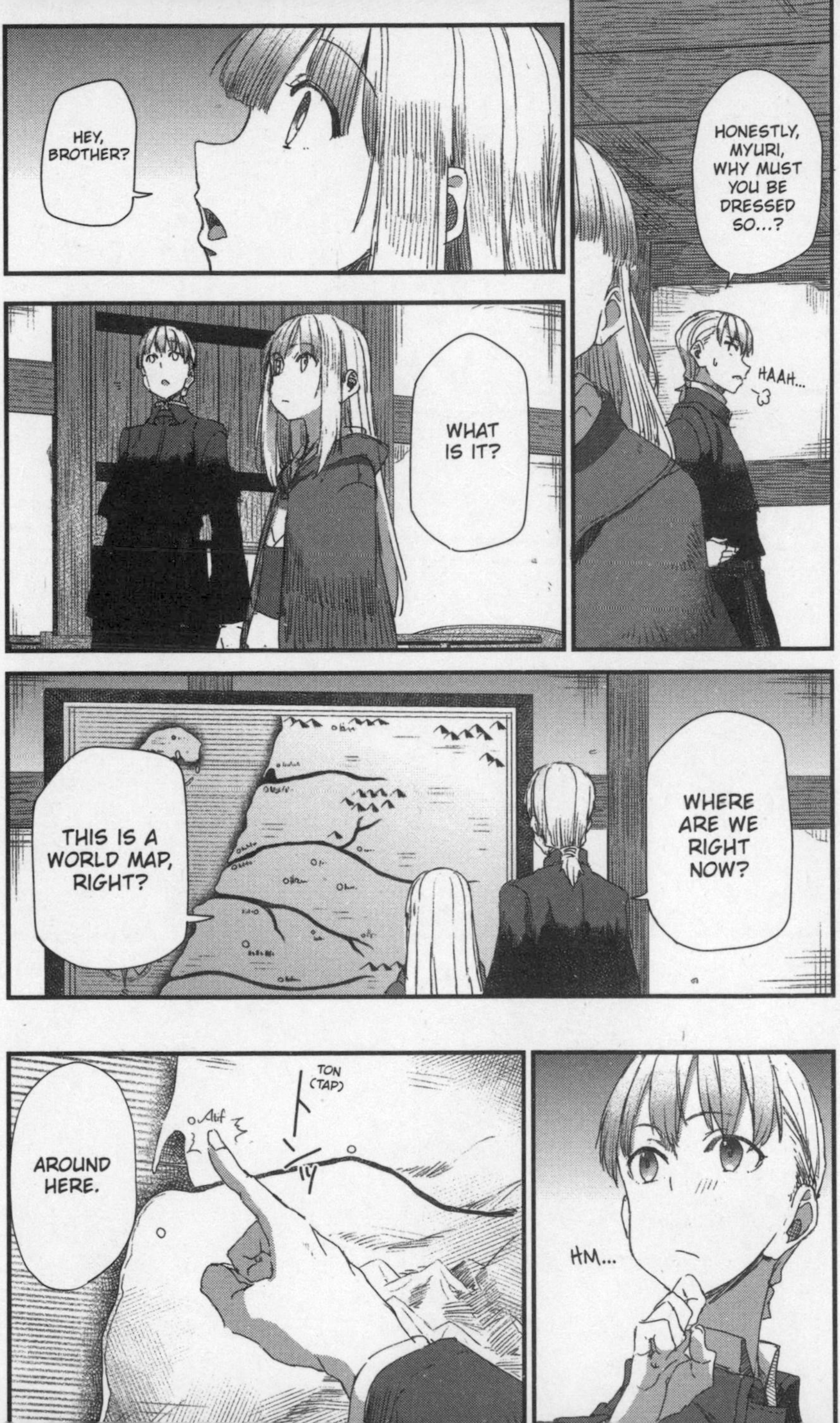
HONESTLY, MYURI, WHY MUST YOU BE DRESSED SO...?
HAAH...
HEY, BROTHER?
WHAT IS IT?
WHERE ARE WE RIGHT NOW?
THIS IS A WORLD MAP, RIGHT?
HM...
TON (TAP)
AROUND HERE.

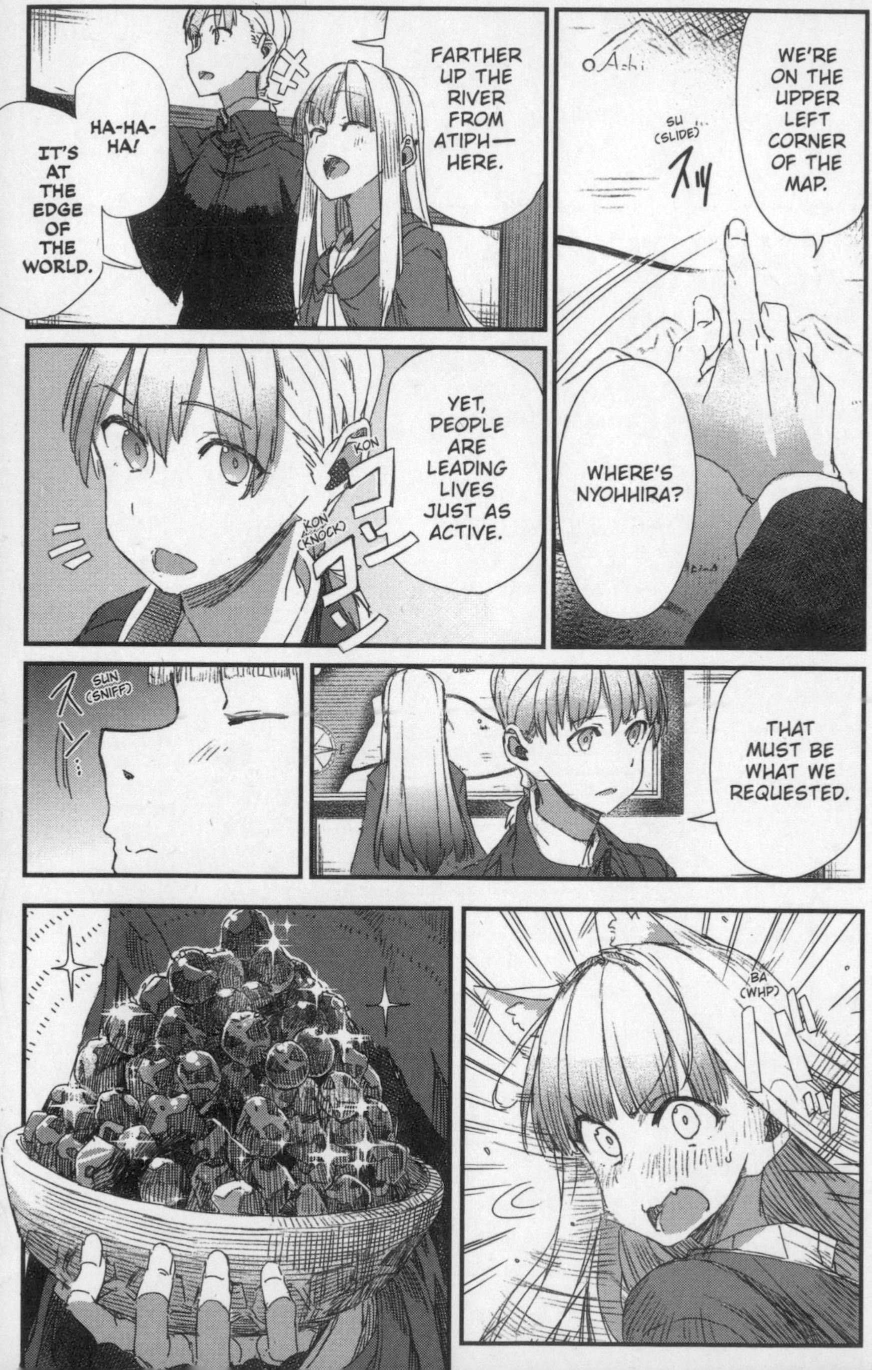
WE'RE ON THE UPPER LEFT CORNER OF THE MAP.
SU (SLIDE)
WHERE'S NYOHHIRA?
FARTHER UP THE RIVER FROM ATIPH—HERE.
HA-HA-HA!
IT'S AT THE EDGE OF THE WORLD.
YET, PEOPLE ARE LEADING LIVES JUST AS ACTIVE.
KON
KON (KNOCK)
THAT MUST BE WHAT WE REQUESTED.
SUN (SNIFF)
BA (WHP)

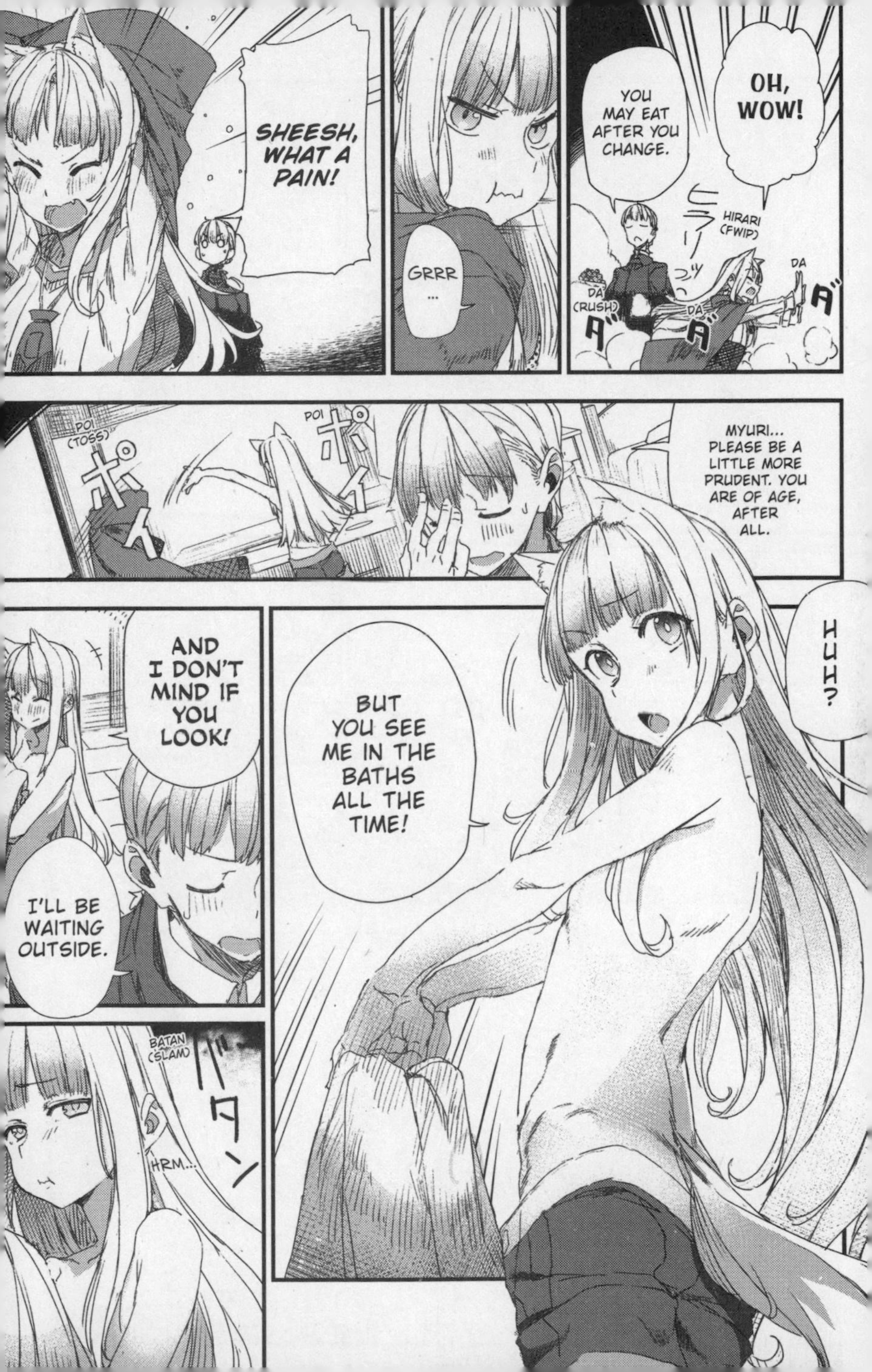
OH, WOW!
YOU MAY EAT AFTER YOU CHANGE.
HIRARI (FWIP)
DA (RUSH)
DA
DA
GRRR ...
SHEESH, WHAT A PAIN!
MYURI... PLEASE BE A LITTLE MORE PRUDENT. YOU ARE OF AGE, AFTER ALL.
POI
POI (TOSS)
HUH?
BUT YOU SEE ME IN THE BATHS ALL THE TIME!
AND I DON'T MIND IF YOU LOOK!
I'LL BE WAITING OUTSIDE.
BATAN (SLAM)
HRM...

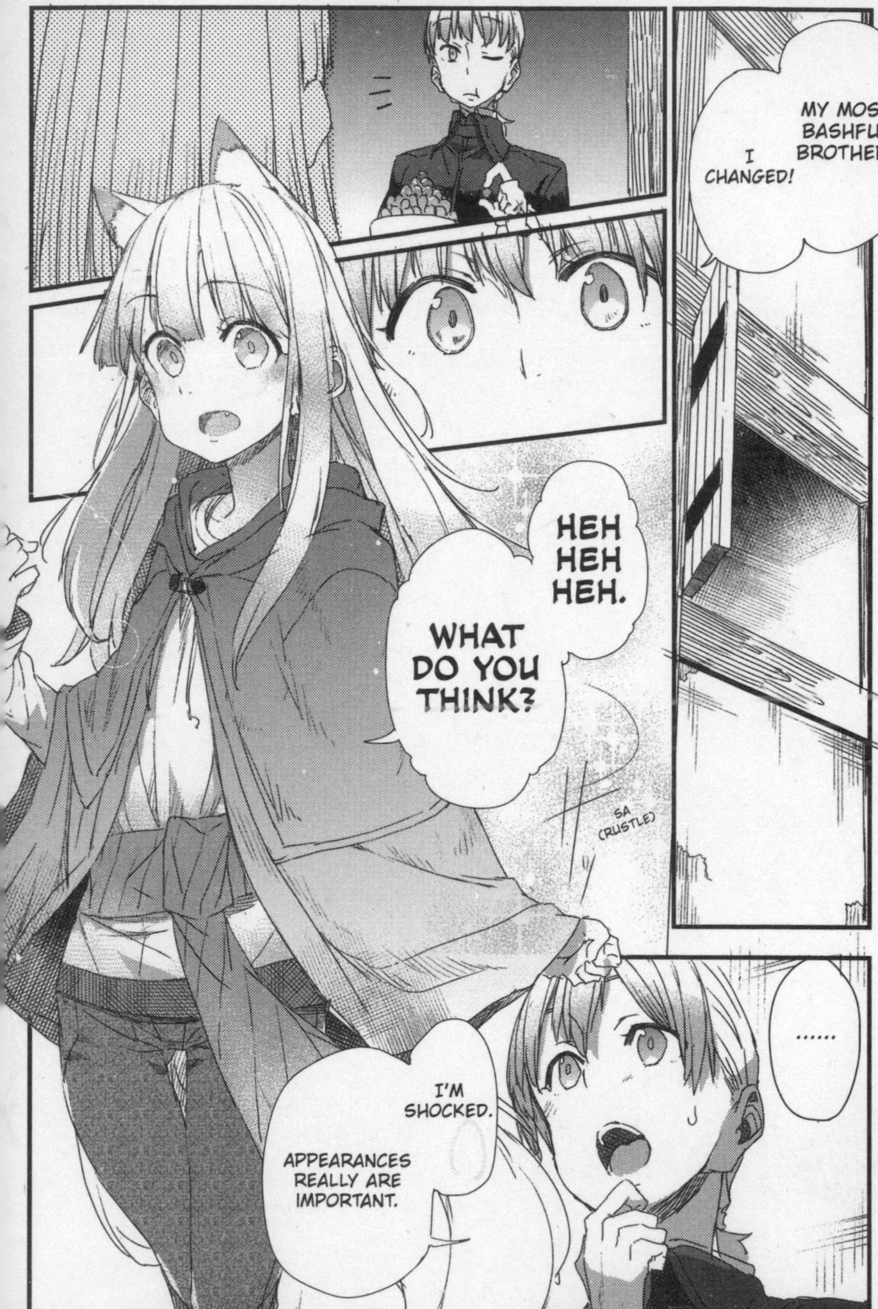
MY MOST BASHFUL BROTHER!
I CHANGED!
HEH HEH HEH.
WHAT DO YOU THINK?
SA (RUSTLE)
......
I'M SHOCKED.
APPEARANCES REALLY ARE IMPORTANT.

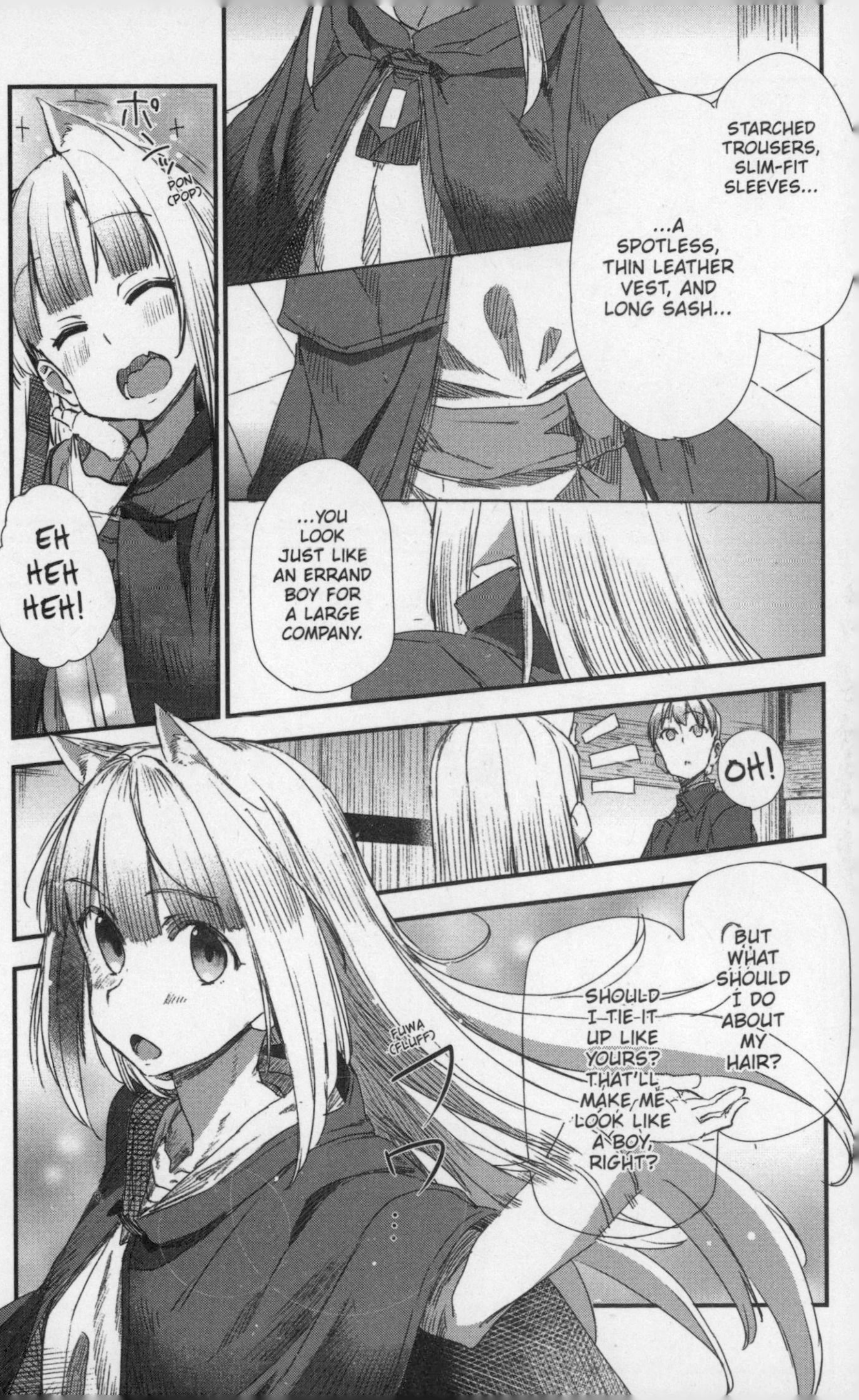
STARCHED TROUSERS, SLIM-FIT SLEEVES...
...A SPOTLESS, THIN LEATHER VEST, AND LONG SASH...
...YOU LOOK JUST LIKE AN ERRAND BOY FOR A LARGE COMPANY.
PON (POP)
EH HEH HEH!
OH!
BUT WHAT SHOULD I DO ABOUT MY HAIR?
SHOULD I TIE IT UP LIKE YOURS? THAT'LL MAKE ME LOOK LIKE A BOY, RIGHT?
FUWA (FLUFF)

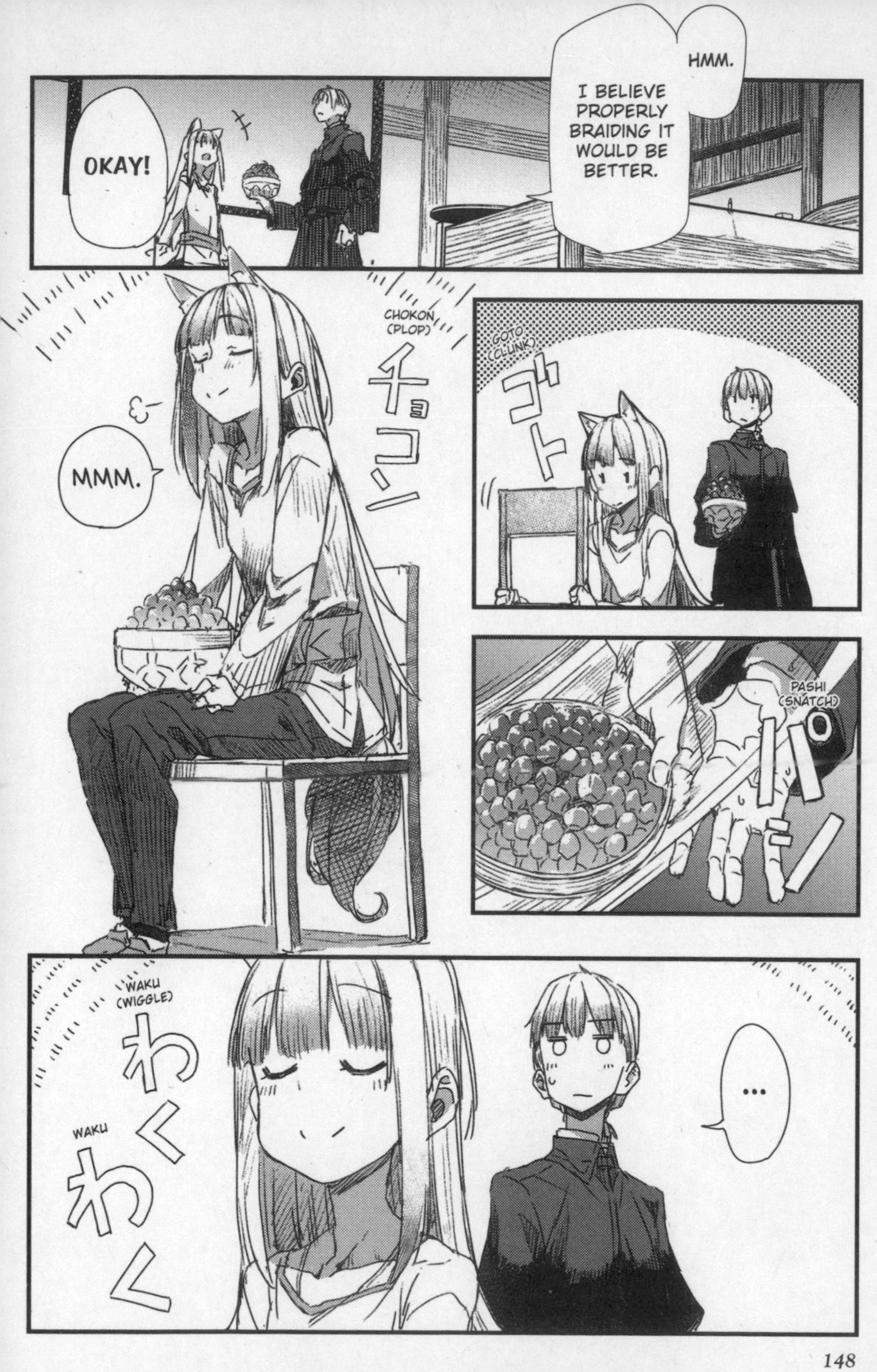
HMM.
I BELIEVE PROPERLY BRAIDING IT WOULD BE BETTER.
OKAY!
GOTO (CLUNK)
ゴト
PASHI (SNATCH)
CHOKON (PLOP)
チョコン
MMM.
...
WAKU (WIGGLE)
WAKU
わくわく

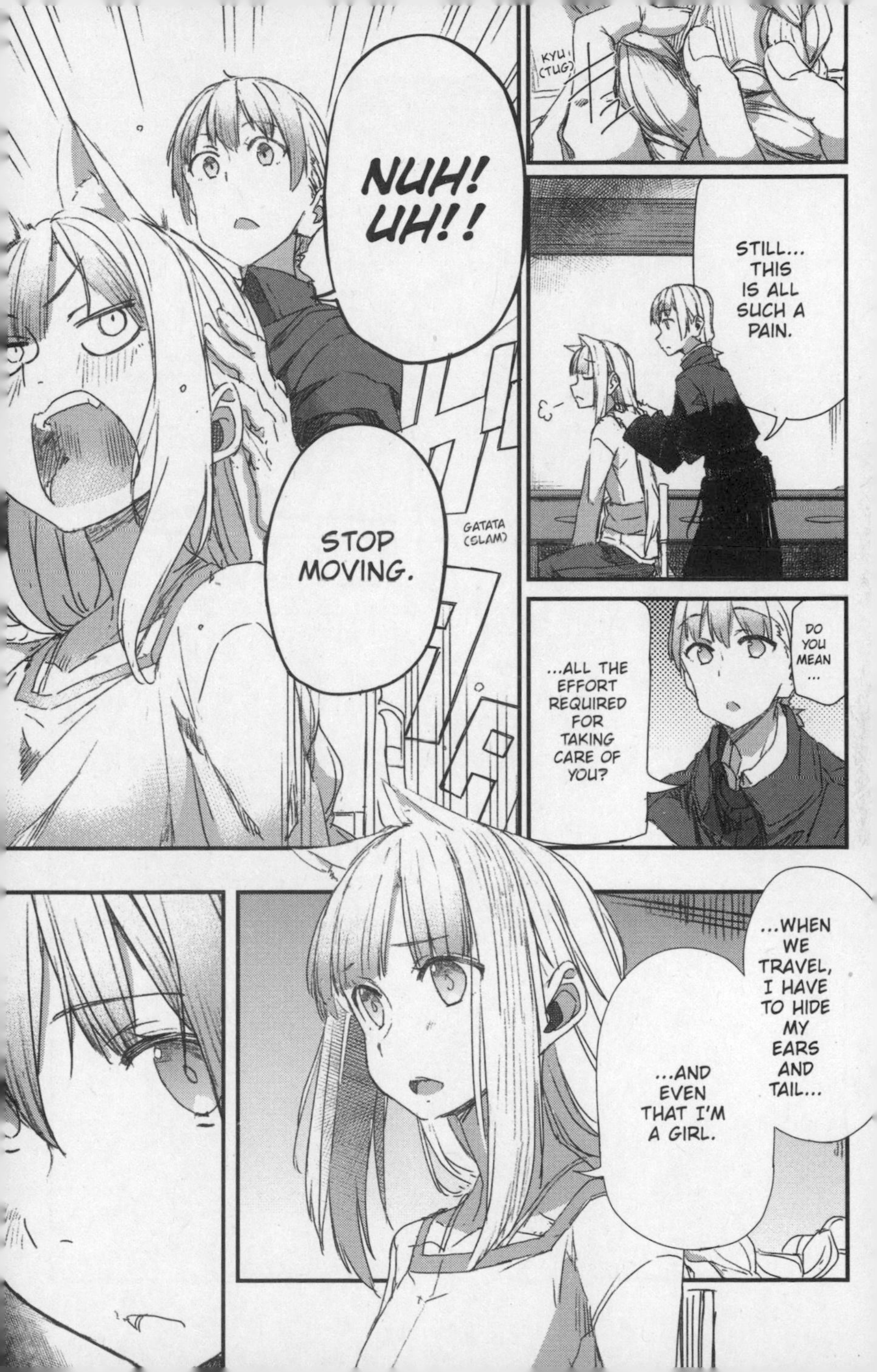
KYU (TUG)
STILL... THIS IS ALL SUCH A PAIN.
DO YOU MEAN ...
...ALL THE EFFORT REQUIRED FOR TAKING CARE OF YOU?
NUH! UH!!
GATATA (SLAM)
STOP MOVING.
...WHEN WE TRAVEL, I HAVE TO HIDE MY EARS AND TAIL...
...AND EVEN THAT I'M A GIRL.

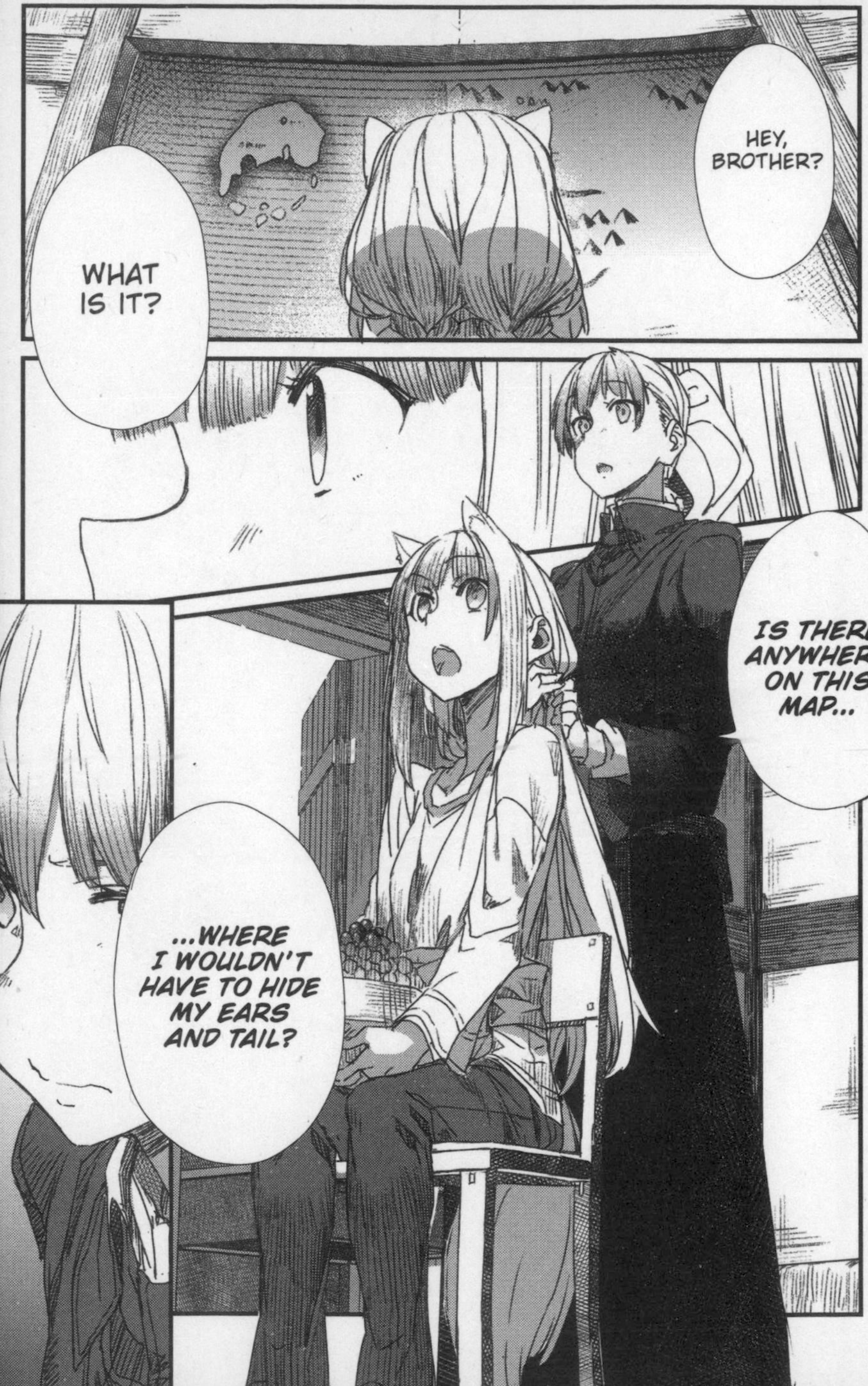
HEY, BROTHER?
WHAT IS IT?
IS THERE ANYWHERE ON THIS MAP...
...WHERE I WOULDN'T HAVE TO HIDE MY EARS AND TAIL?

WOLF & PARCHMENT

WOLF
&
PARCHMENT

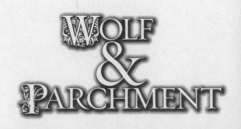

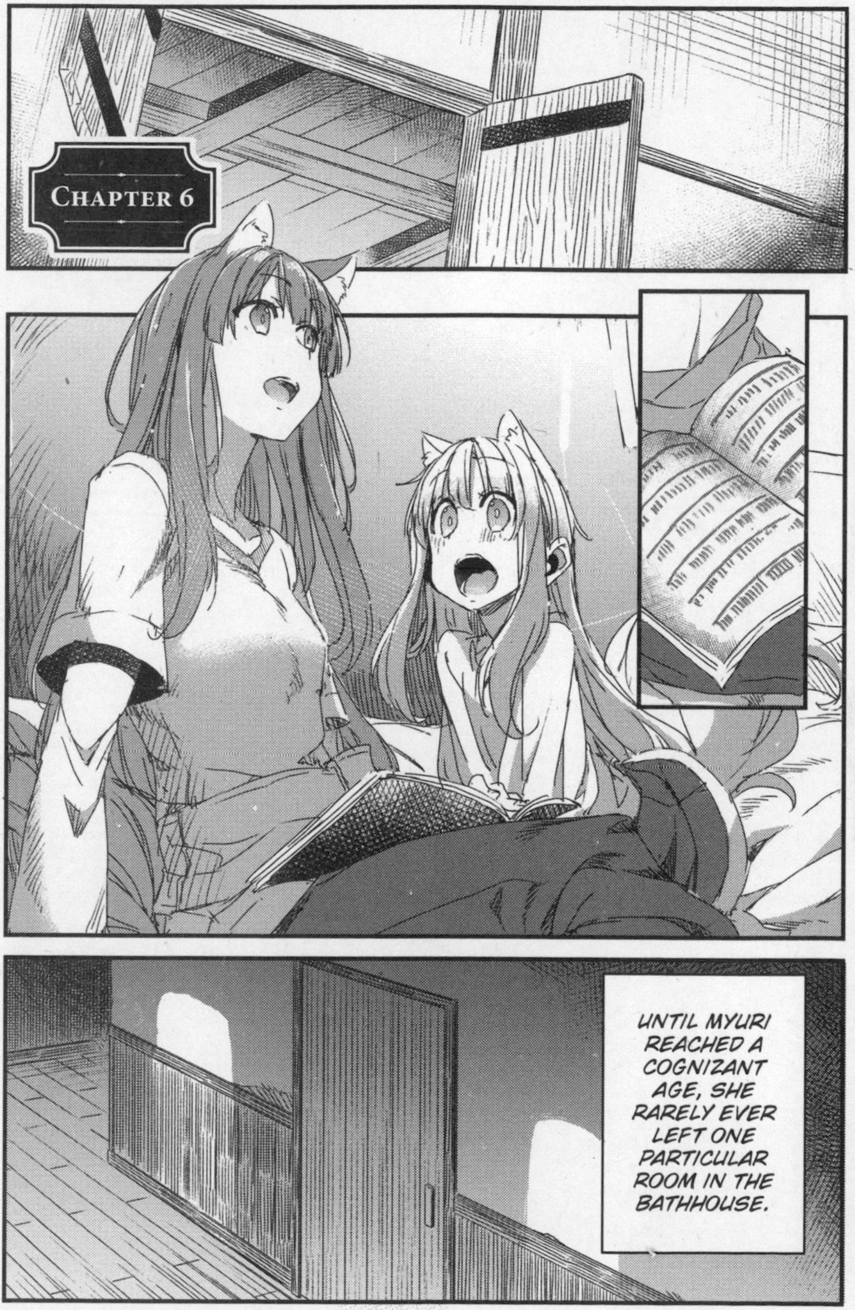
CHAPTER 6
UNTIL MYURI REACHED A COGNIZANT AGE, SHE RARELY EVER LEFT ONE PARTICULAR ROOM IN THE BATHHOUSE.

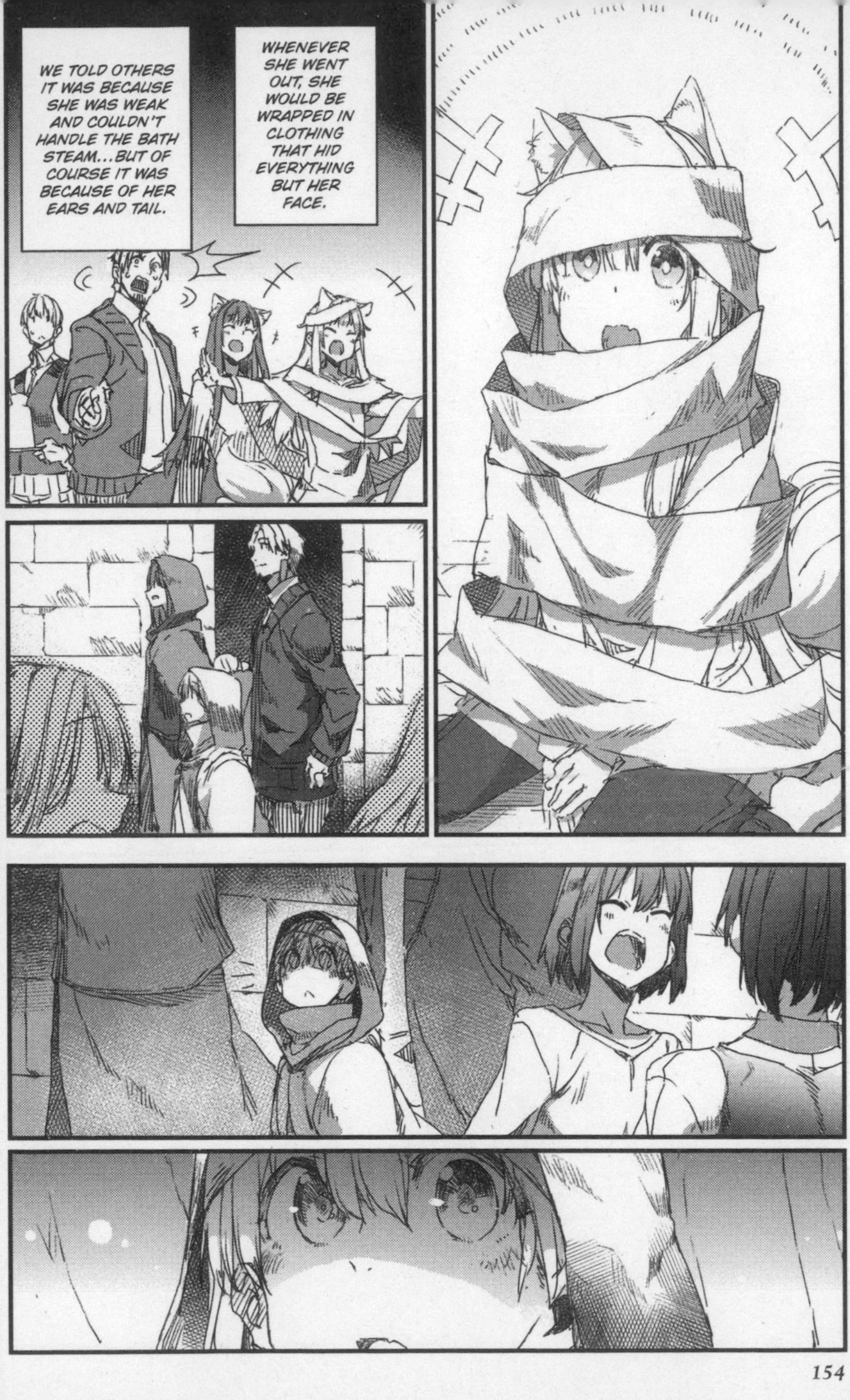
WHENEVER SHE WENT OUT, SHE WOULD BE WRAPPED IN CLOTHING THAT HID EVERYTHING BUT HER FACE.
WE TOLD OTHERS IT WAS BECAUSE SHE WAS WEAK AND COULDN'T HANDLE THE BATH STEAM...BUT OF COURSE IT WAS BECAUSE OF HER EARS AND TAIL.

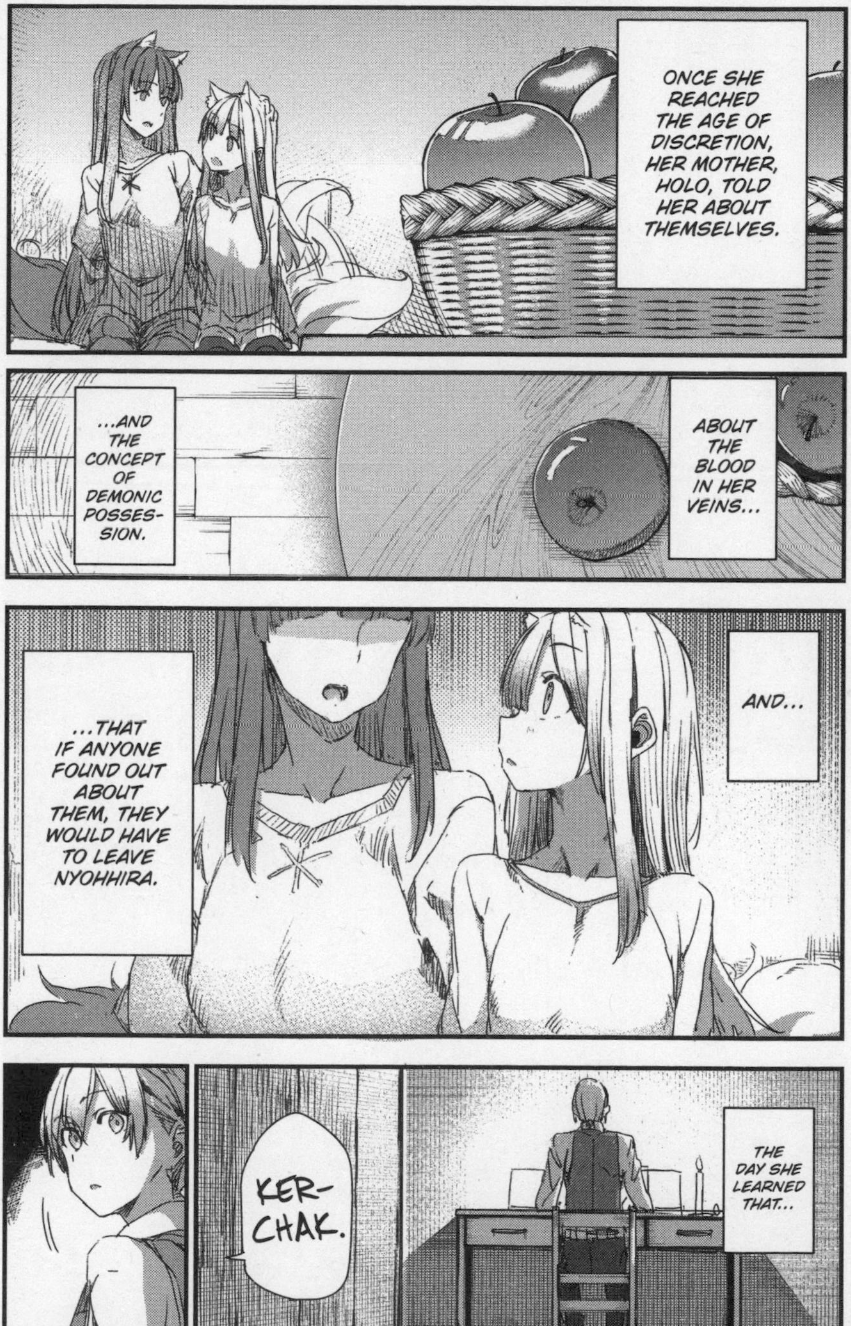
ONCE SHE REACHED THE AGE OF DISCRETION, HER MOTHER, HOLO, TOLD HER ABOUT THEMSELVES.
ABOUT THE BLOOD IN HER VEINS...
...AND THE CONCEPT OF DEMONIC POSSES-SION.
AND...
...THAT IF ANYONE FOUND OUT ABOUT THEM, THEY WOULD HAVE TO LEAVE NYOHHIRA.
THE DAY SHE LEARNED THAT...
KER-CHAK.

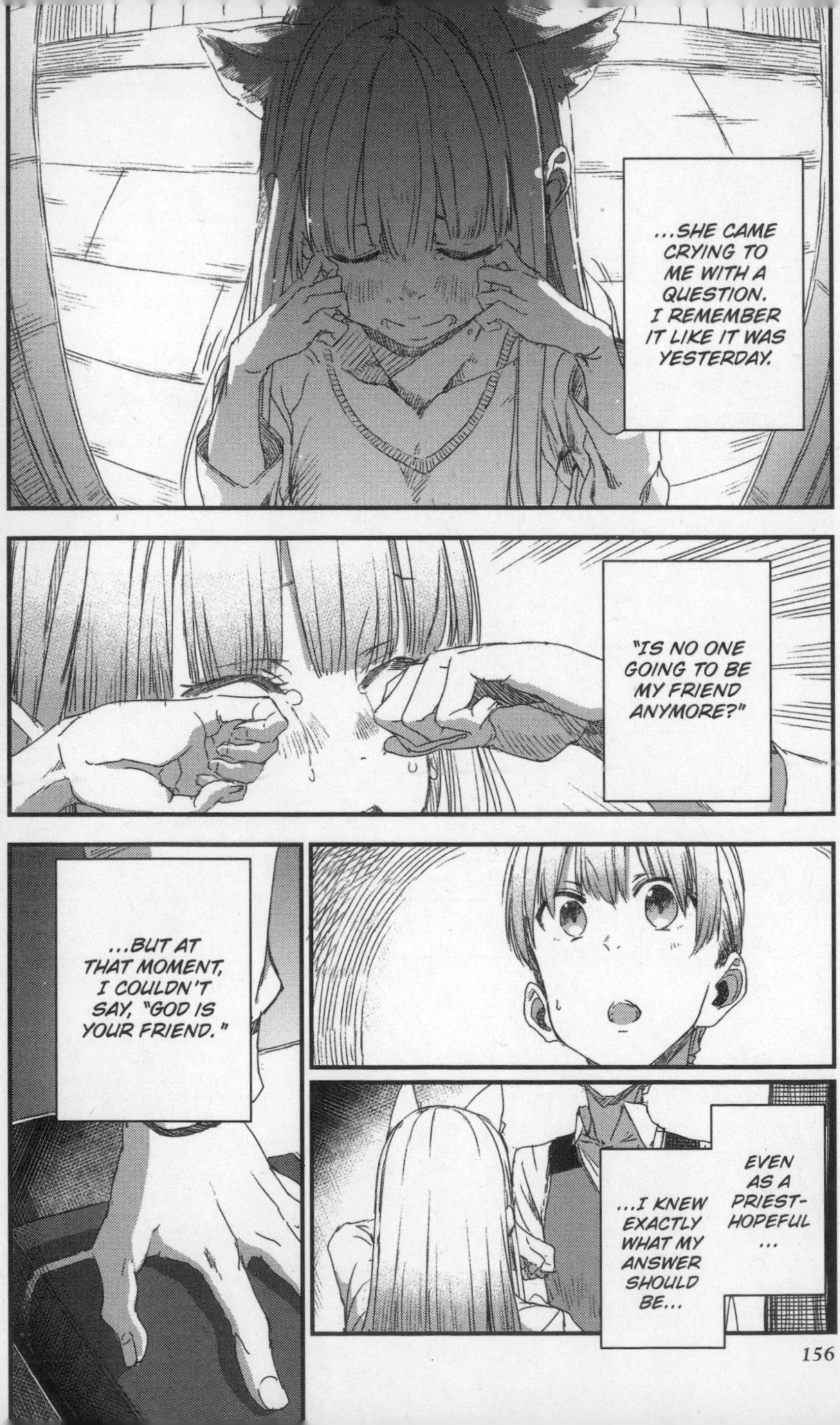
...SHE CAME CRYING TO ME WITH A QUESTION. I REMEMBER IT LIKE IT WAS YESTERDAY.
"IS NO ONE GOING TO BE MY FRIEND ANYMORE?"
EVEN AS A PRIEST-HOPEFUL...
...I KNEW EXACTLY WHAT MY ANSWER SHOULD BE...
...BUT AT THAT MOMENT, I COULDN'T SAY, "GOD IS YOUR FRIEND."

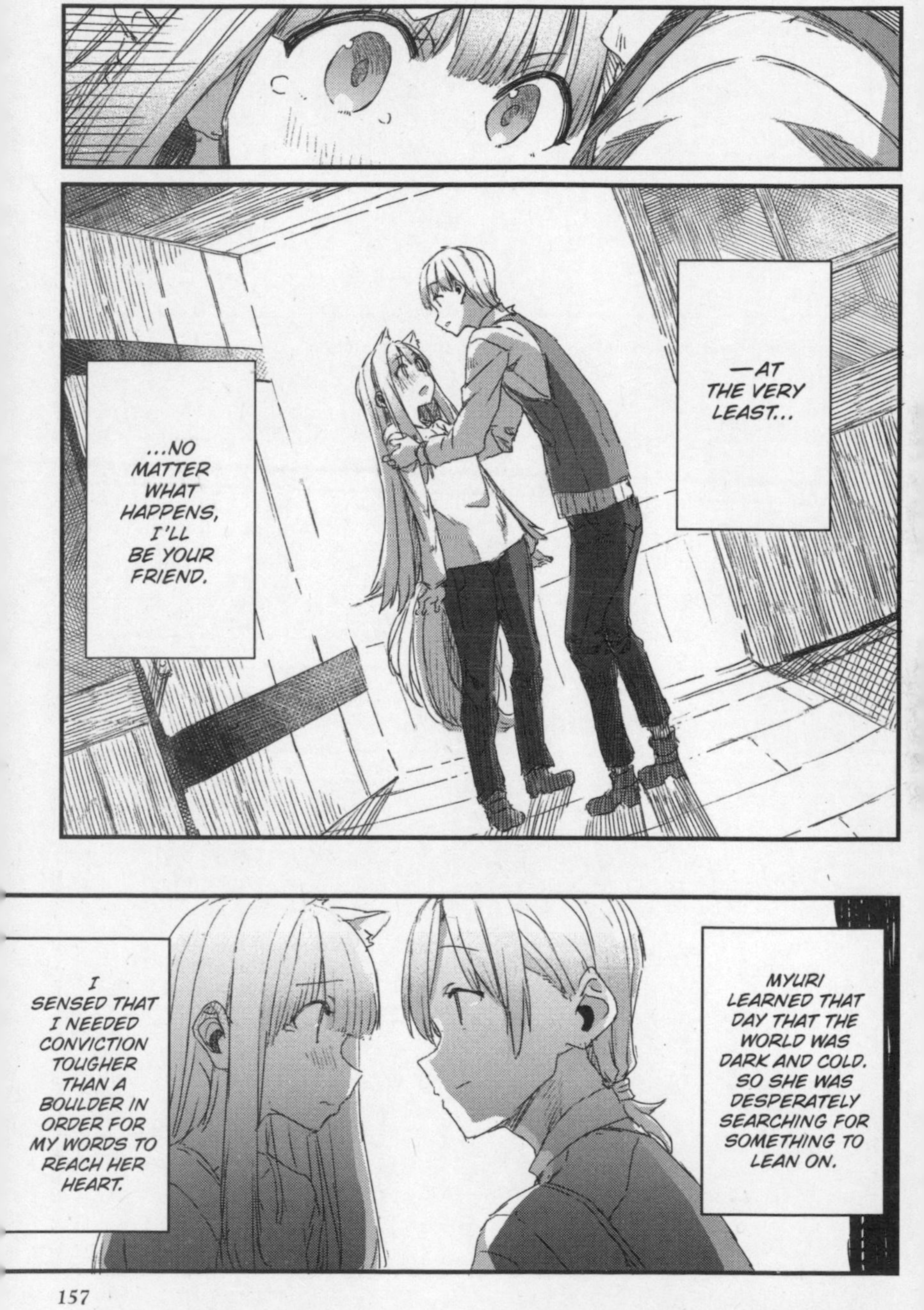
—AT THE VERY LEAST...
...NO MATTER WHAT HAPPENS, I'LL BE YOUR FRIEND.
MYURI LEARNED THAT DAY THAT THE WORLD WAS DARK AND COLD. SO SHE WAS DESPERATELY SEARCHING FOR SOMETHING TO LEAN ON.
I SENSED THAT I NEEDED CONVICTION TOUGHER THAN A BOULDER IN ORDER FOR MY WORDS TO REACH HER HEART.

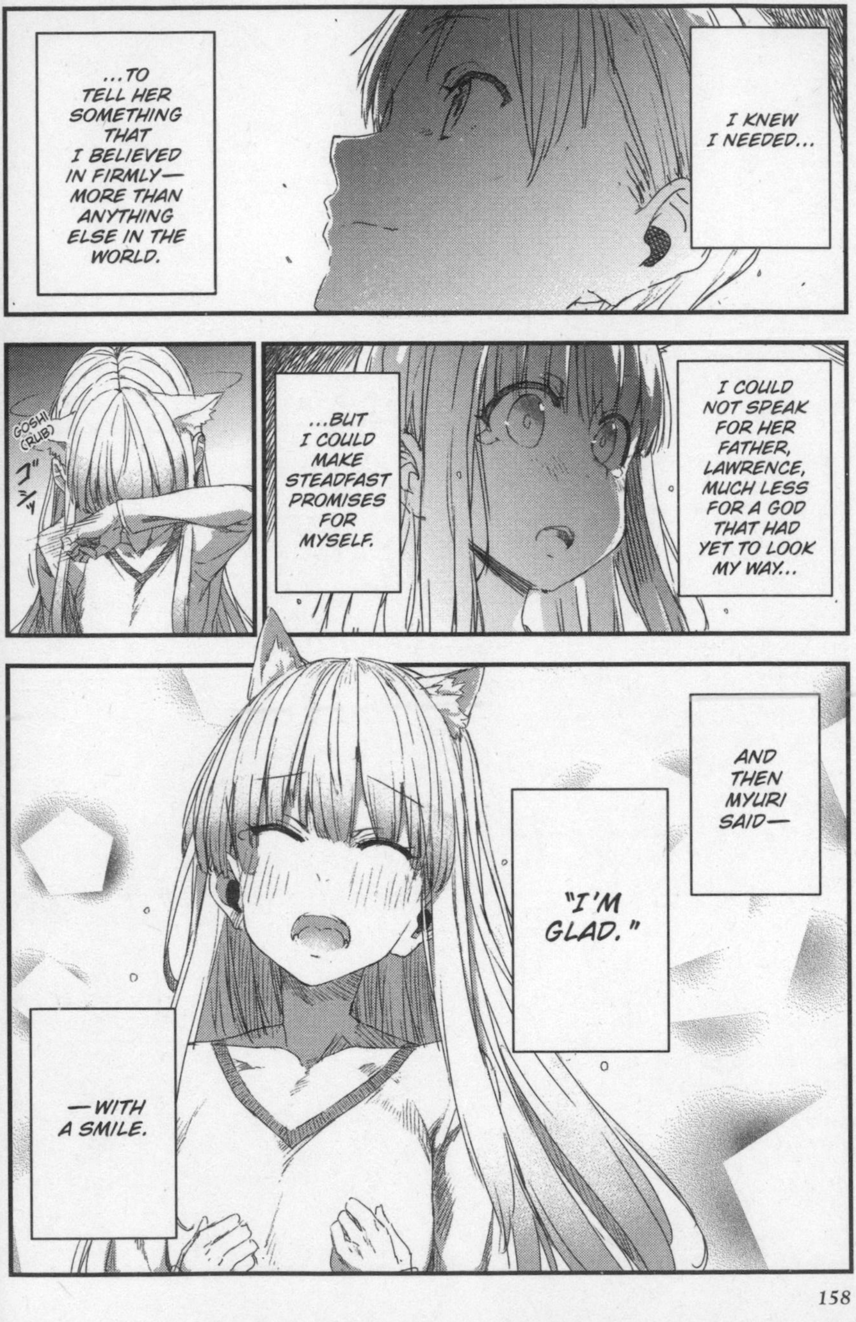
I KNEW I NEEDED...
...TO TELL HER SOMETHING THAT I BELIEVED IN FIRMLY—MORE THAN ANYTHING ELSE IN THE WORLD.
I COULD NOT SPEAK FOR HER FATHER, LAWRENCE, MUCH LESS FOR A GOD THAT HAD YET TO LOOK MY WAY...
...BUT I COULD MAKE STEADFAST PROMISES FOR MYSELF.
ゴシッ
GOSHI (RUB)
AND THEN MYURI SAID—
"I'M GLAD."
—WITH A SMILE.

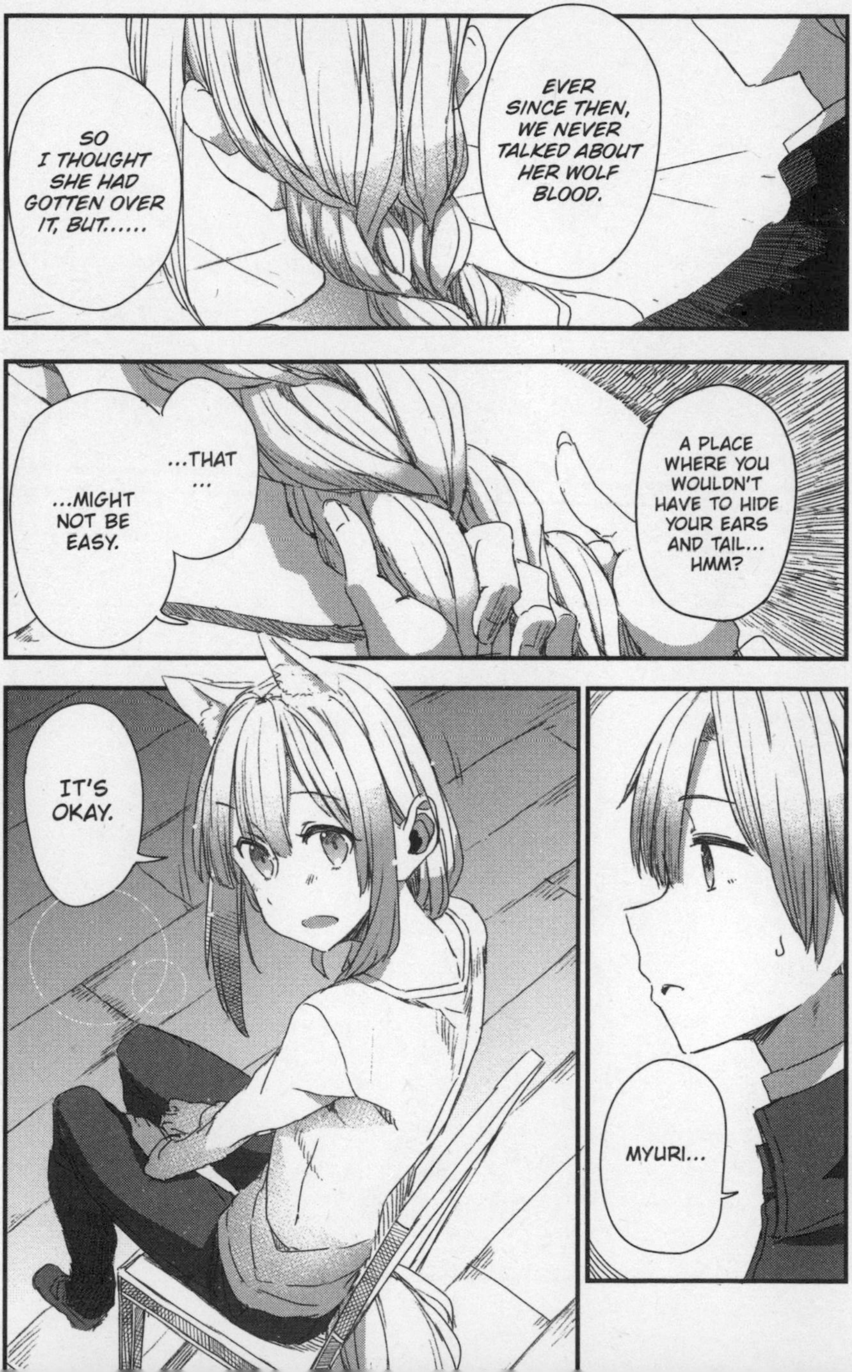
EVER SINCE THEN, WE NEVER TALKED ABOUT HER WOLF BLOOD.
SO I THOUGHT SHE HAD GOTTEN OVER IT, BUT......
A PLACE WHERE YOU WOULDN'T HAVE TO HIDE YOUR EARS AND TAIL... HMM?
...THAT ...
...MIGHT NOT BE EASY.
MYURI...
IT'S OKAY.

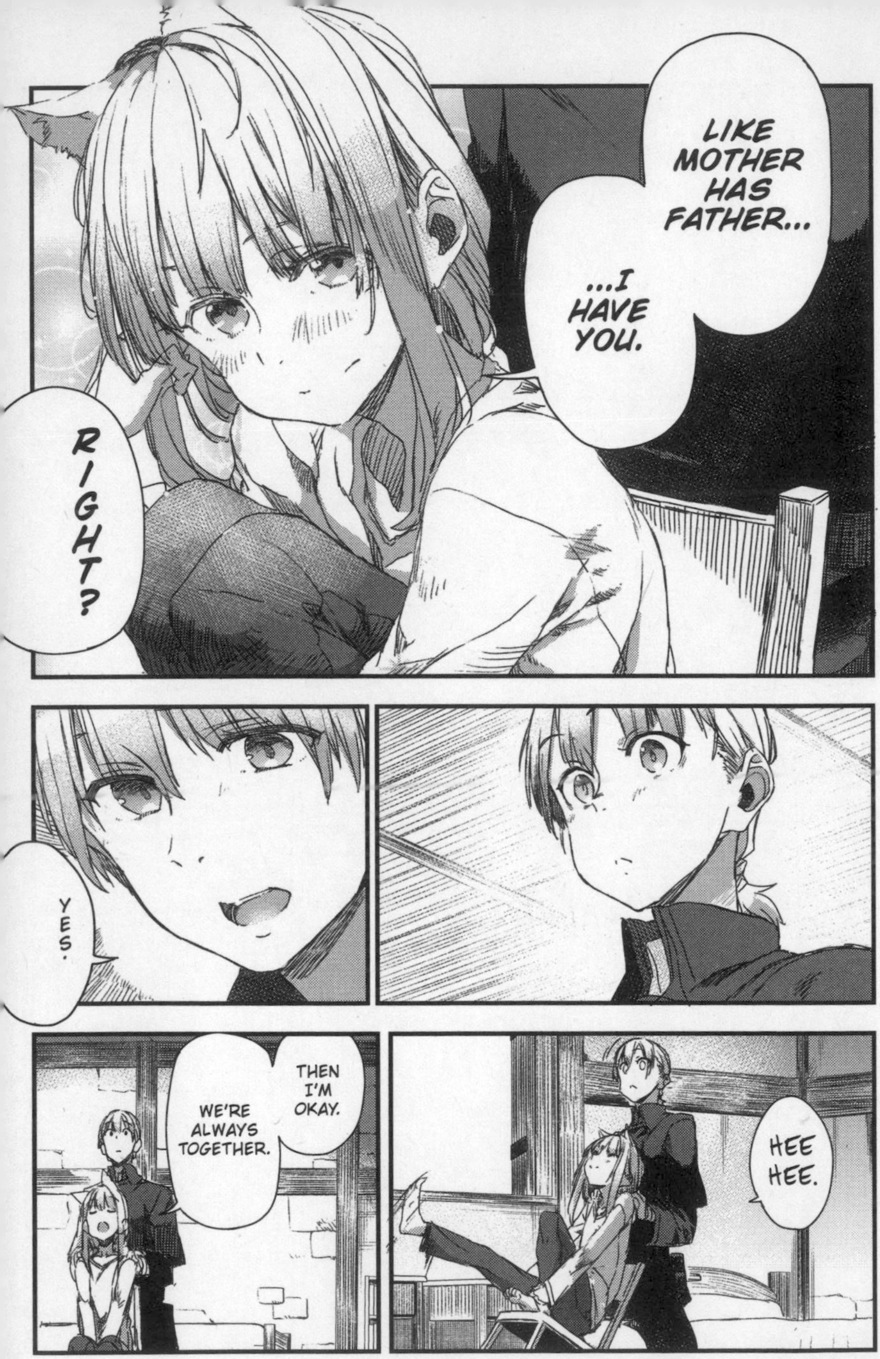
LIKE MOTHER HAS FATHER...
...I HAVE YOU.
RIGHT?
YES.
HEE HEE.
THEN I'M OKAY.
WE'RE ALWAYS TOGETHER.

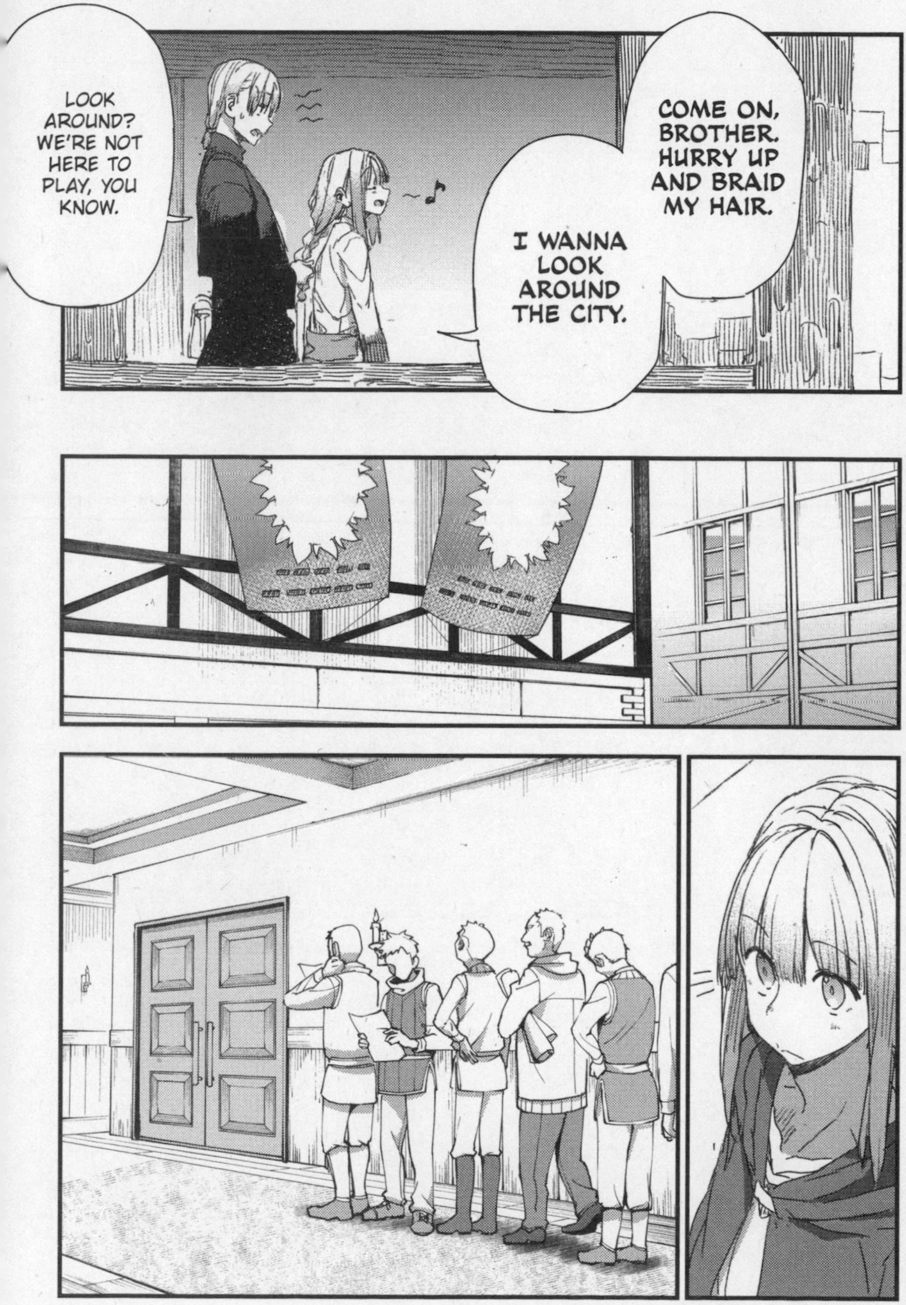
COME ON, BROTHER. HURRY UP AND BRAID MY HAIR.
I WANNA LOOK AROUND THE CITY.
LOOK AROUND? WE'RE NOT HERE TO PLAY, YOU KNOW.

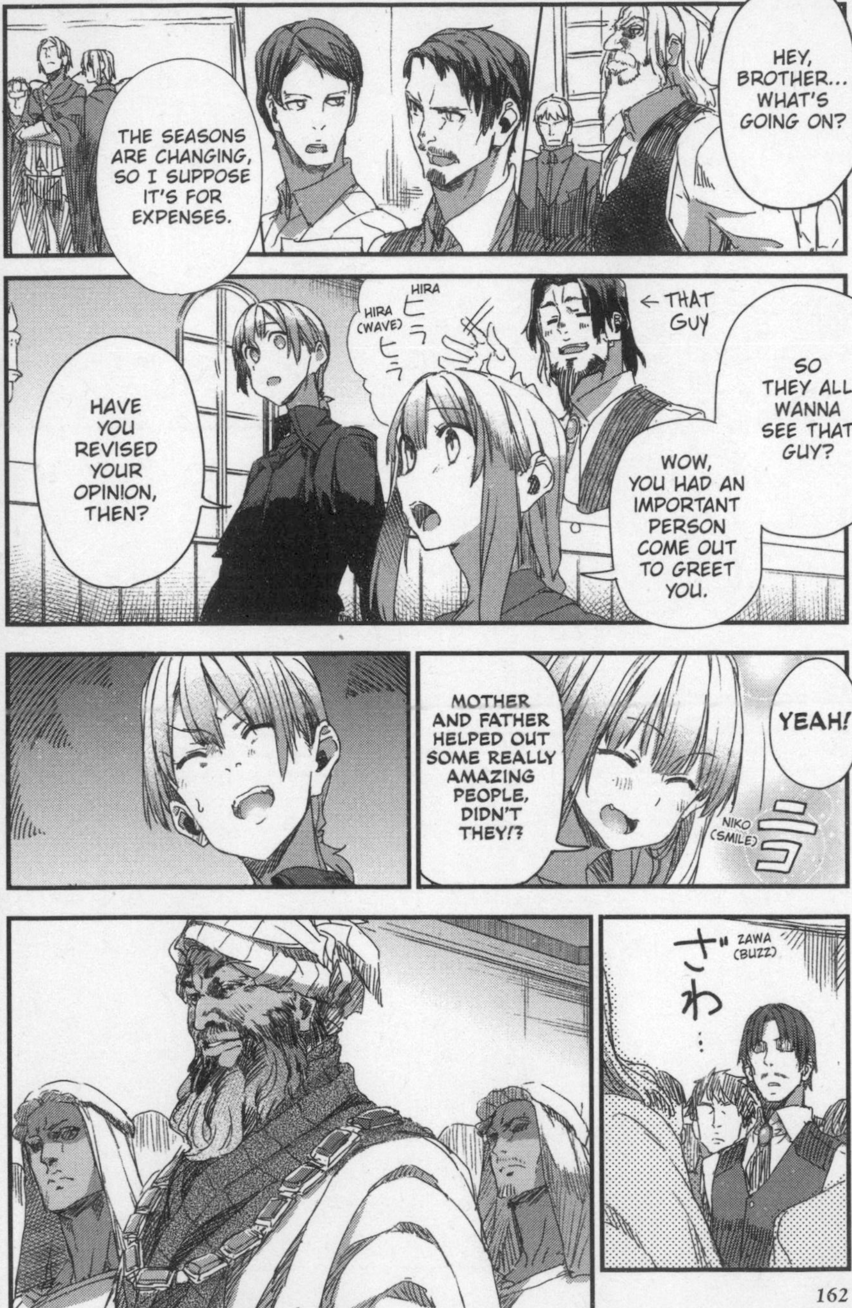
HEY, BROTHER... WHAT'S GOING ON?
THE SEASONS ARE CHANGING, SO I SUPPOSE IT'S FOR EXPENSES.
SO THEY ALL WANNA SEE THAT GUY?
← THAT GUY
ヒラヒラ HIRA HIRA (WAVE)
WOW, YOU HAD AN IMPORTANT PERSON COME OUT TO GREET YOU.
HAVE YOU REVISED YOUR OPINION, THEN?
YEAH!
ニコ NIKO (SMILE)
MOTHER AND FATHER HELPED OUT SOME REALLY AMAZING PEOPLE, DIDN'T THEY!?
ざわ… ZAWA (BUZZ)

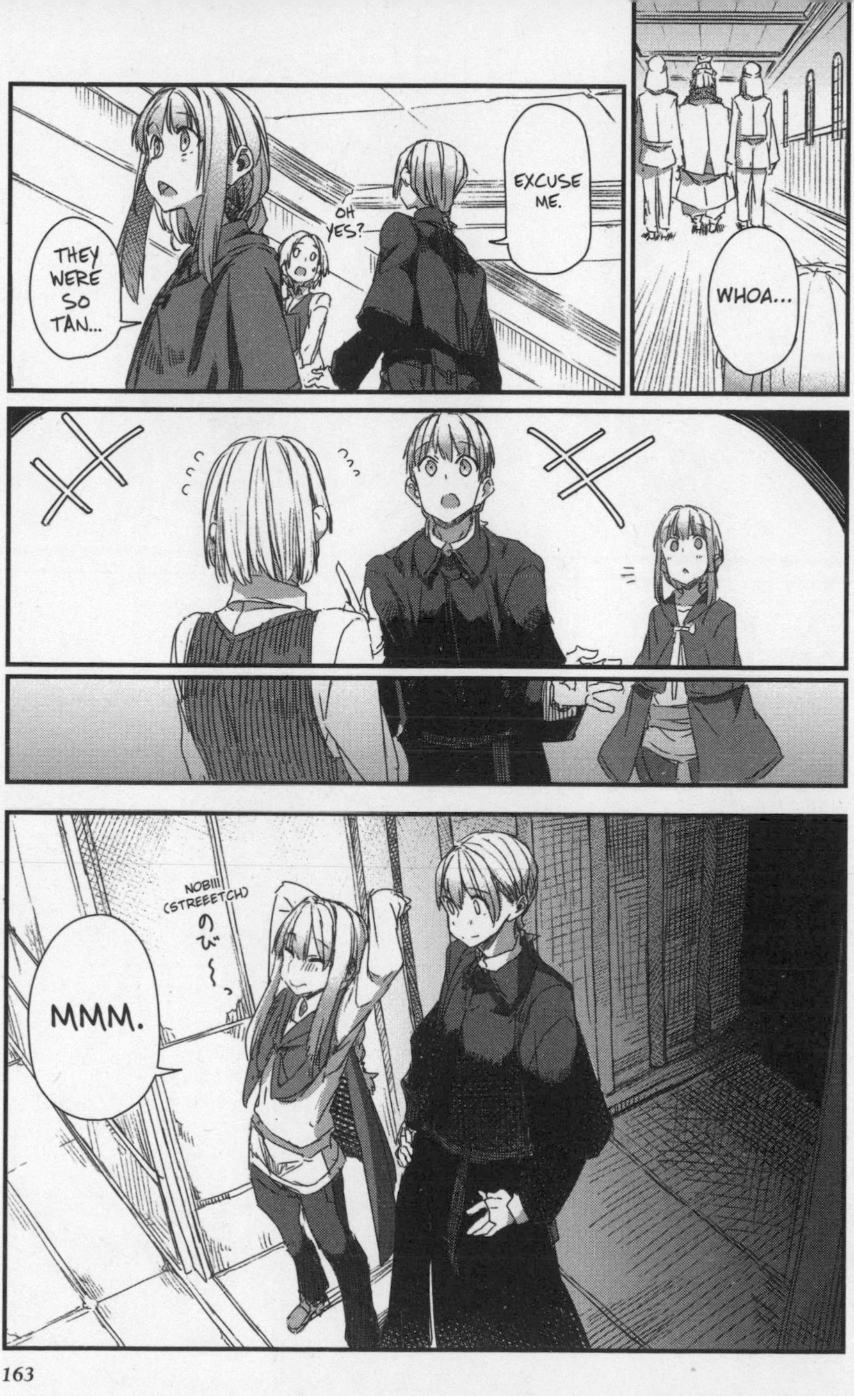
WHOA...
EXCUSE ME.
OH YES?
THEY WERE SO TAN...
NOBIII (STREEETCH)
のび～っ
MMM.

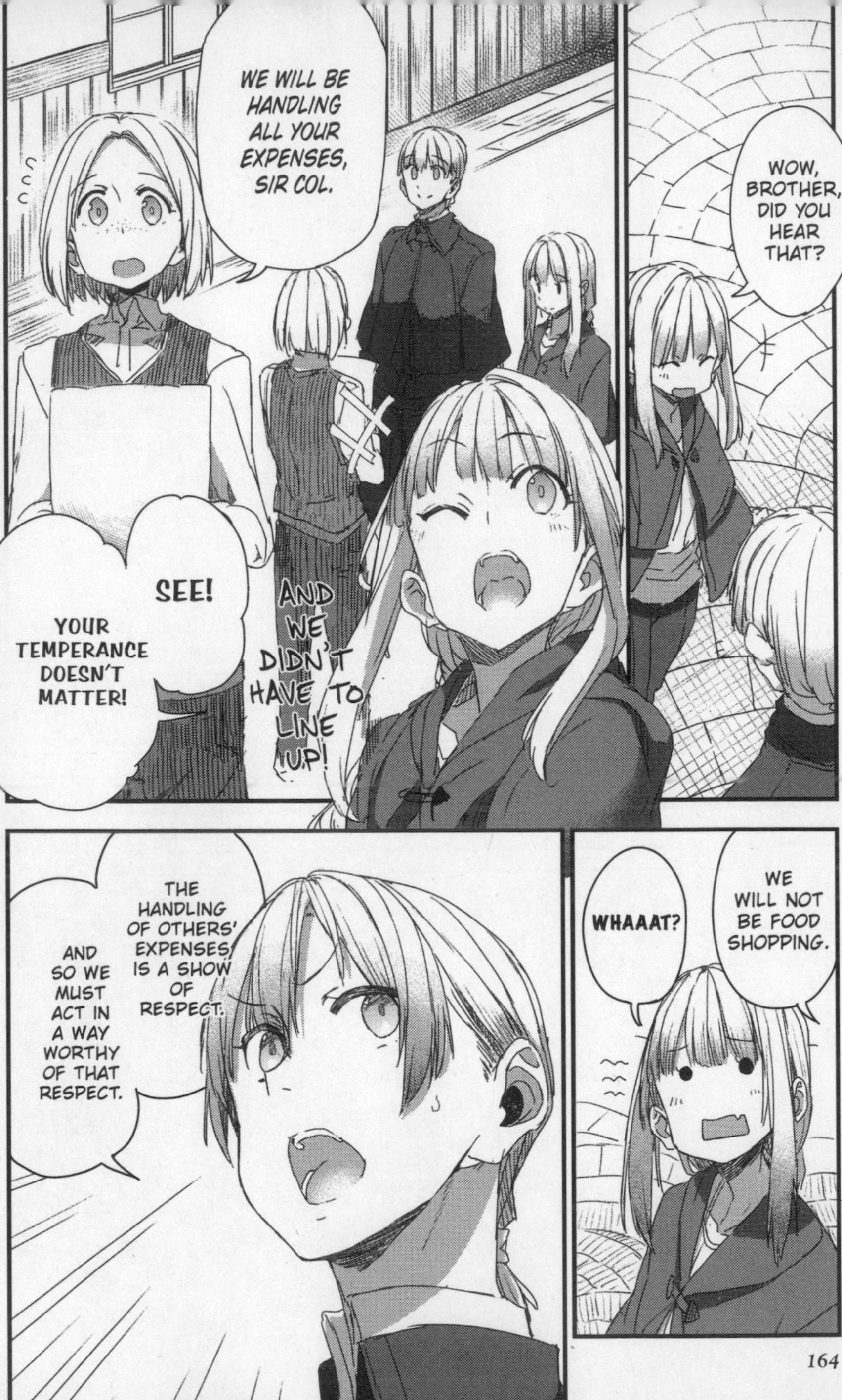
WOW, BROTHER, DID YOU HEAR THAT?
WE WILL BE HANDLING ALL YOUR EXPENSES, SIR COL.
SEE!
YOUR TEMPERANCE DOESN'T MATTER!
AND WE DIDN'T HAVE TO LINE UP!
WE WILL NOT BE FOOD SHOPPING.
WHAAAT?
THE HANDLING OF OTHERS' EXPENSES IS A SHOW OF RESPECT.
AND SO WE MUST ACT IN A WAY WORTHY OF THAT RESPECT.

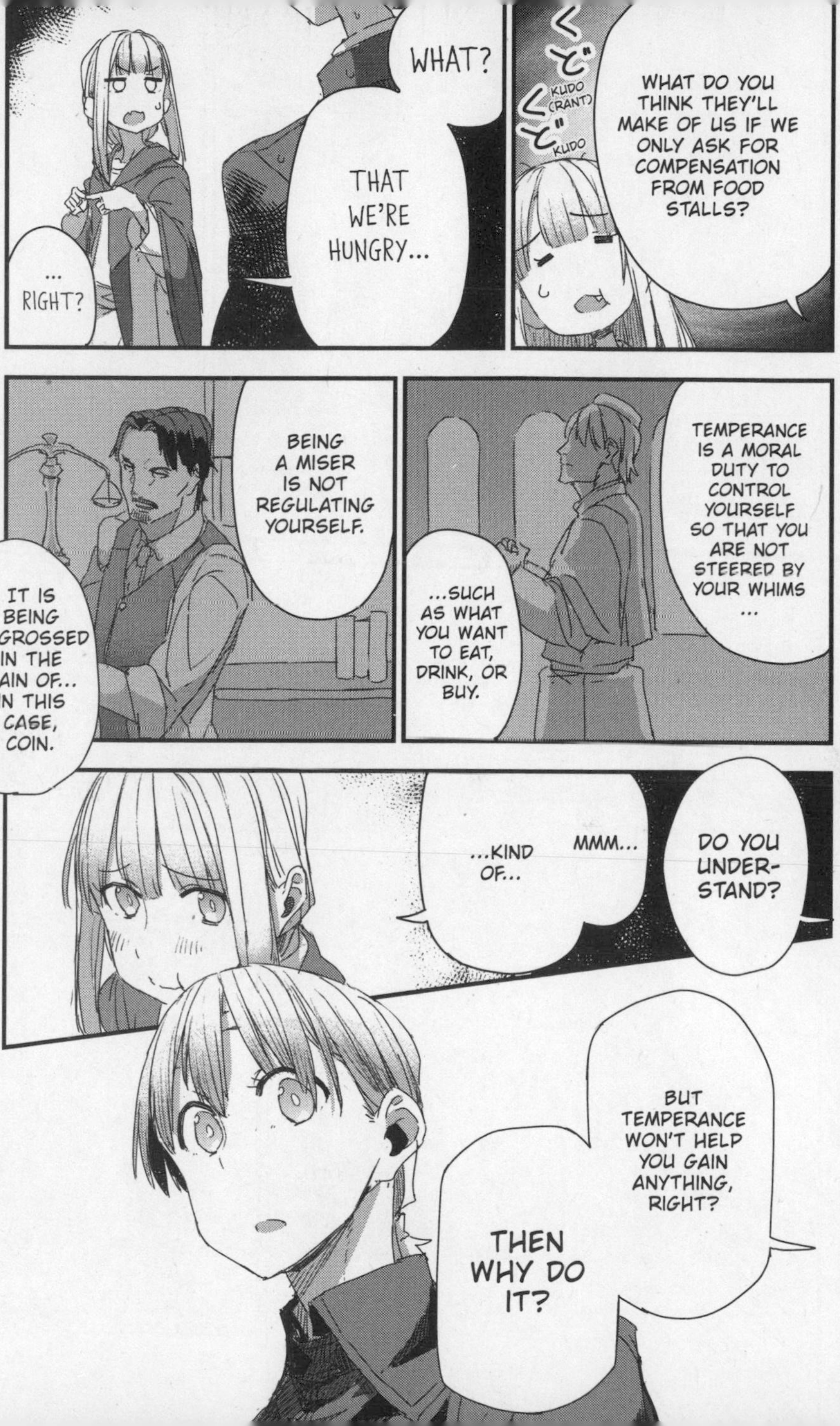
くどくど
KUDO (RANT) KUDO
WHAT DO YOU THINK THEY'LL MAKE OF US IF WE ONLY ASK FOR COMPENSATION FROM FOOD STALLS?
WHAT?
THAT WE'RE HUNGRY...
...RIGHT?
TEMPERANCE IS A MORAL DUTY TO CONTROL YOURSELF SO THAT YOU ARE NOT STEERED BY YOUR WHIMS...
...SUCH AS WHAT YOU WANT TO EAT, DRINK, OR BUY.
BEING A MISER IS NOT REGULATING YOURSELF.
IT IS BEING ENGROSSED IN THE GAIN OF... IN THIS CASE, COIN.
DO YOU UNDER-STAND?
MMM...
...KIND OF...
BUT TEMPERANCE WON'T HELP YOU GAIN ANYTHING, RIGHT?
THEN WHY DO IT?

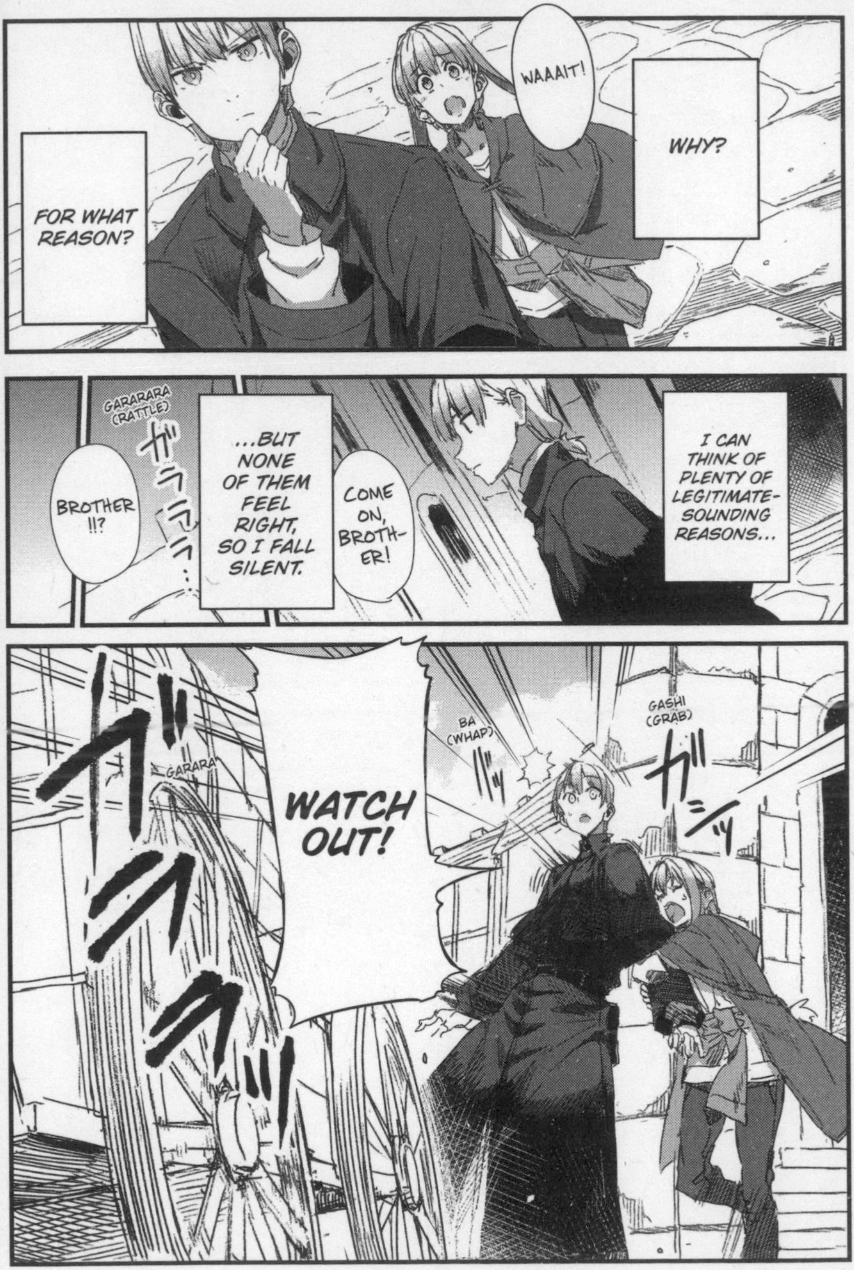
WAAAIT!
WHY?
FOR WHAT REASON?
I CAN THINK OF PLENTY OF LEGITIMATE-SOUNDING REASONS...
COME ON, BROTHER!
...BUT NONE OF THEM FEEL RIGHT, SO I FALL SILENT.
GARARARA (RATTLE)
BROTHER!!?
GASHI (GRAB)
BA (WHAP)
WATCH OUT!
GARARA

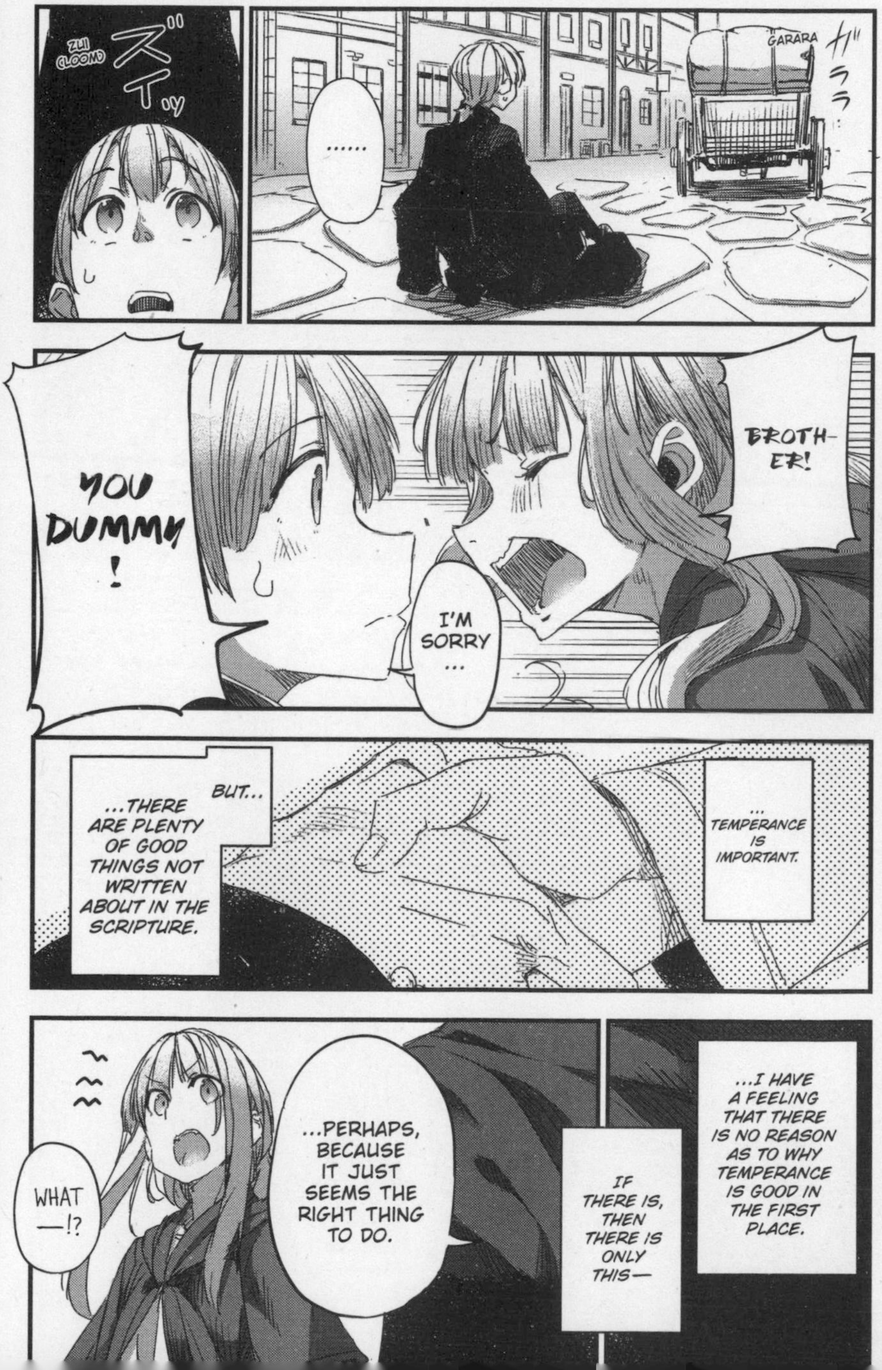
GARARA
ガララ
......
ZUI (LOOM)
ズイッ
BROTH-ER!
YOU DUMMY!
I'M SORRY ...
... TEMPERANCE IS IMPORTANT.
BUT...
...THERE ARE PLENTY OF GOOD THINGS NOT WRITTEN ABOUT IN THE SCRIPTURE.
...I HAVE A FEELING THAT THERE IS NO REASON AS TO WHY TEMPERANCE IS GOOD IN THE FIRST PLACE.
IF THERE IS, THEN THERE IS ONLY THIS—
...PERHAPS, BECAUSE IT JUST SEEMS THE RIGHT THING TO DO.
WHAT—!?

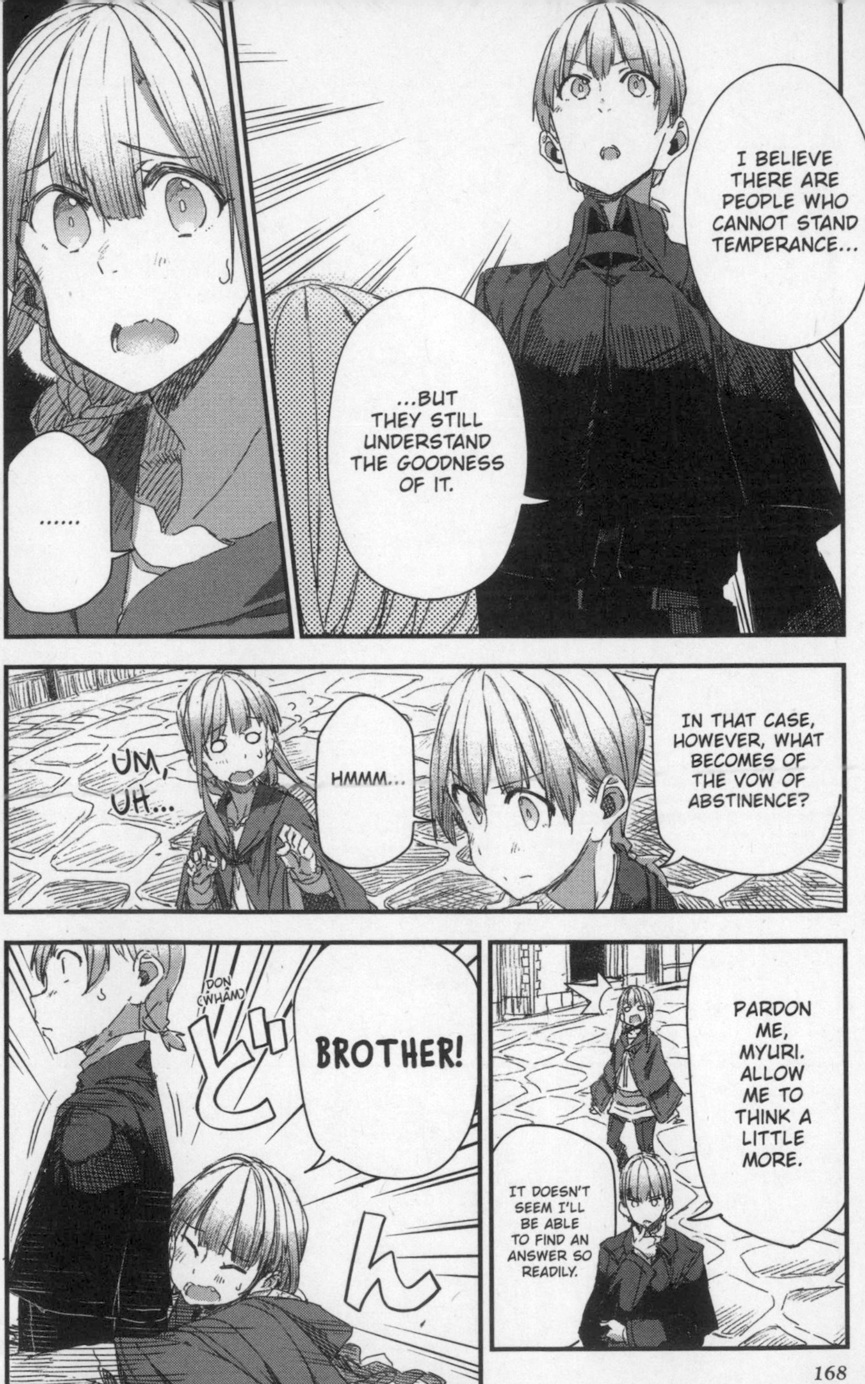
I BELIEVE THERE ARE PEOPLE WHO CANNOT STAND TEMPERANCE...
...BUT THEY STILL UNDERSTAND THE GOODNESS OF IT.
......
IN THAT CASE, HOWEVER, WHAT BECOMES OF THE VOW OF ABSTINENCE?
HMMM...
UM, UH...
PARDON ME, MYURI. ALLOW ME TO THINK A LITTLE MORE.
IT DOESN'T SEEM I'LL BE ABLE TO FIND AN ANSWER SO READILY.
BROTHER!
DON (WHAM)
どん

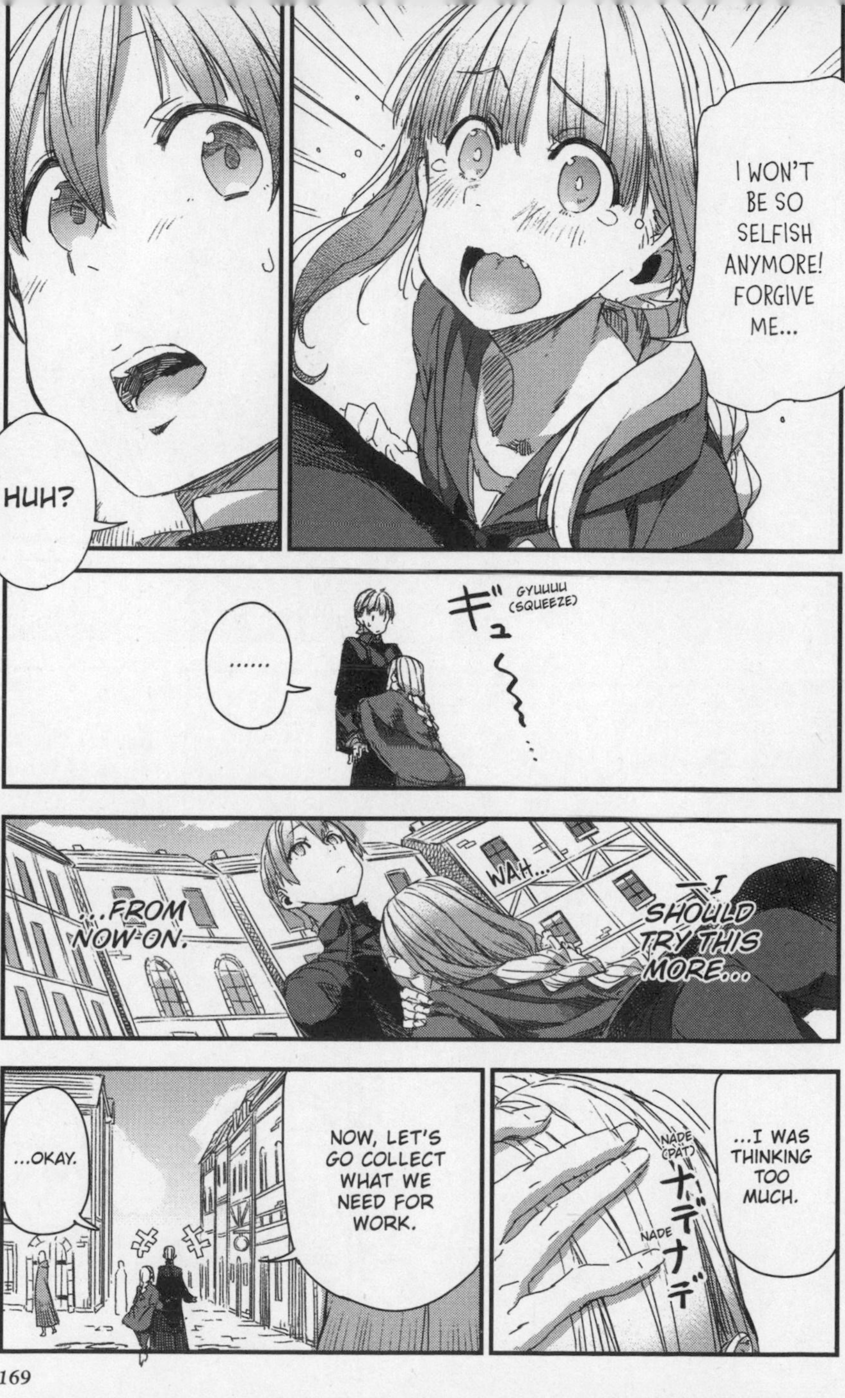
I WON'T BE SO SELFISH ANYMORE! FORGIVE ME...
HUH?
ギュ〜〜…
GYUUUU (SQUEEZE)
......
—I SHOULD TRY THIS MORE...
WAH...
...FROM NOW ON.
...I WAS THINKING TOO MUCH.
NADE (PAT)
ナデナデ
NADE
NOW, LET'S GO COLLECT WHAT WE NEED FOR WORK.
...OKAY.

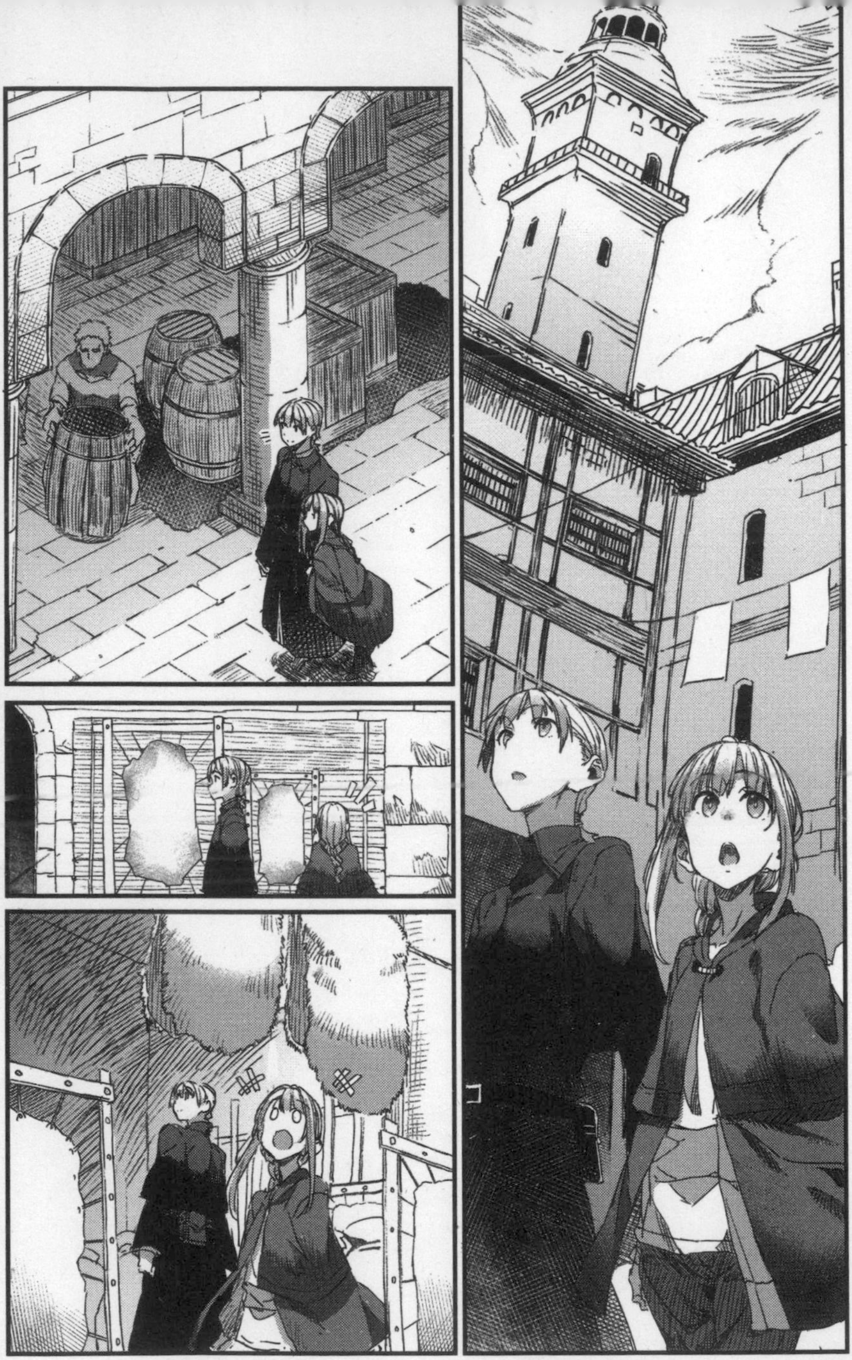

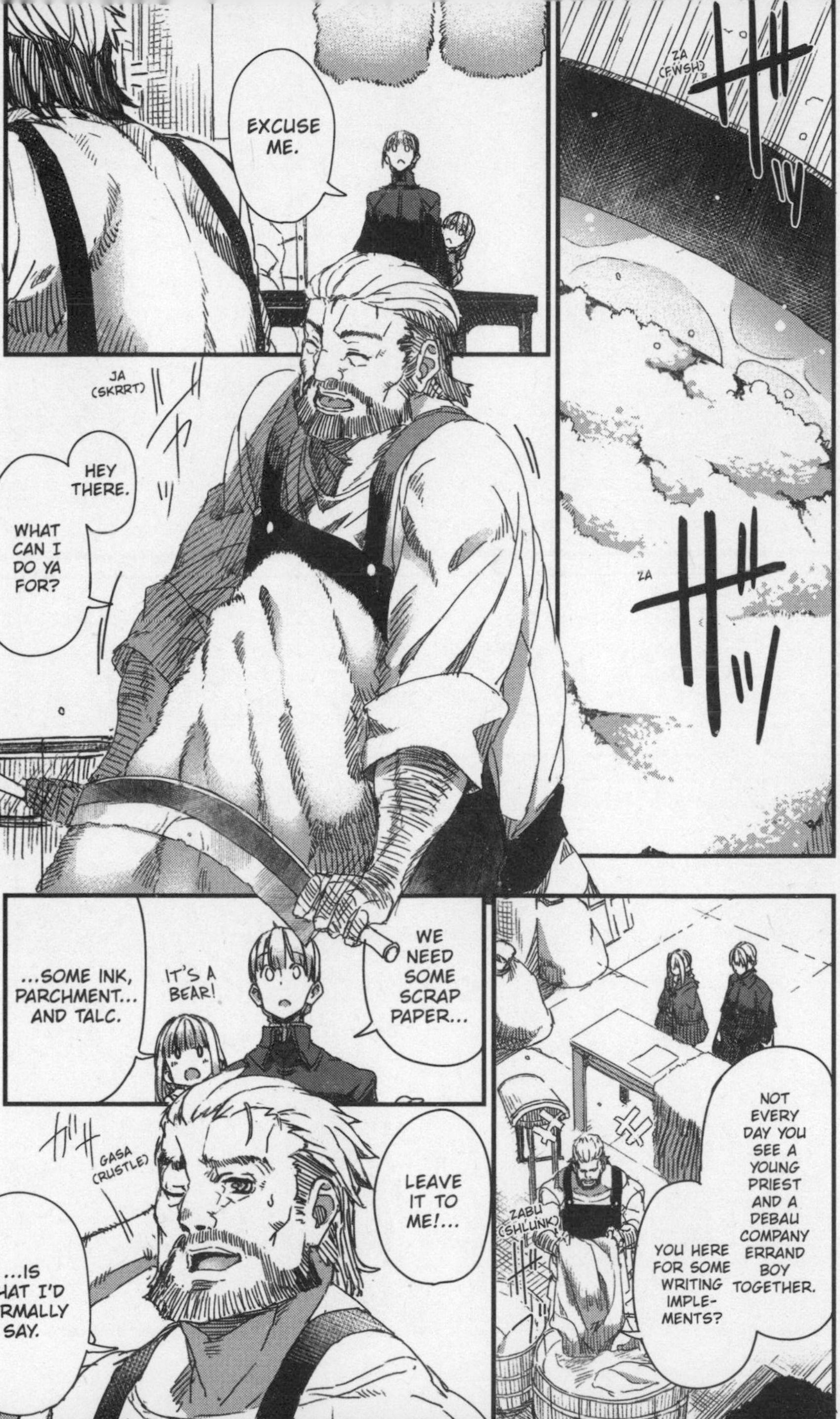
ZA (FWSH)
ZA
EXCUSE ME.
JA (SKRRT)
HEY THERE.
WHAT CAN I DO YA FOR?
NOT EVERY DAY YOU SEE A YOUNG PRIEST AND A DEBAU COMPANY ERRAND BOY TOGETHER.
YOU HERE FOR SOME WRITING IMPLE-MENTS?
ZABU (SHLUNK)
WE NEED SOME SCRAP PAPER...
IT'S A BEAR!
...SOME INK, PARCHMENT... AND TALC.
LEAVE IT TO ME!...
GASA (RUSTLE)
...IS WHAT I'D NORMALLY SAY.

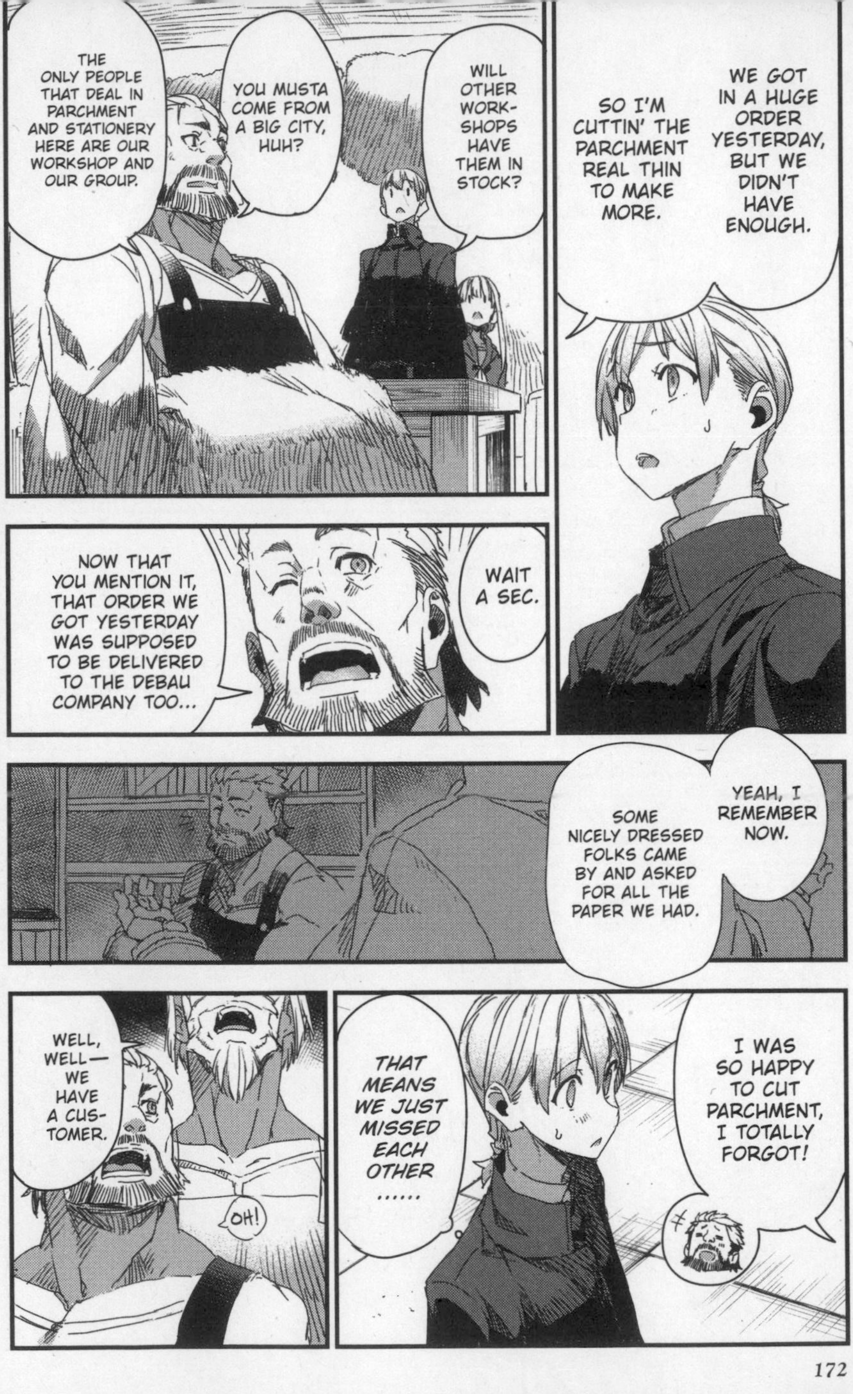
WE GOT IN A HUGE ORDER YESTERDAY, BUT WE DIDN'T HAVE ENOUGH.
SO I'M CUTTIN' THE PARCHMENT REAL THIN TO MAKE MORE.
WILL OTHER WORK-SHOPS HAVE THEM IN STOCK?
YOU MUSTA COME FROM A BIG CITY, HUH?
THE ONLY PEOPLE THAT DEAL IN PARCHMENT AND STATIONERY HERE ARE OUR WORKSHOP AND OUR GROUP.
WAIT A SEC.
NOW THAT YOU MENTION IT, THAT ORDER WE GOT YESTERDAY WAS SUPPOSED TO BE DELIVERED TO THE DEBAU COMPANY TOO...
YEAH, I REMEMBER NOW.
SOME NICELY DRESSED FOLKS CAME BY AND ASKED FOR ALL THE PAPER WE HAD.
I WAS SO HAPPY TO CUT PARCHMENT, I TOTALLY FORGOT!
THAT MEANS WE JUST MISSED EACH OTHER ......
WELL, WELL— WE HAVE A CUS-TOMER.
OH!

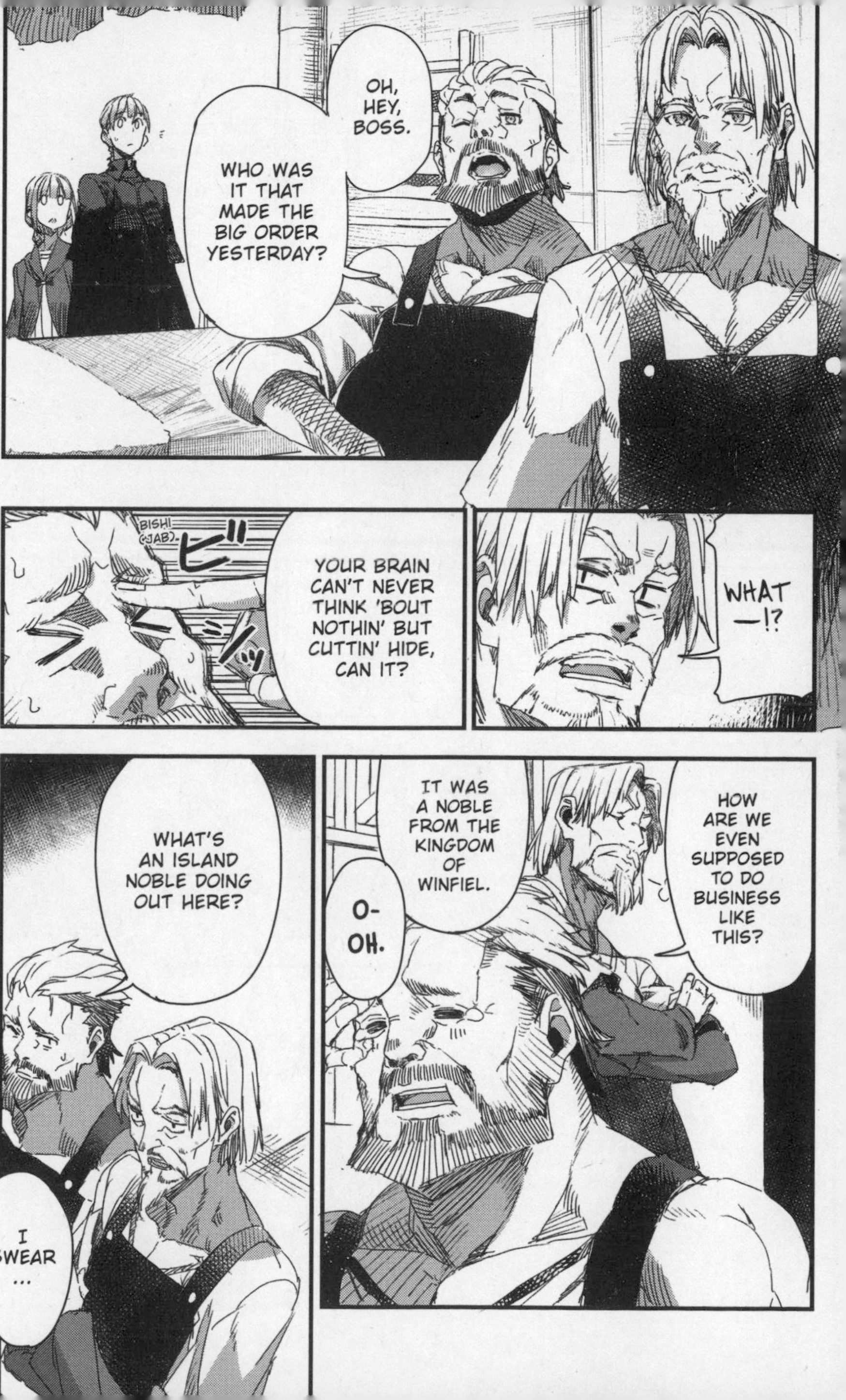
OH, HEY, BOSS.
WHO WAS IT THAT MADE THE BIG ORDER YESTERDAY?
WHAT—!?
BISHI (JAB)
YOUR BRAIN CAN'T NEVER THINK 'BOUT NOTHIN' BUT CUTTIN' HIDE, CAN IT?
HOW ARE WE EVEN SUPPOSED TO DO BUSINESS LIKE THIS?
IT WAS A NOBLE FROM THE KINGDOM OF WINFIEL.
O-OH.
WHAT'S AN ISLAND NOBLE DOING OUT HERE?
I SWEAR...

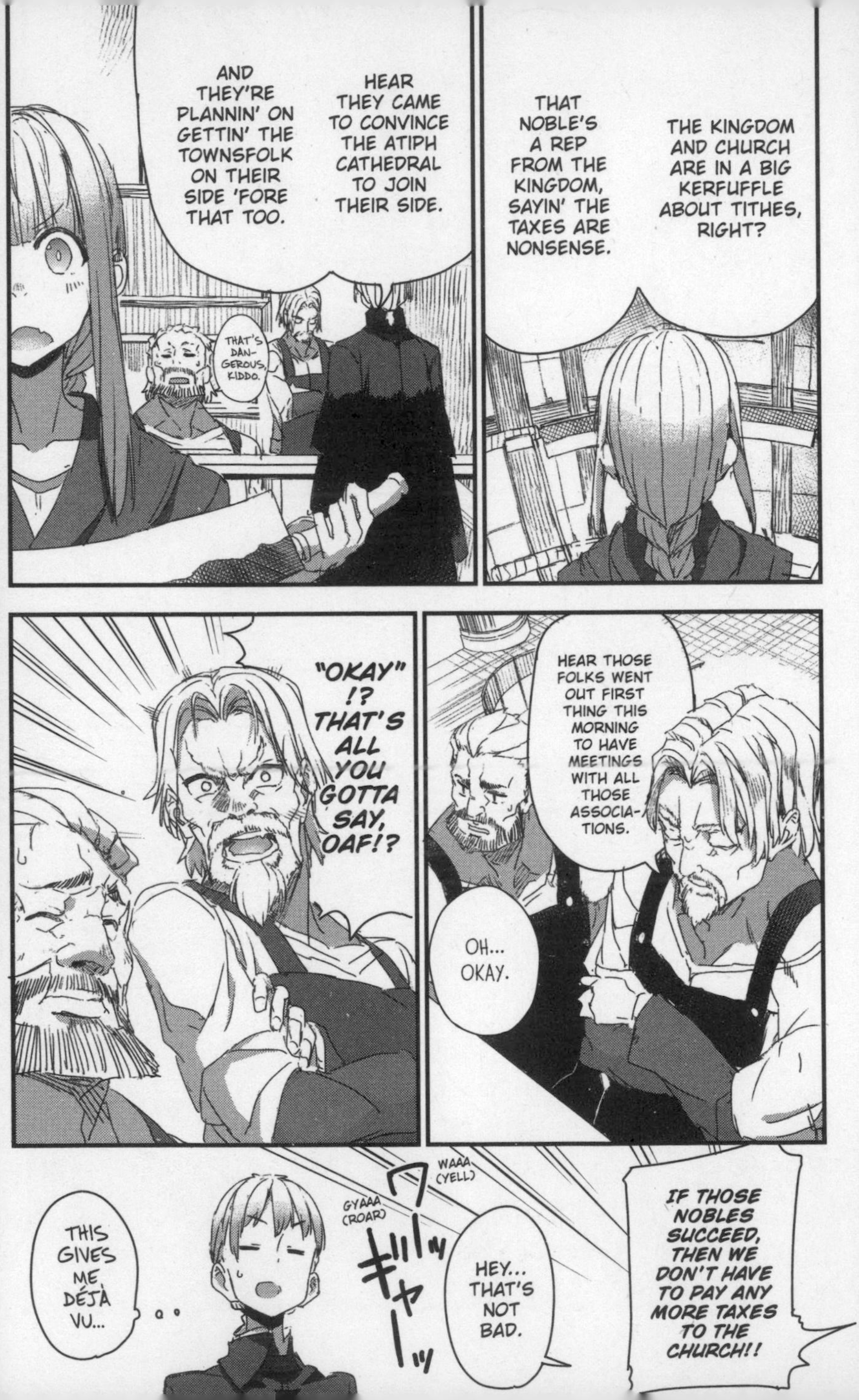
THE KINGDOM AND CHURCH ARE IN A BIG KERFUFFLE ABOUT TITHES, RIGHT?
THAT NOBLE'S A REP FROM THE KINGDOM, SAYIN' THE TAXES ARE NONSENSE.
HEAR THEY CAME TO CONVINCE THE ATIPH CATHEDRAL TO JOIN THEIR SIDE.
AND THEY'RE PLANNIN' ON GETTIN' THE TOWNSFOLK ON THEIR SIDE 'FORE THAT TOO.
THAT'S DAN-GEROUS, KIDDO.
HEAR THOSE FOLKS WENT OUT FIRST THING THIS MORNING TO HAVE MEETINGS WITH ALL THOSE ASSOCIA-TIONS.
OH... OKAY.
"OKAY" !? THAT'S ALL YOU GOTTA SAY, OAF!?
IF THOSE NOBLES SUCCEED, THEN WE DON'T HAVE TO PAY ANY MORE TAXES TO THE CHURCH!!
WAAA (YELL)
GYAAA (ROAR)
HEY... THAT'S NOT BAD.
THIS GIVES ME DÉJÀ VU...

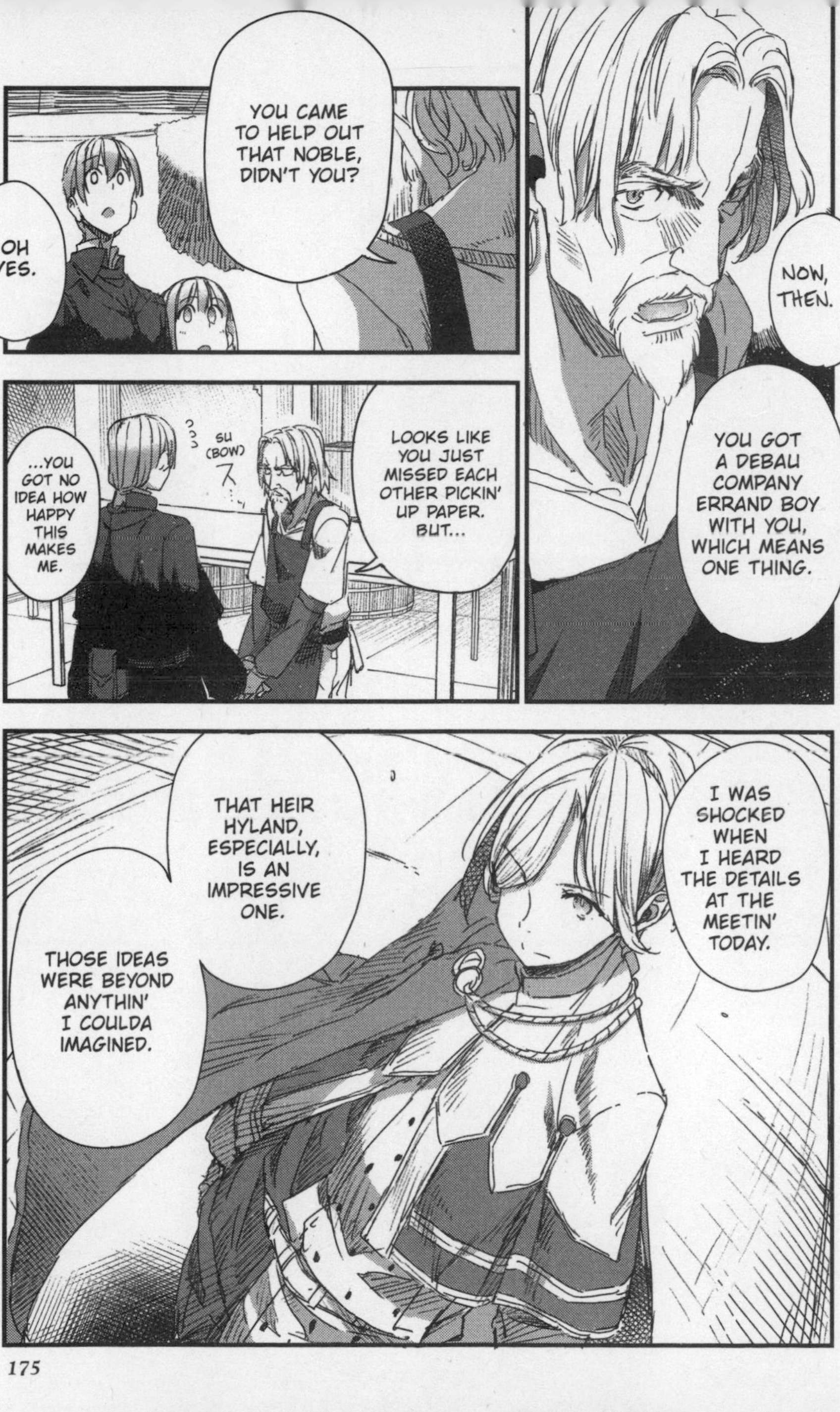
NOW, THEN.
YOU GOT A DEBAU COMPANY ERRAND BOY WITH YOU, WHICH MEANS ONE THING.
YOU CAME TO HELP OUT THAT NOBLE, DIDN'T YOU?
OH YES.
LOOKS LIKE YOU JUST MISSED EACH OTHER PICKIN' UP PAPER. BUT...
SU (BOW) ス
...YOU GOT NO IDEA HOW HAPPY THIS MAKES ME.
I WAS SHOCKED WHEN I HEARD THE DETAILS AT THE MEETIN' TODAY.
THAT HEIR HYLAND, ESPECIALLY, IS AN IMPRESSIVE ONE.
THOSE IDEAS WERE BEYOND ANYTHIN' I COULDA IMAGINED.

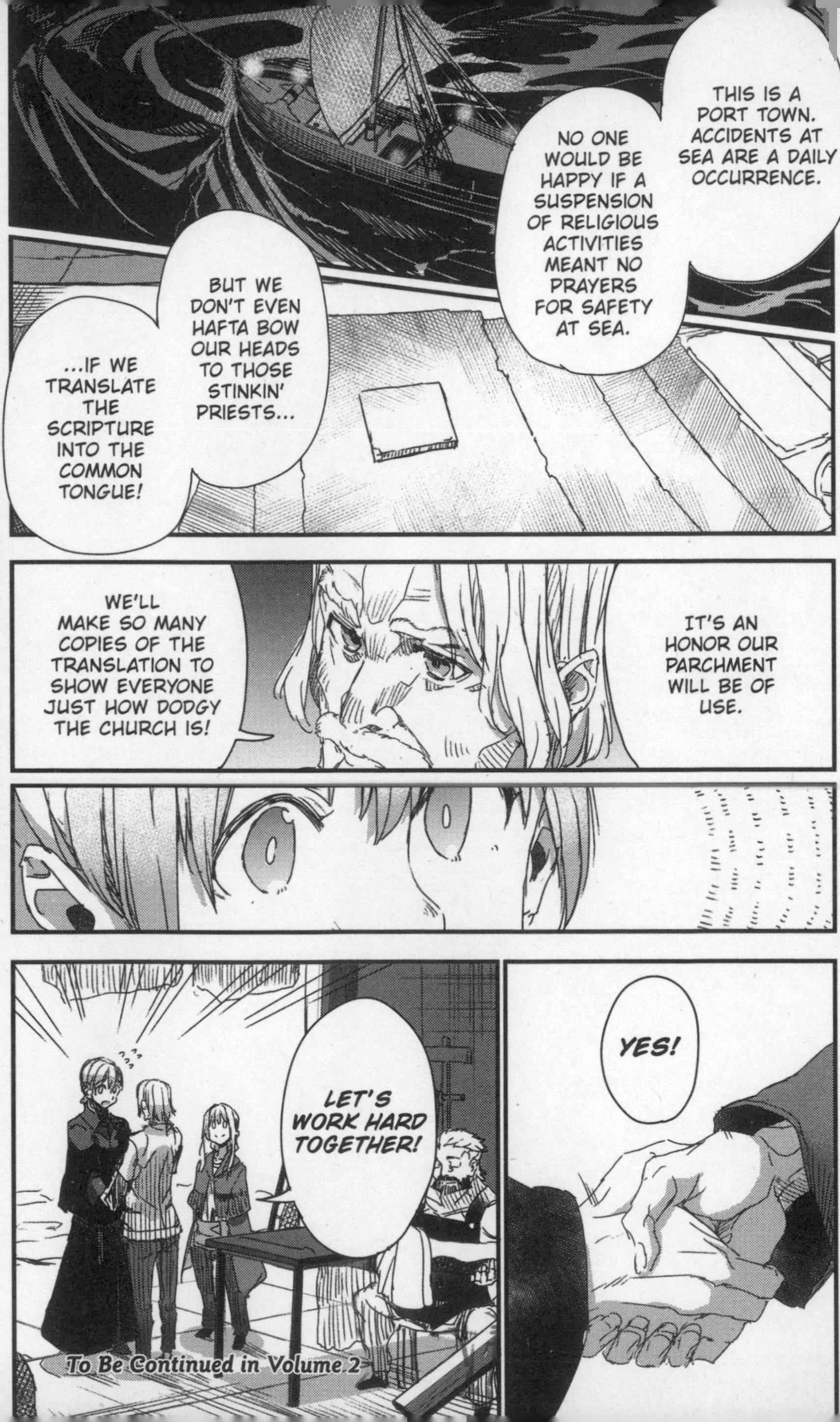
THIS IS A PORT TOWN. ACCIDENTS AT SEA ARE A DAILY OCCURRENCE.
NO ONE WOULD BE HAPPY IF A SUSPENSION OF RELIGIOUS ACTIVITIES MEANT NO PRAYERS FOR SAFETY AT SEA.
BUT WE DON'T EVEN HAFTA BOW OUR HEADS TO THOSE STINKIN' PRIESTS...
...IF WE TRANSLATE THE SCRIPTURE INTO THE COMMON TONGUE!
IT'S AN HONOR OUR PARCHMENT WILL BE OF USE.
WE'LL MAKE SO MANY COPIES OF THE TRANSLATION TO SHOW EVERYONE JUST HOW DODGY THE CHURCH IS!
YES!
LET'S WORK HARD TOGETHER!
To Be Continued in Volume 2

WOLF & PARCHMENT

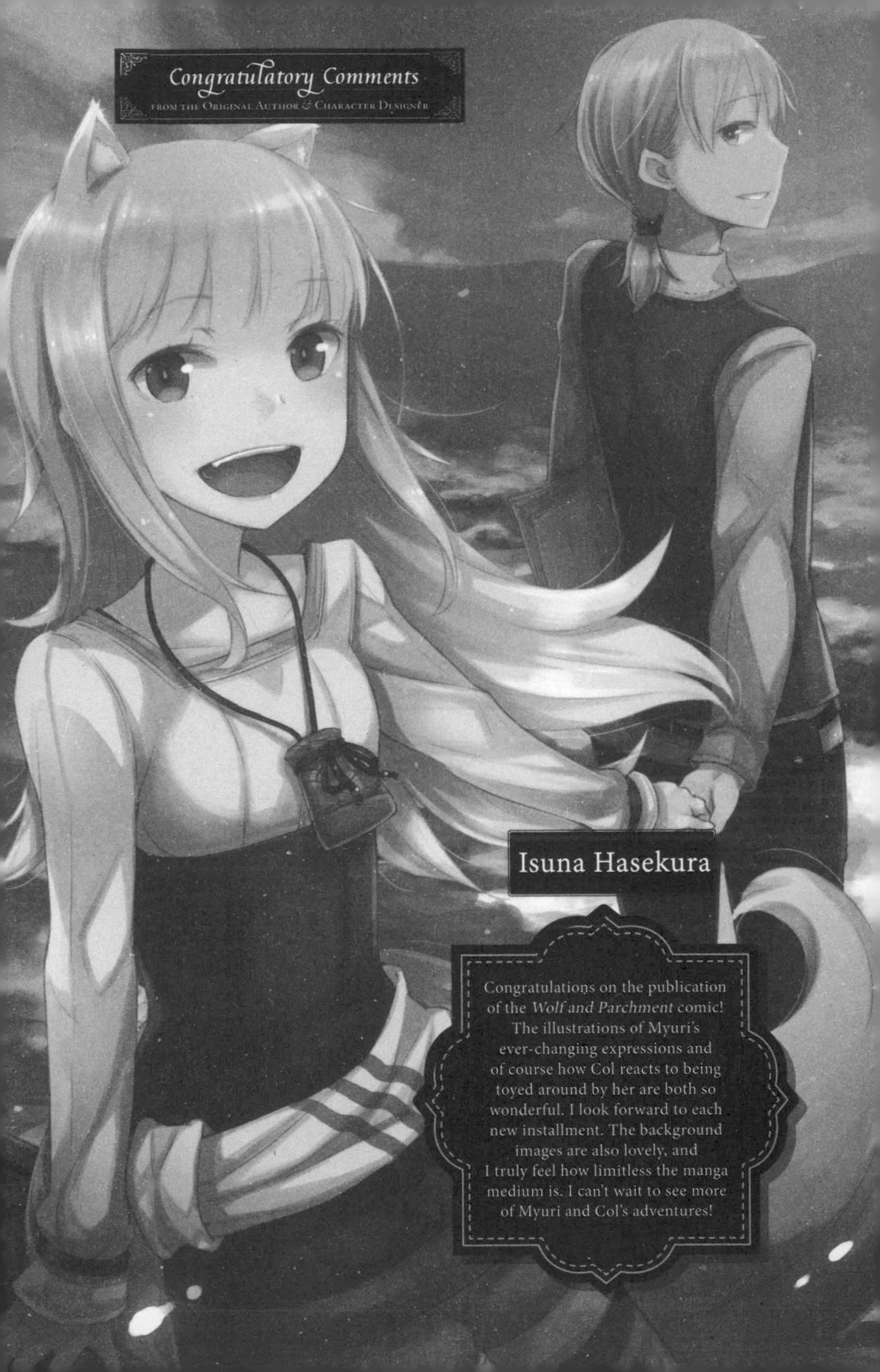
Congratulatory Comments
FROM THE ORIGINAL AUTHOR & CHARACTER DESIGNER
Isuna Hasekura
Congratulations on the publication of the *Wolf and Parchment* comic! The illustrations of Myuri's ever-changing expressions and of course how Col reacts to being toyed around by her are both so wonderful. I look forward to each new installment. The background images are also lovely, and I truly feel how limitless the manga medium is. I can't wait to see more of Myuri and Col's adventures!

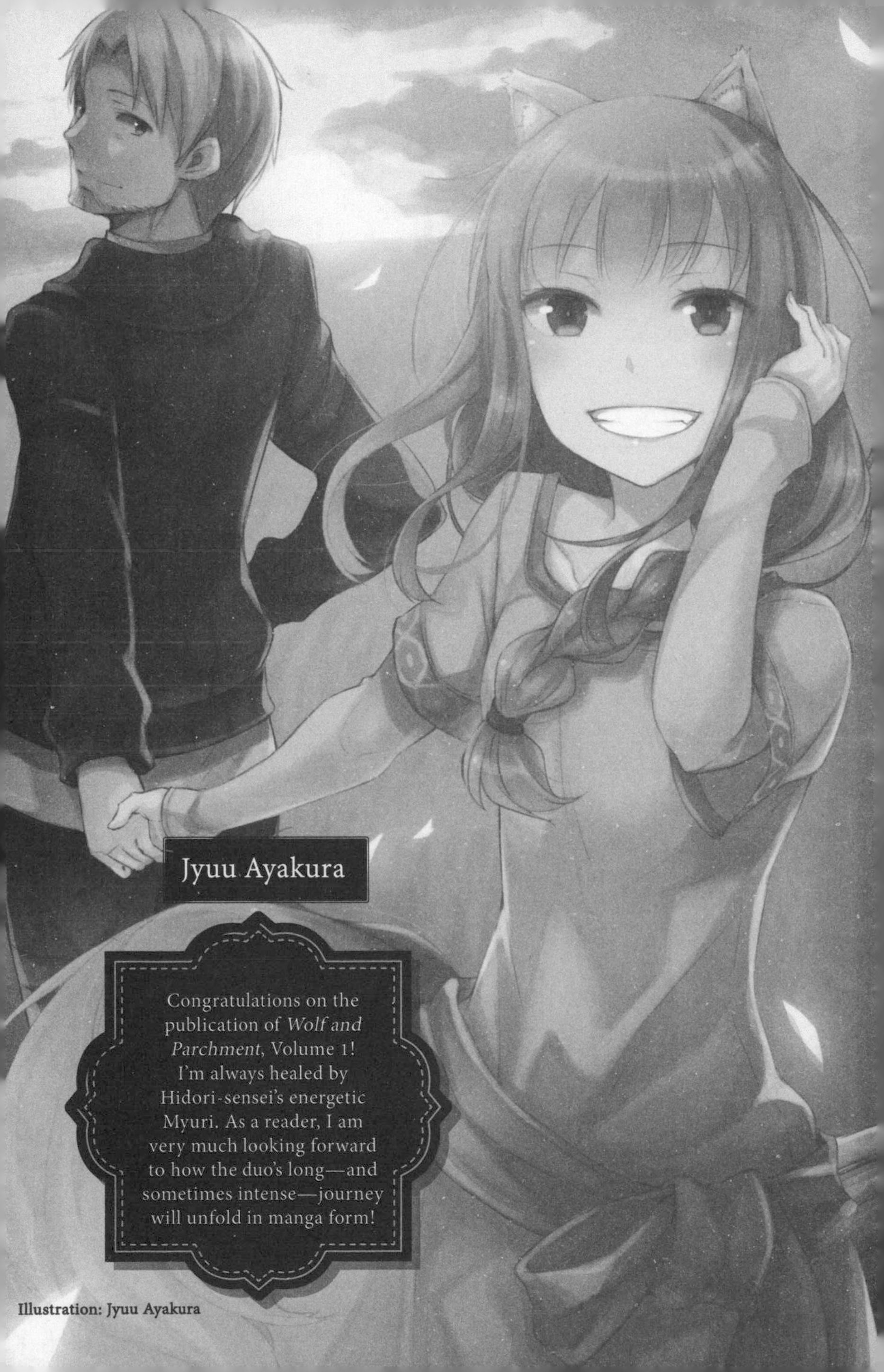
Jyuu Ayakura
Congratulations on the publication of *Wolf and Parchment*, Volume 1! I'm always healed by Hidori-sensei's energetic Myuri. As a reader, I am very much looking forward to how the duo's long—and sometimes intense—journey will unfold in manga form!

Illustration: Jyuu Ayakura

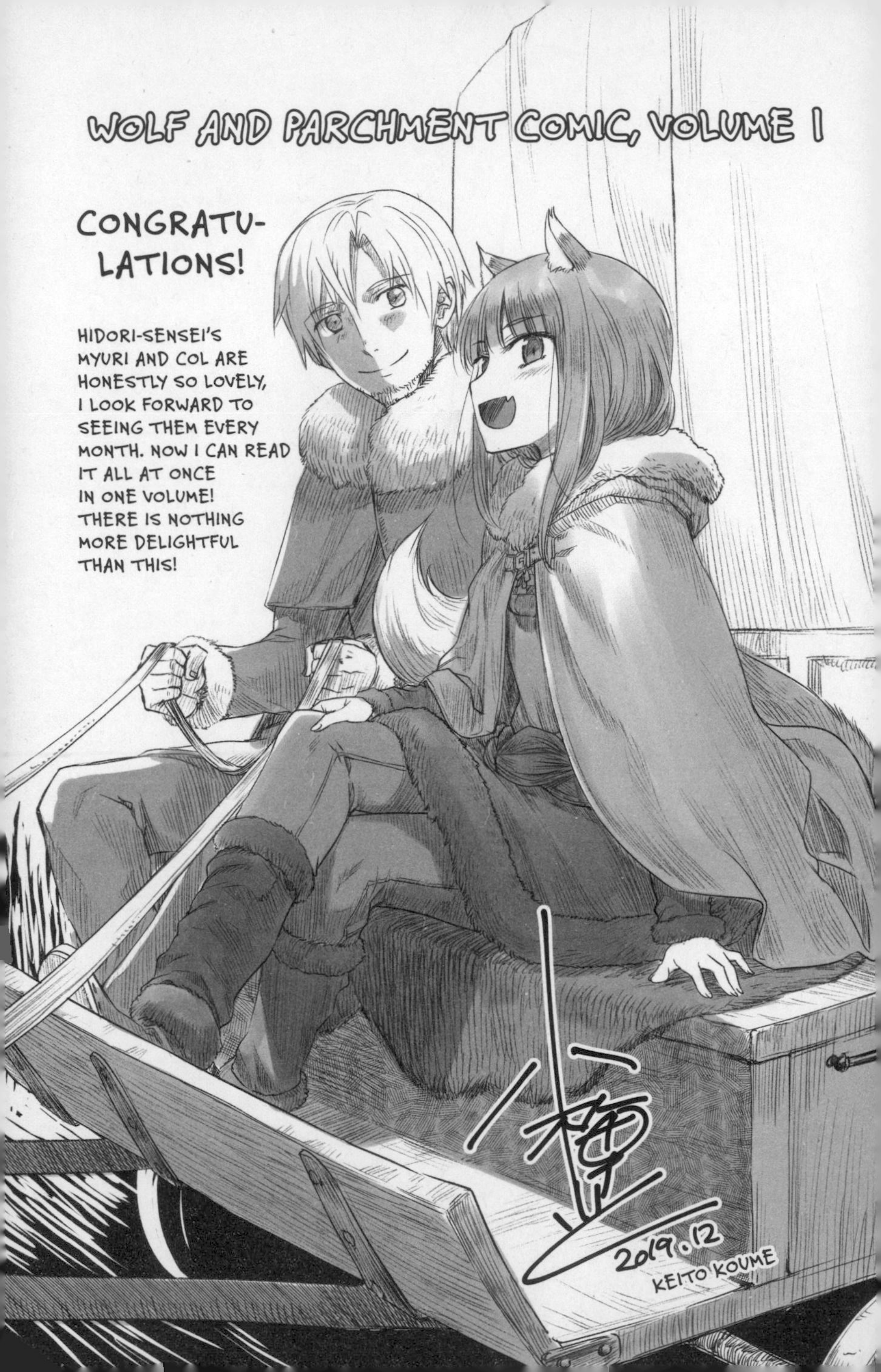
WOLF AND PARCHMENT COMIC, VOLUME 1
CONGRATU-LATIONS!
HIDORI-SENSEI'S MYURI AND COL ARE HONESTLY SO LOVELY, I LOOK FORWARD TO SEEING THEM EVERY MONTH. NOW I CAN READ IT ALL AT ONCE IN ONE VOLUME! THERE IS NOTHING MORE DELIGHTFUL THAN THIS!
2019.12
KEITO KOUME

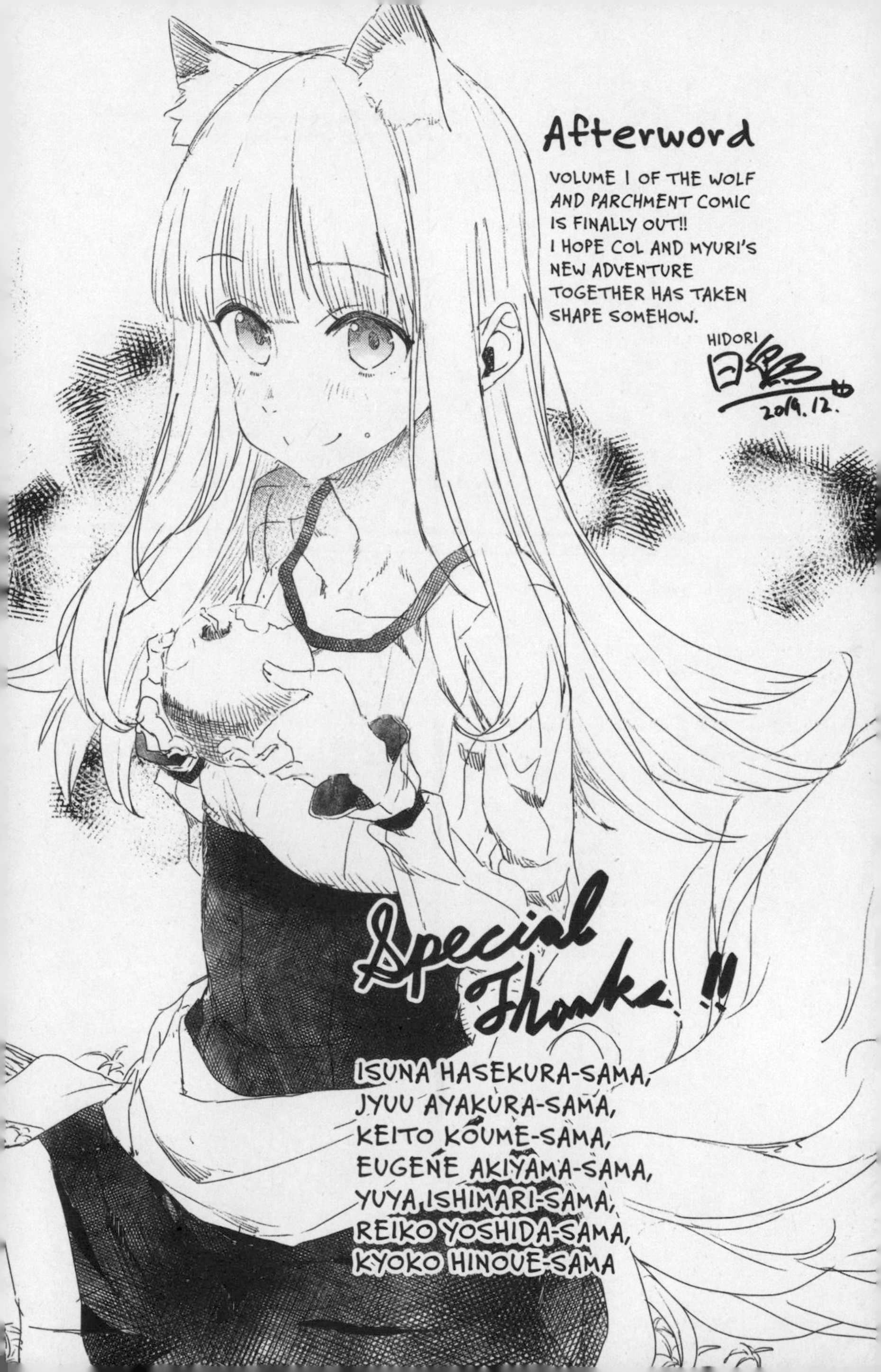
Afterword
VOLUME 1 OF THE WOLF AND PARCHMENT COMIC IS FINALLY OUT!! I HOPE COL AND MYURI'S NEW ADVENTURE TOGETHER HAS TAKEN SHAPE SOMEHOW.
HIDORI
2019.12.
Special Thanks!!
ISUNA HASEKURA-SAMA,
JYUU AYAKURA-SAMA,
KEITO KOUME-SAMA,
EUGENE AKIYAMA-SAMA,
YUYA ISHIMARI-SAMA,
REIKO YOSHIDA-SAMA,
KYOKO HINOUE-SAMA

WOLF & PARCHMENT 1

ISUNA HASEKURA ॐ HIDORI

Character design: Jyuu Ayakura

Translation: JASMINE BERNHARDT ॐ Lettering: CHIHO CHRISTIE

SHINSETSU OKAMI TO KOSHINRYO OKAMI TO YOHISHI Vol. 1
©Isuna Hasekura/Hidori 2019
First published in Japan in 2019 by KADOKAWA CORPORATION, Tokyo.
English translation rights arranged with KADOKAWA CORPORATION, Tokyo through Tuttle-Mori Agency, Inc., Tokyo.

English translation © 2020 by Yen Press, LLC

Yen Press
150 West 30th Street, 19th Floor
New York, NY 10001

Visit us at yenpress.com ॐ facebook.com/yenpress ॐ twitter.com/yenpress
        yenpress.tumblr.com ॐ instagram.com/yenpress

First Yen Press Edition: December 2020

Yen Press is an imprint of Yen Press, LLC.
The Yen Press name and logo are trademarks of Yen Press, LLC.

The publisher is not responsible for websites (or their content) that are not owned by the publisher.

Library of Congress Control Number: 2020946745

ISBNs: 978-1-9753-1875-8 (paperback)
        978-1-9753-1876-5 (ebook)

10 9 8 7 6 5 4 3 2 1

WOR

Printed in the United States of America